The International Relations of the Persian Gulf

Gregory Gause's masterful book is the first to offer a comprehensive, narrative account of the international politics in the Persian Gulf across nearly four decades. The story begins in 1971 when Britain ended its protectorate relations with the smaller states of the lower Gulf. It traces developments in the region from the oil revolution of 1973–74 through the Iranian Revolution, the Iran–Iraq War and the Gulf War of 1990–91, to the toppling of Saddam Hussein in the American-led invasion of Iraq in 2003, bringing the story of Gulf regional politics up to the end of 2008. The book highlights transnational identity issues, regime security and the politics of the world oil market, and charts the changing mix of interests and ambitions driving American policy. The author brings his considerable experience as a scholar and commentator on the Gulf to this riveting account of one of the most politically volatile regions on earth.

F. GREGORY GAUSE, III, is Professor of Political Science at the University of Vermont. During 2009–10 he is the Kuwait Foundation Visiting Professor of International Affairs at the Kennedy School of Government, Harvard University. His previous publications include *Oil Monarchies: Domestic and Security Challenges in the Arab Gulf States* (1994) and *Saudi–Yemeni Relations: Domestic Structures and Foreign Influence* (1990).

The International Relations
of the Persian Gulf

F. Gregory Gause, III

CAMBRIDGE
UNIVERSITY PRESS

CAMBRIDGE UNIVERSITY PRESS
Cambridge, New York, Melbourne, Madrid, Cape Town, Singapore,
São Paulo, Delhi, Tokyo, Mexico City

Cambridge University Press
The Edinburgh Building, Cambridge CB2 8RU, UK

Published in the United States of America by Cambridge University Press,
New York

www.cambridge.org
Information on this title: www.cambridge.org/9780521137300

First published 2010
4th printing 2011

Printed in the United Kingdom at the University Press, Cambridge

A catalogue record for this publication is available from the British Library

ISBN 978-0-521-19023-7 Hardback
ISBN 978-0-521-13730-0 Paperback

For Gregory and Emma, who have waited too long

Contents

Maps and tables

Maps

Tables

Acknowledgments

It is a pleasure to thank those who helped me as I was writing this book. I owe a great debt of gratitude to the late Arthur Ross and the Arthur Ross Foundation. Mr. Ross financially supported an earlier project of mine at the Council on Foreign Relations which turned into the book *Oil Monarchies*. When I had a sabbatical in the 2001–02 academic year to work on the present book, I turned to Mr. Ross again for support. He very graciously agreed to give me another grant to supplement my sabbatical salary. He was even more gracious when the events of 2001 postponed the completion of what I had thought would be a much shorter book. I also gratefully acknowledge the financial support of Columbia University, where I taught from 1987 to 1995, and the University of Vermont, where I have been on the faculty ever since. I received sabbaticals, leaves and travel grants from both institutions during which I worked on various aspects of this book.

I have been at this project since the end of the 1980s, when I thought it might be interesting to examine the Iran–Iraq War and the effects of the Iranian Revolution on the international politics of the Persian Gulf region. That was two wars ago, and events have conspired to extend this research much longer than I had originally intended. In those two decades I incurred a number of personal debts. I want to thank the people of the region – Iranians, Saudis, Iraqis, Kuwaitis, Omanis, Jordanians, Egyptians, Syrians, Bahrainis, Qataris and Emiratis – who received me on my research trips to their countries and in their diplomatic offices on my trips to Washington and New York. They educated me about their region. Many of them became friends. They are too numerous to mention here, but I am grateful to them all.

I began the project when I was a member of the political science department at Columbia University. My years there were like a second graduate education, during which I had the opportunity to learn from leading scholars in the fields of international relations, comparative politics and Middle East studies. My Columbia colleagues know how much I appreciate them. I did much of the research and most of the writing for this book during my time in the political science department of the University of Vermont. My Vermont colleagues are marvelous – smart, collegial, funny. I presented various parts of the book to them at faculty seminars and benefited from their comments. They make coming to work fun. I value both my professional relationships and my personal friendships with them.

I owe a debt of thanks to colleagues who read parts of the manuscript as I was writing it. Special thanks to Arang Keshavarzian of New York University, who read the whole manuscript and provided very useful comments. Robert Jervis, the dean of American international relations scholars and my Columbia colleague, read the chapter on the Iraq War with a careful eye and made numerous helpful suggestions. Mark Gasiorowski of Louisiana State University, Michael Barnett of the University of Minnesota, Fred Lawson of Mills College and Robert Kaufman of Pepperdine University read parts of the manuscript along the way at various times. My thanks to them all. I also thank the two anonymous reviewers at Cambridge University Press for their useful comments.

Particular thanks go to my editor at Cambridge University Press, Marigold Acland. Marigold was always interested in the project, even as new wars added to its length and to the amount of time it took to finish it. She always asked me about it when we ran into each other and encouraged me to keep at it. Her assistant at the Press, Sarah Green, has been very helpful in shepherding the manuscript to publication.

My wife Cindy has been with me on this project from the beginning. We got married during the Iran–Iraq War, had our first child just one month before Saddam Hussein invaded Kuwait, moved to Vermont during the "dual containment" period in American policy toward the Gulf and had our twentieth wedding anniversary when sectarian violence in Iraq was heating up. Needless to say, she uses different milestones to chart the history of our relationship. She has a bemused toleration for my fascination with the Middle East and an unwavering commitment to us as a family. I would be bereft without her. Both of my children were born during this project. Gregory is now in college and Emma is in high school, which is some indication of how long I have been at this. They have never known me when I wasn't working on "the book." I hope that they are ready for the change. They have waited a long time, so the book is dedicated to them.

Note on the text and bibliography

All translations are mine unless otherwise indicated.

Due to space constraints, there is not a full bibliography in this volume. Every source cited in the notes has a full bibliographic citation at its first mention in each chapter. Subsequent citations are in short form. A full bibliography along with a complete list of interviews conducted during the research is posted at www.uvm.edu/~fgause/gulfbook_biblio.htm.

1 The Persian Gulf as a security region

This book will tell the story of the international politics of the Persian Gulf region, the site of three large-scale international wars since 1980: the Iran–Iraq War of 1980–88, the Gulf War of 1990–91 and the Iraq War, which began with the American invasion of 2003 and continues to today. The year 1971 is the starting point for the study because it marks an important turning point in the region's history. Bahrain, Qatar, the United Arab Emirates (UAE) and Oman become independent in that year, ending decades as British protectorates. Kuwait, the other small monarchical state in the area, gained its independence from London in 1961. With the end of formal British protection of these smaller states, the larger regional powers – Iran, Iraq and Saudi Arabia – could contest for regional influence in a much less constrained environment. With the oil revolution of the early 1970s underway, these three states had much greater resources to commit to their contest for influence. The narrative ends in 2008, but not because the story is over.

A number of themes will tie together this narrative of Gulf international politics. The wars themselves are central to the story, to be sure. I will try to convince you that Saddam Hussein's war decisions in 1980 and 1990 (and even his behavior in the lead-up to the 2003 war) and the alliance decisions of regional powers are best explained by leaders' concerns about their own hold on power domestically, and how regional events and regional rivals could affect their own security at home. They view threats primarily through the lens of regime security rather than more conventional balance of power considerations, though the latter are certainly not absent from their calculations. Threats to regime security in the Gulf region are particularly salient to rulers because of the power and importance of transnational identities in the region – ethnic identities in their Arab and Kurdish manifestations, Muslim identity, sectarian Sunni and Shi'i identities. Because ambitious rulers can use these identity issues to mobilize support across state borders, Gulf rulers have to be worried not just about conventional power threats, but also about ideological threats which their neighbors can use to stir up regime challenges from within their own polities.

The arc of American involvement in the region is another theme that will knit together the narrative. When Britain gave up its historic role as protector of the small Gulf states, the United States was mired in Vietnam and had no stomach for taking on new international security obligations. But the importance of the region's oil resources, the repercussions of regional events such as the Iranian Revolution, growing American ambitions in the post-Cold War world and the 9/11 attacks led to progressively costly and sustained American military involvement in the region, culminating in the invasion and occupation of Iraq. I devote a whole chapter at the end of the book to examining the American decision to invade Iraq in 2003, which I see as a major departure from the past pattern of American policy in the Gulf. Before the 2003 war, American foreign policy in the Persian Gulf was relatively simple to understand. Washington wanted to maintain itself as the dominant regional power, because of the oil resources there. Because the United States was the dominant force in the area, "stability" was Washington's Gulf mantra. Irruptions in the status quo, such as the Iranian Revolution and Iraq's invasion of Kuwait, challenged American dominance and, where possible, had to be reversed. But 2003 was something different. I will make the argument that the 9/11 attacks changed the perceptions of the major decision-makers in the George W. Bush administration about American interests in the region, devaluing stability as a predominant American concern and substituting for it an ambitious effort to remake both the international and the domestic politics of the region. I will argue that other factors, including oil, were less important to this decision than many assume.

A third theme that will tie together the narrative is oil itself. The changes in the world oil market since the early 1970s are both causes and effects of regional international political outcomes. Oil has been a uniting factor among regional states during certain periods and an object of regional contestation in other periods. The narrative will link developments in the world oil market and regional states' oil policies to the regional security issues on their agenda and examine American actions in the region in light of American policy on oil issues.

No book can do everything, and I alert the reader to gaps in this account. I do not speak Persian, and thus was not able to delve into the indigenous literature on Iranian foreign policy. I use a number of very good English-language studies of Iranian decision-making as the basis for my discussion of Iranian policy. However, I was not able to do in-depth analysis of important Iranian war decisions, such as the 1982 decision to continue fighting into Iraqi territory after Iraqi troops had been expelled from Iran or the 1988 decision to accept a cease-fire in the Iran–Iraq War.

The important Iranian decisions to remain neutral in the two Iraqi–American wars also do not get the attention they deserve. I look forward to scholars with the necessary language skills enlightening me and other English-language readers about these episodes.

In the rest of this introductory chapter, I will make the case that the events under study are best understood by viewing the Persian Gulf as a distinct regional security complex. I will examine the rather meager literature on the international politics of the Gulf. I will frame the questions of war and alliance decision-making in their larger theoretical contexts. Those who are not particularly interested in these theoretical issues can skip the following sections and go right to the beginning of the narrative of Gulf international politics in Chapter 2.

The Persian Gulf as a regional security complex

My contention is that the best way to understand the security outcomes in the Persian Gulf – the wars that occur there, the alliances that are formed, even, to some extent, the problems of consolidating centralized states – is to view the area as a regional security complex. This approach stands in contrast to two alternative starting points of inquiry. The first starts with the foreign policies of specific states, and thus would seek to understand the security dynamics of the Gulf by looking at Saudi foreign policy, Iranian foreign policy and so on. The second starts with the global level, looking at how a specific region fits into the global security dynamic. Both of these alternative approaches have important gaps which prevent them from helping us understand the totality of the security picture in the Gulf. A focus on regional state foreign policies loses the dynamic of their interaction and takes us away from larger questions about why the region is so conflict-prone. Works limited to Iranian foreign policy, for example, cannot help us appreciate the regional impact of the Iranian Revolution. Thus, Iraq's attack on Iran comes from out of the blue, or out of the frame, in such analyses. The global approach is certainly necessary for understanding why the United States invaded Iraq in 2003. It does not explain how and why regional parties over time invited the United States to play a much greater role in regional security issues, allowing Washington to build the military infrastructure in the Gulf that made the Iraq War possible.

The concept of regional security complexes was first introduced by Barry Buzan, though he builds on the insights of earlier scholars who wrote about international systems. Buzan defines regional systems by the mutuality of threat/fear felt among the members toward each other. He urges analysts to focus on the degree to which certain geographically grouped states spend most of their time and effort worrying about each other, and not other states.[1] Those states with intense security interdependence over time qualify as regional security complexes.[2] In simple terms, regional systems should include states whose primary security focus is one another, manifested over time in the wars they fight and the time and resources they devote to dealing with one another. Note that this conception of regional system does not privilege positive interactions such as efforts at regional integration. Systems are defined by the intensity and durability of their security interactions, whether positive or negative.

If we accept this approach to defining regional security complexes, does the Persian Gulf area qualify? To my mind, without a doubt. The area has seen three major wars since 1980. Iran, Iraq, Saudi Arabia and Kuwait were either direct combatants or played important roles in all of them. Even when they were not active combatants, their alliance choices in these wars were centrally important to how those conflicts turned out. The Persian Gulf system certainly includes these four states. It also includes the other Gulf monarchies, whose security concerns (expressed in the time and resources devoted to their relations with the members of the system) are also primarily Gulf-focused. The states that border the Persian Gulf are certainly members of the system.

Does it make analytical sense to include other states in the Gulf regional security complex? We would be hard-pressed to say that most of Turkey's foreign policy energies, even its security focus, is on the Gulf states. Turkey is important to understanding the Gulf complex, but not a member. Likewise with Syria and Jordan. They both border Iraq; Jordan also borders Saudi Arabia. But their security attentions are focused as much to their west as to their east. Yemen's security policy is intensely focused on Saudi Arabia, but only marginally on issues arising from the Persian Gulf. While all these countries will play a role in the narrative chapters to follow, it is Iraq, Iran, Saudi Arabia and the smaller Gulf monarchies that form the Persian Gulf regional security complex, because they focus intensely on each other and devote the bulk of their security resources to relations with each other, and have done so for decades.

Why hive the Gulf off from the larger Middle East as a separate security complex? The vast majority of authors who have studied security issues in

---

[1] Barry Buzan, *People, States and Fear* (Boulder, CO: Lynne Rienner, 1991), Chapter 5.
[2] Barry Buzan and Ole Waever, *Regions and Powers: The Structure of International Security* (Cambridge: Cambridge University Press, 2003), Chapter 3, particularly pp. 45–49. David Lake makes a similar argument in "Regional Security Complexes: A Systems Approach," in David A. Lake and Patrick Morgan (eds.), *Regional Orders: Building Security in a New World* (University Park: Penn State University Press, 1997), pp. 48–49.

the region do not do so.[3] Very few scholars have focused exclusively on the Gulf as a regional security complex. I made an effort to do so in the early 1990s, the beginning of my interest in this topic.[4] Two Arab authors, Abd al-Khaleq Abdulla and Muhammad al-Sa'id Idris, used the framework of a Gulf regional security system in their interesting and important books published in the late 1990s.[5] More recently, in the wake of the Iraq War, Arshin Adib-Moghaddam presented a constructivist account of Gulf regional conflicts.[6] I will discuss insights from all three of these works below. But here the point is that very few scholars have looked at the Persian Gulf as its own regional unit.

The Gulf states are certainly part of a larger Middle Eastern system. Iran, Saudi Arabia and Iraq have all committed resources in a sustained way, over time, to issues in the Eastern Mediterranean – the Arab–Israeli conflict and Lebanon. Transnational identities of Arabism and Islam connect the Gulf to the Levant. There are important analytical questions about the international politics of the Middle East that can be answered only by taking this larger regional perspective. However, simply folding the Gulf states into the larger Middle East security complex runs the analytical risk of having Arab–Israeli questions drive the analysis of regional international politics. It would be a profound analytical error to see the conflicts in the Gulf as simply extensions of a presumed-dominant regional conflict pattern defined by Arab–Israeli issues. The international politics of the Persian Gulf region have a dynamic quite separate from that of the Arab–Israeli region, even though events in one area certainly affect the other. To understand that dynamic, we need to concentrate on events and processes in the Gulf itself.

One more definitional question about membership in the Persian Gulf regional security complex confronts us: is the United States a member of

---

[3] The most recent examples of such an approach are: Fred Halliday, *The Middle East in International Relations: Power, Politics and Ideology* (Cambridge: Cambridge University Press, 2005); Raymond Hinnebusch, *The International Politics of the Middle East* (Manchester: Manchester University Press, 2003); and Fred H. Lawson, *Constructing International Relations in the Arab World* (Stanford: Stanford University Press, 2006). This is also the approach of Buzan and Waever, *Regions and Powers*, Chapter 7, though they identify the Gulf as a "sub-complex" of the larger Middle East complex.

[4] F. Gregory Gause, III, "Gulf Regional Politics: Revolution, War and Rivalry," in W. Howard Wriggins (ed.), *Dynamics of Regional Politics: Four Systems on the Indian Ocean Rim* (New York: Columbia University Press, 1992).

[5] Abd al-Khaleq Abdulla, *Al-nizam al-'iqlimi al-khaliji* [The Gulf Regional System] (Beirut: Al-Mu'assasa al-Jami'iya lil-Dirasat wa al-Nashr wa al-Tawzi', 1998); Muhammad al-Sa'id Idris, *Al-nizam al-'iqlimi lil-khalij al-'arabi* [The Regional System of the Arab Gulf] (Beirut: Markaz Dirasat al-Wihda al-'Arabiya, 2000).

[6] Arshin Adib-Moghaddam, *The International Politics of the Persian Gulf: A Cultural Genealogy* (London: Routledge, 2006).

the system? Here the theorists of regional security differ.[7] I think that it would be foolish to think about the dynamics of the Persian Gulf regional security complex without including the United States as a member. However, the intensity of its involvement has changed over time. The United States was less involved in Gulf security issues in the 1970s than it was in the 1980s, less involved in the 1980s than in the 1990s, less involved in the 1990s than in the 2000s. I can also imagine, in the wake of its Iraq debacle, that the United States might play a much less direct role in Gulf security dynamics in the future. I emphasize that there are security dynamics independent of American involvement in the region: the triangular contest for influence among Iraq, Iran and Saudi Arabia which helps explain the Iran–Iraq War and Saddam's invasion of Kuwait; the transnational identity factors which draw ambitious leaders into cross-border involvements and exacerbate the security dilemma; the sometimes cooperative, sometimes conflictual dynamics generated by the fact that the Gulf states are major oil producers. But it is hard to argue with the fact that the United States determined the outcome of one Gulf war in 1991 and profoundly changed the distribution of regional power in 2003 by destroying what had been an important pole of regional power. The United States is directly involved in the region, but it does not completely control events in the Gulf.

The structure of the Gulf security complex

At the most basic level, the structure of any international system is defined by the distribution of power within it. The Persian Gulf is a tripolar regional system. Iran, Iraq and Saudi Arabia are the major players. Each has been able to extend its influence over other members of the system at various times; none is so powerful as to be able to control the politics and policies of the others. The relations of power within this three-cornered regional game have varied over time. Iran under the shah clearly was the most powerful regional actor and usually got its way in the pre-Revolution period. The oil revolution of 1973–74 strengthened all three players, but improved the position of Saudi Arabia, the biggest oil producer of the three, the most relatively. The chaos of the Iranian Revolution seemed to catapult Iraq to the forefront of the regional power rankings. Then the Iran–Iraq War and the Gulf War reduced Iraqi power relative to that of its neighbors. But through these changes the tripolar structure of the region endured.

---

[7] For opposing positions, see Patrick Morgan, "Regional Security Complexes and Regional Orders," in Lake and Morgan (eds.), *Regional Orders*, pp. 28–33; and Buzan and Waever, *Regions and Powers*, Chapter 3, particularly pp. 48–49, 63–64, 80–81, and Chapter 14, particularly pp. 450–51.

Structures, however, are not immutable. The American invasion in 2003 basically destroyed Iraq as a pole of power in the Gulf for the foreseeable future. Iraq since the invasion has been a playing field, not a player, in regional politics. Iran and Saudi Arabia now contest for influence both within Iraq, in the Gulf more generally and in the Middle East as a whole.

Up to 2003, regional tripolarity defined the structure of the Persian Gulf security complex. The competition among Iran, Iraq and Saudi Arabia for regional dominance set the Gulf's security agenda. There was a second triangular competition in the region as well, with the smaller Gulf monarchies maneuvering between Saudi Arabia – their close neighbor, self-proclaimed protector and, at times, overbearing patron – and either Iraq or Iran. The Saudis were able to consolidate their leading position in the other monarchies through the Gulf Cooperation Council, founded in 1981 in reaction to the Iranian Revolution and the Iran–Iraq War. However, the smaller Gulf states have now found a new patron and protector, the United States, which allows them (if they want it) a bit of room to maneuver within the Saudi orbit.

The Persian Gulf regional security complex has its own structure, but it is also embedded in an international system. For most of the period of this study, global politics were bipolar, defined by the Cold War between the United States and the Soviet Union. Each superpower played a role in the region, supporting local allies and checking each other's regional ambitions. There has been much less theorizing about global unipolarity and its effects on regional conflicts, both because the situation is still relatively new (existing only since the collapse of the Soviet Union in 1991) and because there are so few similar historical periods.[8] One thing is certain: even in unipolarity, the United States found no reason to disengage from the Persian Gulf. The sensible assumption that unipolarity would remove a check on great power interventionism in important regions was borne out in the Gulf. From 1990, the American role in the Gulf became progressively more militarized and more direct, culminating in the occupation of Iraq in 2003. Idris explicitly links the end of global bipolarity to the change in the Gulf, from local actors driving the security agenda to US control becoming the dominant security factor.[9]

While agreeing that global unipolarity removed an important constraint on American military involvement in the Persian Gulf, I dispute the

---

[8] On the general issue of how regional and global structures interact, see two works by Benjamin Miller: *When Opponents Cooperate: Great Power Conflict and Collaboration in World Politics* (Ann Arbor: University of Michigan Press, 1995); and *States, Nations and the Great Powers: The Sources of Regional War and Peace* (Cambridge: Cambridge University Press, 2007).

[9] Idris, *Al-nizam al-'iqlimi lil-khalij al-'arabi*, pp. 15, 576.

contention that global unipolarity led to American "control" of the Gulf region. Even with its heavy military involvement, the United States has not been able to dictate completely the politics of the region, either before 2003 or after. Iran continues to defy the American order and challenge American influence in Iraq and elsewhere in the Middle East. Iraqi parties themselves have challenged the US effort to remake their domestic politics. Even Saudi Arabia, while generally following the American policy line, has deviated on important tactical questions regarding policy toward Iraq, the Arab–Israeli peace process and oil production. The hegemon cannot always get its way.

Transnational identities and foreign policy decisions

Structure, at the regional and the global level, constrains the choices of the players in the Gulf game but does not dictate specific policy choices. The Gulf regional structure was tripolar both before and after the Iranian Revolution, but the behavior of all the regional states changed dramatically with that domestic Iranian political event. There was a regional war during the period of global bipolarity (Iran–Iraq War), a regional war as bipolarity was transitioning to unipolarity (Gulf War) and a regional war under unipolarity (Iraq War). The United States was the sole global power during both the Bill Clinton and George W. Bush administrations, but American policy in the Gulf was significantly different under those two presidents. Unipolarity was the permissive condition for the United States to go to war in Iraq in 2003, but unipolarity did not cause that war. Structure alone cannot answer the questions of why states in the Gulf (or great powers involved in the Gulf) go to war and why they choose the allies they do.

So what drives foreign policy behavior in the Gulf? At first glance, this seems to be a simple story of power grabs, easily explained by classic "balance of power" (what international relations theorists call Realist) dynamics. Many Realists see shifts in power and disparities in power as the driving forces of conflict, and the Gulf during the period under study saw both important power shifts and enduring power imbalances. Oil exacerbates these conflicts in three ways that Realists would have no trouble understanding. First, because it is a strategic commodity, it draws outside powers into the region. Second, because ownership of oil comes with control of the territory that sits over the oil, the possession of territory in the Gulf is that much more important and valuable for a state.[10] So border disputes, always a potential cause of conflict, become

---

[10] Michael L. Ross, "Blood Barrels: Why Oil Wealth Fuels Conflict," *Foreign Affairs*, Vol. 87, No. 3 (May/June 2008), pp. 2–9.

even more salient when the territory in dispute has oil under it. A cursory look at the wars in the Gulf could lead one to see each as a fight for regional dominance and the expansion of oil control: Iraq attacking a weakened Iran in 1980, invading the oil-rich Iranian province of Khuzestan; Iraq attacking small but oil-rich Kuwait in 1990; and the United States attacking oil-rich Iraq in 2003. Third, oil has given the regional powers the wherewithal to build large militaries and arm them with modern weapons. While states can go to war with small, ill-armed militaries, the chances of success would seem to increase as a state's military resources grow. The major wars in the Gulf in the modern period have all occurred since the oil price revolution of the early 1970s.[11]

While this simple story is appealingly parsimonious, and the factors it highlights are certainly part of the dynamics of Persian Gulf security, in the end it is not a satisfactory framework for understanding the region. These factors are constants; they cannot explain why specific wars occurred when they did nor how important political events such as the Iranian Revolution and the 9/11 attacks led to changes in regional dynamics. The argument will be made in the chapters that follow that oil was not the primary driver of any of the Gulf wars. Border disputes might have been the pretext of the Iran–Iraq and Iraq–Kuwait conflicts, but they were not the cause. I will argue throughout the book that regional states acted more against perceived threats to their own domestic stability emanating from abroad than to counter unfavorable changes in the distribution of power or to take advantage of favorable power imbalances. They chose their allies based not on classic balance of power considerations, balancing against the strongest regional state, but on how their own domestic regime security would be affected by the outcome of regional conflicts. The most important and distinctive factor in the Gulf regional security complex is not power imbalances but the salience of transnational identities.

The Persian Gulf region is characterized by a number of important transnational identities – Arab, Kurdish, Muslim, Shi'i, Sunni, tribal. Arab identities cross every border in the Gulf region, including the Iraq–Iran border, with the large Arab minority community in Khuzestan province (southwestern Iran). The Kurdish identity spans the Turkish-Iraqi-Iranian borders. Iran, Iraq and Bahrain are majority Shi'i countries; there are important Shi'i minorities in Kuwait, Saudi Arabia and the United Arab Emirates. The larger Muslim identity transcends all the

[11] For Abd al-Khaleq Abdulla, Gulf regional politics are an exclusively Realist story. He identifies four reasons for the high level of regional conflicts: regional power imbalances, the Saudi-Iraqi-Iranian rivalry for regional dominance, border disputes and great power intervention: Abdulla, *Al-nizam al-'iqlimi al-khaliji*, pp. 128–32.

region's borders. Important tribes cross the borders of the Arab states. This fact does not discount the importance of state identities. Iran has a millennial history as a political unit and a strong sense of nationalism among its population. The Arab monarchies of the Gulf are newer creations, but have also developed some degree of citizen loyalty and identification. Iraq suffers from serious domestic cleavages, exacerbated by Saddam Hussein's rule and by the American occupation since 2003, but there remains among many Arab Iraqis an identification with their state. But these cross-border identities in the Gulf are real, presenting both opportunities and challenges to Gulf leaders.

These identities affect regional international politics in two important ways. First, they offer ambitious leaders access to the domestic politics of their neighbors, using ties with groups across borders as levers of influence on other governments.[12] Transnational identities also increase the likelihood of war, because leaders can come to believe that important constituencies in target states will rally to support the invading army. The shah of Iran supported Kurdish opponents of the Iraqi regime in the 1960s and early 1970s, and since that time governments in both Baghdad and Tehran have cultivated ties with the Kurdish opponents of the other. Saddam Hussein thought his attack on southwestern Iran in 1980 would be facilitated by the Arab population there; Ayatollah Ruhollah Khomeini likewise thought that Iraqi Shi'a, though Arab, would rally to his side when Iranian forces carried the offensive into Iraq in 1982. Saddam tried to exploit both Arab nationalist and Islamist ideological tropes to gain regional support for his invasion of Kuwait in 1990. Even where such identities have not contributed to war, they can cause tensions between the countries encouraging such transnational identification and the countries targeted for such efforts. Revolutionary Iran has cultivated ties with Islamist groups across the Arab world, mostly Shi'i but some Sunni. Ayatollah Khomeini portrayed his revolution as a model for the entire Muslim world, not only Shi'i Muslims. Saudi Arabia has encouraged the spread of its own brand of Wahhabi Sunni Islam across the Sunni Muslim world for decades.

Second, these transnational identities are seen as threats by leaders to their own regimes' stability. I will make the case that Saddam Hussein's decisions to go to war in both 1980 and 1990 were strongly affected by his perception that regional and international (in the case of 1990) powers were exploiting the pluralism of Iraqi society to try to weaken his regime's

---

[12] For an excellent account of how one of these transnational networks works on the ground, see Laurence Louer, *Transnational Shia Politics: Religious and Political Networks in the Gulf* (London: Hurst and Company, 2008).

hold on power. The Iranian Revolution was a threat to the regime stability of Saudi Arabia and the smaller Gulf states, and helps explain why they aligned with Iraq in the Iran–Iraq War. The United States after 2003 saw Iran as a threat to Iraqi stability not because it particularly feared that the Iranian army would come across the border, but because of Iran's ability to affect Iraqi politics through its ties to Shi'i (and other) groups in Iraq. So the reality of transnational identities in the Gulf both increases the likelihood that ambitious leaders will seek to exploit those identities to expand their influence and increases the sense of threat felt by the regimes that are the targets of those ambitious leaders. The possibilities of conflict already present in the region for the Realist reasons set out above are thus exacerbated by the salience of these transnational identities.

Scholars who have focused on the international politics of the Persian Gulf have noted the importance of these transnational ideological and identity challenges to the Gulf security agenda. Muhammad al-Sa'id Idris holds that the major variable explaining the level of conflict in the Gulf regional system is the ideological complementarity of the regimes. When there are ideological conflicts among the ruling elites, as during the 1980s when Iran sought to export its revolution, conflict will increase, in his view. He stresses that threats to domestic regime security in the Gulf are easily internationalized, as neighbors seek to exploit domestic weaknesses to expand their influence.[13] Abd al-Khaleq Abdulla, who approaches the Gulf from a balance of power perspective, recognizes that the Iranian Revolution is a major turning point because the new Iranian regime sought to export its Islamist ideology regionally.[14]

Arshin Adib-Moghaddam not only highlights the centrality of identity issues but emphasizes them to the exclusion of material factors. He characterizes the Iran–Iraq War as a "legitimacy contest between two ideological constructs: Iraqi pan-Arabism and Iranian Islamism," asserting that "the struggle for hegemony in the Persian Gulf … was primarily cultural."[15] He likewise portrays the 2003 Iraq War as part of a wider regional "clash of neo-fundamentalism [in the region] and neo-conservatism [in the United States]. Both ideational currents, albeit to a different degree and in dissimilar proportions, transgressed rules, norms and institutions of international society, exacerbating regional conflict and disorder."[16] The relative tranquility of the 1991–2001 period in the Gulf is attributable to "the reassertion of sovereignty norms over transnational

[13] Idris, *Al-nizam al-'iqlimi lil-khalij al-'arabi*, pp. 192–96, 212–18, 569–73.
[14] Abdulla, *Al-nizam al-'iqlimi al-khaliji*, pp. 136–38.
[15] Adib-Moghaddam, *International Politics of the Persian Gulf*, p. 23.
[16] Adib-Moghaddam, *International Politics of the Persian Gulf*, p. 125.

Pan-Arabism or Islamist loyalties."[17] For Adib-Moghaddam, it is ideas all the way down.

Adib-Moghaddam's emphasis on the self-perception of individual state actors as the sole driver of their foreign policies deemphasizes the important way in which transnational identities also constitute threats to other actors. It is when identity assertion begins to threaten the regime security of others in the region that conflicts arise and alliance patterns change. That sense of regime threat is the material link between ideas and action in the Gulf. Adib-Moghaddam is also on shaky ground when he divorces changes in ideas from changes in power. For example, the relative stability of 1991–2001 mentioned above certainly benefited from Iran's deemphasis on the revolutionary Islamist aspect of its foreign policy. That change is partly attributable to the death of Ayatollah Khomeini, the most revolutionary of Iran's leaders, in 1989. But it is also attributable to the fact that Iranian efforts to export the revolution had not only largely failed (with the exception of Lebanon), but had also cost the Iranian state in terms of its blood, treasure and relations with other regional states. The power situation cannot be divorced from the ideological map when assessing state behavior.

The framework I suggest for understanding Persian Gulf regional politics accepts the important insight that identities and ideas do matter in international security by showing how ideas can affect leaders' perceptions of their material interests. Transnational ideas about identity and politics can be power resources for ambitious leaders and can be threats to the regimes against which they are directed. It is only when those ideas are matched to the tangible power resources available to a state or political group that they become drivers in security decision-making. Ideas are important, but not to the exclusion of concerns about power. It is at the intersection of ideational and material factors that we will find the explanations of the wars and alliances we see in the Gulf.

American policy in the Persian Gulf

Understanding American behavior in the Persian Gulf requires different frameworks of analysis. While the political fortunes of a number of US presidents were affected by events in the Gulf, regime security considerations were not the driving factor in American policy decisions in the region. What drove American policy for most of the period under study was the US interest in Persian Gulf oil. In the pre-World War II period,

---

[17] Adib-Moghaddam, *International Politics of the Persian Gulf*, p. 69.

Washington wanted to make sure that American companies had access to oil opportunities in what was then a British area of influence. After World War II, Cold War considerations joined the economic interest in continued American access to Gulf oil. Washington wanted to make sure that the Soviet Union and its regional allies could not control the region. As the Cold War developed, the strategic considerations began to trump the economic ones in American policy toward the Gulf. Washington did nothing to prevent the wave of nationalizations of American oil companies' interests in the region in the 1970s. It did not respond when its closest regional allies, Saudi Arabia and Iran, took steps in 1973 that drove the price of oil up by 400 percent, sending the United States and most of the rest of the world into a prolonged economic recession. If anything, American relations with those two countries became even closer and more cooperative after the 1973 oil shock. The key for the United States at that time was to have regional allies in the Gulf against the Soviet Union.[18]

The American policy of relying on regional allies to protect its strategic interests in the Persian Gulf was dealt a blow by the Iranian Revolution of 1979. The shah's regime, a reliable American ally in the Cold War, was replaced by the Islamic Republic. While the new Iranian regime was hardly an ally of the Soviets, it was no longer the "policeman" of American regional security interests that the shah had been. At that point, the United States began to take a more direct military role in the region: the formation of a regional military command in the early 1980s, the deployment of naval forces to the Gulf in 1987–88, the Gulf War of 1990–91, the development of a system of bases in the monarchical states after the Gulf War, and the Iraq War of 2003 and the subsequent occupation of Iraq. The end of the Cold War did not derail this progression. Once the Soviet enemy no longer justified the strategic commitment to the Gulf, the hostility of regional states – Iran and Iraq – was the rationale for the American military presence. Washington's strategic interest in oil both predated the Cold War and outlived it.

The major change in American policy toward the Persian Gulf was not the end of the Cold War, but the beginning what President George W. Bush termed the "global war on terrorism". Far from being a culmination of past trends in Gulf policy, the Iraq War marked a significant

---

[18] The other framework for understanding the American commitment to the Gulf stresses the economic over the strategic interest in oil, in terms both of the desire of specific American corporations to control Gulf oil and of overall American economic security. See Michael T. Klare, *Blood and Oil: The Dangers and Consequences of America's Growing Dependency on Imported Petroleum* (New York: Henry Holt, 2004), Chapter 2, for an intelligent synopsis of this argument.

change in American goals in the region. Until September 11, 2001, American policy was largely aimed at preserving a geopolitical status quo in which American interests in access to oil were secured. Not every challenge to that favorable status quo could be reversed. Washington had to live with the Iranian Revolution, as much as it might have wished otherwise. But some such challenges could be met with American military force, most notably the Iraqi invasion of Kuwait in 1990. The United States restored Kuwaiti sovereignty, but at that time did not consider the unseating of Saddam Hussein's regime as a necessary part of securing American interests in the region. During the 1990s the unipolar power was content to live with a Persian Gulf in which two of the major states were ruled by hostile regimes. As long as the oil flowed, Washington could accept that reality.

After the attacks of 9/11, the Bush administration fundamentally changed the purpose of American policy in the Persian Gulf. Changing the status quo, including the domestic political arrangements of Gulf states, replaced preserving it. The result of that change was the American invasion of Iraq in 2003. Unipolarity is a permissive cause of this war, but not an explanation for it. The absence of a great power competitor certainly smoothed the path to war for the United States in 2003, but unipolarity had obtained for thirteen years before Washington decided to attack Iraq. It was the new understanding of American regional interests in the wake of 9/11 that drove the war decision. Unipolarity just made it easier to get there.

The rest of the book

With these general analytical frameworks established, I turn to the narrative account of the international politics of the Persian Gulf from 1971 to the present. Chapter 2 will cover the period from the end of British protection for Bahrain, Qatar, the UAE and Oman in 1971 until the Iranian Revolution of 1979, with some general background on the pre-1971 period. The oil revolution of 1973–74 is a central part of the narrative here. Chapter 3 will discuss the international repercussions of the Iranian Revolution, including a focus on Saddam Hussein's decision to initiate the Iran–Iraq War. Chapter 4 covers the Gulf War of 1990–91, again with a focus on Saddam's rationale for initiating the conflict, and subsequent regional events in the 1990s. Chapter 5 looks at the Gulf connections to the 9/11 attacks, the repercussions of those attacks on the Saudi–American relationship, the Iraq War of 2003 and the subsequent American occupation of Iraq. Chapter 6 analyzes the American decision to go to war against Iraq in 2003, weighing various possible explanations

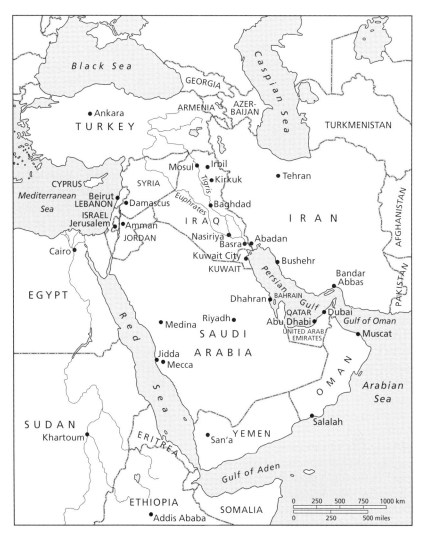

Map 1 The Persian Gulf and the broader Middle East

for the decision against the evidence of administration deliberations and the documentary record established by various investigations of the intelligence community's work. Chapter 7 is a brief conclusion, reviewing the major themes of the volume and speculating about the future of international politics on the Persian Gulf.

2 The emergence of the Gulf regional system, 1971–1978

The formal end of British protectorate status for the smaller states of the lower Persian Gulf in 1971 marked the beginning of a new stage in the international politics of the region. British power had been on the decline for decades in the area. London had effectively ceded primacy to the United States in Saudi Arabia during World War II, and in Iran in the aftermath of the 1953 coup against the government of Muhammad Mossadegh. The 1958 military coup that brought down the Hashemite monarchy in Iraq ended British influence in Baghdad. However, the British military and political commitment to the smaller Arab states of the region served as a brake on the ambitions of the larger regional states. That commitment was manifested tangibly in 1961, when Iraq threatened newly independent Kuwait. British forces returned to the shaykhdom to deter any Iraqi military adventure and to assert London's continuing interest in the region.[1] The small British military presence in the region, combined with its commitments to the other Gulf emirates and Oman, in effect prevented Iran, Iraq and Saudi Arabia from competing openly for influence in the area. The United States, its hands more than full with the war in Vietnam, welcomed the British role in the Gulf.

The announcement in 1968 that London would end its military presence in the region and its protectorate relationships with the Emirates and Oman opened up the Persian Gulf as an arena of regional contestation. Iran, Iraq and Saudi Arabia began to maneuver to assert their influence in what would become, in 1971, the newly independent states of Bahrain, Qatar, the United Arab Emirates and Oman, as well as in already independent Kuwait. Ironically, as the British were leaving the region in 1971, its international importance was growing exponentially as a result of the dramatic increases in oil prices between 1970 and 1974. With Britain gone, and the United States unwilling to "fill the vacuum" militarily and politically in the region, the regional states were able to act with much

---

[1] The most comprehensive study of the 1961 Kuwait crisis is Mustafa M. Alani, *Operation Vantage: British Military Intervention in Kuwait 1961* (Surbiton, UK: LAAM, 1990).

more independence on oil questions than might otherwise have been the case.

While the oil price increases had enormous effects on the domestic politics and societies of the Gulf states, and on the level of international interest in the region, no regional power could exploit this change to dominate the region. Iran, Iraq and Saudi Arabia were all major oil producers, and all built up their military and economic power as a result of the oil price revolution. Their competition for influence continued, though with the stakes much greater and the means at their disposal increased. Despite the social upheavals occasioned by the oil price rise and the political changes that came after the British withdrawal, this was the most stable period of modern Gulf international politics. The shah's Iran and Saudi Arabia came to an understanding supporting the territorial and political status quo after the British withdrawal. They were hardly military allies. The Saudis remained wary of the shah's hegemonic ambitions; the shah, ironically, saw the Saudis as dangerously unstable. However, they were both pro-American monarchies that were perfectly comfortable with the domestic political arrangements in the new Gulf states. Their common superpower ally, the United States, encouraged this Saudi–Iranian rapprochement. Iraq – republican, Arab nationalist, and allied with the Soviets – was the odd man out. It actively opposed the new disposition in the Gulf for some years, but in 1975 sought out better relations with both Tehran and the Arab Gulf monarchies. The collapse of the shah's regime in early 1979 ended that rapprochement and began a new period of open conflict in regional international politics.

The British withdrawal

If we focus simply on questions of power and interest, it is extremely difficult to explain why Britain chose to give up its protectorate agreements with the Arab states of the Gulf in 1971. The rulers of those states did not seek independence from London, nor were there widespread popular movements challenging the British role. The strategic and economic importance of those states was growing, as the late 1960s saw the beginnings of the changes in the world oil market that would send prices skyrocketing in the 1970s. The reason for the decision lies in British domestic politics, particularly the politics within the Labour Party.[2]

---

[2] I have developed this argument at greater length in an earlier article: "British and American Policies in the Persian Gulf, 1968–1973," *Review of International Studies*, Vol. 11, No. 4 (October 1985), pp. 247–73.

In the general retreat from empire after World War II, London had very consciously maintained its role in the Gulf area, including the Crown Colony at Aden and the surrounding protectorates of South Arabia. It committed a substantial number of forces, and took a substantial number of casualties, in fighting the independence movement that developed in southern Arabia in 1963. However, when the Labour Party, under Prime Minister Harold Wilson, came to power in 1964, new pressures were developing on what remained of Britain's role "east of Suez." One was financial, as the British economy was less and less able to sustain the military expenditures required of a world power. But the more important pressure was political, from within the Labour Party. As early as 1965 parliamentarians from the left wing of the party were offering motions both in the House of Commons and in the party's parliamentary caucus calling for an end to Britain's "colonial" role in Asia. Wilson's government resisted these pressures at first, but in 1966 announced that it would leave the British base at Aden by the end of 1967. The British-protected Federation of South Arabia collapsed in November 1967, becoming the People's Republic of South Yemen. In 1969 it changed its name to the People's Democratic Republic of Yemen (PDRY), the only avowedly Marxist state in the Arab world.[3]

For the British-protected rulers in the Gulf, this was hardly an encouraging precedent. Rulers in South Arabia whose titles (shaykh, sultan, amir) and legitimacy claims were very similar to their own were swept from power by Marxist ideologues. Those rulers' longstanding relations with Britain not only did not save them, but in the end contributed to their downfall. Events in South Arabia dealt British credibility in the Middle East its most serious blow since the Iraqi revolution of 1958. Recognizing this, the Wilson government during 1967 reaffirmed Britain's commitment to its Gulf protectorates. However, the same month that British forces left Aden, the pound fell precipitously as Britain's balance of payments deficit worsened. The government was forced to go to the International Monetary Fund for a loan, and in so doing had to accept its conditions, which included substantial cuts in government spending.

As part of those cuts, Wilson committed to withdraw militarily from the Gulf, Singapore and Malaysia by the end of 1971. In response, Shaykh Zayid, the ruler of Abu Dhabi, told a British emissary that he and his

---

[3] For a careful but critical assessment of the British withdrawal from southern Arabia, focusing on British policy-making, see Glen Balfour-Paul, *The End of Empire in the Middle East* (Cambridge: Cambridge University Press, 1991), Chapter 4. In my book *Saudi–Yemeni Relations: Domestic Structures and Foreign Influence* (New York: Columbia University Press, 1990), Chapter 3, I discuss events in this period in southern Arabia.

fellow rulers would be willing to bear the entire cost of the British military presence in the area. Shaykh Rashid of Dubai seconded Zayid's offer.[4] Moreover, Saudi Arabia, worried about the spread of the radical ideologies that had blossomed in newly independent South Yemen, conveyed to London its willingness to help fund a continued British presence.[5] None of these offers was explored. Withdrawal from the Gulf was not an economic necessity, but a political one, part of the price extracted by Labour's left wing for its support for the Wilson government's 1968 emergency budget.[6]

With the end of a political dispensation that had endured for more than a century in sight, the question of "what comes next" for the smaller Gulf states came immediately to the fore. It was accepted by all concerned that Oman, with a long independent history, substantial territory and a comparatively large population, would become an independent state. The fate of the other nine protected states was more uncertain. Britain immediately proposed that they federate into a single state and began consultations to push the leaders in that direction. While the amirs of Abu Dhabi and Dubai, putting aside a long history of enmity between their families, began working together to form a viable federation, other leaders were less enthusiastic about giving up their nominal independence.[7] The shah's Iran viewed the British announcement as the opening it had long sought to assert its dominance in the Gulf and immediately revived the historical Persian claim to sovereignty over Bahrain and to a number of islands near the mouth of the Gulf. Saudi Arabia supported Bahrain against the Iranian claim and the idea of a federation among the nine states, but also pressed Abu Dhabi on border disputes in the Buraymi Oasis area and elsewhere.[8] As recently as 1955 British-officered forces from Oman and the Trucial States had expelled Saudi forces from Buraymi. While the prospect of British withdrawal was disquieting for the Saudis in terms of

[4] *The Times* (London), January 22, 1968, p. 1; J. B. Kelly, *Arabia, the Gulf and the West* (New York: Basic Books, 1980), pp. 49–50; Faisal bin Salman al-Saud, *Iran, Saudi Arabia and the Gulf: Power Politics in Transition 1968–1971* (London: I. B. Tauris, 2003), p. 23.
[5] Interview with Hermann Eilts, US Ambassador to Saudi Arabia, 1970–74, Boston, December 1981.
[6] This conclusion is shared by D. C. Watt, "The Decision to Withdraw from the Gulf," *Political Quarterly*, Vol. 39, No. 3 (July/September 1968), pp. 310–21. See also Balfour-Paul, *The End of Empire*, p. 124.
[7] Frauke Heard-Bey, *From Trucial States to United Arab Emirates*, 2nd edn. (London: Longman, 1996), pp. 341–45.
[8] For a general discussion of territorial issues in the Gulf during this period, see Lenore G. Martin, *The Unstable Gulf* (Lexington, MA: D. C. Heath, 1984), Chapter 3. For an overview of the shah's approach to Gulf questions at this time, see R. K. Ramazani, *Iran's Foreign Policy, 1941–1973: A Study of Foreign Policy in Modernizing Nations* (Charlottesville: University Press of Virginia, 1975), Chapter 16.

general Gulf stability, it opened up the possibility of settling some old scores and extending Saudi influence throughout the peninsula. Further complicating the geopolitical picture in the Gulf was the July 1968 coup in Iraq which brought to power the Ba'thist regime of Ahmad Hassan al-Bakr and Saddam Hussein. The new regime was weak at home, still consolidating its hold over a divided army and society and facing a new outbreak of Kurdish separatist violence in the north. However, it was truculent abroad, at least at the rhetorical level. It paraded Arab nationalist slogans against the British and the Arab monarchs of the Gulf. It publicly supported the Popular Front for the Liberation of the Occupied Arab Gulf, a Marxist group with ties to the new South Yemeni regime, which was operating out of the rebellious Dhufar province in southern Oman. It also provided a base for a small group of ethnic Arab activists from the southwestern Iranian province of Khuzestan, on the border with Iraq, who asserted the province's Arab identity and sought independence from Iran. In April 1969 the Ba'thist government threatened to close the Shatt al-Arab waterway to Iranian shipping unless Iran complied with a number of conditions, claiming the right to control the waterway which had been codified in the 1937 Iran–Iraq treaty but which had not been exercised by Iraq in the past.

For the shah, this challenge provided a golden opportunity to make clear to all the new hierarchy of Persian Gulf regional power. Within days of the Iraqi moves, his government abrogated the 1937 treaty and claimed Iranian control over the eastern half of the waterway. With the Iranian navy escorting Iranian vessels, Iraq could do nothing but protest verbally. Iran and Iraq both moved troops to the border area (Iraqi forces also took up positions in Kuwait, with the post facto acquiescence of the Kuwaiti government), but the crisis passed without serious clashes.[9] The shah also provided support for Iraqi Kurdish separatists and for Arab officers who tried to organize a military coup in January 1970 to oust the Ba'th, leading Baghdad to expel the Iranian ambassador and the staff of the Iranian consulates in a number of Iraqi cities.[10]

---

[9] Iran called attention to the troop concentrations in a letter to the United Nations Security Council: *New York Times*, May 10, 1969, p. 10. On the Iraqi forces in Kuwait, see Majid Khadduri, *Socialist Iraq: A Study in Iraqi Politics Since 1968* (Washington, DC: Middle East Institute, 1978), pp. 155–56.

[10] On this period of Iraqi–Iranian relations, see Phebe Marr, *The Modern History of Iraq* (Boulder, CO: Westview Press, 1985), pp. 220–22; Charles Tripp, *A History of Iraq* (Cambridge: Cambridge University Press, 2000), pp. 201–02; Ramazani, *Iran's Foreign Policy*, pp. 416–19. Abd al-Ghani al-Rawi, an Iraqi army officer and deputy prime minister in the previous Iraqi regime, revealed that he had had extensive dealings with Iranian intelligence in 1969, including one long meeting with the shah himself, in planning an effort to overthrow the Ba'thist regime. The effort was aborted by the arrests of a large

The one outside power that had the means, the interest and (potentially) the local support to assume the British role of managing the international politics of the Gulf was the United States, but Washington at that time had no desire to take up the burden. Bogged down in Vietnam, and facing a Congress and public increasingly disenchanted with American military involvement abroad, the United States immediately ruled out any new military commitments in the area. It focused on bringing its two regional allies, Saudi Arabia and Iran, together to cooperate on Gulf security issues. That was easier said than done, as the two states had numerous differences, most importantly the Iranian claim to Bahrain. Washington's first attempt to broker a summit between the shah and King Faysal in February 1968 fizzled because of the Bahrain issue, though American and other mediation led to a brief stop by the shah in Saudi Arabia in June 1968 and a longer visit in November 1968. The shah signaled to the Saudis informally that he was willing to give up his claim to Bahrain, and the two states resolved an offshore boundary dispute in the period between the visits.[11] The common interest of Riyadh and Tehran in stabilizing the post-British Gulf began to manifest itself.

It fell to the Richard Nixon administration, coming into office in January 1969, to formulate a more coherent American policy toward the post-British Gulf, though the result did not substantially differ from that of its predecessor. Deliberations within the administration started from the premise that the United States would take on no new military commitments in the area. Rather, in keeping with the Nixon Doctrine, Washington would look to regional allies to maintain Gulf stability. The only debate within the administration was over whether Iran alone should assume that role or whether Saudi Arabia should also be included in the picture.

By the end of 1971, the American "twin pillar" policy in the Gulf had taken shape. Iran would be supported politically and sold considerable amounts of American arms, so that it could act as the American proxy in the region. Saudi Arabia would also be encouraged to expand its military through arms purchases, though it was seen as a distinctly

number of his confederates in Iraq in January 1970. See his memoirs, published in *al-Hayat*, July 7, 2003, p. 9; July 8, 2003, p. 9. Majid Khadduri contends that in the aftermath of the January 1970 arrests Iran and Iraq were "on the verge of war." Contemporary sources do not report such a crisis, and Khadduri himself does not mention it in his earlier works. See Khadduri, *The Gulf War: The Origins and Implications of the Iraq–Iran Conflict* (New York: Oxford University Press, 1988), pp. 49–52.

[11] Gause, "British and American Policies," p. 259; al-Saud, *Iran, Saudi Arabia and the Gulf*, Chapter 3; Shahram Chubin and Sepehr Zabih, *The Foreign Relations of Iran: A Developing State in a Zone of Great-Power Conflict* (Berkeley: University of California Press, 1974), pp. 215–18.

junior partner in security matters. Oil price increases in 1970 and 1971 would allow both states to fund this military expansion. Total arms transfers from the United States to Iran increased from $103.6 million in 1970 to $552.7 million in 1972; those to Saudi Arabia increased from $15.8 million in 1970 to $312.4 million in 1972. The United States would maintain its small naval force of three ships in the Gulf, stationed since World War II in Bahrain, but would take on no other formal security commitments.[12] Despite the recognition in Washington of the importance of the oil resources of the region, the policy at this time was premised on a desire to avoid any direct American responsibility for security issues.

The outlines of the transition to a post-British Gulf were thus falling into place by 1970. Britain was definitely leaving; the United States was definitely not going to try to assume the British role. Iran and Saudi Arabia, joined together by their pro-Western international stance, their monarchical domestic systems and their antipathy to Ba'thist Iraq, would cooperate to secure an orderly transition. But the details remained to be worked out. A solution to the Bahrain issue came first, based on a face-saving formula for Iran to withdraw its claim. In January 1969 the shah publicly suggested that Bahrainis make their own choice as to their political future. This comment became the basis for a United Nations mission to Bahrain to determine the views of the inhabitants, which reported to the Security Council Bahrainis' desire for independence. The council accepted this finding in May 1970, and the Iranian parliament ratified its renunciation of sovereignty over Bahrain a few days later.[13] The Conservative victory in the British elections of June 1970 raised the prospect that London would reassess withdrawal, and there was sentiment for such a reassessment in the new government. Iran, asserting its regional primacy, immediately expressed its opposition to any change in the British timetable. More surprising, Saudi Arabia, which had in 1968 encouraged Britain to stay in the Gulf, had by 1970 changed its tune. With security issues on their way to being settled, Riyadh began to see the benefits of asserting its own dominant role over the smaller Arab states. In March 1971, after consultations with the Iranians, the Saudis and the Gulf rulers, the Conservative government announced that it would retain the policy of withdrawal.[14]

---

[12] Gause, "British and American Policies," pp. 258–66.
[13] Al-Saud, *Iran, Saudi Arabia and the Gulf*, pp. 51–54; Heard-Bey, *From Trucial States to United Arab Emirates*, pp. 338–39; Ramazani, *Iran's Foreign Policy*, pp. 414–16.
[14] Gause, "British and American Policies," pp. 253–58.

The political status of the smaller shaykhdoms was the last unresolved question in the transition. As the date for the formal end of the protectorate approached, both Bahrain and Qatar began to establish institutions of self-government outside the negotiations for federation. With the UN finding of a popular desire for independence, along with diplomatic progress toward securing relations with both the shah's Iran and Saudi Arabia, Bahrain privately informed the other states in June 1971 that it would pursue independence. In July 1971 six of the seven current members of the United Arab Emirates announced their intention to form their new state; the seventh member, Ra's al-Khaymah, remained outside the federation for reasons that will be discussed below. Bahrain and Qatar declared their intentions to pursue independence shortly after the UAE announcement.[15]

One issue remained before the formal transfer of power from Britain to the new states, and it would have enduring consequences. The shah had made a magnanimous gesture (in his view, at least, and it was seen as such in both London and Washington) on Bahrain, but still intended to assert Iran's dominant role in the Gulf. The symbol of that dominance became control over three islands near the Strait of Hormuz, at the mouth of the Gulf – Abu Musa, Greater Tunb and Lesser Tunb.[16] The first was under the control of the emirate of Sharjah, the latter two under Ra's al-Khaymah. Britain had supported the emirates' claims, which settled the matter de facto while Britain controlled the area. Iran insisted on controlling the islands, publicly threatened to take them by force if necessary and made its acceptance of the UAE contingent upon such control. British diplomats floated a number of compromise plans to try to settle the issue, based on the idea that Iran would exercise control over the islands while acknowledging nominal Arab sovereignty.

At the eleventh hour, and clearly under duress, Sharjah reached an agreement with Iran over Abu Musa that placed the sovereignty issue in abeyance while acknowledging Iran's right to occupy part of the island. Ra's al-Khaymah turned down a similar offer. On November 30, 1971, the day before Britain's protectorate treaties with the shaykhdoms were terminated, Iranian troops landed on the three islands. On Abu Musa they were greeted by a Sharjah welcoming committee; on the Tunbs they were greeted by gunfire. There were a number of casualties on both sides, and

---

[15] The most comprehensive account of the federation negotiations is in Heard-Bey, *From Trucial States to United Arab Emirates*, Chapter 9.

[16] An excellent, balanced, short account of the history of the islands issue can be found in Richard N. Schofield, "Border Disputes in the Gulf: Past, Present and Future," in Gary G. Sick and Lawrence G. Potter (eds.), *The Persian Gulf at the Millennium* (New York: St. Martin's Press, 1997), pp. 127–66.

perhaps as many as seven deaths.[17] Neither Britain nor the new United Arab Emirates took military action. In protest against this passivity, among other issues, Ra's al-Khaymah refused to join the United Arab Emirates when the state was officially proclaimed on December 2, 1971. It formally acceded to the federation in February 1972. The shaykh of Sharjah who signed the deal on Abu Musa with Iran was assassinated in a palace coup in January 1972 that seemed to be linked to Iraq; his brother was installed as his successor after the intervention of UAE forces.[18]

With the creation of the UAE and the independence of Bahrain, Qatar and Oman at the end of 1971, the transition from British control was complete. While British diplomacy in those last years had concentrated primarily on the fate of the nine southern shaykhdoms and their relations with Iran and Saudi Arabia, London also used that time to clean up some loose ends. Without fanfare, it ended its treaty commitment to defend Kuwait. In 1970 Britain deposed Sultan Sa'id of Oman, notorious for his opposition to modernizing the country, and replaced him with his more vigorous and open-minded son, Qabus.[19] The islands dispute was the only real black mark, with enduring consequences, on what had been a successful and peaceful transfer of power after over a century of British control.

But the smoothness of the British withdrawal did not signal complete regional agreement on security issues. Iran and Iraq were still at loggerheads, with Iraq breaking off diplomatic relations with Iran (and Britain) over the islands issue. Iraqi–Kuwaiti relations remained a flashpoint, dormant at the end of 1971 but not for long. In April 1972 Iraq and the Soviet Union signed a fifteen-year treaty of friendship and cooperation, culminating a steady improvement in the relationship since the Ba'thist coup of 1968. While this move was an understandable attempt to balance American military and political support for both Iran and Saudi Arabia, it emphasized the developing superpower rivalry in the region and exacerbated suspicions of Iraq held by its conservative Gulf neighbors. The

---

[17] The fullest account of British diplomacy on the islands issue is in al-Saud, *Iran, Saudi Arabia and the Gulf*, Chapter 6.

[18] The coup attempt was led by the former ruler of Sharjah, who had been deposed by the British in 1965. He had spent part of his time in exile in Iraq, which was bitterly critical of the Iran–Sharjah deal. See Ali Mohammed Khalifa, *The United Arab Emirates: Unity in Fragmentation* (Boulder, CO: Westview Press, 1979), p. 106. See also Nadav Safran, *Saudi Arabia: The Ceaseless Quest for Security* (Cambridge, MA: Harvard University Press, 1985), p. 137; Tim Niblock, "Iraqi Policies Towards the Arab States of the Gulf, 1958–1981," in Tim Niblock (ed.), *Iraq: The Contemporary State* (London: Croom Helm, 1982), p. 145.

[19] A revisionist account of Sultan Sa'id's rule can be found in Calvin H. Allen and W. Lynn Rigsbee, II, *Oman Under Qaboos: From Coup to Constitution, 1970–1996* (London: Frank Cass, 2000). The picture even they paint of his rule is not terribly flattering.

Dhufar rebellion in Oman, to be discussed below, festered despite the change of ruler in Muscat.

Saudi Arabia and the smaller states did not view Iran as an enemy, but they also did not see it as an ally, either. Despite a concerted effort by Tehran to charm the Arab monarchs after the Bahrain issue was settled, Saudi Arabia and the smaller states resisted Iranian efforts to formalize security cooperation in an explicit Gulf security pact.[20] Even Saudi relations with the smaller monarchies were not completely settled. Riyadh withheld diplomatic recognition of the UAE until 1974, when a border agreement satisfactory to the Saudis was reached. In that agreement the Saudis recognized the Emirati claim to the Buraymi Oasis, but in exchange secured important concessions in the oil-rich area of Shaybah, claimed by Abu Dhabi, and for a small strip of territory on the Gulf that separated Qatar from the UAE.[21] There were also unsettled border issues between Bahrain and Qatar, Saudi Arabia and Qatar, the UAE and Oman, and Saudi Arabia and Oman that would arise from time to time. As the subsequent history of the Gulf demonstrates, there were plenty of unresolved issues over which the states could contend.

The Gulf and the oil revolution of the 1970s

While the political arrangements surrounding the British withdrawal were being worked out, profound changes were occurring in the structure of the world oil market. For decades the major world oil issue had been how to manage oversupply. The international oil companies had since the 1920s colluded to limit the amount of oil produced in the world, to prevent a price collapse. Producer countries were largely at the mercy of these companies, who were the only buyers, shippers and refiners of crude oil with which they could deal. An object lesson in the power relations of the world oil market was meted out to the Iranian government of Prime Minister Mossadegh in 1951–53. Mossadegh nationalized British Petroleum's holdings in Iran, after the company had refused to renegotiate the terms of its concession. In response, BP (then known as the Anglo-Iranian Oil Company) persuaded the other international oil companies to boycott Iranian oil. Production increases elsewhere, including Kuwait and Saudi Arabia, made up for the lost Iranian oil. Economic problems radicalized the Iranian political scene. In the end, with

---

[20] For a review of Iranian diplomacy on this issue and the Arab monarchies' lukewarm responses, see Laurie Ann Mylroie, "Regional Security After Empire: Saudi Arabia and the Gulf," Ph.D. dissertation, Harvard University, 1985, Chapter 2.
[21] On the UAE–Saudi border issue, see Kelly, *Arabia, the Gulf and the West*, pp. 210–12.

assistance from American and British intelligence agencies, the shah's forces deposed Mossadegh and restored monarchical control over the government. While the shah did not reverse the popular nationalization measure, control over the Iranian oil industry basically reverted to Anglo-Iranian and the other multinational companies, which were brought into the Iranian consortium after the fall of Mossadegh.[22]

By 1970, when another ambitious Middle Eastern leader decided to challenge the status quo in the world oil market, things had changed. Muammar Qaddafi, a young officer in the Libyan army, had taken power in September 1969. In June 1970 he informed Occidental Petroleum, a small American oil company operating in Libya, that it would have to increase Libya's share of the profits of its operations from 50 percent to 55 percent, and to raise the price of its oil by 30 cents per barrel (a significant amount at a time when the price of a barrel of oil was around $2.00). Occidental resisted but, threatened with nationalization, eventually capitulated. The other producers in Libya followed suit shortly thereafter.

In less than twenty years, from the Iranian crisis to the Libyan demands, the structure of power in the world oil industry had shifted. The most important reason for that shift was skyrocketing world demand for oil. Whereas in the early 1950s lost Iranian oil production could be easily replaced from other sources, by 1970 there was limited spare oil production capacity anywhere in the world. Oil production in the United States peaked in 1970. US imports of oil increased dramatically from the late 1960s. World demand for oil and world supply of oil had come into a precarious balance. That change gave producer governments more power in their dealings with oil companies. Another shift was the entrance into the world oil market of a group of smaller, "independent" oil companies, challenging the established cartel of the seven "majors" (Exxon, Mobil, Texaco, Chevron, Gulf, Shell and BP). Producer governments could play the majors off against the independents in search of better deals. It is no coincidence that Libya focused its pressure on Occidental, an independent that had no other sources of crude oil, rather than on Exxon, which also operated in Libya, but had oil resources across the globe upon which to draw. Producer countries had also improved their own level of technical sophistication and cooperation. In 1960 Iran, Iraq, Saudi Arabia, Kuwait

---

[22] For an overview of the development of the world oil industry, see Daniel Yergin, *The Prize: The Epic Quest for Oil, Money and Power* (New York: Simon & Schuster, 1991). Chapter 23 deals with the Iran crisis. For a detailed account of American involvement in the Mossadegh coup, see Mark J. Gasiorowski, "The 1953 Coup d'Etat in Iran," *International Journal of Middle East Studies*, Vol. 19, No. 3 (August 1987), pp. 261–86; Mark Gasiorowski, "The CIA Looks Back at the 1953 Coup in Iran," *Middle East Report*, No. 216 (Fall 2000), pp. 4–5.

and Venezuela had formed the Organization of Petroleum Exporting Countries (OPEC) as a forum for coordinating among themselves in dealing with the oil companies.[23]

The import of Qaddafi's coup against Occidental was not lost on the rulers of the Gulf states. In November 1970 the shah successfully insisted that the consortium of companies marketing Iranian oil increase Iran's share of the profit from 50% to 55%. In January and February 1971 representatives of the oil companies and the Gulf governments met in Tehran, and the companies agreed to extend the 55% profit-sharing arrangement to all Gulf countries, and to increase prices by 35 cents per barrel immediately and on an annual basis thereafter. A separate company–government negotiation, involving Mediterranean producers, convened shortly thereafter. Under Libyan leadership, the governments demanded an increase in the price per barrel of 90 cents, and the companies agreed. Successive negotiations in 1972 and early 1973 led to further price increases in both the Gulf and the Mediterranean. The "posted price" (a benchmark price for a particular grade of Saudi oil, from which prices for other grades of oil were set and profit calculations were made) of Gulf oil rose from below $2 per barrel at the beginning of 1970 to $2.90 by June 1973.[24] With both prices and their share of the profit increasing, all the Gulf governments enjoyed substantial increases in their revenue, which tripled if not quadrupled between 1969 and 1973 for each major Gulf oil producer (see Table 1).

The producer states also began to assert more direct control over their oil industries. In the Gulf, this process worked in different ways in different states, but all with the same effect: transferring the real decision-making power on oil questions from the companies to the governments. Iraq nationalized the Iraqi Petroleum Company (owned by BP, Shell, Exxon, Mobil and Compagnie Française des Pétroles) in June 1972. In Iran, the industry had already been officially "nationalized" since 1951, but in the early 1970s the National Iranian Oil Company took over operational control of the Iranian fields from the international consortium, which became a service contractor to the NIOC. Saudi Arabia negotiated

---

[23] These changes in the world oil market are discussed in detail in Yergin, *The Prize*, Chapters 24–28; and Dankwart A. Rustow, *Oil and Turmoil: America Faces OPEC and the Middle East* (New York: W. W. Norton, 1982), Chapters 3–4.

[24] Figures on posted prices taken from Rustow, *Oil and Turmoil*, pp. 141–42. Accounts of the negotiations among the companies and the producer countries can be found in Rustow, *Oil and Turmoil*, pp. 133–43; Yergin, *The Prize*, Chapter 28; Ian Skeet, *OPEC: Twenty-Five Years of Prices and Politics* (Cambridge: Cambridge University Press, 1988), Chapter 3; James Bamburg, *British Petroleum and Global Oil, 1950–1975: The Challenge of Nationalism* (Cambridge: Cambridge University Press, 2000), Chapter 18.

Table 1 *Oil revenues of the Gulf states, 1969–1978 (billions of US dollars)*

Year	Iran	Iraq	Saudi Arabia	Kuwait	UAE
1969	0.9	0.5	0.9	0.8	0.2
1970	1.1	0.5	1.2	0.8	0.2
1971	1.9	0.8	1.9	1.0	0.4
1972	2.4	0.6	2.7	1.4	0.6
1973	4.4	1.8	4.3	1.7	0.9
1974	17.8	5.7	22.6	6.5	5.5
1975	18.4	7.5	25.7	6.4	6.0
1976	20.2	8.5	30.8	6.9	7.0
1977	21.2	9.6	36.5	7.5	9.0
1978	19.3	10.2	32.2	8.0	8.2

Source: Ian Skeet, *OPEC: Twenty-Five Years of Prices and Politics* (Cambridge: Cambridge University Press, 1988), Appendix 3.

a "participation agreement" with Aramco (the Arabian–American Oil Company, owned by Exxon, Mobil, Chevron and Texaco), by which the Saudi government would receive a 25% share of the company in 1973, with a commitment to increase that share to 51% by 1982. Qatar and Abu Dhabi negotiated similar agreements with the oil companies operating in their territory.[25]

With the value of the US dollar, the currency in which international oil transactions are priced, cut by devaluations in 1971 and 1973, and with global energy demand continuing to rise despite the price increases of the previous three years, OPEC members pushed for higher prices. They demanded a new negotiation with the oil companies, which convened on October 8, 1973, in Vienna, just two days after Egypt and Syria had launched a surprise attack on Israeli forces in the Sinai Peninsula and on the Golan Heights. Initially the negotiations proceeded with little reference to the Middle East turmoil. The oil companies offered a 15% increase in the posted price; the OPEC negotiators, led by Saudi Arabia's oil minister, Ahmad Zaki Yamani, demanded a 100% increase. The talks broke down. The ministers from OPEC's "Gulf committee" – Iran, Iraq, Saudi Arabia, Kuwait, Qatar and the UAE – reconvened in Kuwait on October 16. They announced a unilateral decision to raise the posted price of oil by 70%, to $5.11 per barrel. For decades the major oil

---

[25] Discussions of the various ways by which the producer governments gained control over their oil industries can be found in Yergin, *The Prize*, pp. 483–85; Skeet, *OPEC*, pp. 74–81; Bamburg, *British Petroleum*, pp. 467–74.

companies had set oil prices, with no voice for producer governments. Now the opposite was the case.[26]

The unilateral price increase of October 1973 followed a logic that had been established with Libya's first challenge to Occidental in 1970. It reflected changes in the power of the actors in the world oil market, and the market realities of demand growing at a much faster rate than supply. However, what had been a process internal to the dynamics of the world oil market now became entwined with the geopolitics of the Arab–Israeli conflict and American relations with the states of the Gulf. By the time the Gulf committee met in Kuwait, Israel had turned the tide of its early battlefield setbacks, pushed the Syrian forces back toward Damascus and crossed the Suez Canal, beginning an encirclement of the Egyptian forces in Sinai. On October 17, the Gulf Arab oil ministers met in Kuwait to deploy the "oil weapon" in the Arab–Israeli conflict. They agreed to an immediate cut of 5% in their production levels, with a promise to cut 5% more every month until Israel withdrew from the territories occupied in the 1967 War. Only Iraq dissented from the decision. After urging a more radical course of complete economic warfare against the United States (complete oil embargo, nationalization of all American concerns, withdrawal of all assets from US banks, and so forth), rejected by the other states, Iraq *increased* its oil production and benefited from skyrocketing prices.

Three days later, Saudi Arabia took the step that it had resisted in Kuwait City. On October 20, Riyadh announced a complete embargo on the sale of Saudi oil to the United States. It was joined immediately by Kuwait and the UAE. In that period, not only had the United States publicly announced a $2.2 billion military aid package for Israel, but the Israeli army had also tightened its noose around the encircled Egyptian forces in Sinai. While President Nixon had committed to achieving a cease-fire in a meeting with Arab foreign ministers on October 17, Secretary of State Henry Kissinger waited until October 20 to depart for Moscow for cease-fire negotiations with the Soviets. He was informed of the Saudi embargo announcement while in the air. In a telling sign of how power had shifted in the world oil market, the Saudis ordered Aramco to enforce the embargo on sales to the United States. Aramco complied.

The combination of the decisions of October 16, 17 and 20 sent the world oil market into an unprecedented panic. The actual loss of oil to the world market, in retrospect, was not that great. In December 1973, the most severe point in the oil production reductions, about 5 million

---

[26] Yergin, *The Prize*, pp. 599–606; Bamburg, *British Petroleum*, p. 477.

barrels per day (mbd) of Arab oil were taken off the market, compared to production in October 1973. Increased production elsewhere made up about 600,000 barrels, for a net loss of 4.4 mbd, about 9 percent of total non-communist world oil production. The real demand pressures generated by this loss of oil production, combined with the enormous uncertainty over the future of oil supplies, led to unimagined increases in oil prices. Iran declared all its existing oil contracts null and void in December 1973, and held an auction for Iranian oil. Bids ranged as high as $17.00 per barrel. On December 22–23, 1973, the OPEC oil ministers met in Tehran to set a new price. Saudi Arabia, worried that a global recession would kill demand for oil, argued for $8 per barrel. Iran and Iraq, seeking maximum short-term revenues, pushed for a high price, and prevailed. OPEC adopted a benchmark price of $11.65 per barrel, effective January 1, 1974. In three months, oil prices had quadrupled.[27]

The Saudi decision to embargo oil to the United States did not, by itself, cause the oil price crisis of 1973–74. However, it was the most dramatic and unexpected element of that crisis, and a significant gamble on the part of King Faysal of Saudi Arabia, given his country's close economic and security relations with Washington. The reason for his willingness to take such a risky step lies in changed inter-Arab relations.

Before Anwar Sadat and Hafez al-Asad had come to power in their countries, the Egyptian and Syrian governments had regularly targeted Saudi Arabia in their propaganda as an American toady standing in the way of Arab unity. Sadat's predecessor, Gamal Abd al-Nasir (Nasser), had sent Egyptian troops to North Yemen in the 1960s and menaced Saudi Arabia with "accidental" Egyptian air strikes across the Saudi–Yemeni border. Both Sadat and Asad, however, saw the Saudis as a potential ally. The propaganda blitz from Cairo and Damascus ended. Sadat kept the Saudis informed about his plans, including his decision to go to war with Israel in 1973.[28] This improved state of inter-Arab relations greatly increased Saudi security, and King Faysal was therefore willing to go to great lengths to support the Egyptian and Syrian governments in the

---

[27] The most readable accounts of the events in the world oil market in this period are Yergin, *The Prize*, Chapter 29; and Bamburg, *British Petroleum*, Chapter 19. Skeet, *OPEC*, Chapter 5, supplies a number of important technical details, but little of the political context.

[28] In April 1973 Sadat informed King Faysal of his decision to go to war. Faysal in turn informed the Central Intelligence Agency station chief in Jidda, saying that, if the United States did not do something to head off an Arab–Israeli war, he would be under enormous pressure to use the "oil weapon" against the United States: personal communication with Ray Close, CIA station chief in Saudi Arabia at that time, via e-mail, May 31, 2002.

1973 war. Another ignominious Arab defeat could destabilize those governments and perhaps bring to power leaders who would follow Nasser's confrontational policy toward Riyadh.

United States foreign policy on oil issues during the early 1970s had effectively supported friendly governments such as Iran and Saudi Arabia in their dealings with the oil companies, even American companies. Washington refused to intervene on behalf of the companies in their Gulf negotiations, despite a number of direct entreaties to do so. The Nixon administration saw some oil price increase as inevitable, with the silver lining of helping both Iran and Saudi Arabia to build up their militaries so they could act as Washington's "twin pillars" in the Gulf.[29] It was only with the enormous price increases of late 1973 that the Nixon administration began to focus on the strategic implications of the changes in the world oil market. One of the signs of this new focus was the intensity with which Washington engaged in Arab–Israeli mediation from that point. Because an Arab–Israeli war had led to such economic upheaval, preventing Arab–Israeli wars became an even more important part of American Middle East policy than it had been previously. The connection between oil and the Arab–Israeli conflict was reinforced by the Saudi insistence that the United States commit itself to a Syrian–Israeli mediation, on the model of Kissinger's first Egyptian–Israeli shuttle, before it would lift the oil embargo.[30]

Unprecedented tensions emerged in US relations with Iran and Saudi Arabia over oil issues, another sign of the new geopolitical reality wrought by the oil revolution. American diplomats pushed the shah and the Saudis to work to lower oil prices. Neither American ally was willing to forego the enormous windfall that the oil price increases brought them. A number of American officials in 1973 and 1974 made not-so-veiled threats about the use of force to secure oil supplies, both during the embargo and afterwards. However, whatever impulses there might have been in Washington for confrontation were quickly overcome by moves to deepen American cooperation with both Iran and Saudi Arabia, both to solidify the US position in a region whose geopolitical importance had increased substantially and to make sure that the "petrodollars" now in the hands of these countries were recycled through the American economy. Oil would not disappear from the American agenda in its relations with its Gulf allies, and would occasionally lead to serious tensions, but oil

---

[29] Gause, "British and American Policies," p. 265; Rustow, *Oil and Turmoil*, p. 136; Bamberg, *British Petroleum*, pp. 454, 457–60, 464, 468, 470–73. See also Henry Kissinger, *Years of Upheaval* (Boston: Little, Brown, 1982), pp. 854–71.
[30] Kissinger, *Years of Upheaval*, pp. 945–53, 974–76.

disagreements would generally be dealt with in a framework of cooperative, not conflictual, relations.

The termination of the oil embargo was directly related to Arab–Israeli diplomacy. Arab oil producers, led by Saudi Arabia, canceled their scheduled 5 percent production cut for January after Kissinger's shuttle diplomacy had put together the December 21 Geneva conference, bringing Arab states, Israel and the superpowers together in a public forum for the first time. The Saudis, followed by most of the other Arab producers, lifted the embargo on oil sales to the United States in March 1974 after the American commitment to negotiate a disengagement agreement between Syria and Israel. In June 1974 Washington and Riyadh signed a wide-ranging agreement on expanded economic and military cooperation. In January 1975, Kissinger said that, if oil supplies to the West were cut off, the United States could not rule out the use of force against oil producers. Less than a week later, the United States announced a $750 million contract to sell sixty fighter jets to Saudi Arabia. The deed speaks louder than the words. In the 1975 fiscal year alone, Saudi Arabia concluded military sales agreements worth nearly $2 billion with the United States.[31]

Without the impediment of an oil embargo, American relations with Iran accelerated even faster. On November 2, 1973, the two countries agreed to establish a joint economic commission. Less than one year later, US companies had signed contracts and joint ventures with Iran that totaled $11.9 billion. In March 1975 Washington and Tehran negotiated an economic accord that committed Iran to spend $15 billion on American goods and services over the next five years. Iran also sent tens of thousands of students to American campuses for higher education in the 1970s. Between 1972 and 1977, American military sales to Iran totaled $16.2 billion.[32] The "twin pillar" policy of American reliance on Iran and Saudi Arabia to secure American interests in the Gulf did not change as a result of the oil revolution of 1973. Rather, those events deepened the American dependence upon, and involvement in, those two countries.

The regional political effects of the oil revolution were numerous and varied. First, all the regional states got much richer, as Table 1 indicates. That wealth came directly into the hands of these governments from the international economy. The governments then distributed this money through their societies as they saw fit, giving them enormous power over

---

[31] Safran, *Saudi Arabia*, pp. 172–75.
[32] James A. Bill, *The Eagle and the Lion: The Tragedy of American–Iranian Relations* (New Haven: Yale University Press, 1988), pp. 200–15.

those societies.[33] That power did not ensure political stability. The social dislocations of sudden wealth, in terms of urbanization, inflation and corruption, contributed to the outbreak of the Iranian Revolution in the late 1970s. However, in the immediate term this new wealth helped to smooth the transition to independence for the smaller Gulf monarchies. General prosperity helped reduce social tensions in Bahrain, where the Sunni ruling family was governing a Shi'i majority population. Oil-rich Abu Dhabi was able to maintain the loyalty of the poorer shaykhdoms to the new UAE through the judicious use of its wealth. The stability of the new states reduced the opportunities for meddling in their domestic politics by the larger regional powers, reducing the chances of confrontations among them. Cooperation among Iran, Iraq and Saudi Arabia in the negotiations with the international oil companies in the early 1970s underscored the fact that they shared at least some common interests, at a time when the British withdrawal opened up new possibilities of conflict and rivalry among them. Conflict and rivalry did not disappear, as Iranian–Iraqi tensions and the dispute over the Gulf islands indicate. But, to some extent, the oil boom of the early 1970s lent greater stability to regional political relations at a time of transition.

Second, their new oil wealth also allowed the three major regional powers to engage in a frantic and fantastic arms buildup. Between 1975 and 1979, Iran, Saudi Arabia and Iraq accounted for 56 percent of all the arms imports in the Middle East, which amounted to more than one-quarter of all those in the Third World.[34] This acquisition of large amounts of sophisticated weaponry might have played some deterrent role on regional conflict in the 1970s. It was only after the Iranian Revolution, when the new Iranian government cut itself off from the United States, its major weapons supplier, that Iraq launched a war against Iran. However, this arms buildup also gave regional actors the confidence to assert themselves more openly in Gulf politics. The ambitions of both the shah of Iran in the 1970s and Saddam Hussein in the 1980s and early 1990s to be the "strong man" of the Gulf were fed by their ability to acquire large amounts of sophisticated military technology. The

---

[33] The domestic political consequences of great oil wealth, what has been termed the "rentier state" phenomenon, have been examined in a rich and varied scholarly literature in the 1980s and 1990s. Among the most important contributions to that literature are: Jill Crystal, *Oil and Politics in the Gulf: Rulers and Merchants in Kuwait and Qatar* (Cambridge: Cambridge University Press, 1990); Kiren Aziz Chaudhry, *The Price of Wealth: Economies and Institutions in the Middle East* (Ithaca: Cornell University Press, 1997); Terry Lynn Karl, *The Paradox of Plenty: Oil Booms and Petro-States* (Berkeley: University of California Press, 1997); and Michael Herb, *All in the Family: Absolutism, Revolution and Democracy in the Middle Eastern Monarchies* (Albany: State University of New York Press, 1999).

[34] Stockholm International Peace Research Institute, *SIPRI Yearbook 1980*, Table 3.7.

arms race in the Gulf exacerbated the existing security dilemma among the major powers, but it did not create it. Iran, Iraq and Saudi Arabia had viewed each other with suspicion for decades. The arms race certainly raised the destructiveness of regional wars when they did occur in the 1980s and 1990s.

The third consequence of the oil boom for regional politics was to give the local states greater independence from their outside power patrons, at least during the 1970s. The most obvious manifestation of that new independence was Saudi Arabia's decision to impose an oil embargo on the United States in October 1973. It would later refuse to support the American-brokered peace between Egypt and Israel in 1979. Iran made it clear to Britain in 1970, when the Conservatives returned to power, that it would oppose a continued British military presence in the region. Iran also took the lead in late 1973 and early 1974 in pushing oil prices up. The shah remained a leader of the "price hawks" in OPEC through the 1970s, despite the American preference for stable prices at lower levels. Iraq took some distance from the Soviet Union, diversifying its sources of arms purchases (with France in the late 1970s becoming a major supplier of arms to Iraq) and vehemently criticizing the Soviet invasion of Afghanistan in 1979.

All these manifestations of independence from the superpowers can be traced, directly or indirectly, to the new power that increased oil revenues brought to Saudi Arabia, Iran and Iraq. However, this increased power did not substantially change the pattern of local or international alignments in the region. Iran and Saudi Arabia remained close to the United States, and Iraq to the Soviet Union. If anything, their superpower patrons were even keener to maintain close relations with their local allies because of their increased geopolitical and economic importance. All three regional powers remained wary of each other, with Saudi Arabia and Iran enjoying somewhat better relations than either had with Iraq. The regional distribution of power was not fundamentally altered. None of the three major regional powers gained relative to the other two, for each benefited enormously from the oil windfall. The pre-1973 "balance" continued, although at a much higher level of armaments.

Regional interventions: the Kurds and the Dhufar rebellion

Regional rivalries in the Gulf during the 1970s were pursued, in great part, through outside intervention in the domestic politics of neighboring states. The two most important cases of such intervention were the Kurdish issue in Iraq and the Dhufar rebellion in Oman. In both cases the shah of Iran intervened in these domestic disputes to extend Iran's power and assert his role as "policeman" of the Gulf. In the former he backed the Kurdish opponents of the Ba'thist regime in Baghdad; in the latter he supported the Omani sultan against leftist rebels.

When the Ba'th Party came to power in Iraq in 1968, it immediately sought to placate the Iraqi Kurdish minority. While it succeeded in gaining the support of some Kurdish factions, it was unable to reconcile with the major Kurdish party, the Kurdish Democratic Party (KDP), led by the redoubtable Kurdish chieftain Mustafa Barazani. The KDP attacked government and oil facilities, pressuring the Ba'th at a time when it was still weak internally and facing Iranian pressure along the border. In March 1970 the Iraqi government offered a wide-ranging autonomy agreement to Barazani, who accepted. However, by 1972 fighting had resumed in Iraqi Kurdistan. The Baghdad government had not completely implemented the March 1970 agreement and Barazani had not severed his ties to Iran. Israel also continued its support for the Kurdish insurgents. With the Iraqi nationalization of its oil industry and its conclusion of a friendship treaty with the Soviet Union in 1972, the United States also began to support the Kurdish insurgency. Between 1972 and March 1974, Baghdad and the KDP leadership alternated between talks and hostilities. In March 1974 the Ba'thist government issued an autonomy law for Iraqi Kurdistan and gave Barazani two weeks to accept it and join the ruling regime. The KDP rejected the law, which fell short of their demands to have Kirkuk included in the Kurdish autonomous areas and to have real financial and police powers accorded to the regional authority. The Kurdish areas rose in full rebellion against Baghdad, with open support from the shah (border tensions had resumed between Iran and Iraq at the same time) and (barely) covert support from the United States and Israel.[35]

In the Dhufar province of southern Oman, what had originally been manageable tribal unrest had by the early 1970s developed into an ideological movement aimed at overthrowing the sultan. The turning point in this process was the victory of the Marxists in South Yemen in 1969. With Soviet and Chinese support, the government in Aden encouraged leftist elements to take control of the Dhufari movement, which adopted the name "Popular Front for the Liberation of Oman." With a secure base across the border and military supplies from the communist powers, the PFLO had effective control of most of Dhufar province by 1970. In that year the British deposed Sultan Sa'id, replacing him with his more

---

[35] On the Iraqi Kurdish question during this period, see Marr, *The Modern History of Iraq*, pp. 222–23, 232–36; and David McDowall, *A Modern History of the Kurds* (London: I. B. Tauris, 2000), Chapter 16.

vigorous son Qabus, as was mentioned above. The new sultan actively confronted the rebels, both militarily and politically. He increased government spending in the region and offered inducements for tribal and rebel leaders to join the government. The Omani army, with British and Jordanian advisers, took the fight to the PFLO. They were joined by thousands of Iranian forces and F-5s from the Iranian air force. In December 1975 Sultan Qabus declared that the rebellion had been crushed and the government was in control of all of Dhufar. Despite the end of the fighting, Iranian forces remained in Oman at the request of the sultan.[36]

Iraq also tried to play the game of intervention in the affairs of its Gulf neighbors, though much less successfully than Iran. Iraq supported the Dhufari rebels in Oman and their sponsor, the Marxist government of South Yemen. Circumstantial evidence points to Iraqi complicity in the coup attempt against the shaykh of Sharjah in 1972 mentioned above. The Iraqi media were very critical of Saudi policy, both its relations with the United States and its cooperation with Iran on security issues, at times openly calling for popular revolt against the Saudi regime. Iraqi pressure on Kuwait was more overt. With Iran effectively in control of the Shatt al-Arab, Baghdad looked to expand its access to the Gulf through Kuwaiti territory. It pressed for control over two Kuwaiti islands, Warba and Bubiyan, that controlled access to the Iraqi port of Um Qasr. In December 1972 Iraq moved troops toward the border, and in March 1973 they occupied a Kuwaiti border post. Saudi Arabia strongly supported Kuwait in the crisis, and Arab League pressure led to an Iraqi withdrawal.[37]

From the Algiers Agreement to the Iranian Revolution, 1975–1978

A major turning point in regional relations occurred in March 1975. Iraq and Iran, which had confronted one another over their various border and political disputes for years, reached an agreement on all their outstanding differences. Iraq recognized Iranian sovereignty over half of the Shatt al-Arab river, acquiescing to a longstanding Iranian demand. In return, Iran agreed to turn over to Iraq disputed territory along their central frontier

---

[36] Joseph A. Kechichian, *Oman and the World* (Santa Monica, CA: RAND, 1995), pp. 99–101. Kechichian reports that more than 100 Iranian soldiers died in the Dhufar fighting. See also Mylroie, "Regional Security After Empire," pp. 115–20.

[37] Niblock, "Iraqi Policies Towards the Arab States of the Gulf," pp. 139–45; Marr, *The Modern History of Iraq*, pp. 220–22; Mylroie, "Regional Security After Empire," Chapter 3.

and, more importantly, to end its support for the Iraqi Kurdish rebellion. The agreement was explicitly based on "the principles of territorial integrity, border inviolability and noninterference in internal affairs."[38] This diplomatic deal was signed by Saddam Hussein and the shah at the OPEC meeting in Algiers, after mediation by Jordan and Algeria.

The dispute over the Shatt al-Arab, a river formed from the confluence of the Tigris and Euphrates, had been an irritant in Iranian–Iraqi relations for decades, and would reemerge at the outset of the Iran–Iraq War in 1980. In 1937 the new state of Iraq and Iran agreed on Iraqi sovereignty over the whole river, with the important exception of an eight-kilometer stretch from the mouth of the Gulf to the Iranian port of Abadan. In that part of the river, the boundary would be the midpoint of the navigable channel, known in maritime law as the thalweg. This would give Iran sovereign rights of access to the port of Abadan, where the Anglo-Iranian Oil Company had built an enormous oil refinery. However, tensions between the two countries following the overthrow of the Iraqi monarchy in 1958 scuttled the 1937 agreement. Iraqi president Abd al-Karim Qasim asserted Iraqi sovereignty over the entire Shatt al-Arab. As mentioned above, after the Ba'thist coup in 1968 Iran unilaterally abrogated the 1937 agreement and asserted equal rights in the Shatt by force.[39]

While resolution of the border disputes was an important part of the Algiers Agreement, a more fundamental agreement – for each to accept the legitimacy and durability of the other's domestic political regime – underlay the specifics of territorial control and riparian rights. Since the Ba'thist takeover in 1968 both states had attempted to foment domestic political problems for the other. The shah's support for Iraq's Kurdish opposition was by far the most significant of those efforts. Iranian forces actually joined the fighting on the Kurdish side in early 1975, and provoked clashes elsewhere along the border to draw off Iraqi forces from the Kurdish front.[40] Much of the Iraqi army was tied down in confronting the rebellion. Saddam Hussein later said that, in the year before the Algiers Agreement was signed, Iraq suffered 60,000 casualties (dead and wounded) in the fighting.[41] With the Algiers Agreement, Iranian support

---

[38] The text of the Algiers Agreement can be found in Khadduri, *The Gulf War*, pp. 199–200.

[39] For the historical background on the Iran–Iraq border dispute, see Richard Schofield, *Evolution of the Shatt al-Arab Boundary Dispute* (Wisbech, UK: Menas Press, 1986); and Khadduri, *The Gulf War*, pp. 12, 35–41, 49–52.

[40] Kenneth M. Pollack, *Arabs at War: Military Effectiveness, 1948–1991* (Lincoln: University of Nebraska Press, 2002), p. 179.

[41] Foreign Broadcast Information Service, Middle East-Africa (FBIS-MEA), 80–216, November 5, 1980, p. E2. In an interview with the author (New York, March 9, 1995), Iraqi foreign minister Tariq Aziz said that Iraqi casualties in the north before the Algiers Agreement were between 15,000 and 16,000, still a substantial number.

for the Kurdish rebellion ended, also cutting off the Israeli and American supply routes to the Iraqi Kurdish forces. Mustafa Barazani and over 100,000 of his followers crossed the border into Iran; thousands of other Iraqi Kurdish fighters surrendered to government forces.[42] The Ba'thist government clearly made the greater territorial compromise in ceding its claim to all of the Shatt al-Arab, but in return bought some breathing space for consolidating its hold over the country.

Iraq's willingness to settle its differences with Iran was but one aspect of a general turn in Baghdad's foreign policy away from ideological confrontation and toward state-to-state cooperation, not just with Iran but also with the Gulf monarchies. While Iranian military pressure through the Kurds was the major reason for this switch, it also reflected the Ba'thist government's appreciation that its previous policies had isolated it both in the Gulf and in the larger Arab region. The shift began at the Rabat Arab summit of October 1974, with Iraq welcoming a proposal that Jordan sound out Iran about the possibilities of a settlement of their differences and generally exhibiting a new willingness to work with Egypt and Saudi Arabia.[43] Baghdad followed the Algiers Agreement with a charm offensive toward Saudi Arabia and the smaller Gulf monarchies. High-level Iraqi officials, including Vice President Saddam Hussein and President Ahmad Hassan al-Bakr, visited the kingdom, and ranking Saudis, like Crown Prince Fahd, paid return visits to Baghdad. Iraq ended propaganda efforts critical of the Saudi rulers and suspended covert activities in the kingdom.[44] In June 1975 the two states settled outstanding border issues, agreeing to divide equally the diamond-shaped "neutral zone" carved out by the British in the 1920s. In early 1976 Iraq ended its support for the Dhufari rebels and established diplomatic relations with Oman. After an increase in border tensions in 1976, Iraq and Kuwait agreed in 1977 to mutual troop withdrawals and to the establishment of a committee to resolve the border issue. In July 1977 Kuwait reopened its border with Iraq, closed since 1972.

---

[42] McDowall, *A Modern History of the Kurds*, p. 338; on Iranian moves along the border south of the Kurdish areas, see Dilip Hiro, *The Longest War: The Iran–Iraq Military Conflict* (New York: Routledge, 1991), p. 16.

[43] Interview with Tariq Aziz (March 9, 1995, New York). See also Mylroie, "Regional Security After Empire," pp. 147–51.

[44] Sa'ad al-Bazzaz, *Harb tulid 'ukhra: al-tarikh al-sirri li-harb al-khalij* [One War Leads to Another: The Secret History of the Gulf War] (Amman: Al-Ahliya Publishing and Distribution, 1993), p. 207; Mylroie, "Regional Security After Empire," pp. 140–49; Marion Farouk-Sluglett and Peter Sluglett, *Iraq Since 1958: From Revolution to Dictatorship* (London: I. B. Tauris, 1990), pp. 200–02; Safran, *Saudi Arabia*, pp. 265–66; Marr, *The Modern History of Iraq*, p. 244.

The easing of tensions in relations among the Gulf states did not, however, end the competition for regional influence among them. Iraq and Saudi Arabia resisted Tehran's efforts to organize a Gulf security pact under Iranian leadership. Saudi Arabia distanced itself slightly from Iran as it improved relations with Iraq. The Saudis also more openly asserted their leadership of the smaller Gulf monarchies. Saudi pressure played a role in the decisions by the amir of Bahrain to suspend his country's elected National Assembly in August 1975 and by the amir of Kuwait to do the same in August 1976 (how much is difficult to ascertain, as domestic developments in both countries also pushed the rulers in this direction). In late March–early April 1976 King Khalid, who had succeeded his half-brother Faysal after the latter's assassination in March 1975, became the first Saudi monarch to visit the Gulf states. Khalid urged the other Arab monarchs to resist Iranian pressure to subscribe to the shah's proposed security plan and pushed Saudi Arabia's alternative – a series of bilateral agreements on internal security cooperation.[45]

Feeling generally more secure in the Gulf, the Saudis also took more assertive positions within OPEC between 1975 and 1978. At the September 1975 OPEC meeting in Vienna, Saudi Arabia strongly opposed an Iranian proposal, backed by Iraq, for a 15% price increase, arguing for a 5% hike and eventually agreeing to a compromise of 10%. At the May 1976 OPEC meeting in Bali, Iraq and Iran both publicly attacked the Saudi position that prices should remain stable, but the Saudi position prevailed. The December 1976 OPEC meeting in Doha witnessed the organization's first public split. Iran and Iraq were both pushing for a major price increase. Saudi Arabia, joined by the UAE and with the strong support of Washington, was adamant that prices be increased only 5%. The other members announced a 10% increase for January 1977, with a further 5% increase in July 1977; the Saudis and the Emiratis demurred, announcing a 5% increase. Riyadh did more than oppose its fellow OPEC members. It also increased oil production, pressuring prices downward and encouraging other OPEC members' customers to buy cheaper Saudi oil. The Iraqi oil minister called Saudi Arabia "a defeatist and uncompromising reactionary cell," while the Iranian newspaper *Kayhan* called Saudi oil minister Yamani "a stooge of capitalist circles, a yellow belly, a traitor." But the Saudi production increase, along with direct American diplomatic pressure on Iran, had its effects. In June 1977 OPEC members agreed to forego their planned 5% price increase, and Saudi Arabia agreed to bring its prices up 5% in line with other OPEC members. With Iran

---

[45] The diplomacy behind the various Gulf security proposals during this period is exhaustively covered by Mylroie, "Regional Security After Empire," Chapter 4.

switching positions and joining the Saudis, OPEC agreed to freeze prices during 1978.[46] The Saudi willingness to confront Iran and Iraq on price issues during this period stemmed from a number of factors. In general, Riyadh was not as hawkish on prices as either Tehran or Baghdad. It had the world's largest oil reserves and sought to maintain world demand for oil at the highest possible level for the longest possible time. Relations with the United States also played a role. After the strain of 1973–74, the Saudis had reestablished very close relations with Washington, and the United States avidly sought price restraint from its oil producing allies. Confronting the OPEC hawks won Saudi Arabia points in Washington. Iran's shift from price hawk to price moderate during 1977 was a response to American pressure and entreaties as well as recognition that the Saudis were cutting into Iranian market share. But part of Riyadh's willingness to go it alone during this period, against both Iran and Iraq, came from the relative security the Saudi leadership felt in the post-Algiers Agreement Gulf. The risk that differences on oil issues would lead to more direct political or military confrontations was lower than before. Saudi Arabia did not need Iranian support against a potential Iraqi threat as much as it had previously, and thus it could afford a split with Iran on oil issues.

The same environment of regional security that allowed the Saudis to take more independent positions on oil issues also permitted the two most independent-minded of the smaller monarchies, Kuwait and Oman, to take some distance from Saudi Arabia. Sultan Qabus, despite promises to the contrary, never completely abandoned his reliance on security ties with Iran. Only with the Iranian Revolution did the last Iranian troops leave Oman. In August 1976 Kuwait signed a $400 million arms deal with the Soviet Union, an assertion of independence from the vehemently anti-communist Saudis. Both countries politely demurred from Saudi proposals in the fall of 1976 that the Arab monarchies form an organization for internal security cooperation that would exclude Iraq (of special concern to Kuwait) and Iran (ally of Oman).[47]

---

[46] Skeet, *OPEC*, Chapter 6; quotes from p. 135. For a detailed account of American oil diplomacy in this period, see Andrew Scott Cooper, "Showdown at Doha: The Secret Oil Deal That Helped Sink the Shah of Iran," *Middle East Journal*, Vol. 62, No. 4 (Autumn 2008), pp. 567–91. Cooper's contention that Iran's loss of market share, and the concomitant loss of revenue, created an economic crisis that helped spur the revolution is well supported. His implication that there was some explicit Saudi–American deal to weaken the shah's regime is less convincing.

[47] Safran, *Saudi Arabia*, p. 269.

Perhaps the most telling sign of the relative stability in relations among the Gulf states in the period after the Algiers Agreement was that none of his Gulf neighbors, even Iraq, sought to exploit the shah's growing domestic problems. On the contrary, as demonstrations snowballed in Iran, the Ba'thist government expelled Ayatollah Khomeini from Najaf in October 1978, where he had been fulminating against the shah since 1963.[48] Khomeini decamped to Paris, where access to the Western media paradoxically strengthened his leadership role in the gathering political storm in Iran. In fact, the shah's domestic problems to a certain extent brought the Gulf countries together, as the Ba'thist regime in Iraq had no interest in seeing Shi'i militancy succeed across the border, and the Saudis had an equal distaste for anti-monarchical movements. After over two years of opposing each other's Gulf security proposals, the three major states in the summer of 1978 engaged in intensive negotiations aimed at increasing their level of cooperation on domestic security issues. The negotiations came to naught, however, as mutual suspicions remained high and as the shah's regime became increasingly unstable at home.[49]

While Iraq did not seek to exploit the shah's domestic problems directly, the weakening of Iran combined with events in the Arab–Israeli arena presented the Ba'thist regime in 1978 with an unprecedented opportunity to assert its leadership in the Arab world. Egyptian president Anwar Sadat's trip to Jerusalem in November 1977 had split the Saudi-Egyptian-Syrian triangle that had fought the 1973 war and dominated inter-Arab politics. With the Camp David accords between Israel and Egypt in September 1978, the Saudis faced a difficult choice. On the one hand, their most important Arab ally, Egypt, and their superpower patron, the United States, expected support for the agreement. On the other hand, Iraq was mobilizing support in the Arab world to oppose the accords, putting itself forward as an alternative leader to Egypt. The Ba'thist regime even patched up its longstanding feud with the Syrian Ba'thist government, though only temporarily, to present a united rejectionist front.

---

[48] Official Iraqi sources insist that their decision to expel Khomeini was not made at the behest of the shah's regime, which they contend asked Iraq to allow Khomeini to stay. Rather, the decision stemmed from an Iraqi fear that, if Khomeini continued his anti-shah activities, it would give Iran a pretext to break the Algiers Agreement, to obstruct the transfer of territory still held by Iran to Iraq under the terms of that agreement and to renew efforts to meddle in Iraqi domestic politics. This logic was set out in a series of articles on Iran–Iraq relations published in *al-Thawra* newspaper in June 1979 (see specifically FBIS-MEA-79-116, June 14, 1979, pp. E4–E5) and reiterated in Arab Ba'th Socialist Party-Iraq, *The Central Report of the Ninth Regional Congress, June 1982* (Baghdad: n.p., 1983), pp. 172–73.

[49] *New York Times*, June 18, 1978, p. 1; Safran, *Saudi Arabia*, pp. 273–75.

Caught between these two powerful poles, the Saudis temporized. They attended the Arab summit meeting in Baghdad in November 1978, called by Iraq to condemn Egypt, but argued that any tangible sanctions against Egypt should be postponed until an actual peace treaty with Israel was signed. The Iraqis accommodated the Saudis, knowing that having Riyadh as a member of the anti-Camp David front would strengthen their position immeasurably. Rather than threatening Riyadh publicly, as they would have done before 1975, the Ba'thist leadership left up to the Saudi imagination the costs of defiance, emphasizing its desire for cooperative relations. With the shah's regime looking increasingly shaky, the need for the Saudis to maintain good relations with Iraq loomed large in the Saudi strategic picture. As the shah's regime collapsed and Egypt signed its treaty with Israel in early 1979, the Saudis would revisit this difficult choice.[50] Iraq, with Iran in chaos and most of the Arab world solidly behind it against Sadat's Egypt, appeared ready to assume the leading role both in Arab politics and in the Gulf.

Conclusion

The period between the British withdrawal from the Gulf in 1971 and the fall of the monarchy in Iran in January 1979 was the most stable in the recent history of the Gulf. While there were regional crises, there was no major war. Considerable mistrust existed among the regional states, but so did the basis for compromise and conciliation. The great powers were involved in the region, but not nearly to the extent that they – particularly the United States – would be subsequently.

The major reason for this relative stability was the fact that disputes over the domestic bases of political legitimacy among the regional states were muted during the first part of the period, and non-existent in the second. While the major regional powers jockeyed for geopolitical position and advantage, they did not actively threaten the domestic political stability of their neighbors, or, when they did, they were willing to compromise rather than push an opponent to the brink of regime collapse. With their core interest – regime stability – unthreatened, the regional powers saw no need to risk international war. Power is important here. The status quo states had a considerable power advantage over the one potential regional revolutionary, Ba'thist Iraq. However, that power imbalance served a

---

[50] The best account of Saudi policy during this period is Safran, *Saudi Arabia*, Chapters 9–10.

moderate regional agenda, one that accepted the reality and the legitimacy of the regimes in all the Gulf states.

From 1971 to March 1975, the preponderance of regional power was overwhelmingly in the hands of monarchical regimes. The Saudis might not have trusted the shah's ultimate intentions, and the smaller Arab monarchies had their own worries about Riyadh's ambitions. They were united not only in their international alignments, but also in their domestic political arrangements. The shah's power was not a threat to regime stability in the Arab monarchies; it provided support. Iraq could do little to challenge the Iranian-led and American-supported monarchical alignment in the region – just the reverse. Iran did what it could to destabilize the Ba'thist regime within Iraq itself.

But Iranian efforts were meant to pressure Iraq, not change the Iraqi regime. When Iraq agreed to acknowledge Iranian power in the region with the Algiers Agreement of March 1975, the shah ceased his support for the Iraqi Kurdish opposition forces. In the reassessment of its regional policy that accompanied the Algiers Agreement, Baghdad dropped the revolutionary rhetoric that had frightened the Arab monarchs of the Gulf and very publicly ceased its support for revisionist movements in the region. For that brief period, from the Algiers Agreement to the fall of the shah, none of the regional powers sought change in the domestic arrangements of its neighbors. This was not an alliance or a security concert. Iraq, Iran and Saudi Arabia all pursued foreign policies aimed at maximizing their own power and displayed considerable mistrust of each other's power and ultimate intentions. However, the most sensitive issue and core concern of each regime – its own hold on power domestically – was not challenged by other regional players. Even as the shah's regime tottered, neither Iraq nor Saudi Arabia sought to gain advantage through intervention in Iranian domestic politics. Rather, to the extent that they could (which was not much), they supported the shah against his domestic opponents. Gulf regional politics during this period were moderate not only because the status quo states had the upper hand in terms of power, but also because the agenda pursued by those states was limited.

The limited nature of the aims of the regional states is even more noticeable when we remember that the oil revolution of the 1970s provided numerous incentives for more grandiose ambitions. Each of the major regional states was much richer and more capable of contemplating an aggressive foreign policy, and all built up their militaries at dizzying rates. The weaker Gulf states were much more attractive targets, as the oil on which they sat was a much more precious prize than it had ever been before. The United States and the Soviet Union were less willing and less able to play a major military role in the region than they would be subsequently, so the international constraints on regional adventurism were not nearly what they would become. Yet there was relative peace, compared to what came after. That is partly attributable to old-fashioned balance of power politics, but the operations of the balance of power failed to restrain conflict subsequently. It was the moderation of the regional agenda, the acceptance by the major players of sovereignty and legitimacy of the other regional players, that sets this period apart from what followed in the Gulf.

3   The Iranian Revolution and the Iran–Iraq War

The Iranian Revolution is a pivot of modern Middle Eastern history. It was that rarest of political events – a real social revolution, on a par with the French, Russian and Chinese revolutions. Its impact, like that of its historical counterparts, was not contained by Iran's borders. Among its regional effects, it substantially changed the geopolitics of the Persian Gulf. It destroyed the American–Iranian alliance, one of the "twin pillars" upon which American policy in the region was built. It ushered in a new global oil crisis, with prices nearly doubling between 1978 and 1980. It led directly to the Iran–Iraq War, which was not only a battle for regional dominance but also a struggle over the political future of the area, with revolutionary Islam challenging the status quo of Ba'thist Arab nationalism in Iraq and monarchy in the Gulf states. It made allies out of former enemies – if only for a time – and altered the pattern of regional alignments developed in the 1970s.

The Iran–Iraq War lasted for nearly eight years, costing each side close to 200,000 dead and perhaps twice that number wounded.[1] It left the

---

[1] It has become the conventional wisdom that there were a million deaths in the Iran–Iraq War. It is difficult, even if wounded are included, to see how overall casualty figures on the two sides for the war could be that great. In a September 23, 2000, report from the Islamic Republic News Agency, the director general of the Statistics and Information Department at the Islamic Revolution Martyrs Foundation, an agency of the Iranian government, put the number of Iranian dead during the war at 188,015, the vast majority on the battle front, and 16,780 as a result of air, artillery and missile attacks on cities. Other Iranian officials have put the total number of Iranian dead slightly higher, as high as 220,000. Estimates of the Iranian wounded range between 320,000 and 400,000. Iraq never published an official count of its war dead and wounded. A former head of Iraqi military intelligence estimated Iraq's war dead at 180,000. On the rough estimate that Iraqi wounded would not be more than two-thirds of Iran's number, and assuming the upper range totals for all figures, total killed and wounded on both sides in the war might be as high as 1 million, but deaths could not be more than 400,000. For the casualty figures and estimates cited here, see Lawrence Potter and Gary Sick, "Introduction," in Lawrence Potter and Gary Sick (eds.), *Iran, Iraq and the Legacies of War* (New York: Palgrave Macmillan, 2004), p. 8, note 5. Phebe Marr reports total military casualties for Iraq in the war of 380,000, of which about 125,000 dead, though she does not cite a source for these figures: *The Modern History of Iraq*, 2nd edn. (Boulder, CO: Westview Press, 2004), p. 207.

region poorer by hundreds of billions of dollars in lost oil production, physical destruction and wasted human and economic capital. However, the war's political and strategic effects were not commensurate with its devastating human and economic toll. Neither Iran nor Iraq was able to impose its will on the other. The end of the war found the combatants in roughly the same position as when the war started, with two important exceptions: Saddam Hussein's Iraq was armed to the teeth and facing real economic problems as a result of the war; and the United States had by the end of the war become more directly involved militarily in the region than at any previous time.

The geopolitical effects of the Iranian Revolution, 1979–1980

The causes of the Iranian Revolution and the course of post-revolutionary Iranian domestic politics are fascinating topics, but beyond the scope of this work.[2] I concentrate here on the regional and international repercussions of the revolution, which were immediate and considerable, in three areas – the regional politics of the Gulf, the world oil market and superpower policies in the region.

Political fallout in the Gulf

After months of escalating tensions, demonstrations and riots, on January 19, 1979, the shah left Iran. On February 1, 1979, Ayatollah Khomeini, who had emerged as the focal point of the growing revolutionary opposition, returned to Iran. He was greeted at the airport in Tehran by 2 million Iranians and promptly appointed his own government. On February 11, 1979, the last remnants of the imperial order collapsed and the revolutionaries took control of the country.

Every other Gulf state felt the reverberations of the Iranian Revolution in its own politics. Those reverberations were greatest among Shi'a in the Arab states, and thus the domestic political impact was most noticeable in the Shi'i majority states, Iraq and Bahrain, and in states with important

---

[2] Some of the better contributions to the question of why and how the revolution happened are: Nikki R. Keddie, *Roots of Revolution: An Interpretive History of Modern Iran* (New Haven: Yale University Press, 1981); Ervand Abrahamian, *Iran Between Two Revolutions*, (Princeton: Princeton University Press, 1982); Mohsen M. Milani, *The Making of Iran's Islamic Revolution*, 2nd edn. (Boulder, CO: Westview Press, 1994); and Said Amir Arjomand, *The Turban for the Crown: The Islamic Revolution in Iran* (New York: Oxford University Press, 1988). An excellent account of the early years of post-revolution politics is Shaul Bakhash, *The Reign of the Ayatollahs* (New York: Basic Books, 1984).

Shi'i minorities, Kuwait and Saudi Arabia (in the oil-producing Eastern Province). For all the regional elites, the example of a popular revolution unseating an apparently strong regime which had superpower backing was extremely disturbing. Even more disturbing were the signs that the revolutionary government in Tehran would actively encourage similar movements in neighboring states. Those domestic disturbances and Iran's apparent desire to "export" the revolution led to important changes in the foreign policies of all the Arab states of the Gulf.

As the shah's regime fell, a wave of Shi'i unrest swept the Arab states. In Iraq, Shi'i opposition and the government reaction to it were particularly violent. Massive demonstrations in the Iraqi shrine cities of Najaf and Karbala followed the arrest of Ayatollah Muhammad Baqir al-Sadr in June 1979, on the eve of his scheduled trip to Tehran. Al-Da'wa (The Call), the major Iraqi Shi'i opposition group at the time, was emboldened by the success of the Iranian Revolution to attack regime symbols and personnel. Both underground Shi'i groups and members of the clerical hierarchy (though not all of them) were, by the fall of 1979, calling for violent opposition to the government. In March 1980 the government made membership in the Da'wa Party punishable by death. In April 1980 an attempt was made on the life of the deputy prime minister, Tariq Aziz, by Shi'i militants. The regime responded by executing Ayatollah al-Sadr and his sister, arresting thousands and deporting tens of thousands of Iraqis of Iranian origin to Iran.[3]

In Bahrain, demonstrations organized by pro-Iranian Shi'i clerics occurred in August 1979 and in April, May and June 1980. Kuwait witnessed a similar demonstration, in front of the American embassy in Kuwait City, in November 1979, at the outset of the Iranian hostage crisis. In Saudi Arabia, leaflets circulated among the Shi'i minority throughout 1979 supporting the Iranian Revolution. In late November of that year, Saudi Shi'a in towns throughout the Eastern Province, in defiance of a government ban, publicly observed '*ashura*, the Shi'i holy day that commemorates the martyrdom of Imam Hussein. Riots ensued, with several protesters and members of the Saudi National Guard killed. Unrest emerged again in early February 1980 in the Shi'i city of Qatif, on the first anniversary (in the Muslim lunar calendar) of Ayatollah Khomeini's return to Iran.[4] On November 20, 1979,

---

[3] Charles Tripp, *A History of Iraq* (Cambridge: Cambridge University Press, 2000), pp. 220 – 21, 229–30; Marion Farouk-Sluglett and Peter Sluglett, *Iraq Since 1958: From Revolution to Dictatorship* (London: I. B. Tauris, 1990), pp. 198–200; Joyce N. Wiley, *The Islamic Movement of Iraqi Shi'as* (Boulder, CO: Lynne Rienner, 1992), pp. 52–58.

[4] R. K. Ramazani, *Revolutionary Iran: Challenge and Response in the Middle East* (Baltimore: Johns Hopkins University Press, 1986), pp. 49–50; Christin Marschall, *Iran's Persian Gulf*

the Saudi regime was shaken by the takeover of the Grand Mosque in Mecca by Sunni Islamists, who condemned the ruling family and called for an uprising against them. It took the security services two weeks to regain control of the mosque. While the organizers of the mosque take-over were hardly sympathetic to the Iranian Revolution on ideological or doctrinal issues (they criticized the Saudis for being too lenient toward the Shi'a in the kingdom), their actions added to the sense that, in the wake of the Iranian Revolution, the Islamist political challenge was shaking all the Gulf regimes.[5]

The sense of threat felt by the rulers of Iraq and the Arab monarchies of the Gulf in the wake of the revolution was exacerbated by the clearly stated intention of elements of the new Iranian regime, in particular Ayatollah Khomeini, to "export" the revolution to neighboring states. Even before he came to power in Tehran, in late 1978 Khomeini appointed "repre-sentatives" to the Shi'i communities of Kuwait and Bahrain, who were subsequently arrested and expelled from those countries after Shi'i dem-onstrations there.[6] Once the revolutionaries had come to power, Ayatollah Sadeq Rouhani threatened that, unless the Bahraini govern-ment adopted an "Islamic form of government similar to the one estab-lished in Iran," he would urge Iran to revive its territorial claim to Bahrain.[7] In January 1980 Iranian Radio announced in an Arabic-language broadcast plans to create a force to "export the Islamic revolu-tion."[8] In February 1980, following new disturbances in the Eastern Province of Saudi Arabia, Iranian radio stations called openly for a revolt

  Policy: From Khomeini to Khatami (New York: Routledge/Curzon, 2003), pp. 34–35; Nadav Safran, *Saudi Arabia: The Ceaseless Quest for Security* (Cambridge, MA: Harvard University Press, 1985), pp. 357–58; Colin Legum *et al.* (eds.), *Middle East Contemporary Survey*, Vol. IV: *1979–80* (New York: Holmes and Meier, 1981), pp. 397, 403–04, 688–89. The best account of the Saudi Shi'i uprising is Toby Craig Jones, "Rebellion on the Saudi Periphery: Modernity, Marginalization and the Shi'a Uprising of 1979," *International Journal of Middle East Studies*, Vol. 38, No. 2 (May 2006), pp. 213–33.

  [5] The group that took over the Grand Mosque was, ideologically, the precursor of the Sunni Islamist opposition that emerged in Saudi Arabia in the 1990s and of al-Qaeda. The best accounts in English of the ideology of the group and the politics of the takeover can be found in Joseph Kechichian, "Islamic Revivalism and Change in Saudi Arabia," *Muslim World*, Vol. 80, No. 1 (January 1990), pp. 1–16; Joseph Kechichian, "The Role of the Ulama in the Politics of an Islamic State: The Case of Saudi Arabia," *International Journal of Middle East Studies*, Vol. 18, No. 1 (February 1986), pp. 53–71; and Thomas Hegghammer and Stephane Lacroix, "Rejectionist Islamism in Saudi Arabia: The Story of Juhayman al-'Utaybi Revisited," *International Journal of Middle East Studies*, Vol. 39, No. 1 (February 2007), pp. 103–22. For a riveting account of these events, see Yaroslav Trofimov, *The Siege of Mecca* (New York: Doubleday, 2007).

  [6] Joseph Kostiner, "Shi'i Unrest in the Gulf," in Martin Kramer (ed.), *Shi'ism, Resistance and Revolution* (Boulder, CO: Westview Press, 1987), pp. 177–78; Marschall, *Iran's Persian Gulf Policy*, pp. 26–29, 34–35.

  [7] Ramazani, *Revolutionary Iran*, p. 49; Marschall, *Iran's Persian Gulf Policy*, p. 34.

  [8] "Chronology," *Middle East Journal*, Vol. 34, No. 2 (Spring 1980), p. 171.

against the Al Saud.[9] In April 1980 Iranian pilgrims held demonstrations in Mecca and Medina calling for the overthrow of the Saudi regime.[10] As early as June 1979 Iranian ayatollahs, including Khomeini, were condemning the Ba'thist regime in Iraq as "despotic" and "criminal," warning Iraq's rulers of "the wrath of God and the anger of the Muslim people" following the arrest of Ayatollah Muhammad Baqir al-Sadr.[11] By April 1980 Iran was making explicit threats to unseat the regime in Baghdad.[12]

The trajectory of events in Tehran did nothing to reduce the fears of the Arab rulers. The first post-revolutionary government appointed by Khomeini, headed by Prime Minister Mehdi Bazargan, attempted to reassure neighboring states that the new regime had no hostile intentions against them. However, Bazargan resigned in November 1979, after the takeover of the American embassy in Tehran. He was succeeded by politicians more closely identified with Khomeini's revolutionary views. For example, when Ayatollah Rouhani threatened to revive the Iranian claim to Bahrain, he was quickly repudiated by Bazargan's foreign minister. However, within months that foreign minister was gone, while Rouhani remained close to Khomeini.

With Iran in political chaos and its military apparently collapsing from disorder during and purges following the revolution, Iraq seemed to emerge as the new dominant power in the Gulf. It had oil money, an army that had successfully put down the Kurdish rebellion in the mid-1970s and evident regional ambitions. As mentioned in the previous chapter, Baghdad made its bid for Arab leadership immediately after the Camp David accords with the Baghdad summit of November 1978. Iraq's charm offensive toward the Gulf monarchies since the Algiers Agreement helped to insure their attendance at the meeting. Syria, with Egypt now out of the Arab–Israeli war equation, needed Iraqi support and also attended. Despite a long history of animosity between the two wings of the Ba'th Party ruling in Damascus and Baghdad, Hafez al-Asad in October 1978 signed a Charter of Joint National Action with his erstwhile Ba'th rivals, committing Syria to eventual political union with Iraq.

The first months of 1979 saw a remarkable confluence of regional events that shifted alignment patterns in the Gulf decisively. The triumph of the Islamic revolutionary forces in early 1979 seemingly ended Iran's

[9] Laurie Ann Mylroie, "Regional Security After Empire: Saudi Arabia and the Gulf," Ph.D. dissertation, Harvard University, 1985, pp. 262–63.

[10] Legum et al. (eds.), Middle East Contemporary Survey, Vol. IV, p. 691.

[11] David Menashri, Iran: A Decade of War and Revolution (New York: Holmes and Meier, 1990), p. 101.

[12] Shahram Chubin and Charles Tripp, Iran and Iraq at War (Boulder, CO: Westview Press, 1988), p. 34.

"policeman" role in the Gulf. While the Arab monarchies in the Gulf had distrusted the shah's regional ambitions, they knew that he did not seek to destabilize them domestically. The new Islamic Republic was weaker militarily, but much more aggressive toward them politically, encouraging domestic opposition and openly proclaiming that monarchy was "non-Islamic." While Iraqi Ba'thism was hardly a more congenial ideology for the monarchs, since 1975 Baghdad had made serious efforts to reassure and cultivate the Arab Gulf rulers. Iraq looked like a potential protector against the new regime in Iran. At the same time, the signing in March 1979 of the Egyptian–Israeli peace treaty placed a stark choice before the monarchies – align with Egypt and the United States, risking domestic backlash and the hostility of Iraq and Syria, or follow through with the commitments made in the Baghdad summit of November 1978 to isolate Egypt. Finally, in February 1979 North and South Yemen engaged in a brief border war, in which the Soviet-allied South seemed to have the upper hand. The fighting ended in early March 1979 after a joint Syrian–Iraqi mediation effort brought the two sides together, highlighting the important regional role the new Syrian–Iraqi alignment could play.[13]

Facing all these pressures, Saudi Arabia and most of the smaller Arab monarchies of the Gulf opted to align with Iraq. They joined with Iraq and Syria in ostracizing Egypt in the Arab world, cutting diplomatic relations and halting aid payments to Cairo. This was a dramatic choice for Saudi Arabia in particular. There is evidence of a serious split at the top level of the Al Saud family over the decision to join the boycott of Egypt, with Crown Prince Fahd leaving the country for some months shortly after the decision.[14] In February 1979 Iraq and Saudi Arabia signed an internal security agreement; in April 1979 Iraqi president Ahmad Hassan al-Bakr became the first head of state of republican Iraq to visit Saudi Arabia. The only exception among the Gulf monarchies in this alignment with Iraq was Oman. It maintained diplomatic relations with Egypt, strengthened ties with the United States and pursued a businesslike relationship with the new government in Iran, particularly regarding their joint management of the Strait of Hormuz.[15]

As these dramatic events unfolded in the region, a fateful change occurred in Iraqi domestic politics. On July 16, 1979, Saddam Hussein

---

[13] On the brief 1979 Yemen War and the regional diplomatic repercussions of its settlement, see my *Saudi–Yemeni Relations: Domestic Structures and Foreign Influence* (New York: Columbia University Press, 1990), pp. 130–36.

[14] For a detailed account of Saudi diplomacy and internal debates during this period, see Safran, *Saudi Arabia*, pp. 261–64, 278–81, 290–94, 304–08.

[15] Joseph A. Kechichian, *Oman and the World* (Santa Monica, CA: RAND, 1995), pp. 102–03, 146–47.

assumed the presidency, after the resignation of President al-Bakr. The circumstances of this transition remain clouded in rumor and speculation. What is clear is that Saddam Hussein had, since the mid-1970s, been the strong man of the regime, asserting control over the party, the military and the oil industry. The confluence of events in 1979, offering opportunities for regional leadership if Iraq were bold enough to grasp them while also presenting threats to the Ba'thist regime at home (Shi'i unrest related to the Iranian Revolution) and to Saddam's personal power in Iraq (the unity plan with Syria), moved him to assert direct control. There had been no previous indication that al-Bakr was looking to give up his position, which implies that Saddam took the initiative to force his resignation. On the other hand, al-Bakr was allowed the luxury of a peaceful retirement with full honors. If Saddam had seen him as a threat, he would certainly have been killed, as were twenty-two senior party members (including five members of the Revolutionary Command Council, the highest organ of the state) who apparently opposed Saddam's ascent in the weeks following the transition. Those killed were accused of plotting with Syria to topple the regime, bringing to an end the brief Syrian–Iraqi unity plan. Saddam's assumption of the presidency and the subsequent purge completed his monopolization of the instruments of power in Iraq. What had been a one-party state increasingly became a personal fiefdom.[16]

The Iranian Revolution and the world oil market – the "second oil shock" of 1979–1981

As convulsive as the Iranian Revolution was in the region, it was even more immediately disruptive in world oil markets. Oil prices had flattened out in the mid-1970s after the oil shock of 1973–74, with relatively small price increases from 1975 through 1978. Given dollar inflation during the period, the real price of oil actually declined from 1976 through 1978 (see Table 2). World demand for oil, despite the huge increase of 1973, continued to grow. After slight declines in 1974 and 1975 from 1973 levels, oil demand turned up again in 1976. In 1979 demand stood at just over 64 mbd, up from just over 57 mbd in 1973.[17]

---

[16] On Saddam's assumption of the presidency, see Marr, *The Modern History of Iraq*, pp. 178–80; Tripp, *A History of Iraq*, pp. 222–23. For an account of the "Syrian plot" that is relatively sympathetic to Saddam, see Majid Khadduri, *The Gulf War: The Origins and Implications of the Iraq–Iran Conflict* (New York: Oxford University Press, 1988), pp. 68–78. I discuss Syrian–Iraqi relations in greater detail in my article, "Balancing What? Threat Perception and Alliance Choice in the Gulf," *Security Studies*, Vol. 13, No. 2 (Winter 2003/04), pp. 273–305.

[17] British Petroleum, *BP Statistical Review of World Energy*, June 1988, pp. 9–10.

Table 2 *Nominal and real oil prices, 1974–1981*

Year	Nominal oil price (per barrel)	Real oil price (per barrel)
1974	$10.73	$ 9.68
1975	$10.73	$ 8.47
1976	$11.51	$ 8.93
1977	$12.39	$ 8.67
1978	$12.70	$ 7.58
1979	$17.25	$ 9.04
1980	$28.64	$13.26
1981	$32.51	$15.55

Source: OPEC Annual Statistical Bulletin 2002, www.opec.org/Publications/AB/pdf/
AB002002.pdf.
Notes: Oil prices: Arabian Light crude at official prices, yearly average.
Real price: nominal price adjusted for inflation and exchange rates, 1973 as base year.

Strikes in the Iranian oil sector began in the fall of 1978, with production falling from more than 6 mbd in September 1978 to 2.4 mbd in
December 1978. The chaos of the revolution pushed oil production down
below 1 mbd in January and February 1979, recovering a bit in March
1979 to 2.4 mbd, but nowhere near the pre-revolutionary level.[18] In a
period of less than six months, nearly 10 percent of world oil production –
Iran's pre-revolutionary share – was taken out of the market.

In the face of this supply shortfall, Saudi Arabia in the fall of 1978
increased its production from just above 8 mbd in September to more
than 10 mbd for the remainder of the year. However, on January 20, 1979,
shortly after the shah had left Iran, Saudi Arabia announced that it would
set its official production rate for the first quarter of 1979 at 9.5 mbd. In
effect, this meant a reduction of Saudi production of about 1 mbd, at a
time when the effects of the chaos in Iran were still being felt in the
markets. Spot prices nearly doubled the official OPEC price of $13.34
per barrel in February 1979. In April 1979, Saudi Arabia reverted to its
previous "production ceiling" of 8.5 mbd, as Iranian production began to
climb from its low point in January–February 1979. Still, Tehran's production by that point remained well below the pre-revolutionary level.[19]
The system of official OPEC prices basically collapsed, as state oil
companies either canceled long-term contracts with buyers or forced
those buyers to take more expensive "spot" oil along with the cheaper,

---

[18] Ian Skeet, *OPEC: Twenty-Five Years of Prices and Politics* (Cambridge: Cambridge
University Press, 1988), pp. 157–58.
[19] Skeet, *OPEC*, p. 158; Dankwart A. Rustow, *Oil and Turmoil: America Faces OPEC and the
Middle East* (New York: W. W. Norton, 1982), pp. 183–84.

officially priced "contract" oil. At the OPEC meeting in March 1979, the organization abandoned the official price system. Saudi oil minister Ahmad Zaki Yamani bluntly characterized the pricing system as a "free-for-all." Panic buying, similar to that of late 1973, drove the market as buyers, fearing the worst, built up their reserve stocks, adding to the upward pressure on prices.[20]

Why the Saudis cut production twice in the face of massive market uncertainties at this time is unclear. The moves were depicted by Riyadh as simply a return to business as usual – their 8.5 mbd production ceiling. But market conditions were anything but usual. Technical factors very possibly played a role. It is not certain that Saudi Arabia could have sustained production at over 10 mbd for an extended period of time. Moreover, production problems in Saudi fields, related to a fire during this period, might have made it impossible to sustain production of even 9.5 mbd.[21] The decision to reduce to 8.5 mbd in April 1979 could have been in reaction to increased Iranian production and a belief that the crisis would ameliorate as a result.[22] Other analysts have pointed to political motives, speculating that a coolness in Saudi–American relations and a desire to placate the new Islamic Republican regime in Iran were behind the decisions.[23]

For whatever reason, during this brief period the Saudis seemed to abandon their normal role of working to smooth out price spikes by providing more oil to the market. The result was to fuel the panic in the markets, driving prices higher. Gas lines reappeared in the United States, recalling the crisis atmosphere of the 1973–74 oil embargo. President Jimmy Carter's approval rating dropped as quickly as prices rose. Carter personally appealed to the Saudis for an increase in production. In July 1979 Riyadh announced that it would push its output back up to 9.5 mbd.[24] This step did little to quiet the markets, which were further shaken by the political upheavals of late 1979: the takeover of the Grand Mosque in Saudi Arabia in November, the beginning of the American hostage crisis in Iran in the same month and the Soviet invasion of Afghanistan in December. By the June 1980 OPEC meeting, Iran had increased its official price to $35 per barrel, with other states following suit.[25] It appeared that prices would only go up.

---

[20] Daniel Yergin, *The Prize: The Epic Quest for Oil, Money and Power* (New York: Simon & Schuster, 1991), pp. 686, 689.

[21] Lawrence Axelrod, "Saudi Oil Policy: Economic and Political Determinants, 1973 – 1986," Ph.D. dissertation, Columbia University, 1989, pp. 124–32.

[22] This is the interpretation of Skeet, *OPEC*, p. 163.

[23] Safran, *Saudi Arabia*, pp. 401–02; Yergin, *The Prize*, p. 690.

[24] Yergin, *The Prize*, pp. 689–96.   [25] Skeet, *OPEC*, pp. 168–69.

The oil price increases of 1979–80, like those of 1973–74, had little effect in and of themselves on the regional balance among Iran, Iraq and Saudi Arabia. They were all oil producers, and they all benefited from the increased revenue. Both Iraq and Saudi Arabia were able to acquire even more military hardware, and the increased revenue provided the material support for Saddam Hussein's ambitions to make Iraq the predominant regional power. In Iran, the oil price increase helped the new revolutionary government maintain some semblance of a functioning economy and reduced the negative effects of the oil production cuts. The second oil shock's immediate international political effects were more pronounced on the United States. Along with the contemporaneous regional political changes, the oil price increases refocused American strategy on the Gulf region, where for the second time in less than a decade political events led directly to the kind of domestic economic problems that American politicians cannot afford to ignore.

The superpowers and the Iranian Revolution

The Soviet Union openly welcomed the Iranian Revolution as a major setback for the United States, despite the obvious ideological differences. But the Soviets were also worried about the spillover effects of the revolution. Afghanistan was of particular concern. The unstable pro-Soviet regime there was facing growing opposition. In December 1979 Soviet forces invaded Afghanistan to support their client regime, safe in the knowledge that American–Iranian hostility (the hostage crisis had begun just one month earlier) precluded any kind of joint response. Tehran immediately condemned the Soviet invasion and began to back resistance movements among the Afghan Shi'i minority. In effect, Moscow sacrificed any possibility of supplanting Washington as Iran's major foreign patron by going into Afghanistan.

If the Iranian Revolution was a mixed blessing for the Soviet Union, it was an unmitigated disaster for the United States, the most damaging single blow to American interests in the Middle East in the post-World War II period. The revolution brought down the most important US ally in the Gulf, the shah, the anchor of the "twin pillar" policy. He was replaced with a virulently anti-American regime. The chaos of the revolution brought on the second oil shock, causing gas lines to form in the United States and inflation to soar. While the Soviets saw their move into Afghanistan as defensive, in Washington it was seen as an aggressive extension of the Soviet empire toward a vital American sphere of influence, and something that would not have happened had the shah still been in power. The Iranian Revolution was not just a blow to US interests in the region, but a serious Cold War setback as well.

The effects of the Iranian hostage crisis on the United States cannot be overestimated. The hostage crisis took what was a very important geopolitical challenge for the United States and turned it into a national obsession. On November 4, 1979, supporters of Ayatollah Khomeini took over the US embassy in Tehran, and held the American diplomats and staff there as hostages. The organizers said that their takeover was aimed at preventing the United States from plotting to reinstall the shah, who on October 22 had entered the United States for medical treatment. Given the American-supported coup against Prime Minister Mossadegh in 1953, the accusation resonated in Iranian public opinion.

The focus of the hostage takers, however, was as much on Iranian domestic politics as it was on the United States. They suspected Prime Minister Bazargan of trying to normalize relations with the United States. That suspicion was well founded, as Bazargan and his foreign minister, Ibrahim Yazdi, had a range of contacts with American officials both in the embassy in Tehran and in Washington. Moreover, Khomeini and those around him had, since the shah's admission to the United States, publicly spoken of a "plot" being hatched there to restore him. They linked this purported threat to the revolution to "moderates" like Bazargan. While Bazargan worked to end the takeover, Khomeini publicly supported the hostage takers. Bazargan resigned as prime minister on November 6. According to James Bill, "the embassy takeover reinforced the extremist phase of the revolution because it continued to radicalize the rule of politics in Iran."[26]

On both sides of the American–Iranian divide, domestic politics came to dominate relations, which themselves were dominated by the hostage crisis. In Iran, control over the hostages became a bargaining chip in factional infighting, and no politician would allow himself to be out-flanked on the issue of anti-Americanism.[27] In the United States, the media and the public focused intently upon the fate of the hostages, to the extent that the hostage crisis was the dominant American news story for over a year. Public opinion was intensely hostile toward Iran in general and Ayatollah Khomeini in particular. President Carter became obsessed

---

[26] On the origins of the hostage crisis, see James A. Bill, *The Eagle and the Lion: The Tragedy of American–Iranian Relations* (New Haven: Yale University Press, 1988), Chapter 8, quote from p. 297; and Gary Sick, *All Fall Down: America's Tragic Encounter with Iran* (New York: Random House, 1985), Chapters 8–10.

[27] On Iranian factional politics in this period, see Bakhash, *The Reign of the Ayatollahs*, Chapters 3–6, as well as sources cited in note 33.

with the hostage issue, and his failure to end the crisis before the November 1980 presidential election contributed to his defeat by Ronald Reagan.[28] The abject failure of an American military effort to rescue the hostages in April 1980, with the destruction in the Iranian desert of one of the eight helicopters sent on the mission and the death of eight American servicemen, seemed to symbolize post-Vietnam American weakness and Carter's personal inability to muster American power against Iran's defiant revolutionaries.

The hostage crisis finally ended on January 20, 1981, the last day of Carter's presidency. The Iranian government ceased to see any benefit in its prolongation. The crisis, which was a blatant violation by Iran of international law, had alienated many governments from the new regime and subjected it to a number of international sanctions. Facing a war with Iraq, which began in September 1980, the leaders of the Islamic Republic began to see the value in ending this particular irritant in their international relations. While Iranian politics was still roiled by factional infighting between President Abol Hassan Bani Sadr and clerical elements in the Islamic Republic Party, the hostage crisis had served one of its purposes by providing a lever for ejecting moderate Islamists such as Bazargan from power. On the American side, the incoming Reagan administration was happy to see its predecessor clean up the last details of a distasteful episode. In a final insult to Carter, the Iranians waited until after Reagan had taken the oath of office before releasing the hostages. While the hostage crisis was over, the bitterness which suffused Iranian–American relations would not soon dissipate.

While the hostage crisis was the focus of American Gulf policy between November 1979 and January 1981, the larger set of crises surrounding the Iranian Revolution, including the second oil shock and the Soviet invasion of Afghanistan, called for a new American approach to the region. The old "twin pillar" policy was in tatters. Reliance on Iraq, a Soviet ally and leader of Arab opposition to the Camp David accords, as a regional security partner was not possible. This left Saudi Arabia as the United States' only significant partner in the Gulf, and Saudi–American relations were strained over Arab–Israeli, oil and other issues.[29] Moreover, given its small population relative to Iran, its military weakness compared to Iraq and its generally cautious approach to regional politics, Saudi Arabia could hardly assume the shah's role of "regional policeman." The

---

[28] For a detailed account of American policy on the hostage crisis, by one of its makers, see Sick, *All Fall Down*, Chapters 10–15.
[29] Safran, *Saudi Arabia*, pp. 398–406.

Carter administration decided that the only course of action was to prepare for a more direct American military role in the Gulf, a policy course that would accelerate over the next twenty-five years.

President Carter presented the American response to the crises of 1979 in his State of the Union address in January 1980. He announced that the United States would use all means at its disposal to prevent any "outside power" from gaining control of the Gulf region. To back up the Carter Doctrine, the US military created the Rapid Deployment Joint Task Force (RDJTF), consisting of a number of existing units of the armed services. These units were to be coordinated by a new joint command structure, while the United States worked to develop conventional airlift and sealift capabilities to get those units to the Gulf when necessary.[30]

Making the Carter Doctrine and the RDJTF work required access to regional bases. Saudi Arabia and the smaller Gulf monarchies, the obvious candidates for such access arrangements, were mostly cool to the idea. Given the example of the shah, none wanted to appear too close to Washington, nor did they want to confront directly Iran or Iraq, both of which opposed the new American policy. Arab opposition to the American-brokered Egyptian–Israeli peace also factored into their reluctance. Only Oman accepted the new American strategy in the region. As early as 1975 Oman had agreed to American requests for access to the old British airbase on Masirah Island in the Arabian Sea. In June 1980 it became the only Gulf state to sign a formal military facilities agreement with the United States.[31] The other Gulf states rebuffed American pressures to sign similar facilities agreements, even while permitting existing military access agreements with the United States, such as Bahrain playing host to the small American naval force in the Gulf, to continue.

The Iran–Iraq War, 1980–1988

Saddam Hussein's decision to launch a large-scale attack on Iran on September 22, 1980, began the longest and most devastating war in modern Middle Eastern history. It would last nearly eight years, ending in the summer of 1988. The war can be divided into three periods: (1) September 1980 to the summer of 1982, when Iraqi forces were occupying Iranian territory; (2) summer 1982 to the end of 1986, during which time Iranian forces were on the offensive and most of the war was fought in Iraqi territory; and (3) 1987 to the summer of 1988, when Iraqi forces

---

[30] Charles A. Kupchan, *The Persian Gulf and the West: The Dilemmas of Security* (Boston: Allen and Unwin, 1987), Chapter 5.
[31] Kechichian, *Oman and the World*, pp. 144–50.

regained the initiative, eventually leading Iran to accept a cease-fire in July 1988. In each period, battlefield dynamics both affected and were affected by regional states' policies, superpower policies and the oil market.

The Iraqi war decision

While responsibility for initiating the Iran–Iraq War rests squarely upon Saddam Hussein, from an analytical perspective the causes of the war can be traced directly to the Iranian Revolution.[32] First, the very fact of the revolution – a mass-based, Islamically inspired, successful opposition to an authoritarian regime – was a threat to the domestic political stability of all the neighboring Arab states. As discussed above, the revolution had a strong and immediate effect among Shi'i communities throughout the Arab side of the Gulf. The strength of the revolution's ideological appeal was made all the more threatening to the rulers of those states by the active rhetorical, and in some cases material, support given by the new revolutionary government to opposition forces in those states. More moderate leadership elites in Iran, less threatening in the eyes of neighboring rulers, were quickly swept away, increasing the sense of threat the revolution represented.

Second, the chaos that the revolution brought to Iranian politics made the country seem weak in the conventional attributes of national power, and therefore not as formidable a military opponent, even as its danger as an ideological opponent was increasing. Violent factional infighting was the norm in Tehran in 1979–80, and regional separatist movements seemed to be tearing the country apart. The upper officer corps of the Iranian armed forces was decimated by purges; the military machine built by the shah at the cost of billions of dollars seemed to have collapsed.[33] The revolutionary regime had willingly, even recklessly, sabotaged Iran's relationship with its former superpower ally and weapons supplier, the United States, and isolated itself from the international community through the hostage crisis. To an ambitious neighbor like Saddam Hussein, the domestic consequences of the revolution created a power vacuum in the region that Iraq could easily exploit. The Iran–Iraq War can

---

[32] The dynamics linking revolutions to international wars, upon which this brief analysis of the effects of the Iranian Revolution is based, are explored by Stephen M. Walt, *Revolution and War* (Ithaca: Cornell University Press, 1996). See Chapter 5 for his account of the Iranian Revolution.

[33] For accounts of domestic Iranian politics in the immediate post-revolutionary period, see Keddie, *Modern Iran*, Chapter 10; Bakhash, *The Reign of the Ayatollahs*, Chapters 3–5; Milani, *The Making of Iran's Islamic Revolution*, Chapters 8–9; Arjomand, *The Turban for the Crown*, Chapters 7–8.

be understood only as the result of a set of circumstances that made Iran seem both militarily weak *and* politically threatening to the domestic stability of neighboring regimes. And those circumstances trace directly back to the Iranian Revolution itself.

While both threat and opportunity played into Saddam Hussein's decision to go to war, the evidence indicates that the threat posed by the revolution was the more important factor.[34] The weakening of Iran in conventional power terms, which began in late 1977 as the revolutionary movement gathered steam, did not immediately excite Iraqi ambitions. On the contrary, Baghdad expelled Ayatollah Khomeini from Iraq in October 1978 and engaged in security consultations with the shah's government, as was discussed above. When the shah fell in February 1979, Iraq's first reactions were mildly welcoming to the new regime. Iraq's president, Ahmad Hassan al-Bakr, sent a congratulatory message to Khomeini upon the establishment of the Islamic Republic. Iraq publicly supported Iran's withdrawal from the Central Treaty Organization (CENTO) and offered to support Iranian membership in the Non-Aligned Movement. As late as July 1979 Iraq extended an invitation to the Iranian prime minister, Mehdi Bazargan, to visit Baghdad.[35]

Relations soon deteriorated, however. In June 1979 Ayatollah Muhammad Baqir al-Sadr, the most politicized of the major Iraqi Shi'i religious leaders, was arrested on the eve of a scheduled trip to Tehran. Violent demonstrations ensued in the cities of Najaf and Karbala, and in Shi'i areas of Baghdad itself, which were suppressed with force. Al-Sadr was released shortly thereafter to house arrest in Najaf.[36] Several prominent Iranian ayatollahs, including Khomeini, condemned the Iraqi regime as "despotic" and "criminal," warning Iraq's rulers of "the wrath of God and the anger of the Muslim people."[37] Iranian media charged Iraq with instigating disturbances among Iranian Arabs in Khuzestan province.[38] The Iraqi media answered in kind, accusing the new Iranian government of following in the footsteps of the shah in trying to exploit domestic divisions within Iraq.[39] Border clashes in the Kurdish areas ensued, with Iraq using its air force against Iranian villages where Iraqi

---

[34] I make this argument at greater length in my article, "Iraq's Decisions to Go to War, 1980 and 1990," *Middle East Journal*, Vol. 56, No. 1 (Winter 2002), pp. 47–70.

[35] Ramazani, *Revolutionary Iran*, pp. 57–59.

[36] Tripp, A *History of Iraq*, pp. 220–21; Chubin and Tripp, *Iran and Iraq at War*, p. 25.

[37] Menashri, *Iran*, p. 101.

[38] Foreign Broadcast Information Service, Middle East and Africa (FBIS-MEA), 79-107, June 1, 1979, p. E1.

[39] See the series of articles in *al-Thawra*, FBIS-MEA-79-115, June 13, 1979, pp. E1–E3; FBIS-MEA-79-116, June 14, 1979, pp. E1–E6; FBIS-MEA-79-117, June 15, 1979, pp. E1–E5.

Kurdish insurgents were based.[40] In July 1979 Masoud and Idris Barazani, the sons of Iraqi Kurdish leader Mustafa Barazani, crossed the border into Iran and received support from the revolutionary government.[41]

In the midst of these events, Saddam Hussein became president of Iraq on July 16, 1979. An explanation that focused purely upon Saddam's ambitions would expect a militant change in Iraqi policy toward Iran from that time. However, that did not happen. On the contrary, the two governments sought in the short term to reduce the tensions. Border skirmishes subsided. In early September 1979 Iranian foreign minister Ibrahim Yazdi even invited Saddam to visit Iran.[42] To some extent, this deescalation might be attributable to Saddam's need to consolidate his own power. But it can also be attributed to the Iraqi leader's view of the political situation in Iran. He clearly differentiated between the government of Iran, headed by Prime Minister Bazargan, who tried to maintain correct relations with Iran's neighbors, and the revolutionary circles around Ayatollah Khomeini. In the long analysis of Iran–Iraq relations published in the Iraqi newspaper *al-Thawra* in June 1979, it was acknowledged that "there were many trends, wings and groupings in the Iranian Revolution … What caught our attention was the fact that a large percentage of the direct and indirect offenses were made by the group that is considered to belong to Khomeini."[43] The series of articles ended with the admonition that "there is still sufficient patience to give certain Iranian circles the opportunity to arrange matters and to favor the ideas of good and reason over forces, intrigues and malice."[44] Saddam himself made this point to the Iraqi National Assembly in November 1980: "During the first few months after Khomeini came to power … I used to make all kinds of excuses to my colleagues to give the Persians more time. I used to remind my colleagues in the leadership of the state of confusion and chaos we were in in 1963."[45]

The political ferment among Iraq's Shi'i majority continued. In July 1979, while under house arrest, Ayatollah Muhammad Baqir al-Sadr called for violent opposition to the regime. Shortly thereafter major Iraqi Shi'i political groups announced the formation of the Islamic Liberation Movement, ready to "resort to all means" to bring down the Ba'thist

---

[40] Anthony H. Cordesman and Abraham R. Wagner, *The Lessons of Modern War, Volume II: The Iran–Iraq War* (Boulder, CO: Westview Press, 1990), p. 27.

[41] Dilip Hiro, *The Longest War: The Iran–Iraq Military Conflict* (New York: Routledge, 1991), p. 35.

[42] Menashri, *Iran*, p. 102.   [43] FBIS-MEA-79-116, June 14, 1979, p. E2.

[44] FBIS-MEA-79-117, June 15, 1979, p. E5.

[45] FBIS-MEA-80-216, November 5, 1980, p. E3.

regime. In October 1979 the Organization of the Iraqi Ulama, which had previously avoided overt political opposition, declared its support for the use of violence against the government. The Da'wa Party, the major Iraqi Shi'i party, formed a military wing by the end of the year.[46]

The regime, usually loath to admit to any domestic opposition (at least within the Arab population of Iraq), was by its standards quite open about the threat that Shi'i militancy posed. In May 1980 the Iraqi interior minister told an interviewer that, while there were fewer than 1,000 members of the Da'wa Party, "the number of misguided supporters and religious sympathizers is considerable."[47] The report of the 1982 Ba'th Party regional congress was even more open. It admitted that the Iranian Revolution had led to an upsurge of support for religious-political movements in Iraq, and that the intense social transformations that Iraq had undergone presented a large number of potential recruits to those movements. It even acknowledged that the religious-political movement had infiltrated the junior ranks of the party itself.[48]

In the midst of this rising tide of Shi'i opposition in late 1979, Iranian politics became more militant. Prime Minister Bazargan resigned in November 1979, in the wake of the takeover of the US embassy in Tehran. With the victory of the more radical forces around Khomeini, there was a marked turn in Iranian government rhetoric against the Ba'thist regime.[49] Statements about the need to export the Iranian revolutionary model around the region became more frequent, and by 1980 Iranian government officials were making explicit calls for the Iraqi people to overthrow the Ba'th regime.[50] In March 1980 the Iranian ambassador left Baghdad and a number of Iranian consulates in the country were closed. Iran claimed the ambassador was recalled; Iraq contended that he was asked to leave "due to his blatant interference in Iraq's internal affairs."[51]

In late March 1980 the Iraqi government retroactively made membership in the Da'wa Party a capital offense, after having earlier that month executed ninety-six members of the organization. On April 1 a member of one of the Shi'i opposition groups attempted to kill Deputy Prime

[46] Wiley, *Islamic Movement*, pp. 54–55; Tripp, *A History of Iraq*, p. 229.
[47] FBIS-MEA-80-097, May 16, 1980, p. E2.
[48] Arab Ba'th Socialist Party-Iraq, *The Central Report of the Ninth Regional Congress, June 1982* (Baghdad: n.p., 1983), pp. 272–77, 280.
[49] Ramazani, *Revolutionary Iran*, p. 59, identifies the fall of Bazargan as the turning point in Iranian–Iraqi relations.
[50] Khadduri, *The Gulf War*, p. 82; Walt, *Revolution and War*, pp. 238–39; Chubin and Tripp, *Iran and Iraq at War*, p. 34; Menashri, *Iran*, pp. 157–58.
[51] FBIS-MEA-80-048, March 10, 1980, p. E1.

Minister Tariq Aziz while he was speaking at al-Mustansiriya University in Baghdad.[52] A number of students attending the talk were killed, though Aziz himself escaped injury. During the funeral procession for some of those killed, according to the Iraqi media, a bomb was thrown from a window of an "Iranian school" in Baghdad as the procession went past.[53] In retaliation the Iraqi government executed Ayatollah Muhammad Baqir al-Sadr and his sister, who was also a Shi'i activist, publicized what it alleged were the organizational links between the Da'wa Party and the Iranian regime, and began to expel tens of thousands of Iraqi Shi'a of Iranian origin from the country.

These events of March–April 1980 were the final straw for Saddam Hussein and the spur for the Iraqi war decision. His rhetoric underwent an immediate change. Previously, he had warned the Iranians not to interfere in Iraq, but he had never attacked the Iranian leadership personally nor had he overtly threatened war. From this point, he began to threaten Iran in the most obvious way. He went to al-Mustansiriya University after the attack on Aziz and told the students: "It is not our tradition to make threats, but we tell you, by God, by God, by God and in the name of every particle of earth in Iraq that the pure blood that was shed in al-Mustansiriyah University will not go in vain … [W]e tell those cowards and dwarfs who try to avenge al-Qadisiyah [the battle in which the Muslim Arab army defeated the Persian Empire in 637 CE] that the spirit of al-Qadisiyah as well as the blood and honor of the people of al-Qadisiyah who carried the message on their spearheads are greater than their attempts."[54] This was the first use by Saddam of the imagery of the battle of al-Qadisiya to clothe his conflict with the Iranians in the banners of Islam and Arab history. Later in April, Saddam referred to the Iranian ruler as "that mummy Khomeini" and told his listeners "we hope that the Iranian people will find someone other than Bani-Sadr [then president of Iran] who will have better relations with the Arabs and the Muslims, and find someone else than this rotten man Khomeini."[55] By late July 1980 Saddam was all but promising a war: "We are not the kind of people to bow to Khomeini. He wagered to bend us and we wagered to bend him. We will see who will bend the other."[56]

When news of Ayatollah Baqir al-Sadr's execution reached Iran, the Iranian reaction matched the hostility being exhibited by Saddam. Ayatollah Khomeini reiterated his previous calls to the Iraqi people and

---

[52] Wiley, *Islamic Movement*, p. 55.   [53] FBIS-MEA-80-068, April 7, 1980, pp. E5–E7.
[54] FBIS-MEA-80-066, April 3, 1980, p. E3.
[55] FBIS-MEA-80-076, April 17, 1980, pp. E2–E5.
[56] FBIS-MEA-80-144, July 24, 1980, pp. E4–E5.

the Iraqi army to overthrow the regime, accusing the Ba'th of launching a "war against Islam."[57] The Iraqi media began reporting regular border clashes in June 1980.[58] Iraq also increased more non-conventional attacks on Iran. On April 29, gunmen attempted to assassinate Iranian foreign minister Sadeq Qotbzadeh, who was on a visit to Kuwait; on April 30 Iranian Arabs backed by Iraq seized the Iranian embassy in London, holding it for five days; in early June a bomb exploded at the Iranian embassy in Kuwait. In March 1980 two Iranian generals were received in Baghdad and allowed to use Iraq as a base to plan a military coup. Former Iranian prime minister Shahpur Bakhtiyar was permitted to set up a radio station in Iraq, which began broadcasting in May 1980.[59]

Sources that have reported on the timing of the Iraqi decision to go to war almost unanimously place the decision in the spring of 1980, after the events of March–April. Fuad Matar, Saddam's official biographer, identified early April as the turning point in Saddam's approach toward Iran.[60] According to R. K. Ramazani, Arab diplomats pointed to April 1980 as the time that Iraq began its preparations to go to war with Iran.[61] Edgar O'Ballance reports that Saddam ordered his chief of staff to start preparations for war in May 1980, though he provides no source for that information.[62] Anthony Cordesman and Abraham Wagner, based on interviews with those involved, state that Iraqi officials began to "consult" with colleagues in the Arab Gulf states in May 1980 about their intention to attack Iran, and that Saddam informed several Arab Gulf state leaders about his plans in July and August.[63]

The gap between the war decision and the actual initiation of conflict in the beginning of September 1980, with the full-scale invasion on September 22, 1980, is attributable to two factors. The first is planning and organization, which would take some months to achieve. The second is the effort by Iranian exiles in Iraq to organize a military coup to overthrow the Islamic regime in Tehran. That effort, termed the "Nuzhih plot" for the air force base from which it was launched, was fully supported by Iraq and planned on Iraqi territory. Begun on July 9, 1980, it was a spectacular and immediate failure, leading to a number of arrests and an

---

[57] Quoted in Hiro, *The Longest War*, p. 35.

[58] FBIS-MEA-80-109, June 4, 1980, p. E1; FBIS-MEA-80-118, June 17, 1980, p. E4; FBIS-MEA-80-123, June 24, 1980, p. E1.

[59] Mark Gasiorowski, "The Nuzhih Plot and Iranian Politics," *International Journal of Middle East Studies*, Vol. 34, No. 4 (November 2002), pp. 645–66.

[60] Fuad Matar, *Saddam Hussein: The Man, the Cause and the Future* (London: Third World Centre for Research and Publishing, 1981), pp. 13, 135.

[61] Ramazani, *Revolutionary Iran*, p. 60.

[62] Edgar O'Ballance, *The Gulf War* (London: Brassey's Defence Publishers, 1988), p. 48.

[63] Cordesman and Wagner, *Lessons*, pp. 38–39, notes 25 and 26.

extensive purge of the Iranian armed forces.[64] Coming after the fall of the Bazargan government in November 1979, the collapse of the Nuzhih plot was the last chance that the Iraqis saw for eliminating the Khomeini regime from within. Had the coup succeeded, Saddam might still have seen some geopolitical benefit in a short and victorious war with a weak and chaotic Iran. We will never know. However, the failure of the coup underlined to the Baghdad leadership the durability of the Islamic revolutionary regime on its border, a regime that was actively working to bring about the demise of Ba'thist rule in Iraq.

September 1980 to June 1982: the Iraqi invasion

On September 17, 1980, Saddam Hussein formally abrogated the 1975 Algiers Agreement, dramatically ripping up a copy of the document before the Iraqi parliament. Five days later, on September 22, the Iraqi air force struck Iranian oil facilities and military bases, and Iraqi ground forces launched attacks across the border in the north, the center and the south of the country. The main offensive thrust was on the southern front, into the Iranian province of Khuzestan. Despite overwhelming numerical and tactical advantages, the Iraqi forces could make little progress. Much to the Iraqis' surprise, what was left of the Iranian air force quickly mobilized to meet the Iraqi attack. Baghdad responded by abandoning the air, dispersing most of its aircraft to bases in western Iraq and friendly neighboring Arab states. It regrouped its air forces back into Iraq a week later, but generally kept them out of the battle. The only major Iranian city that the Iraqis captured in their initial thrust was Khorramshahr, and that only after a month of fighting. They failed to secure the major oil port, Abadan, or the provincial capital, Ahvaz. By the beginning of November 1980, as careful observers of the war wrote, "the momentum of the Iraqi invasion was over."[65]

In an effort to consolidate his limited gains, Saddam Hussein indicated early on that he was willing to accept a cease-fire, though not the withdrawal of his troops in Iran.[66] Even though Iran was at a military disadvantage, Ayatollah Khomeini had no intention of accepting even a limited defeat. He rejected a UN Security Council resolution for a cease-fire and identified Iran's war aims as not only repelling the invasion, but also punishing "the criminal Ba'th leaders."[67] In October 1980, he told

---

[64] For a complete account of the Nuzhih coup attempt, based on interviews with those involved, see Gasiorowski, "The Nuzhih Plot and Iranian Politics."

[65] Cordesman and Wagner, *Lessons*, pp. 183–93, quote from p. 193.

[66] Hiro, *Longest War*, p. 42.   [67] Quoted in Khadduri, *The Gulf War*, p. 89.

Map 2 Iran–Iraq frontier

Iranians that "you are fighting to protect Islam and he [Saddam Hussein] is fighting to destroy Islam … There is absolutely no question of peace or compromise and we shall never have any discussions with them, because they are corrupt." He went on to say that Iraqi withdrawal from Iran would not be enough to end the fighting; Saddam Hussein must also give up power in Iraq.[68]

Unwittingly, the Iraqi leader had given the new revolutionary regime, still beset by internal divisions and domestic competitors for power, the ideal cause around which to rally popular support. The war allowed Khomeini to link Iranian nationalist sentiment to his Islamic revolutionary platform and to brand his domestic opponents not only as "enemies of Islam," but also as traitors to the nation. If there is one thing at which revolutions have historically excelled, it is the mobilization of mass-based, popular military forces.[69] Iran proved to be no exception. It poured reinforcements into the fronts, both regular forces and the newly created formations of the revolution, the Revolutionary Guard (Pasdaran) and the Basij, the popular "mobilization battalions" that provided much of the cannon fodder for Iran's "human wave" attacks as the war dragged on. By January 1981 Iran began to go on the offensive. In April 1981, the Revolutionary Guard and Basij won a victory on the northern front, near the Iranian Kurdish town of Qasr e-Shirin. It was not particularly important militarily, but politically it strengthened those in Tehran who thought that the revolutionary formations should play a greater role in the battle.[70] In June 1981 Ayatollah Khomeini removed Iranian president Abol Hasan Bani Sadr, who had developed into a rival of the clerical Islamic Republican Party for real leadership of the regime. Bani Sadr had become identified with the regular military, and his departure signaled the ascendance of the Revolutionary Guard and other popular formations in the Iranian war strategy.[71]

The clarification of power in Tehran allowed for more direct cooperation among the regular army, the Revolutionary Guards and the other irregular units. In September 1981 Iranian forces lifted the Iraqi siege of Abadan. In November–December 1981 they drove Iraqi forces that had been threatening Ahvaz from the north back to the border. In March 1982 the Iranians pushed Iraqi forces back from Dezful, in the northern part of Khuzestan, with the Iraqis fleeing in disarray. Finally, in April–May 1982 Iranian forces recaptured the only major city held by the Iraqis, Khorramshahr. On June 10, 1982, Saddam Hussein ordered all Iraqi forces to withdraw from Iran.[72]

---

[68] Quoted in Chubin and Tripp, *Iran and Iraq at War*, p. 38.

[69] Theda Skocpol, "Social Revolutions and Mass Military Mobilization," *World Politics*, Vol. 40, No. 2 (January 1988), pp. 147–68.

[70] Kenneth M. Pollack, *Arabs at War: Military Effectiveness, 1948–1991* (Lincoln: University of Nebraska Press, 2002), pp. 193–95; Cordesman and Wagner, *Lessons*, pp. 111–18.

[71] Bakhash, *The Reign of the Ayatollahs*, Chapter 6.

[72] Cordesman and Wagner, *Lessons*, pp. 119–43; Pollack, *Arabs at War*, pp. 193–202.

Saddam's gamble had failed. The Arab residents of Khuzestan had not risen up to support the Iraqi invasion. The early Iraqi victories had not shaken Khomeini's regime in Tehran, just the opposite. The Iranian military, despite its revolutionary disarray, reorganized itself and proved more than a match for the Iraqi army. The superpowers, as we will see below, had not stepped in to stop the fighting after Iraq's early gains. In June 1982, as the rout of Iraqi forces was completed, an extraordinary meeting of Iraq's Revolutionary Command Council (RCC), military command and Ba'th Party command was held in the absence of Saddam Hussein. That meeting generated a cease-fire proposal that offered a return to the status quo before the war, accepting the border set by the Algiers Agreement. One informed observer of Iraqi politics speculates that, had Iran accepted this offer, it is questionable whether Saddam could have retained power.[73] However, following the line Ayatollah Khomeini established at the outset of the war, Tehran refused all cease-fire offers. Saddam was able to reassert his leadership as Iraq prepared its defenses and awaited Iran's next move. In late June 1982 he reshuffled the RCC, the Regional Command of the Ba'th Party and the cabinet, reducing the number of members of the RCC (the highest organ of the state) and filling each of these bodies, even more so than previously, with his own close associates, kinsmen and protégés. He personally killed the minister of health, who had the temerity to suggest at a cabinet meeting that perhaps Saddam could temporarily step down as president to facilitate a cease-fire with Iran.[74]

One of the great surprises of the first stage of the Iran–Iraq War was the relative lack of involvement of the superpowers. Given the history of the Arab–Israeli wars, in which both Moscow and Washington worked to bring about quick ends to hostilities, and the enormous importance of Gulf oil to the world economy, this hands-off attitude was unexpected. One could even speculate, though there is no documentary evidence to confirm it, that Saddam Hussein might have expected the superpowers to step in and end the fighting after his initial victories, as they had in the 1967 Arab–Israeli War.[75]

The Soviet Union, Iraq's superpower ally, was strongly against Baghdad's move against Iran. The Soviets declared their neutrality at the outset of the war and imposed an arms embargo on the combatants,

---

[73] Tripp, *A History of Iraq*, pp. 235–36.
[74] Tripp, *A History of Iraq*, pp. 236–37; Farouk-Sluglett and Sluglett, *Iraq Since 1958*, pp. 210–13, 264–65.
[75] This is the contention of Sa'd al-Bazzaz, who in the late 1980s and during the Gulf War was the editor of the Iraqi newspaper *al-Jumhuriya*. See his *Harb tulid 'ukhra* [A War Gives Birth to Another] (Amman, Jordan: Al-Ahliya lil-Nashr wa al-Tawzi', 1993), pp. 208–09.

which affected Iraq directly and Iran hardly at all. Moscow also took a number of steps that signaled a slight tilt toward Iran during the first months of the war. They maintained commercial relations with Iran, supplying it with jet fuel, and assured the Iranian leadership that the Soviet Union would respect their border, allowing Tehran to move troops to the Iraqi front. Iran quickly became dependent upon close Soviet allies as its main weapons suppliers: Syria, Libya, North Korea and Warsaw Pact countries. As the tide of the battle turned in 1981, the Soviets reengaged with their Iraqi allies, lifting the arms embargo against Iraq in June 1981, ostensibly in response to the Israeli attack on Iraq's Osirak nuclear facility earlier that month.[76] Moscow remained formally neutral in the conflict, repeatedly urging the two sides to end the fighting.

If Moscow hoped to curry favor with both sides in the war, Washington was in the position of having little leverage with either side. American hostages were still being held in Iran when Iraq attacked, making it politically impossible, even if the Carter administration had wanted, to back Iran. Iraq had been estranged from the United States for some time. While Washington's intense focus on the hostage crisis might have made an American tilt toward Iraq at the outset of the war a logical move, there is no evidence that the United States gave Saddam Hussein a "green light" to attack Iran.[77] The memoirs of President Carter and those in his administration involved in Gulf issues unanimously record American surprise at the Iraqi invasion.[78] Washington's first policy reaction was to try to prevent the spread of the conflict down the Gulf. Carter's national security adviser (NSA), Zbigniew Brzezinski, reports that on September 26, 1980, Washington received an urgent call from Saudi Arabia relaying information that Iraq was planning to stage air attacks on Iranian targets from "the territory of some of the Arabian Gulf states."[79] According to a contemporary press account, Washington

---

[76] Chubin and Tripp, *Iran and Iraq at War*, p. 221; Oles M. Smolansky with Bettie M. Smolansky, *The USSR and Iraq: The Soviet Quest for Influence* (Durham, NC: Duke University Press, 1991), pp. 231–37.

[77] For one version of this charge, see Hiro, *The Longest War*, pp. 71–72.

[78] Gary Sick records that, just weeks before the onset of the war, Washington had received an encouraging signal from Tehran of its willingness to open talks in Germany on the hostages, and Deputy Secretary of State Warren Christopher met with Iranian minister of state Sadegh Tabatabai in Bonn on September 16 and 18, 1980, to begin negotiations: *All Fall Down*, pp. 308–15. In a personal communication, Sick reiterated that, to his knowledge, no one in the White House encouraged the Iraqi attack on Iran, or even had knowledge of it.

[79] Zbigniew Brzezinski, *Power and Principle: Memoirs of the National Security Advisor, 1977–1981* (New York: Farrar, Straus and Giroux, 1983), p. 452.

intervened with the government of Oman to head off an attack from its territory.[80] The official American position was neutrality at the outset of the war and support for UN Security Council resolution 479, which called for a cease-fire.

When it found itself closed out of both Iraq and Iran, the United States' first reaction to the war was to bolster ties with the one Gulf power still in the American corner, Saudi Arabia. The Saudis, confronted with a real war practically on their borders, similarly turned to their long-time American ally for support. Riyadh requested a demonstration of American military support, and Washington immediately responded by dispatching Airborne Warning and Control Systems (AWACS) aircraft to the kingdom. The new Reagan administration, coming to power in January 1981, quickly announced that it would sell AWACS to Saudi Arabia and pushed the sale through a reluctant Congress in October 1981. While the Saudis were grateful for the signals of American support, they were not willing to become too publicly aligned with the United States. Riyadh rejected the Reagan administration's "strategic consensus" initiative in the Middle East, which would have established a formal American military presence in the kingdom. They preferred at that time to keep the Americans (at least publicly) "over the horizon," rather than on Saudi soil.[81]

The superpowers' neutrality does not explain their passivity; they could have been truly neutral but fully engaged in ending the conflict in short order. Their stance at the outset of the war undoubtedly reflected Cold War tensions, making real superpower cooperation to end the conflict impossible. It also reflected a lack of military instruments in the area. The Soviet Union was increasingly tied down in Afghanistan and had little naval power in the area. The United States could bring naval power to bear, if it chose, but in 1980 had only begun the process of building a military infrastructure for projecting power to the Gulf region. Their economic and military supply leverage was also limited. Oil money gave both combatants the wherewithal to buy military supplies on the open market, and Iraq had already stockpiled a considerable arsenal of Soviet weaponry and French fighter planes. If two major regional powers, with their own resources, wanted to fight, it would not be easy for the super-powers to stop them.

On the American side, there was one other reason behind the early passivity: the surprisingly small impact the war had on the global oil market. To be sure, the initial Iraqi attack on Iran sent oil prices spiraling.

[80] Bernard Gwertzman, "US Said to Act to Prevent Attack by Iraq from Oman," *New York Times*, October 4, 1980, pp. 1, 2.
[81] Safran, *Saudi Arabia*, pp. 410–16.

Iran and Iraq each targeted the other's oil facilities in the early days of the war, taking over 3 mbd of exports off the market. Prices shot toward the $40 per barrel level. However, little noticed at the time, demand for oil had begun to decline during 1980. Total non-communist world oil consumption in 1980 was, on average, 2.6 mbd less than it had been in 1979. Saudi Arabia, in response to the onset of hostilities, also raised its production by nearly 1 mbd, averaging 10.4 mbd for the last quarter of 1980. By mid-1981, the spot market price had fallen back to the official OPEC price range, in the low $30s per barrel.[82] Demand continued to fall in 1982. OPEC sought to maintain its official price, but as 1982 wore on it became increasingly clear that market realities were driving prices lower. The bottom would fall out of the world oil market a few years later.

The Iran–Iraq War did not lead to a new oil crisis. With plenty of oil in the market to meet falling demand, there was little need for the United States to take immediate steps to halt the fighting. It was only toward the end of this period, into 1982, as it became clear that Iran had turned the tide in the fighting and was poised to carry the war into Iraq, that the United States "tilt" toward Iraq began. In February 1982 Iraq was removed from the American list of state sponsors of terrorism, despite considerable evidence of continuing Iraqi support for Palestinian groups labeled by Washington as terrorist. This step opened up the possibility for Iraq to receive export credits from the United States and removed controls on American companies to sell Iraq "dual-use" technologies.[83] In early 1982 the United States also began supplying Iraq with intelligence data on Iranian force deployments.[84] This was the beginning of what would develop into considerable support from Washington for the Iraqi war effort.

As the superpowers reacted to the new strategic situation in the Gulf, important regional powers also picked sides and sought to take advantage, where possible, of the war.[85] For their own reasons, both Jordan and Egypt rallied to Iraq's side. The monarchical government in Jordan was understandably worried about the potential threat emanating from revolutionary Iran. Jordan's economy, already strongly tied to Iraq's, became

---

[82] Skeet, *OPEC*, pp. 169–77.

[83] Bruce W. Jentleson, *With Friends Like These: Reagan, Bush and Saddam, 1982–1990* (New York: W. W. Norton, 1994), pp. 33, 42.

[84] Jentleson dates the beginning of the intelligence sharing to June 1982: *With Friends Like These*, p. 46. Wafiq al-Samara'i, an officer in Iraqi military intelligence who eventually rose to become deputy director of Iraqi military intelligence in the Gulf War, reports that Baghdad began to receive American intelligence information in late March 1982: *hatam al-bawaba al-sharqiya* [The Destruction of the Eastern Gate] (Kuwait: Dar al-Qabas, 1997), p. 127.

[85] For a fuller discussion of Jordanian, Syrian and Saudi alliance decisions in the Iran–Iraq War, see Gause, "Balancing What?"

even more reliant on the Iraqi market as the Jordanian port of Aqaba became the major seaport for goods headed to Iraq. Jordan was Iraq's most immediate and vocal supporter in the war, hosting the Arab summit meeting of November 1980 that sought to put an Arab imprimatur on Iraq's war effort. Egypt also backed Iraq, to some extent out of President Sadat's distaste for the Islamic revolution (he had given refuge to the deposed shah, who died and was buried in Cairo) and its anti-Americanism, but mostly as a way to reintegrate itself into the Arab world after its peace treaty with Israel. The Egyptian arms industry supplied the Iraqi army with low-technology exports, Egyptian advisers assisted the Iraqi military, and over 1 million Egyptians went to Iraq to work, filling jobs left by Iraqis in the military. Egypt's strategy was a great success, though it took some time for its formal reintegration into Arab councils. As Iran turned the tide of battle in 1981–82, Jordanian and Egyptian support for Iraq was bolstered by classic balance of power concerns about a potential Iranian victory.

Syria was, from the outset, Iran's most important regional ally during the war. Damascus criticized Baghdad for attacking the new Iranian government, whose hostility toward Israel (replacing the de facto alliance the shah had had with Israel) made it a potential ally against Israel, and for diverting Arab energies from the Israeli front. The more immediate concern for the regime of Hafez al-Asad, however, was the risk a victorious Saddam Hussein would pose to it. The hostility between the two Ba'th regimes reached new heights with the breakdown in mid-1979 of the short-lived Syrian–Iraqi "unity" agreement signed in the aftermath of the Egyptian–Israeli peace, amidst Iraqi charges of Syrian interference in Iraqi domestic politics. Saddam Hussein answered in kind, supporting al-Asad's Muslim Brotherhood opponents. Given the risks to his own regime of an empowered Saddam, al-Asad provided political cover for Iran in the Arab world, blocked efforts at various Arab summits to support Iraq, supplied Iran with weapons and did what he could to weaken Iraq. The most significant step in this regard was Damascus' 1982 decision to cut off the flow of Iraqi oil through a Syrian pipeline to the Mediterranean. With Iraq's Persian Gulf ports closed, this had been Iraq's major oil export route.

Saudi Arabia and the smaller Gulf monarchies faced a dangerous and unavoidable dilemma at the outset of the war: support Iraq and run the risks of eventual Iraqi hegemony in the area, or act to balance Iraqi power by supporting Iran, despite the ideological threat of the Islamic revolution. Two Iranian air attacks on a Kuwaiti border post in November 1980 underscored the risk that the fighting could directly involve them and their oil shipments in the Gulf. Saudi Arabia and most of the other monarchies chose to throw in their lot with Baghdad. Iraqi ships and warplanes were permitted to take shelter in Saudi Arabia and other Gulf states during the first days of the fighting, despite Iranian threats to attack Iraqi forces wherever they were.[86] The Saudis permitted their Red Sea ports to be used for the shipment of military material and other supplies to Iraq.[87] Kuwaiti ports were virtually turned over to the Iraqis as the war went on.[88] Saudi Arabia, Kuwait and the UAE supported Iraq financially, with "loans" and, in the case of the first two, oil production undertaken on the Iraqi account.[89] Only Oman, furthest from the fighting and sharing management of the Strait of Hormuz with Iran, tried to maintain businesslike relations with Iran during the first years of the conflict, and even they were tense.[90]

As fighting bogged down in early 1981, the Saudis began to see a silver lining in the war clouds. With Iran and Iraq engaged with each other, Riyadh could consolidate its leadership among the smaller Gulf monarchies. In the past these states had used Iran, Iraq and foreign powers such as Britain and the United States to offset Saudi influence. However, the immediate security threats presented by the Iranian Revolution and the war underlined their vulnerability, and drove them closer to Riyadh. In May 1981 these extraordinary circumstances led the five smaller monarchies to put aside their fears of Saudi dominance and agree to the formation of the Gulf Cooperation Council (GCC), which has endured to the present. Although its founding documents stress economic and cultural cooperation, the security threats they faced from the revolution and war are clearly what brought the smaller states formally under the Saudi umbrella.[91] The security rationale for the GCC became much more apparent in December 1981, when Saudi and Bahraini authorities uncovered a plot to overthrow the Bahraini government. Officials in both countries charged that Iran armed and trained the saboteurs, and the evidence for some Iranian complicity in the plot is strong. Coordination among the Gulf monarchies on security issues at both the bilateral and the GCC levels intensified.[92]

[86] *New York Times*, October 3, 1980, p. A10; FBIS-MEA-80-191, September 30, 1980, p. i.
[87] Safran, *Saudi Arabia*, p. 369; Ramazani, *Revolutionary Iran*, pp. 72–73.
[88] Personal interviews, Kuwait, May 1997.
[89] Gerd Nonneman, *Iraq, the Gulf States and the War* (London: Ithaca Press, 1986), pp. 96 – 97; Hiro, *The Longest War*, pp. 76–77.
[90] Kechichian, *Oman and the World*, pp. 102–04; personal interview, Oman, March 1990.
[91] On the formation of the GCC, see R. K. Ramazani, *The Gulf Cooperation Council: Record and Analysis* (Charlottesville: University Press of Virginia, 1988); Emile Nakhleh, *The Gulf Cooperation Council: Politics, Problems and Prospects* (New York: Praeger, 1986); and Erik R. Peterson, *The Gulf Cooperation Council* (Boulder, CO: Westview Press, 1988).
[92] Ramazani, *Revolutionary Iran*, pp. 51, 131–32; Mylroie, "Regional Security after Empire," pp. 339–50.

July 1982 to February 1987: Iran on the offensive

The Islamic Republican government in Iran, having driven almost all Iraqi forces out of its territory by June 1982, could have declared victory in the Iran–Iraq War and accepted one of the various cease-fire plans on offer internationally (the UN Security Council had passed yet another cease-fire resolution on July 12, 1982). There was some public discussion of Iran's options among top-level Iranian officials after the recapture of Khorramshahr in May 1982, with voices counseling moderation and others urging continuation of the conflict into Iraq. Ayatollah Khomeini ended this debate on June 21, 1982, publicly calling (once again) for the overthrow of Saddam Hussein. He did not hide his desire to spread the Islamic revolution throughout the region, saying that Saddam's overthrow would lead to the Iraqi people establishing an Islamic government, and "if Iran and Iraq unite and link up with one another, the other, smaller nations of the region will join them as well."[93] The ayatollah succumbed to much the same temptations that had seduced Saddam to war in the fall of 1980. Now it was Iraq that seemed an easy target for revived Iranian military power, and Khomeini expected active support from Iraqi Shi'a for Iran's effort to dislodge Saddam. On July 13, 1982, Iranian forces launched an assault on the Iraqi city of Basra.

Iranian domestic politics added to the push for war. The preceding months had been particularly brutal and violent, as the revolutionary regime battled its domestic opponents to consolidate its rule. After his removal from the presidency in June 1981, Abol Hassan Bani Sadr joined forces with the Mujahidin e-Khalq (MEK), the Islamic-Marxist militant group that had emerged as the regime's most potent challenger. Just weeks after Bani Sadr's removal from office, on June 28, 1981, a powerful explosion at the headquarters of the ruling Islamic Republican Party (IRP) killed Ayatollah Muhammad Beheshti, one of the architects of the revolution and IRP secretary-general, along with scores of government officials. On August 30, 1981, another bomb blew up the prime minister's office, killing Iran's president, prime minister and chief of the national police. By September 1981 MEK and other leftist groups were openly confronting the Revolutionary Guard in the streets of Iranian cities. The regime responded with a ruthless program of mass arrests and public executions, in which thousands were killed.[94]

---

[93] Quoted in Bakhash, *Reign of the Ayatollahs*, p. 232.
[94] Bakhash, *Reign of the Ayatollahs*, pp. 219–24; Milani, *The Making of Iran's Islamic Revolution*, pp. 186–89.

By the summer of 1982 the regime had basically defeated its domestic opponents, but the consolidation process was hardly complete. Continuing the war with Iraq would allow Khomeini and the IRP to continue to brand their foes as traitors to the nation as well as enemies of the state. The MEK contributed to that line by openly allying with Saddam Hussein. MEK leader Masud Rajavi publicly met with Iraqi deputy prime minister Tariq Aziz in Paris on January 9, 1983, and MEK forces established bases in Iraq.[95] Iran countered by organizing its own Iraqi opposition group, the Supreme Council of the Islamic Revolution in Iraq (SCIRI), headed by Muhammad Baqir al-Hakim. Al-Hakim was the scion of a prominent Iraqi Shi'i clerical family who had left Iraq at the outset of the Iran–Iraq War.

Iranian forces launched a series of offensives along the northern, central and southern fronts between July 1982 and the end of 1984. In the north, Iran was able to neutralize the Kurdish Democratic Party-Iran (KDP-I) forces, which had been in revolt against the central government since the revolution and had been supported by Iraq. With the assistance of Iraqi Kurdish forces from the Kurdish Democratic Party, the Iranians then began to take the fight across the border into Iraqi Kurdistan, though they realized only modest territorial gains. Likewise on the central front, Iranian offensives in this period pushed Iraqi forces back into Iraq and led to the capture of modest amounts of Iraqi territory. The largest Iranian offensives were on the southern front, aimed at cutting Basra off from the rest of Iraq. Major efforts in July–August 1982 and February–March 1984 resulted in large numbers of casualties but only small territorial gains for Iran. The Iraqi military, which had not distinguished itself in its offensive operations in Iran, proved more adept at defense. Saddam Hussein, realizing that he was now in a fight for his regime's survival, took steps to depoliticize the promtion process and advance officers with a record of success on the battlefield. Iraq also began to use chemical weapons against Iranian troop formations.[96]

The Iraqi leadership did not relish the prospect of a long war with a country whose population trebled its own. With Iran uninterested in ending the conflict, Baghdad looked to expand the battlefront, both into Iran with air and missile attacks on Iranian cities and into the waters of the Persian Gulf. The latter effort was aimed not only at cutting Iran's oil exports, and thus its source of wealth, but also at forcing international

---

[95] Hiro, *The Longest War*, p. 100.
[96] For extensive discussions of developments on the battlefield during this period, see Cordesman and Wagner, *Lessons*, Chapter 6; O'Ballance, *The Gulf War*, Chapters 6–9; Pollack, *Arabs at War*, pp. 203–13.

powers to take a more active role in stopping the conflict. Iraq began targeting Iranian cities near the southern border with air and missile attacks during the Iranian offensive of February–March 1984; Iran responded with artillery attacks on Basra and air raids on Baghdad and other Iraqi cities.[97] While both sides continued over the course of the war to attack each other's cities, Iraq was able over time to mount many more of these attacks. With all but unfettered access to the international arms market and financial support from the Gulf monarchies, Baghdad could obtain more and better missiles and more advanced aircraft both from the Soviets and from Western countries, most notably France. Tehran, with fewer friends and less money, could not keep pace in the arms race.

Baghdad began a concerted campaign against Iran-bound shipping in 1984, after they had integrated recently obtained French aircraft and air-to-surface missiles into their air force. The Iranians responded with air attacks in the Gulf on ships headed to and from Kuwait and Saudi Arabia. In the only direct Saudi involvement in the Iran–Iraq War, in June 1984 Saudi air force F-15s shot down one Iranian jet flying over Saudi territorial waters and damaged another. After that engagement, the Iranian air force avoided Saudi airspace, but continued to strike at ships elsewhere in the Gulf. The "tanker war" saw sixty-two successful attacks by both sides on oil tankers in 1984 and fifty in 1985.[98] However, these attacks did not affect the oil market. While insurance rates rose, Iran found captains and crews willing to take the risk of calling at Iranian ports, increased its own protection of those ships and established an effective "shuttle service" taking Iranian oil to tankers outside the range of Iraqi aircraft. Iranian oil exports increased from the first years of the war. Iraq's exports also increased, even though its Persian Gulf oil ports were closed by the war. New pipelines through Turkey and Saudi Arabia brought Iraqi oil to safe ports in the Mediterranean and Red Seas. Neither side could bring the other to its knees through attacks on its civilian populations or through interdiction of oil shipping.

Iran launched offensives through 1984 and 1985, though none as large as the February–March 1984 assault on the southern front. There were no major breakthroughs, as the fighting settled down into a war of attrition.[99] The only significant military defeat Iran was able to inflict on Iraq during this period came in early 1986, with the Iranian capture of the al-Faw

---

[97] O'Ballance, *The Gulf War*, pp. 153–54.
[98] On number of attacks, reported by the shipping insurance firm Lloyd's of London, see John Creighton, *Oil on Troubled Waters: Gulf Wars 1980–1991* (London: Echoes Press, 1992), pp. 63–65, and more generally on the Tanker War, Chapter 7. See also Cordesman and Wagner, *Lessons*, pp. 191–98; O'Ballance, *The Gulf War*, pp. 128–29, 154–56, 170–72.
[99] O'Ballance, *The Gulf War*, Chapters 9–10; Cordesman and Wagner, *Lessons*, Chapter 7.

Peninsula south of Basra, the southernmost tip of Iraq. This was Iran's most dramatic military success since it had carried the war into Iraqi territory in 1982. Iraqi counterattacks against al-Faw failed, as did the Iraqi effort to compensate for the loss of the peninsula by capturing the Iranian city of Mehran along the central front a few months later. The loss of al-Faw reminded all concerned that, despite the desultory fighting of the past few years, Iran was still on the offensive in the war.[100] The US assistant secretary of state for the Near East told his superiors in July 1986 that "the trends in the war ... underscore our long-held view that the longer the war continues, the greater the risk of an Iraqi defeat."[101]

That risk, while real, never came to fruition. Iran was unable to build on its success at al-Faw to break Iraqi defenses, either around Basra or elsewhere along the front, despite a number of offensives through 1986. In early 1987 Iran mounted its largest attack on Basra since 1982. After two months of intense fighting the Iraqi defenses still held. This was the apogee of Iranian military pressure on Iraq. Tehran attacked along the length of the front for the remainder of 1987, but could not achieve a breakthrough. Meanwhile, Iraq exploited its air superiority to continue to harass Iranian shipping and hit Iranian oil facilities as well as to launch air and missile attacks on Iranian border positions and cities.[102]

As Iran took the offensive on the battlefield in this period, the tentative alignment of the Gulf monarchies with Iraq became solidified. Kuwait and Saudi Arabia in particular took a number of steps to support the Iraqi war effort, including financial support, Iraqi access to their port and military facilities, and clandestine transfers (in the Saudi case) of weapons to Iraq.[103] Saudi Arabia allowed Iraq to build an oil pipeline across Saudi territory, linking up to the Saudi pipeline system, to allow Iraqi oil exports to bypass the Persian Gulf. Egypt and Jordan continued to support Iraq as well. Iran's only regional ally remained Syria, which served as a staging ground for arms shipments to Iran.

---

[100] Cordesman and Wagner, *Lessons*, pp. 219–29; Pollack, *Arabs at War*, pp. 217–18.

[101] State Department memo quoted in Jentleson, *With Friends Like These*, p. 56. General Wafiq al-Samara'i reports that in August 1986 a CIA team came to Baghdad and expressed its fears that Iraq was in a very bad military situation, and might not be able to resist the next round of Iranian attacks: *Hatam al-bawaba al-sharqiya*, p. 113.

[102] Cordesman and Wagner, *Lessons*, Chapters 8–9; Pollack, *Arabs at War*, pp. 221–24; O'Ballance, *The Gulf War*, Chapter 11.

[103] King Fahd, in a public speech during the Gulf War, listed the amounts of aid to Iraq, which totaled over $25 billion: *al-Sharq al-Awsat*, January 17, 1991, p. 4. Saudi sources subsequently confirmed that from the time of the closure of the Syrian–Iraqi pipeline in April 1982, Saudi oil revenues from the Kuwait–Saudi Arabia neutral zone were placed "at Iraq's disposal": Omar Al-Zobidy, "Iraq Owes Kingdom SR94b in Debt," *Arab News* (Jidda), June 25, 2001.

While there was little Iran could do to either Cairo or Amman, the proximity of Saudi Arabia and Kuwait made them inviting targets. Iranian forces attacked oil tankers calling at Kuwaiti and Saudi ports, in retaliation for Iraqi attacks on its shipping and oil facilities. After the capture of al-Faw in 1986, Iranian missiles occasionally found their way across the Kuwaiti border, always "by mistake." Iran encouraged Shi'i opposition to the regime in Kuwait, where about one-quarter of the citizen population is Shi'i. In December 1983, a series of coordinated explosions damaged targets in the country. An assassination attempt on the amir of Kuwait in May 1985 was followed by bombings of popular cafes in July 1985, killing eight and wounding ninety. Three times during the period (1984, 1985 and 1988) Shi'i militants hijacked airlines and demanded the release of Shi'i prisoners in Kuwaiti jails. In January 1987 fires erupted at a Kuwaiti oil facility, just as Kuwait was to host an Islamic Conference Organization summit being boycotted by Iran. The Kuwaiti government, in response to this domestic unrest, placed restrictions on the relatively free political system in the country, eventually suspending its elected parliament in July 1986.[104]

The Iranians used the annual pilgrimage to Mecca as a lever of pressure against Saudi Arabia (which had a much smaller indigenous Shi'i community, as a percentage of citizen population, than Kuwait). Ayatollah Khomeini bluntly asserted that the pilgrimage should be as much a political as a religious event. He openly encouraged Iranian pilgrims to demonstrate and agitate while in Saudi Arabia, to call into question the domestic and international legitimacy of the Al Saud regime. In 1982 Saudi authorities expelled about 100 Iranians from the pilgrimage; in 1983 Saudi security clashed with Iranian pilgrims. A brief rapprochement between Tehran and Riyadh in 1984–85, when the Iranians tried to draw Saudi Arabia away from its support for Iraq, ended with the Iranian victory at al-Faw in early 1986. The 1986 pilgrimage saw a return of tensions, as the Saudis confiscated arms and explosives carried by Iranians, and in 1987 clashes between Iranian pilgrims and Saudi security forces left more than 400 dead.[105] Between the attacks on oil shipping in the Persian Gulf and the domestic unrest in the Gulf monarchies

---

[104] Jill Crystal, *Kuwait: The Transformation of an Oil State* (Boulder, CO: Westview Press, 1992), pp. 111–16; Kostiner, "Shi'i Unrest in the Gulf," p. 180.

[105] Iranian efforts to disrupt the 1986 pilgrimage were revealed in a letter from Ayatollah Hussein Ali Montazeri to Ayatollah Khomeini, which was made public during the 1989 leadership struggle in Iran: *New York Times*, May 22, 1989, pp. 1, 8. On the pilgrimage as an issue in Saudi–Iranian relations, see Ramazani, *Revolutionary Iran*, pp. 93–96; and Henner Furtig, *Iran's Rivalry with Saudi Arabia between the Gulf Wars* (Reading, UK: Ithaca Press, 2002), pp. 42–55.

most closely aligned with Iraq, regional tensions remained high throughout this period.

The shift in battlefield fortunes in 1982, as Iran went on the offensive, led to a reassessment by both superpowers of their positions toward the combatants. Both the Soviet Union and the United States worried about the regional consequences of an Iranian military victory, and moved to shore up Iraq. The Soviet Union had announced a resumption of arms shipments to Baghdad (cut off in 1980 when the war began) in July 1981, following the Israeli attack on the Iraqi nuclear facility. However, major new arms shipments did not begin until the summer of 1982, and in the fall of 1982 Soviet-made missiles were being fired by Iraq into Iran. Moscow remained Iraq's major military supplier throughout the war. In 1983 Iran expelled a number of Soviet diplomats from the country on charges of espionage and tried the leaders of the communist Tudeh Party on the same grounds, declaring membership in the party illegal that same year.[106] While Moscow tried to keep channels of communication open to Iran, and permitted a number of its allies (Syria and North Korea more notably) to supply Soviet-made arms to Tehran, in effect it tilted toward Iraq for the remainder of the war.

The United States, which had begun to tilt toward Iraq early in 1982, moved more directly toward supporting Baghdad with the battlefield change of the summer of that year. Diplomatic relations between the two countries were restored in 1984. Intelligence sharing with Baghdad accelerated. Washington permitted American companies to sell Iraq "dual-use" products and technology (including helicopters), ostensibly for civilian use but knowing that Iraq was likely to use them for military purposes. Even while adhering to a formal policy of no military sales to Iraq, the Reagan administration allowed, even in some cases encouraged, allies to provide Iraq with arms, while launching in 1983 Operation Staunch, an effort to prevent third countries from supplying Iran with weapons. Washington also provided Iraq with credits for the purchase of American goods and agricultural products. While acknowledging and even publicly condemning the Iraqi use of chemical weapons in the conflict, the United States continued to build its relations with Saddam Hussein's regime during this period.[107]

This public tilt toward Iraq, however, did not prevent the United States from secretly reaching out to Iran. The Reagan administration engaged in

---

[106] Smolansky and Smolansky, *The USSR and Iraq*, pp. 236–42; Chubin and Tripp, *Iran and Iraq at War*, pp. 220–23.

[107] Jentleson, *With Friends Like These*, Chapter 1. For declassified American documents on the development of the relationship with Iraq in the 1982–84 period, see National Security Archive, "Shaking Hands With Saddam Hussein: The US Tilts Toward Iraq, 1980–84," edited by Joyce Battle, National Security Archive Briefing Book No. 82, February 25, 2003, www.gwu.edu/~nsarchiv/NSAEBB/NSAEBB82/.

secret negotiations with Iran over the years 1984–86, culminating in the sale of American arms, through Israel at first and then directly, to Iran and the provision of American intelligence to Iran. The profits from those sales were used to buy arms for the Nicaraguan opposition force, known as the contras, who opposed the Sandinista regime. Direct American support for the contras at that time was prohibited by Congress. In exchange for the arms and intelligence, Iran agreed to use its influence with its allies in Lebanon to bring about the release of American hostages held there (though more Americans were taken hostage shortly after those in the bargain were released). When the secret dealings were revealed in a Lebanese magazine in November 1986, the relationship ended.[108] The hostility felt by both sides toward the other was hardly ameliorated by this adventure. Revelation of the affair also did nothing to help Iraqi–American relations, as Saddam Hussein learned that he could not trust professions of good will from Washington.

While the unsteady American effort to balance its interests between Iraq and Iran in this period sometimes reads like the plot of a cheap spy novel, the most striking fact about American policy was the country's lack of direct involvement in the conflict. There are two reasons that American forces were not committed to the region, despite the Persian Gulf's central importance in American global strategy. The first was the course of the conflict itself. With neither Iraq nor Iran able to gain a decisive military advantage, Washington could afford to allow the fighting to continue, as it was not changing the regional strategic picture. The second reason for the relative American passivity was the change in the world oil market. The mid-1980s witnessed a collapse in oil prices as dramatic as the price increases of 1973–74 and 1979–80. Oil prices averaged nearly $37 per barrel in 1980. By 1983 they had fallen to an average of $29.55, a substantial decline but still far above prices in the 1970s, even adjusted for inflation. As the 1980s progressed, more oil was brought on to the world market, and demand for oil in both Europe and the United States declined. In the fall of 1985 Saudi Arabia, which had steadily cut its production over the previous years in an effort to put a floor under falling prices, abandoned that strategy and upped production, leading to the price collapse. Saudi production went from 2.3 mbd in August 1985 to 4.6 mbd in December 1985.[109] By 1986 the bottom had dropped out of

---

[108] For a full account of the Iran–contra affair, with declassified documents, see Peter Kornbluh and Malcolm Byrne, *The Iran–Contra Scandal: The Declassified History* (New York: W. W. Norton, 1993). For brief accounts, see Jentleson, *With Friends Like These*, pp. 56–59; Cordesman and Wagner, *Lessons*, pp. 237–42.

[109] US Department of Energy, Energy Information Administration, *Monthly Energy Review*, March 2004, Table 11.1a.

the market, with an average price that year of only $14.43.[110] Daily spot prices actually dropped below $10 per barrel on occasion that year.

The reasons for Saudi Arabia's decision to abandon its role of "swing producer" are much debated. Some have argued that the Saudis increased production and drove down prices as part of a Reagan administration plan to bankrupt the Soviet Union, which was also a major oil exporter.[111] However, it is hard to see why the summer of 1985 would have been a Cold War turning point for the Saudis or for the Reagan administration. Mikhail Gorbachev had just come to power in Moscow; Margaret Thatcher had famously commented that he was a man with whom she could do business. The Reagan administration had been in power since 1981, and the Saudis had pursued a policy from that period of trying to prop up oil prices, not bring them down. Others have argued that the real Saudi target was Iran, still on the offensive and a threat to Saudi Arabia's regional position and domestic stability.[112] Again, it is hard to reconcile this explanation with the timing of the decision. Iran had been a threat to Riyadh at least since it turned the tide on the battlefield in 1982, if not before. Moreover, there was something of a thaw in Saudi–Iranian relations in 1984–85, which was reversed only with Iran's al-Faw offensive in early 1986.

The more likely explanation for the Saudi change in strategy centers on oil market dynamics. Other producers were not matching the Saudi production cuts, and thus the Saudis were not only unable to stop the decline in prices, they were also losing their market share. Falling prices and fewer sales translated into a serious decline in Saudi oil revenues. To break this pattern, the Saudis moved aggressively against both fellow OPEC members and non-OPEC producers, offering profit guarantees to buyers (through the "net-back" pricing system), and recaptured some of their lost market share. The cost of the strategy was the even steeper decline in prices from the end of 1985 and well into 1986. The price collapse put the fear of God (via the fear of bankruptcy) into other OPEC producers, who agreed by the end of 1986 actually to abide by their production quotas. A number of non-OPEC producers also coordinated a cut in production, to convince the Saudis to end the price war. The price collapse had also seriously damaged the United States oil industry, and the United States signaled to Saudi Arabia (during a visit by Vice President George H. W. Bush to Saudi Arabia in April 1986) that it

---

[110] Average annual Brent spot crude prices taken from British Petroleum, *Statistical Review of World Energy 2006*, www.bp.com.
[111] Peter Schweizer, *Reagan's War* (New York: Doubleday, 2002), pp. 238–41.
[112] Hiro, *The Longest War*, p. 213.

wanted prices stabilized at a higher level. All these factors, plus a slight upturn in world demand for oil in the late 1980s, combined to halt the oil price decline. Prices fluctuated between just shy of $15 and just shy of $19 per barrel for the rest of the decade.[113]

March 1987 to August 1988: American intervention and cease-fire

During this period, little over a year in duration, the United States became directly involved in the Iran–Iraq War, with the US Navy confronting Iranian forces in the Persian Gulf. The United States also became more active diplomatically, seeking to pressure Iran into ending the war. At the same time, Iraq turned the tide of battle, recapturing lost territory, subjecting Tehran for the first time in the war to sustained missile attack and threatening to carry the ground war back into Iran. These two changes in the strategic picture led the Iranian leadership to accept a cease-fire in July 1988. Iraq, after some foot-dragging, followed suit a few weeks later.

In November 1986 Kuwait asked both the United States and the Soviet Union for assistance in protecting shipping to and from its ports, which had been subject to Iranian attack for some time. After learning that the Soviet Union had begun negotiations with Kuwait, in March 1987 Washington agreed to put American flags on a number of Kuwaiti tankers and to provide them with naval escorts. To that end, the United States assembled its largest naval force since the Vietnam War and deployed it to the Persian Gulf and Arabian Sea. While Saudi Arabia made no formal request of Washington, the American forces in the Gulf provided protection for Saudi tankers as well. The Soviet Union and a number of West European countries also sent naval forces to protect oil tankers. It is interesting to note that the American naval deployment did not come in response to changes in the regional strategic picture. The high-water mark of Iranian military success in the war was more than a year earlier, with the capture of al-Faw. Washington reacted to prevent the Soviet Union from increasing its influence with Kuwait and the other Gulf monarchies, even though Soviet–American relations were growing increasingly cooperative with the Reagan–Gorbachev détente. Cold War considerations, more than regional power shifts, drove American policy here, though Washington also saw the deployment as an opportunity to reassure both Iraq and the Gulf monarchies in the aftermath of the Iran–contra affair.

Ironically, the first attack on the US Navy in the Iran–Iraq War came not from Iran, but from Iraq. On May 17, 1987, an Iraqi jet fired two

---

[113] Yergin, *The Prize*, Chapter 36; Skeet, *OPEC*, Chapters 10–12.

missiles at the USS *Stark*, killing thirty-seven crew members. Washington accepted Baghdad's explanation that the attack was due to pilot error. The attack on the *Stark* served only to increase American commitment to its intervention in the Gulf, with the Reagan administration finalizing its reflagging agreement with Kuwait just two days later. The tilt to Iraq and the confrontation with Iran was solidified.[114] With this indirect American protection, Iraq accelerated its air campaign against Iran's oil exports. Iran responded by laying mines. In September 1987 US forces attacked an Iranian ship laying mines, killing five crew members and seizing the ship. Iran continued its attacks on shipping, with Revolutionary Guard forces using small speedboats in a version of guerrilla war at sea. In October 1987 an Iranian missile launched from al-Faw struck one of the reflagged tankers approaching Kuwait. The United States responded by destroying two Iranian offshore oil platforms. Iran and the United States were, in effect, engaged in a low-level war at sea.[115]

The second element of the increased American involvement in the war was diplomatic. At the United Nations, the United States pushed for a new Security Council resolution calling for an end to the war. Given the general improvement in Soviet–American relations and the specific fact that Washington and Moscow were both tilting toward Iraq at the time, this effort bore fruit. In July 1987 the Security Council unanimously adopted Resolution 598. The resolution invoked Chapter VII of the UN Charter, which empowered the Security Council to take actions, in the event of a breach of international peace, that are mandatory upon member states. Resolution 598 called for an immediate cease-fire and a withdrawal of all forces to their own territory without delay. In a nod toward Iran, it also called for the secretary general to set up an impartial tribunal to determine responsibility for the conflict. Iraq immediately accepted the resolution, subject to Iranian acceptance. Iran criticized the resolution as biased and providing a cover for American military intervention in the Gulf, but never formally rejected it. It argued that the cease-fire clause should come into effect only when other clauses, specifically on attribution of war guilt, were accomplished. The overall effect of UN Security Council Resolution 598 was to increase international pressure on Iran to end the war.[116]

---

[114] Jentleson, *With Friends Like These*, pp. 62–67.
[115] A detailed account of the naval operations in 1987 can be found in Cordesman and Wagner, *Lessons*, Chapter 9 and Table 10.1 (pp. 365–66) on shipping attacks.
[116] For an insider account of the diplomacy at the United Nations which led to UNSC 598 and subsequent UN activity on the Iran–Iraq War, see Cameron R. Hume, *The United Nations, Iran, and Iraq: How Peacemaking Changed* (Bloomington: Indiana University Press, 1994), Chapters 7–11.

As the United States became increasingly involved in the conflict, militarily and diplomatically, Iraq decisively turned the tide of battle in the spring of 1988. Reflecting its own exhaustion, the Iranian military failed for the first time in years to launch an offensive along the southern front at the beginning of the year. In March 1988 Iraq bombarded Tehran with long-range missiles. Iran responded with missile attacks and air raids on Iraqi cities, but they had little effect. The Iraqi attacks on Tehran, on the other hand, caused considerable panic, given the fear that Iraq would arm the missiles with chemical weapons. Substantial numbers of people fled Tehran in response to the first attacks. In April 1988 Iraq recaptured the al-Faw Peninsula in a lightning two-day campaign. Baghdad followed up that victory in May and June 1988 by retaking other areas along the southern front and pushing substantially into Iranian territory along the central front before retiring back across the border. In all these attacks the Iraqis used chemical weapons. For the first time since 1982, Iran was no longer on the offensive in the war. The momentum of battle had shifted to Iraq.[117]

While Iraqi forces were successfully engaging the Iranians in 1988, Saddam Hussein was intensifying his policy of retribution against Iraqi Kurds for their disloyalty to him in the war. At various points during the war, the major Iraqi Kurdish opposition groups, the Kurdish Democratic Party (KDP) and the Patriotic Union of Kurdistan (PUK), had both allied themselves with Iran and had participated in Iranian attacks along the northern front. Although rivals, the two groups began cooperating on military matters under Iranian sponsorship by 1987. Iranian and Iraqi Kurdish forces had some success in 1987 and early 1988 along the northern front, taking and holding territory in Iraqi Kurdistan. Saddam's response was deadly. In February 1987 he appointed his first cousin, Ali Hassan al-Majid, governor of the Iraqi Kurdish provinces with full powers to end the insurgency. Ali Hassan supervised what came to be called the Anfal campaign (*anfal* in Arabic means the spoils of war), razing thousands of Kurdish villages and relocating 1.5 million Iraqi Kurds. The governor earned his nickname, "Chemical Ali," by ordering a series of chemical weapons attacks between February and September 1988 on Kurdish guerrilla strongholds. The chemical attack on Halabja in March 1988 became notorious around the world. After PUK and Iranian forces captured the town, Iraqi forces bombarded it with chemical weapons, killing between 3,500 and 5,000 people. All told, between 50,000 and 100,000 Iraqi Kurds were killed in the Anfal

[117] Cordesman and Wagner, *Lessons*, Chapter 10; Pollack, *Arabs at War*, pp. 224–28.

campaign. Another 250,000 fled the country, becoming refugees in Iran and Turkey.[118]

Two days after Iraq recaptured al-Faw in April 1988, United States naval forces conducted their largest attack of the reflagging operation on Iran's sea power. On April 13 the USS *Samuel B. Roberts* struck a mine, wounding ten of the sailors aboard. In retaliation, on April 18, American forces sank two Iranian ships and badly disabled another, destroyed two of the oil platforms and attacked a number of Iranian Revolutionary Guard speedboats. There is no evidence that Washington and Baghdad had coordinated on the timing of their campaigns, but that was certainly the impression left in Tehran. Iranian parliament speaker Ali Akbar Hashemi Rafsanjani said on April 19: "Time is not on our side anymore. The world – I mean the anti-Islamic powers – has decided to make a serious effort to save Saddam Hussein and tie our hands."[119]

On the morning of July 3, 1988, the USS *Vincennes* was engaged in a firefight with a number of small Iranian gunboats. An Iran Air civilian passenger plane, which had taken off from Bandar Abbas along the Persian Gulf coast on a regularly scheduled flight to Dubai, following its assigned flight path, approached the area where the *Vincennes* was engaged. Mistaking the plane for an Iranian military craft, the commander of the *Vincennes* ordered it shot down. All 290 people on board died. The United States expressed its regret for the event and paid compensation to the Iranian government and to families of the victims, but many Iranians continue to believe that the United States deliberately targeted a civilian aircraft. Iranians remain particularly aggrieved that the commander of the *Vincennes* was not disciplined for his error and was decorated before his retirement.[120] It was subsequently revealed that many of the details in the official American account of the event were not true.[121] The sanitized version American officials originally put out seems to have been intended to mask the

---

[118] For short descriptions of the Anfal campaign, see Marr, *The Modern History of Iraq*, pp. 200–02; and Tripp, *A History of Iraq*, pp. 243–46. A more detailed account can be found in Middle East Watch, *Genocide in Iraq: The Anfal Campaign Against the Kurds* (New York: Human Rights Watch, 1993).

[119] Cordesman and Wagner, *Lessons*, pp. 375–81, quote on p. 380.

[120] Elaine Sciolino, "Muting Anguish in Iran over '88 Air Disaster," *New York Times*, July 4, 1998. As recently as June 2000, an Iranian admiral said: ""The US downing of the Iranian plane cannot be considered a mistake but (instead) demonstrated the depth of its hostility to Iran" ("Senior Commander Says US Bombed Iranian Plane on Purpose," Islamic Republic News Agency, June 21, 2000; accessed through Gulf 2000 project archives, https://www1.columbia.edu/sec/cu/sipa/GULF2000/).

[121] Joint investigative report by *Newsweek* magazine and ABC News "Nightline." The transcript of the Nightline broadcast of July 1, 1992, can be found at http://homepage.ntlworld.com/jksonc/docs/ir655-nightline-19920701.html.

extent to which US forces were seeking out engagements with Iran. However, there is no evidence that the commander knew that his target was a civilian airliner.

This incident, following on the Iraqi military successes of 1988, finally prompted the Iranian leadership to decide that it was time to end the war. Iranian officials had, even before the downing of the airliner, been advising Ayatollah Khomeini that the prospects for victory were very dim. Khomeini had been told by a senior member of the government that the economy was operating "at a level below zero" and that volunteers for the front were in short supply. The commander of the Revolutionary Guard, Mohsin Rezai, in a letter to Khomeini in late June 1988, advised that the Iranian forces would not win "any victories in the next five years."[122] On July 18, 1988, Iranian president Ali Khamenei informed the UN secretary general Javier Pérez de Cuéllar that Iran accepted UN Security Council Resolution 598. On July 20, Ayatollah Khomeini confirmed the decision in a public statement, in which he compared it to drinking poison. He said that for him it "would have been more bearable to accept death and martyrdom" than to end the war in this way. He implied that he was the last holdout in the Iranian leadership on the decision, saying that "all the high-ranking political and military experts" in the country urged him to accept the cease-fire.[123] Saddam Hussein, buoyed by Iraq's successes and this sign of Iranian weakness, initially refused to accept the Iranian offer, demanding direct talks between the two governments. Under pressure from his Arab allies, the United States and most of the rest of the world, Saddam Hussein finally agreed to the cease-fire on August 6, on the condition that Iran agree to direct talks shortly thereafter.[124] Pérez de Cuéllar on August 8 announced the cease-fire, which went into effect on August 20, 1988. The two sides ended the war in roughly the same positions they were when it began.

---

[122] This unvarnished military advice was referenced by Khomeini in his own letter to leading regime figures explaining why he had decided to accept the cease-fire. That letter was declassified and released by former president Rafsanjani in September 2006. For a discussion of the letter's contents, see Hamid Ahadi, "New Political Linings in Iran," *Rooz on-line*, October 3, 2006, www.roozonline.com/english/017928.shtml. See also Nazila Fathi, "An Old Letter Casts Doubts on Iran's Goal for Uranium," *New York Times*, October 5, 2006.

[123] Robert Pear, "Khomeini Accepts 'Poison' of Ending War with Iraq," *New York Times*, July 21, 1988.

[124] Cameron Hume reports that the ambassadors of the five permanent members of the Security Council in Baghdad pressed the Iraqi government to accept the cease-fire: *The United Nations, Iran and Iraq*, p. 170. Giandomenico Picco, an aide close to Secretary General Pérez de Cuéllar, recounts how the Saudi leadership was instrumental in getting Saddam to agree to the cease-fire proposal: Picco, *Man Without a Gun* (New York: Times Books, 1999), pp. 92–96.

Conclusion

The Iranian Revolution was the most important event in the Persian Gulf region, perhaps in the entire Middle East, in the second half of the twentieth century. It fundamentally redirected the domestic politics of the largest state in the region. It changed regional and international alignments. It caused the second major oil shock in less than a decade. It was a major factor, if not the major factor, in the regional revival of Islamist politics that has dominated the area since. It created the conditions that led to the longest and most damaging, and most senseless, war in modern Middle Eastern history. One cannot exaggerate its importance.

The revolution profoundly changed the regional international politics of the Persian Gulf in two important ways. First, it ended the relative moderation of the regional political agenda that had obtained in the 1970s. I argued in the previous chapter that the Gulf had been a relatively stable place because the major regional powers had come to accept the domestic legitimacy of each other's regimes. The revolution ended that tacit agreement. The very fact that a mass-based, Islamist social revolution had occurred in the neighborhood was an implicit threat to both Ba'thist Iraq and the monarchical Arab states. The fact that the new Iranian revolutionary leadership actively encouraged the export of the revolution made that implicit threat explicit. While Saddam Hussein certainly is responsible for initiating the Iran–Iraq War, it is difficult to imagine that it would have occurred had the monarchical regime continued in Iran. The uncomfortable but stable relationship between Saudi Arabia and the shah was replaced by open hostility. Ayatollah Khomeini proclaimed monarchy un-Islamic, and the two states engaged in a contest for leadership of Islamist political movements. The conflicts between Iran and its neighbors were about regional power, but they were also about defining legitimate domestic political regimes. Thus they could not be compromised the way power conflicts in the 1970s could.

The second important change the revolution brought was in American policy. No longer could the United States rely on a powerful regional ally to safeguard its interests in the world's oil patch. Immediately after the revolution, the United States, with the Carter Doctrine, signaled that it would take a more direct military role in the area. The first manifestation of that role came with the reflagging operation in 1987–88. This period saw the beginning of a trend that would culminate with the American occupation of Iraq in 2003. As with the Iran–Iraq War, the revolutionary government in Tehran was not responsible for this change in American policy. Decision-makers in Washington, Democrats and Republicans, Carter-ites and Reagan-ites, made those decisions. But it is difficult to imagine that they would have seen those decisions as necessary if the monarchical regime had still been in power in Iran.

Unlike the Iranian Revolution, the Iran–Iraq War had little lasting impact on the international politics of the Gulf region, though it profoundly affected domestic political developments in both countries. Both regimes were still in power. Neither gained or lost significant territory. They ended the war much as they had begun it, except for the enormous human and economic costs. In the catalogue of evidence that war can be a senseless endeavor, the Iran–Iraq War is exhibit A.

Ayatollah Ruhollah Khomeini, that most unlikely of modern revolutionaries, died on June 3, 1989. With his passing, a good bit of the fire went out of the Iranian commitment to export the revolution. His successors never gave up their ties to Islamist group in the region, particularly Shi'i Islamists, but they tempered their commitment to the spread of Islamist revolution with greater elements of caution and *Realpolitik* than the Imam, as Khomeini is referred to, would have liked. The other major regional protagonist, Saddam Hussein, continued to play a starring role in Persian Gulf politics, as we will see in the next chapter.

4   The Gulf War and the 1990s

The Gulf War of 1990–91 was the world's first post-Cold War crisis. It appeared to open up the possibility for profound changes in the Persian Gulf region, as the United States, unconstrained by the fear of superpower confrontation, deployed massive force to the area and defeated a major regional power, Iraq, in a brief but intense war. However, after the Gulf War dust settled, not much had changed. Saddam Hussein was weakened and constrained by draconian international sanctions, but he still ruled Iraq (though Iraqi Kurdish areas secured de facto autonomy under American protection). His ambitious effort to redraw the regional map had failed. Kuwait remained an independent state; the regimes in the Gulf monarchies remained in power. The Islamic Republic of Iran gained relatively from the defeat of its Iraqi rival in terms of the regional power game, but could do little to turn that gain into a new position of regional leadership. Rather, and in contrast to its foreign policy in the 1980s, Tehran took a more moderate, diplomatic tack in its relations with its monarchical neighbors and refrained from adventures against a weakened Iraq.

The biggest strategic change, aside from the destruction of Iraq's offensive military capabilities, to come out of the war was the development of a permanent American military infrastructure in the Gulf monarchies. That military presence hardly translated into regional hegemony. Saddam Hussein remained an irritant to the United States throughout the 1990s. American influence in Iran was nil. It is difficult to regard a country as hegemonic in a region when it did not even have embassies in two of the most important regional capitals. American military power was sufficient, however, to sustain the regional territorial and political status quo, which is all that Washington sought during this period. It fought the 1990–91 war to preserve that status quo. It did not like the Iranian regime particularly, but was learning to live with it. It did not like Saddam Hussein's regime, but was not willing to do much to get rid of it. American power was great, but its ambitions in the Gulf during this period were modest. Small wonder, then, that the Gulf strategic picture in January 2001, when

President Bill Clinton left office, was remarkably similar to what it was in January 1993 when he took office.

The Iraqi invasion of Kuwait

Saddam Hussein hoped that the end of the Iran–Iraq War would provide him the opportunity to cement the Arab leadership role that he felt he had earned. He was severely disappointed. Arab states behaved not as grateful friends, but as cold-blooded power balancers. With the Iranian threat reduced, they saw less need for close relations with Baghdad. Saudi Arabia and Kuwait ended their aid payments. A number of the smaller Gulf monarchies, including Kuwait, looked to repair their relations with Iran. Saudi Arabia, still engaged in an ideological struggle with the Islamic Republic for leadership of transnational Islamist politics, did not do likewise, but also made it clear that it would not be following Baghdad's lead in regional politics. Saddam's plan to play the leader of the Gulf Arabs was not accepted by the GCC states. He openly supported anti-Syrian forces in Lebanon as payback for Syria's alliance with Iran, but was unable to break Syria's hold on Lebanese politics.

Even Saddam's biggest diplomatic success of the post-war period, the formation of the Arab Cooperation Council (ACC), did not turn out the way he had hoped.[1] The grouping of Iraq, Egypt, Jordan and North Yemen (Yemen Arab Republic) was established in February 1989. Saddam hoped to turn the ACC into a political-military bloc under his leadership, on the model of what Saudi Arabia had been able to do (politically, not militarily) with the Gulf Cooperation Council. But Egypt, in particular, was not interested in subordinating its political role in the region to Iraq. It was looking for economic benefits from closer ties to Iraq, not to play second fiddle to Saddam's regional ambitions.

While Saddam Hussein clearly was a man on the make after the Iran–Iraq War, in 1989 his means to expand his influence were conventional and diplomatic. The Arab Cooperation Council was hardly a revolutionary initiative. Immediately after it was formed, to allay Saudi fears about the organization, in March 1989 he signed a "non-aggression" agreement with Riyadh. He also sought to sustain the good working relationship he had developed with Washington during the war. That stance was reciprocated by Washington, which continued to see revolutionary Iran as the major threat to its interests in the Gulf. The Reagan administration blocked a strong congressional push in 1988 to sanction

---

[1] For an overview of the ACC, see Curtis R. Ryan, "Jordan and the Rise and Fall of the Arab Cooperation Council," *Middle East Journal*, Vol. 52, No. 2 (Summer 1998), pp. 386–401.

Iraq for its use of chemical weapons. The administration of George H. W. Bush, which came into office in January 1989, set out its Iraq policy in a formal National Security Directive (NSD 26) in October 1989. It sought to achieve "normal relations between the United States and Iraq," offering "economic and political incentives for Iraq to moderate its behavior" and aiming "to increase our influence with Iraq." The Bush administration policy of engagement with Iraq was adopted despite increasing evidence in 1989 that the country was continuing to develop weapons of mass destruction (WMD) and revelations that it had diverted American loans intended to finance agricultural purchases to its weapons programs.[2]

In 1990 the tone of Iraqi foreign policy began to change. By the beginning of 1990 the Iraqi leader had concluded that his conventional diplomatic efforts to reap the fruits of his "victory" against Iran were not working. On the contrary, he had come to believe that domestic, regional and international forces were working against him, to the extent that the survival of his regime was at stake.[3] Iraq's economy was stagnant, with oil prices remaining below $20 per barrel. Domestic discontent was rising, evidenced by a number of coup attempts against him. Low oil prices also limited Saddam's ability to extend Iraq's influence outside its borders. The fall of the Soviet empire in 1989 ended the bipolar international system in which he had successfully played and brought down East European regimes which were not dissimilar to his own. Voices in Israel, Europe and the United States were calling greater attention to Iraq's efforts to obtain nuclear and other non-conventional weapons and to Saddam's human rights abuses. He viewed these disparate events as part of a concerted effort to pressure, if not destroy, his regime. His response to this perceived threat was a much more bellicose stance toward what he saw as his unfaithful allies – the United States and the Gulf monarchies, particularly Kuwait – and a return to anti-Israeli rhetoric to mobilize regional support.

Establishing with certainty when Saddam Hussein decided to attack Kuwait is a difficult task. There are indications from Iraqi sources themselves that the decision was made only a few months before the actual invasion. Sa'd al-Bazzaz, editor of one of the major Iraqi papers during this period, reports on a series of meetings beginning in mid-June 1990

---

[2] For a comprehensive discussion of American policy toward Iraq in the period between the end of the Iran–Iraq War and Iraq's attack on Kuwait, see Bruce W. Jentleson, *With Friends Like These: Reagan, Bush and Saddam, 1982–1990* (New York: W. W. Norton, 1994), Chapters 2–4; quotes from NSD 26 taken from p. 94.

[3] I make this argument in much greater detail in my article, "Iraq's Decisions to Go to War, 1980 and 1990," *Middle East Journal*, Vol. 56, No. 1 (Winter 2002), pp. 47–70.

that formulated the plan for the invasion.[4] Tariq Aziz, foreign minister of Iraq at the time of the war, also spoke of a June war decision and a last-minute choice by Saddam to occupy all of Kuwait.[5] Other sources place the decision to invade slightly earlier in 1990. Iraqi opposition circles claim that they have evidence that the decision was made in March 1990.[6] Wafiq al-Samara'i, deputy director of Iraqi military intelligence during the war, said that the decision was made in April 1990, though he did not offer any direct evidence supporting this claim.[7] Al-Samara'i, who saw Saddam with some frequency, wrote that in the first quarter of 1990 Saddam realized that his policies were failing: "This was reflected in the psychological state of the president, and led him to make statements and follow policies that were more and more spasmodic."[8] Hassan Rouhani, then head of the Iranian National Security Council, reportedly told Arab officials that Saddam Hussein sent a message to Iran in May 1990 that "certain events" would soon take place in the Gulf that Iran should not interpret as being directed against it.[9]

While many people in the countries aligned against Iraq in the Gulf War believe that Saddam had a long-term plan to invade Kuwait, no source that refers specifically to the timing of the decision places it earlier than the spring of 1990. Moreover, the timing of the invasion, before Iraq had developed its nuclear capability, indicates that Saddam thought he had to act quickly to arrest the flow of events against him. Had he waited just a year to attack Kuwait, he very possibly could have brandished a nuclear weapon against those who stood against him. He did not think that he had that time.

The haste with which the decision was made was indirectly reflected in some of the (very mild) self-criticism exercised by Iraqi leaders after the invasion. At a meeting of the Iraqi Revolutionary Command Council and Ba'th Party leadership on January 24, 1991, Taha Yasin Ramadan told his colleagues, "I am not saying that August 2, 1990, was the best day for the

---

[4] Sa'd al-Bazzaz, *Harb tulid 'ukhra* [One War Gives Birth to Another] (Amman, Jordan: Al-'Ahliya lil-Nashr wa al-Tawzi', 1993), pp. 27–36; Sa'd Al-Bazzaz, *Al-janaralat 'akhr man ya'lam* [The Generals Are the Last to Know] (Amman, Jordan: Al-'Ahliya lil-Nashr wa al-Tawzi', 1996), pp. 47–55.

[5] Milton Viorst, *Sandcastles: The Arabs in Search of the Modern World* (New York: Alfred A. Knopf, 1994), pp. 340–41, 344.

[6] Falih Abd al-Jabbar, "Roots of an Adventure: The Invasion of Kuwait – Iraqi Political Dynamics," in Victoria Brittain (ed.), *The Gulf Between Us: The Gulf War and Beyond* (London: Virago Press, 1991), p. 37.

[7] At www.pbs.org/wgbh/pages/frontline/gulf/oral/iraqis.html.

[8] Wafiq al-Samara'i, *Hatam al-bawaba al-sharqiya* [The Destruction of the Eastern Gate] (Kuwait: Dar al-Qabas, 1997), p. 214.

[9] *New York Times*, March 20, 1991, pp. A1, A12.

mother of battles. We had not studied the situation for a year, or even for months, preparing for the mother of battles."[10] One would not dare to criticize a decision of Saddam Hussein in his presence, the implication being that Saddam himself recognized that the decision was rushed. The Ba'th Party also circulated an analysis to ranking party members after the war ended in February 1991 that admitted that Iraq was forced to take a quick decision to invade Kuwait, because of the pressures it was under, even though all necessary preparations for the confrontation had not been made.[11] There is every indication that the decision to invade Kuwait was made relatively shortly before the invasion, with the regime feeling intense pressure to act. What had happened in the period leading up to the decision to trigger it?

The Iraqi leadership steadfastly maintained that there was an international conspiracy against it, meant to weaken Iraq internationally and destabilize it domestically. The first sentence of al-Bazzaz's first book on the Gulf War reads, "There is no doubt that Iraq was feeling danger and the existence of a conspiracy against it."[12] The outlines of the Iraqi argument are well known. Its economic problems were blamed on lower oil prices, which were in turn blamed on the "overproduction" of Kuwait and the UAE, clients of the United States. Small shifts in US policy (such as limits on US credits for Iraqi purchases of American rice and congressional resolutions condemning Iraq for human rights violations) and damaging revelations (such as Iraq's use of the Atlanta branch of an Italian bank to launder arms purchase money) were read as evidence that the United States had adopted a hostile attitude toward Iraq. Media attention to the Iraqi nuclear program, and subsequent British and American efforts to block the export of dual-use technology, was seen as part of a concerted effort to weaken Iraq. Lurking behind many of these efforts, in the Iraqi view, was Israel, seen as preparing for a strike on the Iraqi nuclear establishment similar to the one it had conducted in 1981.[13] Al-Samara'i writes that at the beginning of 1990 military intelligence began receiving a wave of warnings from Saddam's office about Israeli plans to strike at Iraqi non-conventional weapons facilities.[14] Al-Bazzaz

[10] Al-Bazzaz, *Al-janaralat*, p. 200, quoting from minutes of the meeting.
[11] Al-Bazzaz, *Harb*, p. 34.
[12] Al-Bazzaz, *Harb*, p. 17.
[13] Lawrence Freedman and Efraim Karsh, *The Gulf Conflict 1990–1991: Diplomacy and War in the New World Order* (Princeton: Princeton University Press, 1993), Chapters 2–3; Mohamed Heikal, *Illusions of Triumph: An Arab View of the Gulf War* (London: Harper Collins, 1993), pp. 158–231; Amatzia Baram, "The Iraqi Invasion of Kuwait: Decision-Making in Baghdad," in Amatzia Baram and Barry Rubin (eds.), *Iraq's Road to War* (New York: St. Martin's Press, 1993).
[14] Al-Samara'i, *Hatam*, p. 365.

reports that the Iraqi leadership fully expected an Israeli military attack sometime in August 1990.[15]

Saddam himself bluntly described this "conspiracy" to al-Samara'i in March 1990: "America is coordinating with Saudi Arabia, the UAE and Kuwait in a conspiracy against us. They are trying to reduce the price of oil to affect our military industries and our scientific research, to force us to reduce the size of our armed forces ... You must expect from another direction an Israeli military airstrike, or more than one, to destroy some of our important targets as part of this conspiracy."[16]

What is less well known is the internal aspect of the Iraqi regime's fears. In either late 1988 or early 1989 scores of officers were arrested and executed on the charge of working to bring down the government. Hundreds of high-ranking officers indirectly connected to the accused were forced to retire.[17] Iraqi ruling circles came to believe during 1989 that a number of foreign powers, including Iran, Saudi Arabia and the United States, were attempting to infiltrate Iraqi society to collect intelligence and pressure the government.[18] In May 1989, Iraqi defense minister Adnan Khayrallah, who was Saddam's cousin and brother-in-law, died in a helicopter crash (after a number of prominent Iraqi generals had died in similar helicopter accidents since the end of the Iran–Iraq War). Rumors circulated, however, that Khayrallah was killed on Saddam's orders, either because of his involvement in these foreign machinations or because of his inability to insulate the army from them.[19] Other sources report a failed coup attempt in September 1989 and the exposure of a coup attempt, coupled with a plan to assassinate Saddam, in January 1990.[20]

While Saddam Hussein increasingly saw his domestic political and economic situation in 1989 deteriorate, events in the larger world during

---

[15] Al-Bazzaz, *Harb*, p. 345. One does not have to accept that there was a conspiracy against Iraq to accept that this belief could have profoundly affected Iraqi decision-making. It is clear that there was no concerted American policy aimed against Iraq. American policy in this period might better be described as working at cross-purposes. See Jentleson, *With Friends Like These*; and Zachary Karabell, "Backfire: US Policy Toward Iraq, 1988–2 August 1990," *Middle East Journal*, Vol. 49, No. 1 (1995), pp. 28–47.

[16] Al-Samara'i, *Hatam*, pp. 222–23.

[17] Baram, "The Iraqi Invasion of Kuwait," p. 8; al-Bazzaz, *Al-janaralat*, pp. 36–37, 89–90; al-Samara'i, *Hatam*, pp. 184–85; Charles Tripp, *A History of Iraq* (Cambridge: Cambridge University Press, 2000), pp. 249–50.

[18] Al-Bazzaz, *Harb*, pp. 159–60, 210–13.

[19] Tripp, *A History of Iraq*, p. 250; Said K. Aburish, *Saddam Hussein: The Politics of Revenge* (New York: Bloomsbury Publishing, 2000), p. 263.

[20] Freedman and Karsh, *The Gulf Conflict*, pp. 29–30; Amatzia Baram, "Neo-tribalism in Iraq: Saddam Hussein's Tribal Policies, 1991–1996," *International Journal of Middle East Studies*, Vol. 29, No. 1 (1997), pp. 5–6; Amatzia Baram, *Building Toward Crisis: Saddam Hussein's Strategy for Survival*, Policy Paper No. 47, Washington Institute for Near East Policy, Washington, DC, 1998, p. 27; al-Samara'i, *Hatam*, p. 185.

that year reinforced his growing sense of crisis. The fall of the Soviet client states in Eastern Europe increased his fears about the future of his own regime. Al-Bazzaz reports that in the summer of 1989 Saddam and a number of Iraqi experts debated the effect of the end of the bipolar world on Iraq, and concluded that Iraq's international enemies would use the events in Europe to create an impression among Iraqis that it would be easy for them to change their government.[21] This belief helps to explain the intensely negative reaction of the Iraqi government to a Voice of America (VOA) Arabic service broadcast in January 1990 that implicitly compared Saddam to the fallen East European leaders, to the February 1990 State Department human rights report on Iraq and to congressional resolutions critical of his human rights record.[22] They were seen as proof of American involvement in the plots against Saddam's regime. Saddam himself referred to the VOA broadcast in his July 25, 1990, meeting with US ambassador April Glaspie.[23]

Saddam Hussein's sense that international and regional forces were conspiring with his domestic opponents against him had reached the point that, in October 1989, Tariq Aziz raised this issue in his meeting with Secretary of State James Baker in Washington.[24] President Bush tried to reassure Saddam, through Saudi Arabia's ambassador in Washington, Prince Bandar bin Sultan Al Saud, in April 1990, when Saddam, through the Saudis, raised similar suspicions of American intentions.[25] These reassurances had little effect on Saddam, who since the revelation of the Iran–contra affair in 1986 had come to view official American pronouncements with suspicion.[26] Even after the fall of the regime, when he would no longer have an interest in covering for his old boss, Aziz told his American captors that Saddam believed that, after the revelation of the Irangate scandal in 1986, Washington could not be trusted and was out to get him personally.[27]

These domestic and international events had by early 1990 convinced Saddam Hussein that his regime was being targeted. In response, he changed his rhetoric and the tone of his foreign policy. In February 1990

---

[21] Al-Bazzaz, *Harb*, p. 392.

[22] Freedman and Karsh, *The Gulf Conflict*, p. 31.

[23] See text of meeting released by Iraq, reproduced in Micah L. Sifry and Christopher Cerf (eds.), *The Gulf War Reader* (New York: Random House, 1991), pp. 123–24.

[24] James A. Baker, III, *The Politics of Diplomacy* (New York: G. P. Putnam's, 1995), p. 265; Heikal, *Illusions of Triumph*, p. 159; al-Bazzaz, *Harb*, pp. 154–60.

[25] Bob Woodward, *The Commanders* (New York: Simon & Schuster, 1991), pp. 203–04.

[26] Saddam himself referred to this in his interview with Ambassador Glaspie: Sifry and Cerf, *The Gulf War Reader*, p. 123. See also al-Samara'i, *Hatam*, p. 128.

[27] "Comprehensive Report of the Special Advisor to the DCI on Iraq's WMD," September 30, 2004, www.cia.gov/library/reports/general-reports-1/iraq_wmd_2004/index.html (hereafter referenced as the Duelfer Report, after Charles Duelfer, the special adviser), "Regime Strategic Intent" section, p. 31, reporting on interrogation of Tariq Aziz.

Saddam launched an attack on the United States military presence in the Gulf at the founding summit of the Arab Cooperation Council and devoted much of the speech to criticism of Israel.[28] Privately, he told President Husni Mubarak of Egypt and King Hussein of Jordan to pass the word to the Gulf states that he urgently required a new infusion of financial aid.[29] His threat to "make fire eat half of Israel if it tries to do anything against Iraq" followed in early April 1990.[30] The rhetorical temperature escalated from there. At the same time, Iraq's program to develop weapons of mass destruction experienced a number of setbacks. Gerald Bull, a Canadian scientist who was working for Iraq on a "supergun" project, was killed in Belgium on March 22, 1990, by unknown assailants. Over the following weeks, officials in a number of European countries impounded high-technology devices purchased by Iraqi companies fronting for the country's weapons program. These moves seemed to confirm for the Iraqi leadership the extent of the international opposition against them.

This shift in Iraqi foreign policy, the beginning of the process that led to the invasion of Kuwait, came when Saddam concluded that there were international efforts afoot to destabilize him domestically. Further support for this reading of Saddam's motivations in attacking Kuwait comes from statements by Saddam himself and by one of his closest aides at the meeting of the Revolutionary Command Council/Ba'th Party leadership held on January 24, 1991. Saddam told those present that perhaps they had heard some people suggesting that Kuwait should be returned as a way to avoid war. He went on,

You must say to those people, "What were things like before August 2 when Iraq was without Kuwait? They were conspiring against you to starve you, after they had deprived us of our economic capacity ... Even our standard of living at the time, they were planning to push it backwards in their despicable conspiracies, to crush us spiritually and force us to abandon our role.[31]

Taha Yasin Ramadan, Iraq's first deputy prime minister, said at the same meeting:

Yes, the battle is inevitable. If it had happened later our revolutionary base would not have been consolidated and would have been weaker in confronting the size of the hostile forces as they are now. Imagine if we had waited two years, and the Gulf oil policy had continued as it is ...

How were we going to maintain the loyalty of the people and their support for the leader if they saw the inability of the leadership to provide a minimal standard

---

[28] Ofra Bengio (ed.), *Saddam Speaks on the Gulf Crisis: A Collection of Documents* (Tel Aviv: Moshe Dayan Center for Middle Eastern and African Studies, 1992), pp. 37–49.

[29] Freedman and Karsh, *The Gulf Conflict*, p. 45.

[30] Bengio (ed.), *Saddam Speaks on the Gulf Crisis*, pp. 50–61.

[31] Al-Bazzaz, *Al-janaralat*, pp. 227–28.

of living in this rich country? In this situation, could you lead the army and the people in any battle, no matter what its level and under any banner? I think not. I am not deviating from my deep faith in victory in this battle, but whatever the outcome, if death is definitely coming to this people and this revolution, let it come while we are standing.[32]

As regional tensions rose, Iraq ratcheted up the pressure on the smaller Gulf states. At the Arab summit meeting held in Baghdad in May 1990, Saddam told the Arab leaders in a private session that other Arab states were waging "a kind of war against Iraq" by violating their OPEC quotas and depressing oil prices. In January 1990 prices pushed over $20 per barrel, but then had fallen below $16 per barrel by May 1990.[33] Part of the reason for that price fall was the fact that both Kuwait and the United Arab Emirates had been overproducing their OPEC quotas for some time. (They were not the only quota-cheaters in OPEC, but they were the closest geographically to Iraq.) Kuwait had a quota of 1.5 mbd in the January–July 1990 period; the UAE's quota was almost 1.1 mbd.[34] Kuwait's monthly production during that period fluctuated between 1.8 and 2.2 mbd. The UAE's monthly production in that period was about 2 mbd.[35]

Iraq's public pressure began to focus on Kuwait after the May 1990 Arab summit, but relations between the two countries had started to deteriorate at the beginning of the year. Given the history of Iraqi claims on Kuwait, bilateral relations between the countries were never without tensions. Shortly after the Iran–Iraq War, in February 1989, the crown prince of Kuwait, Shaykh Sa'd Abdallah, visited Baghdad. The atmosphere was frosty. The Iraqis proposed that Kuwait cede half of Bubiyan Island, which controls access to the Iraqi port of Um Qasr, to Iraq and that Iraq be allowed to build a naval base on another Kuwaiti island, Failaka.[36]

[32] Al-Bazzaz, *Al-janaralat*, pp. 198–99.

[33] US Department of Energy, Energy Information Administration, "Petroleum Navigator," http://tonto.eia.doe.gov/dnav/pet/hist/rbrted.htm.

[34] Quota figures from chart "OPEC: Crude Oil Production Ceiling Allocations" on the OPEC website, www.opec.org/home/Production/productionLevels.pdf.

[35] US Department of Energy, Energy Information Administration, *Monthly Energy Review*, March 2004, Table 11.1a.

[36] The Iraqi proposal was revealed in the report of a Kuwaiti parliamentary committee established to investigate the government's performance in the months preceding the Iraqi invasion. A detailed account of parts of the report released to the public can be found in *al-Hayat*, August 13, 1995, pp. 1, 6. The Iraqi proposal was confirmed in interviews with current and former Foreign Ministry officials in Kuwait City in May 1997. Such proposals were not unprecedented. In 1975 Iraq proposed that Kuwait "return" Warba Island to Iraq and lease half of Bubiyan for ninety-nine years: *al-Siyasa* (Kuwait), July 8, 1975. In 1981, during the Iran–Iraq War, Iraq renewed its formal request to lease part of Bubiyan: Abd al-Jalil Marhun, "Al-'alaqat al-khalijiya al-'iraqiya madiyan wa hadiran wa ihtimalat al-mustaqbal" [Gulf–Iraqi Relations: Past, Present and Possibilities of the Future], *al-Hayat*, May 25, 1997, p. 13.

However, the atmospherics improved considerably in September 1989, when the amir of Kuwait, Shaykh Jabir, visited Baghdad. He received the highest Iraqi decoration from Saddam, and the Iraqi media lavishly praised Kuwait's role in the Arab world.[37] Privately, Saddam raised both the border issue and debt relief in his talks with the amir. He assured Saddam that Kuwait would not seek repayment on the debt and said that border discussions should continue on the government-to-government level.[38] The border and debt issues were on the bilateral agenda in 1989, but there was no sense of crisis in Iraqi–Kuwaiti relations.

That changed in 1990. In January 1990 Iraq for the first time demanded from Kuwait a "loan" of $10 billion, along with a public announcement of forgiveness of the Iraqi debts built up during the Iran–Iraq War.[39] In February 1990 the Kuwaiti foreign minister, Shaykh Sabah al-Ahmad, visited Baghdad. He was presented with an Iraqi proposal for defense cooperation that, in the words of a subsequent Kuwaiti parliamentary investigation, "would have turned Kuwait into an Iraqi base." In April 1990 Iraqi deputy prime minister Sa'dun Hamadi sent Shaykh Sabah a letter calling into question the validity of the 1963 Iraq–Kuwait border agreement.[40] The bilateral dispute escalated in May 1990 with Saddam's accusation at the Arab summit that some Arab oil producers were conducting "a kind of war" against Iraq by overproducing their OPEC quotas. In June 1990 Hamadi visited Kuwait, renewing the Iraqi demand for $10 billion.[41]

Given the tensions in Kuwaiti society during this period, Saddam also had reason to hope that some Kuwaitis might support his pressure on their government, and later accept his takeover of the country. The amir of Kuwait had suspended the elected parliament in 1986 and was attempting unilaterally to alter the Kuwaiti constitution, replacing the parliament with a body that did not have full legislative powers. Since 1989 leaders of the last parliament had been mobilizing support in Kuwait against this change, with demonstrations, sit-ins and petitions.[42] If Saddam had

---

[37] See coverage in Kuwaiti newspapers al-'Anba, September 24, 1989, p. 1, and al-Ra'i al-'Am, September 24, 1989, p. 1, and September 25, 1989, p. 1.

[38] Personal interview, retired official in the Kuwaiti Foreign Ministry, May 1997, Kuwait City.

[39] Heikal, Illusions of Triumph, p. 209. A number of sources, including personal interviews in Kuwait City in May 1997, indicate that Kuwait responded to the "loan" demand with an offer of a $500 million loan, 5 percent of what the Iraqis were demanding.

[40] Al-Hayat, August 19, 1995, pp. 1, 6. See also Heikal, Illusions of Triumph, p. 210. Interviews in Kuwait City in 1997 with current and former officials in the Foreign Ministry, parliamentarians and political observers confirmed the escalation of Iraqi demands at this time.

[41] Freedman and Karsh, The Gulf Conflict, p. 46.

[42] A number of Kuwaitis believe that these domestic divisions encouraged the Iraqis to invade: personal interviews in Kuwait, May 1997. See also Hassan Ali al-Ibrahim, Al-kuwayt: al-ghazu wa tajdid al-dhat al-wataniya [Kuwait: The Invasion and the Renewal of

hoped to exploit these internal Kuwaiti divisions during the occupation, however, his hopes were not realized. Kuwaitis almost to a person refused to cooperate with the Iraqi occupation authorities, and many actively resisted.

Alarmed by the growing tensions, Saudi Arabia pressured both Kuwait and the UAE to recommit to their quotas at a July 10, 1990, meeting of Gulf oil ministers. (The Saudis, burned by quota-cheaters in the past, had their own reasons to rein in Kuwait and the Emirates as well.) They agreed, and the Saudis also pledged to cut their production temporarily, sending spot market prices up by almost one dollar the day after the meeting.[43] This agreement was ratified at the OPEC meeting of July 27, with OPEC oil ministers reaffirming their commitments to abide by their quotas and setting a target price of $21 per barrel for the organization. Iraq later charged that it had information that Kuwait intended to maintain its quota for only a few months, but with the Iraqi invasion it became impossible to test that assertion.

Despite the results of the July 10, 1990, meeting, Saddam raised the stakes. On July 15, Iraqi troops began to move toward Kuwait. On July 16 Iraqi foreign minister Tariq Aziz delivered a memorandum to the Arab League publicly accusing Kuwait of deliberately harming Iraq by keeping oil prices low, of drilling into Iraqi oil fields and of using the cover of the Iran–Iraq War to push their border posts into Iraqi territory. On July 17, in a public address to the country, Saddam accused Kuwait (and the UAE) of conspiring against Iraq and the Arab nation, and warned that if "words fail to afford us protection, then we will have no choice but to resort to effective action to put things right."[44] Aziz responded on July 24 to a Kuwaiti suggestion that an Arab League committee be established to solve the

National Identity] (Kuwait: n.p., 1995), Chapter 2, particularly pp. 69–70. Al-Bazzaz reports that from mid-July 1990 the Iraqi government attempted to organize a group of Kuwaiti political personalities to come to Baghdad, to develop them as supporters of any Iraqi move that might occur. Very few of the Kuwaitis invited attended the Baghdad meeting: *Al-janaralat*, pp. 65–66. Tariq Aziz later reported that Kuwaiti domestic divisions did not play a role in Iraqi planning in the lead-up to the invasion: personal interview, New York, April 1995.

[43] On the Saudi commitment and the spot price rise, see H. J. Maidenberg, "Oil Prices Surge as Saudis Agree to Reduce Output," *New York Times*, July 13, 1990. After the invasion, King Fahd made a number of public statements to the effect that he did what Saddam had asked him regarding Kuwait's and the UAE's oil production: "I contacted ... the amir of Kuwait and ... the president of the UAE ... and matters returned to their normal state according to the OPEC decisions" (*al-Sharq al-Awsat*, January 8, 1991, p. 3); "I expended much effort to achieve your desire when the difference between you and officials in Kuwait and the UAE occurred concerning the production and price of petroleum. I made the necessary contacts ... and you got what you wanted" (*al-Sharq al-Awsat*, January 17, 1991, p. 3).

[44] Freedman and Karsh, *The Gulf Conflict*, pp. 47–48.

border issue by accusing Kuwait of joining a foreign conspiracy against Iraq: "The situation has been made volatile because some Kuwaiti rulers chose to subscribe to foreign schemes and conspiracies against Iraq and the Arab nation … Once conspirators are kept away from decision-making centers, the air will be clear for the talk about borders. Otherwise, we will not heed maneuvers and sugar-coated statements."[45] What had been since the beginning of the year an escalating problem was now a full-fledged crisis.

Egypt attempted to mediate between Iraq and Kuwait. On July 24, 1990, Egyptian president Mubarak met with Saddam Hussein in Baghdad. Iraqis contend that they told Mubarak that they would not use force against Kuwait as long as there was progress on negotiations. Mubarak subsequently said that Saddam's commitment not to use force was unconditional. What is clear is that Mubarak immediately traveled to Kuwait, told the Kuwaitis that they should "do something for him [Saddam] … and be ready to give him some money," and reassured them about what he thought were Saddam's ultimately peaceful intentions.[46]

One day later, on July 25, 1990, the US ambassador in Baghdad, April Glaspie, was summoned to meet with Saddam Hussein for the first time in her two-year tenure in Baghdad. American policy in the Bush administration had been torn between an overall desire to nurture a friendly relationship with Iraq and the need to respond to Iraq's growing belligerence. The result was a confusing mix of threats and reassurances. In response to evidence that Iraq had diverted agricultural credits toward military uses, the United States refused to issue the second installment of promised credits. However, the program itself was not canceled. Ambassador Glaspie made a number of protests to the Iraqi Foreign Ministry over Iraqi policies in 1990, but the administration continued to oppose congressional sanctions on Iraq. As Iraq escalated its threats in July, the UAE requested an American show of force, and Washington responded by sending six navy ships to the UAE coast. Kuwait, fearful of provoking Saddam, turned down Washington's offer of a similar show of force. As late as July 31, 1990, the assistant secretary of state for the Near East was asked in a congressional hearing what the American reaction would be to an Iraqi attack on Kuwait. He replied that the United States would be extremely concerned, but that he could not get into "what if" answers.[47]

---

[45] *Baghdad Observer* (Iraq), July 25, 1990, pp. 1, 2.

[46] Mubarak's quote is from his interview with the *New York Times*, November 8, 1990, pp. A1, A4. See also Freedman and Karsh, *The Gulf Conflict*, p. 50.

[47] Jentleson, *With Friends Like These*, Chapter 4, provides an excellent review of US policy in the months leading up to the invasion. See also Freedman and Karsh, *The Gulf Conflict*, pp. 50–52.

This was the context in which Glaspie met Saddam for the first and last time. The Iraqis subsequently released a transcript of the meeting, in which the ambassador comes across as very accommodating in the face of Saddam's threats and bluster.[48] She subsequently denied the accuracy of the transcript, saying that she had warned Saddam that the United States would not countenance acts of violence by Iraq against its neighbors. She admitted to a congressional committee that she did not directly tell Saddam that, if Iraq attacked Kuwait, the United States would respond with force. She did tell him that the United States took no position on the substance of the Iraq–Kuwait border dispute.[49] While her meeting with Saddam arose suddenly and she was unable to get specific instructions from Washington, it is clear that she was following the general outlines of American policy, seeking to reassure Saddam about American intentions and to work for an improvement of Iraqi–American relations. At the conclusion of the meeting, Saddam informed her that he had just heard from President Mubarak that the Kuwaitis had agreed to a high-level meeting between the two sides in Saudi Arabia, to be followed by a meeting in Baghdad. Saddam said that he told Mubarak to "assure the Kuwaitis and give them our word that we are not going to do anything until we meet with them."[50] Ambassador Glaspie was reassured by the conclusion of the meeting and left Iraq a few days later on a previously scheduled trip to Washington.

The announcement of the meeting between the two sides, scheduled for the Red Sea port city of Jidda in Saudi Arabia on August 1, 1990, led many to believe that the crisis was about to end. The Kuwaiti press certainly headlined the news that way.[51] There is every reason to believe that Saddam Hussein wanted that impression put out. After the invasion of Kuwait he told a group of army officers that he had avoided the mistake made by Iraqi president Abd al-Karim Qasim, who laid claim to Kuwait in 1961. Saddam said Qasim was too clear about his intentions, allowing Britain to send troops to Kuwait before Iraq could move. This time, Saddam said, Iraq was doing things differently.[52] The meeting with Glaspie, the commitment to

---

[48] For a copy, see Bengio (ed.), *Saddam Speaks on the Gulf Crisis*, pp. 99–110.

[49] The American ambassador to Kuwait used almost exactly the same language in a public statement during a 1973 Iraqi–Kuwaiti border dispute: *al-Qabas* (Kuwait), March 27, 1973. That language was echoed in a cable from Secretary of State Baker to American embassies in the Middle East and Europe one day before the Glaspie–Saddam meeting: *New York Times*, October 25, 1992, p. 14.

[50] Bengio (ed.), *Saddam Speaks on the Gulf Crisis*, pp. 99–110.

[51] The July 26, 1990, headline of the Kuwaiti daily *al-Ra'i al-'Am* was a one-word banner (*'infarajit*) that translates loosely as "Relaxation." Another Kuwaiti daily, *al-Watan*, had as its headline on July 26, 1990: "Mubarak: No Mobilization and No Attack ... Kuwaiti–Iraqi Meeting on Sunday."

[52] Al-Bazzaz, *Al-janaralat*, pp. 73–74.

Mubarak and the willingness to meet with the Kuwaitis at Jidda were all very likely intended to lull potential opponents into a false sense of security, allowing Iraq the advantage of strategic surprise.

The Jidda meeting itself was a dialogue of the deaf. The Kuwaiti delegation, headed by Crown Prince Sa'd Abdallah, brought no proposals to the table. The Kuwaitis believed that Jidda was a preparatory session, before the more serious bargaining that would take place later in Baghdad.[53] Iraqi sources subsequently revealed a memo from the amir to the crown prince before the meeting urging the crown prince not to give in to any Iraqi demands, citing "the opinion of our friends in Egypt, Washington and London."[54] Saudi, Kuwaiti and Iraqi sources confirm that the Saudis, hosts of the meeting, submitted no specific bridging proposals to bring the sides together.[55] The Iraqi delegation, led by Ba'th Party enforcer Izzat Ibrahim al-Duri, not by the more urbane Foreign Minister Tariq Aziz, made no specific demands of the Kuwaitis, but rehearsed their earlier complaints about Kuwaiti behavior and the extent of economic damage Kuwaiti oil policy had caused to Iraq.[56] The meeting ended the evening of August 1, with the Iraqi delegation departing for Baghdad. Within hours, the Iraqi army began its operation against Kuwait. It had begun to configure itself for offensive operations along the border before the end of the Jidda meeting.[57]

Kuwait, along with the rest of the world, was caught unprepared by the Iraqi occupation of Kuwait, which was accomplished within hours on

[53] A member of the Kuwaiti delegation to the talks confirmed that Kuwait did not go to Jidda with an offer: personal interview, Riyadh, May 1991. A member of the Kuwaiti cabinet at the time confirmed that the Kuwaiti delegation did not go to Jidda with real negotiating options: personal interview, Kuwait City, May 1997.

[54] A photographed copy of the memo was published in the *Jordan Times*, February 14–15, 1991, pp. 1, 5. Given Jordan's support for Iraq in the crisis, and the fact that the memo, if real, had to have come from the Iraqi occupation authorities in Kuwait, the Iraqi provenance is clear. While the memo could have been a skillful forgery, the fact that the newspaper reproduced a photograph of it, with handwritten notes purportedly by the amir in the margins, increases the likelihood that it was genuine. Al-Bazzaz reports that Iraqi intelligence in the last week of July informed the leadership that British prime minister Margaret Thatcher told the Kuwaitis not to give the Iraqis anything at Jidda and had promised British support in any confrontation: *Harb*, pp. 55–56.

[55] King Fahd subsequently said, on a number of occasions, that all Saudi Arabia did at Jidda was host the meeting. See his comments in *al-Sharq al-Awsat*, August 15, 1990, p. 7; January 8, 1991, p. 3. Kuwaiti sources in parliament and the Foreign Ministry confirmed in personal interviews that there were no Saudi or Egyptian proposals put forward at Jidda: personal interviews, Kuwait, May 1997. The late Nizar Hamdoon, then deputy foreign affairs minister of Iraq, also confirmed that there were no specific Saudi or Egyptian proposals at Jidda: personal interview, New York, June 1996. This is interesting given the fact that the amir of Kuwait, in the memo referenced above, speculated that the Saudis would push Kuwait to accommodate Iraq.

[56] Sa'dun Hamadi, part of the Iraqi delegation, reported this to al-Bazzaz: *Harb*, pp. 83–84.

[57] Freedman and Karsh, *The Gulf Conflict*, pp. 60–61.

August 2, 1990. Even if force were to be used, the Kuwaiti government was convinced that the Iraqis would do no more than seize disputed areas along the border and the Persian Gulf islands which controlled access to Iraqi ports, as bargaining chips. In subsequent testimony before a Kuwaiti parliamentary committee, Crown Prince Sa'd Abdallah said: "I had the impression that if there was going to be an Iraqi attack it would be limited, in specific places like the Rutqa oil field and maybe Bubiyan Island. It never even occurred to me that Iraq would occupy Kuwait. I said that the most it would do is attack there and then bargain." Foreign Minister Sabah al-Ahmad told the same committee: "I said that maybe Iraq wants to get the two islands – Warba and Bubiyan – and might occupy them. But Iraq occupied the whole country. By God, that never crossed my mind."[58] The view that Iraqi military action, if it occurred, would be limited was shared by American military intelligence.[59] The Kuwaiti parliamentary committee severely criticized the government for "negligence and inadequate readiness, and not taking the simplest security, civil and military steps to deal with the Iraqi threats." It attributed this lack of military preparedness to the government's desire not to provoke Iraq and its fears of offending domestic and regional opinion if it sought direct American military support.[60] Those fears disappeared after Iraq had occupied the country.

The Gulf War

The United States decided very quickly that it would oppose the consolidation of Iraq's control over Kuwait. While there was some sentiment at the first post-invasion meeting of the National Security Council (NSC) that Washington would have to adjust to the new realities, by the NSC meeting on August 3 American policy was forming around the goal of reversing Iraq's invasion.[61] Whether force would be used to achieve that goal was the subject of debate among administration decision-makers. However, as the crisis continued into the fall of 1990, all eventually came around to support the use of force.[62]

---

[58] From sections of the report published in *al-Hayat*, August 19, 1995, pp. 1, 6.

[59] Woodward, *The Commanders*, pp. 207–08.

[60] *Al-Hayat*, August 19, 1995, pp. 1, 6.

[61] Brent Scowcroft, the national security adviser, wrote: "I was frankly appalled at the undertone of the discussion, which suggested resignation to the invasion and even adaptation to a *fait accompli*" (George Bush and Brent Scowcroft, *A World Transformed* [New York: Alfred A. Knopf, 1998], p. 317 for quote; see also pp. 318–24).

[62] President Bush reported that in late August "[n]ot everyone in the Administration yet shared my feeling that it might be time to consider using force. From the beginning of the

Map 3 The Iraq–Kuwait border

The American stand was, in social science parlance, "overdeter-mined." For decades Washington had identified the oil resources of the Persian Gulf as a vital American interest. In one fell swoop, Saddam had become master of 20% of the world's oil reserves, with the possibility of indirect control over the additional 25% of reserves in Saudi Arabia. With Saddam's military power now on the Saudi border, the United States' closest Gulf ally was threatened, if not with immediate attack then with a long-term security problem. Had this been a Cold War crisis, the United States might have been reluctant to confront a Soviet ally directly, for fear of escalation to a superpower confrontation. But the

crisis, Baker was reluctant to contemplate it … He never backed away from any decision to use force or planning for it, but he advised pushing the diplomatic course first and giving sanctions more time" (Bush and Scowcroft, *A World Transformed*, p. 354).

Gulf War turned out to be the first post-Cold War crisis, with the Soviet Union quickly joining the United States in condemning the invasion and acting as an (at times reluctant, but still cooperating) junior partner to the United States as the crisis unfolded. Moreover, Saddam had violated the one core principle upon which practically every member state of the United Nations (some with greater degrees of hypocrisy than others) agreed: that territory in the modern world could not be legitimately obtained by force. The United Nations Security Council churned out numerous resolutions condemning the invasion and calling upon Iraq to withdraw, the first (UNSC Resolution 660) a unanimous resolution (with Yemen abstaining) in a special evening session on August 2/3, less than twenty-four hours after the invasion. Even Iraq's closest Arab partners in the crisis, Jordan and Yemen, refused to recognize officially the Iraqi annexation of Kuwait.

The United States, with the support of other great powers, was ready to act to safeguard its strategic oil interests and to support widely agreed-upon international norms. It was that rare international occasion when interests, values and the international *Zeitgeist* all seemed to point in the same direction. Washington was so sure of its course that it did not follow up on reported Iraqi feelers early after the invasion offering to withdraw from most of Kuwait in exchange for a number of concessions, including parts of Kuwait, debt relief and a large amount of money.[63] But for the United States to act militarily against Iraq, it needed Saudi Arabia to open up its territory to American forces.

At the outset, the Saudis were hesitant, hoping that Arab diplomacy could reverse the consequences of the Iraqi attack. King Fahd put off an offer by President Bush on August 2 to deploy an American F-15 squadron to Saudi Arabia as a show of support.[64] A flurry of Arab diplomatic activity followed the invasion, as both President Mubarak of Egypt and King Hussein of Jordan exerted efforts to end the crisis. The two mediators quickly fell out, accusing each other of bad faith and broken promises. But at the outset they both agreed that the United States should not take any initiatives until they had explored an "Arab solution." They agreed to try to organize a summit of the major Arab leaders. Mubarak said that the summit could occur only if Saddam committed himself, before the meeting, to withdraw from Kuwait. King Hussein later reported that he had

---

[63] This Iraqi offer is reported by Dilip Hiro, *Desert Shield to Desert Storm: The Second Gulf War* (New York: Routledge, 1993), p. 118, based on an article in the British newspaper the *Guardian*. It was also reported by Heikal, *Illusions of Triumph*, pp. 308–11. Memoirs on the American side do not mention the Iraqi offer.

[64] Bush and Scowcroft, *A World Transformed*, p. 321.

obtained a commitment by Saddam to attend the summit and to withdraw his troops from Kuwait. Mubarak contended that the king had failed to get Saddam's commitment to the conditions, and, without those assurances, he could not convene a summit. On August 3, the Arab League foreign ministers condemned the invasion, though in a divided vote in which six members (including Jordan, Yemen and the Palestine Liberation Organization, or PLO) did not support the resolution. Iraq then decided that it would not attend the proposed summit meeting.[65]

Meanwhile, President Bush encouraged King Fahd to receive a US delegation that would lay out American proposals to defend Saudi Arabia. On August 6 the king and other senior members of the Al Saud family received Secretary of Defense Dick Cheney in Riyadh. At that meeting, the king agreed to accept the deployment of American forces in his kingdom. King Hassan of Morocco and President Mubarak had by that time committed to sending forces to Saudi Arabia, allowing the Saudis to portray their decision as an opening to an international coalition, including Muslim countries, aimed at deterring an Iraqi attack on the country. The first contingent of American forces was ordered to the kingdom on August 7.[66] On that same day, Saudi Arabia indicated that it would increase its oil output by 2 mbd, making up close to half of the shortfall created by the end of Kuwaiti and Iraqi oil exports.[67]

There is no evidence that Saddam Hussein intended to continue his military assault into Saudi Arabia. His forces stayed on the Kuwaiti side of the Kuwaiti–Saudi border during this period. However, the ease with which his forces had consolidated their control over Kuwait clearly unnerved the Saudis. They did not allow their official media to report on the invasion for three days. On August 8, Iraq officially annexed Kuwait, making it hard to imagine that a negotiated solution that would meet American demands – unconditional Iraqi withdrawal from Kuwait and restoration of the previous government – could be met.

With these events, the confrontation hardened and local actors began to pick sides. With the decision to accept American forces on their soil, the

---

[65] Freedman and Karsh, *The Gulf Conflict*, pp. 69–71.
[66] Freedman and Karsh, *The Gulf Conflict*, pp. 92–93.
[67] Andrew Rosenthal, "Bush Sends US Force to Saudi Arabia as Kingdom Agrees to Confront Iraq," *New York Times*, August 8, 1990. Saudi Arabia's average oil production in August 1990 was 5.8 mbd, up from 5.4 mbd in July 1990. In September 1990 Saudi production increased to 7.7 mbd and eventually peaked during the crisis at 8.5 mbd in December 1990, making up about 60 percent of the oil production lost from Iraq and Kuwait: US Department of Energy, Energy Information Administration, *Monthly Energy Review*, March 2004, Table 11.1a.

Saudis were wedded to the American position in the crisis. Jordan and Syria surprised many observers with their choices in the crisis. King Hussein, the Arab leader most admired in official circles in the West, was Saddam's most visible Arab ally in the crisis. Hafez al-Asad, hardly the United States' favorite Arab leader, not only condemned the Iraqi invasion of Kuwait but also sent a Syrian division to Saudi Arabia to participate in the international coalition against Iraq. In King Hussein's case, Jordanian domestic politics were the driving force behind his choice to align with Iraq. For al-Asad, a long history of enmity between the Ba'thist regimes in Damascus and Baghdad led to his decision to balance against Saddam Hussein, who would be much stronger in regional politics if he could consolidate his gain in Kuwait.[68]

Yemen, newly united in May 1990 and occupying the Arab seat on the UN Security Council, basically tilted toward Iraq. The Yemeni position very likely arose from its desire to have a strong ally to balance Saudi power in the Arabian Peninsula. The Saudis had opposed past efforts at Yemeni unity and were clearly not pleased by the success of the latest effort. In retaliation, Saudi Arabia in September 1990 adopted measures that, in effect, expelled Yemeni workers living in Saudi Arabia. Some estimates put the number of Yemenis who were forced to leave Saudi Arabia at 750,000.[69] Yasir Arafat and the PLO also sided with Iraq in the crisis, perhaps reflecting support among Palestinians for Saddam's efforts to condition a diplomatic solution to the Kuwait crisis on resolution of the Arab–Israeli conflict.

Egypt, as indicated above, joined the international coalition very early in the game. Like the American decision to oppose the Iraqi invasion, the Egyptian decision to do the same was overdetermined. For balance of power reasons in the Arab world, Mubarak had every reason to oppose Iraqi regional pretensions. His close alignment with the United States would have been called into question if he had not joined the coalition. Egypt's peace treaty with Israel, never particularly popular either at home or in the region, would come under increased pressure if Iraq and Israel engaged in a long confrontation. Saudi Arabia and Kuwait made it worth Egypt's while to take this position, supplying Cairo with cash payments. The United States and other Western allies also expressed their gratitude financially, relieving Egypt of a substantial part of its foreign debt in the

---

[68] For a full discussion of the Jordanian and Syrian alliance decisions, see my article, "Balancing What? Threat Perception and Alliance Choice in the Gulf," *Security Studies*, Vol. 13, No. 2 (Winter 2003/04), pp. 273–305.

[69] For a discussion of Saudi–Yemeni relations in the crisis, see my article, "Saudi Arabia: Desert Storm and After," in Robert O. Freedman (ed.), *The Middle East After Iraq's Invasion of Kuwait* (Gainesville: University of Florida Press, 1993), pp. 219–20.

wake of the crisis.[70] The smaller Gulf monarchies lined up behind their GCC partners Kuwait and Saudi Arabia. While hardly surprising, this move was important for United States forces, which gained access to ports and bases in Bahrain, Qatar, the United Arab Emirates and Oman. Turkey, led by President Turgut Ozal, actively supported the international coalition. It cut the oil pipelines through which Iraqi oil was shipped to the Mediterranean immediately after UN Security Council Resolution 661 of August 6, which mandated a trade and financial boycott of Iraq and occupied Kuwait. Despite serious reservations in Turkish public and elite opinion (including the resignation of his foreign minister, defense minister and chief of staff of the army), Ozal opened up Turkish bases for use by coalition air forces in the attack on Iraq. In exchange, Turkey received foreign aid from coalition partners and strengthened its relations with Washington.[71]

Iran, perhaps the most important regional player in the crisis after Saudi Arabia, played a subtle game that, in the end, tilted toward the coalition and away from Saddam Hussein. So soon after its eight-year war with Iraq, Tehran had no desire to see Saddam Hussein strengthened by his annexation of Kuwait. However, the Iranian leadership was equally leery of American intentions in the region. Saddam made a major effort to court Iran at the outset of the crisis. On August 14 he publicly agreed to all of Iran's conditions for a formal end of the Iran–Iraq War, including a reaffirmation of the Algiers Agreement border in the Shatt al-Arab. Shortly after the invasion Tariq Aziz led an Iraqi delegation on a secret visit to Tehran, where he offered the Iranians further concessions for their support in the crisis, including a promise of $25 billion in reparations for the Iran–Iraq War. Iraq made another effort to secure Iranian support shortly before the January 15, 1991, deadline for withdrawal from Kuwait, once again promising concessions to Tehran.[72] Iranian officials did speak out publicly against the American military buildup in the region. However, the Iranian government did nothing to support Saddam. Aside from some smuggling across the border, Iran abided by UN sanctions against Iraq. It also did nothing to impede the coalition military effort against Iraq.

---

[70] Louis Cantori, "Unipolarity and Egyptian Hegemony in the Middle East," in Freedman (ed.), *The Middle East after Iraq's Invasion of Kuwait*, pp. 335–57.

[71] On Turkish policy in the crisis, see Freedman and Karsh, *The Gulf Conflict*, pp. 82–83, 352–54.

[72] Kuwaiti sources reported on the Iraqi offer to Iran, contending that the Kuwaiti government was informed by Iran about the Iraqi offer: Youssef Ibrahim, "After the War: Iran Organizes and Arms Rebels Fighting Hussein, Diplomats Say," *New York Times*, March 20, 1991.

With the sides basically set, the crisis played out over the following months in a series of mini-dramas which absorbed the attention of the world but basically did not change the dynamics established in its first days. Saddam Hussein worked assiduously to break up the emerging international coalition arrayed against him. His first ploy in this direction was on August 12, 1990, when he explicitly linked his occupation of Kuwait to other regional issues, suggesting he might withdraw from Kuwait if Israel first withdrew from the West Bank and Gaza and if Syria withdrew from Lebanon. This attempt at what became known as "linkage" succeeded in garnering Palestinian support for his position, but failed in its larger effort to break off the Arab members of the coalition. Even the October 8, 1990, eruption of violence on the Temple Mount (Haram al-Sharif) in Jerusalem, in which clashes between Palestinian protestors and Israeli troops led to the death of twenty-one Palestinians, did not shake the commitment of the Arab members of the coalition. Saddam's efforts at linkage and events such as those of October 8 did, however, place the Arab–Israeli issue firmly on the international agenda once again. Other coalition members, particularly France and the Soviet Union, gave some signals that they accepted the logic of linkage, if not Saddam's definition of it.[73] After the crisis, the United States revived the Arab–Israeli peace process, in large measure as redemption of promises to its Arab and European allies in the coalition.

As the Iraqis were failing in their efforts to split the coalition, the United States was developing its military, political and diplomatic strategy for reversing the Iraqi conquest of Kuwait. As early as October 1990 American decision-makers were beginning to doubt whether the sanctions imposed on Iraq by the UN Security Council could induce Saddam Hussein to withdraw.[74] President Bush asked for a military briefing on plans to dislodge the Iraqis from Kuwait in early October. In late October the Bush administration decided to double the number of American forces in the region, to approximately 500,000, in order to provide an offensive option against Iraq. The move was not announced publicly until early November 1990, after the congressional elections.[75] From that point, the administration's management of the crisis was aimed at two goals: (1) to maintain coalition unity in support of the use of military force against Iraq; and (2) to gain public and congressional support in the United States

---

[73] On French and Soviet diplomatic initiatives involving linkage, see Freedman and Karsh, *The Gulf Conflict*, Chapters 11, 19.

[74] President Bush reports in his memoirs that, by late September 1990, "I was frustrated and impatient to resolve the crisis, hoping we could find reason to go in and settle the matter" (Bush and Scowcroft, *A World Transformed*, p. 375).

[75] Freedman and Karsh, *The Gulf Conflict*, Chapter 14 and pp. 211–12.

for the use of force. These two goals sometimes led American diplomacy in seemingly opposite directions.

At the international level, the United States focused on getting a UN Security Council resolution authorizing the use of force against Iraq. Secretary of State Baker spent most of November lobbying in the capitals of the countries represented on the council and shoring up support among coalition members in the region. On November 29, the council voted 12– 2 (Cuba and Yemen voted against) with one abstention (China) for Resolution 678, authorizing the use of "all necessary means" if Iraq did not withdraw from Kuwait by January 15, 1991.

With the international front seemingly secure, the administration turned to mobilizing congressional and domestic support for the war option. The announcement of the doubling of troop strength in the region, made in early November, elicited substantial congressional opposition. Public opinion support for President Bush's handling of the crisis, which had been very high at the outset, began to drop toward the 50 percent mark.[76] While the UN resolution of November 29 eventually strengthened the administration's case for war, since it could point to broad international support, its immediate effect was to stoke congressional and public fears that war was inevitable. To help convince his domestic audience that he was willing to explore a diplomatic solution, on November 30 President Bush publicly invited Iraqi foreign minister Aziz to Washington for direct talks and offered to send Secretary of State Baker to Baghdad. President Bush wrote: "One action I had been contemplating to help strengthen congressional and public support was direct contact with the Iraqis. I wanted to show that we were going the extra mile for peace." But this offer did not mean that he was looking for a real negotiation with Saddam. He envisaged the meetings as opportunities "where Saddam would be told exactly how determined we were – that there was no room for compromise, that unconditional, total withdrawal was the only answer." He wrote further on that he would have been willing to go to war even without congressional approval.[77]

The invitation to Iraq for direct talks was a domestic gambit, but it ran counter to the efforts to build international support for war. A number of members of the coalition were upset by the prospect of a bilateral American–Iraqi deal that would leave Saddam Hussein's military and political power intact.[78] The administration spent much of the next month reassuring

[76] Freedman and Karsh, *The Gulf Conflict*, p. 211.
[77] Bush and Scowcroft, *A World Transformed*, pp. 419, 446.
[78] Brent Scowcroft wrote: "The downside internationally of inviting Tariq Aziz was instantly obvious and genuinely serious. It had shaken the coalition to its core, just as the UN resolution had seemingly cleared away the last hurdle to taking action" (Bush and

coalition members in the Middle East that they were, in fact, going to use force against Saddam, while telling Congress and the American public that there was still a chance for a diplomatic solution. Those twin tracks finally came together on January 9, 1991, when Secretary of State Baker and Foreign Minister Aziz met in Geneva for the only face-to-face contact between high-ranking officials of the two states during the crisis. The maneuvering around that meeting had taken more than a month before the date and place were settled.

It is no exaggeration to say that the eyes of the world were focused on the Geneva Intercontinental Hotel that day. Baker reports in his memoirs, with more than a hint of both satisfaction and wonder, that the New York Stock Exchange and world oil markets gyrated sharply over the course of the six hours of talks.[79] Baker set out a stark choice for Iraq: withdraw from Kuwait by the deadline or experience unparalleled military defeat. He added, for good measure, that any use of weapons of mass destruction by Iraq in the conflict would mean the end of Saddam Hussein's regime. His only assurance to Iraq was that its forces would not be attacked if they withdrew by the deadline. The Iraqi side did not flinch. Aziz refused to accept a letter from Bush to Saddam, complaining that its threatening tone was inconsistent with diplomatic protocol. He rehearsed Iraq's arguments about the origins of the crisis and the justice of its cause, but made no offers, save for an invitation to continue the talks in Baghdad.[80]

The failure of the Geneva talks secured a congressional majority authorizing the use of force.[81] On January 12, 1991, the Senate voted 52–47 to authorize the use of "all necessary means" to enforce the UN Security Council resolutions on the crisis. The House of Representatives approved the same language by a vote of 250–183. The majority of Democrats in both chambers opposed the use-of-force resolution. The Senate vote was particularly close. While one public opinion poll on the eve of the war showed 58 percent support for President Bush's handling of the crisis, majorities also supported compromise to avoid war and feared a long

---

Scowcroft, *A World Transformed*, p. 420). James Baker described the initiative thus: "It confused and confounded our friends, delighted our critics, and fueled whispers about a weakening of America's resolve. At least momentarily, it undermined our credibility with some of our coalition partners, and handed Saddam Hussein a propaganda opening" (*The Politics of Diplomacy*, p. 346).

[79] Baker, *The Politics of Diplomacy*, p. 364.

[80] This account of the Geneva meeting is based on Baker's memoir, *The Politics of Diplomacy*, Chapter 19. Subsequent accounts, including interviews with Aziz, confirm Baker's version of the event.

[81] Baker reports that Senator Sam Nunn, the normally hawkish Democrat from Georgia who was leading the opposition to the use of force against Iraq, observed that, as soon as Baker began his post-meeting press conference with the word "regrettably," any chance of defeating the use-of-force resolution in Congress was lost: *The Politics of Diplomacy*, p. 364.

conflict with many casualties.[82] The president had his authorization, but the American political class and the American public were seriously divided as war approached.

Last-minute diplomatic initiatives by UN secretary-general Javier Pérez de Cuéllar, who saw Saddam Hussein in Baghdad on January 13, and the French foreign minister, who proposed a new UN Security Council resolution linking the solution of all Middle East crises, came to naught.[83] Air attacks on Iraqi targets by American, British, Saudi and Kuwaiti air forces began in the early morning of January 17 (late in the evening of January 16 in the United States). As Iraqi officials had promised for months, Iraq responded to the air attacks with missile strikes on Israel (as well as Saudi Arabia and Bahrain) which continued for weeks. Saddam Hussein was trying to draw Israel into the fight, in hopes that Israeli retaliation would create political problems for his Arab opponents and thus split the coalition. The Israelis, however, did not rise to the bait. In exchange for Israeli restraint, the United States intensified its hunt for Iraqi missile launchers in western Iraq, provided Israel with extensive intelligence on its military operations and supplied Israel with Patriot anti-missile missile batteries.[84] Iraqi missile attacks on Israel continued intermittently throughout the war.

In the face of the coalition's air campaign, most of the Iraqi air force flew to Iran in late January and early February 1991. The Iranian government impounded the planes, later claiming them as reparations for the Iran–Iraq War. Secretary of State Baker responded on February 6, as the air war continued, by telling a congressional committee hearing that Iran was conducting itself "in a very, very credible way throughout the crisis so far."[85]

The coalition air attack on Iraq continued for more than a month, pulverizing the Iraqi military and civilian infrastructure and demoralizing the Iraqi military.[86] The Iraqi army made only one, limited offensive into Saudi Arabia during this period. On the evening of January 29 Iraqi forces

---

[82] Andrew Rosenthal, "Confrontation in the Gulf: Public Opinion: Americans Don't Expect Short War," *New York Times*, January 15, 1991.

[83] Freedman and Karsh, *The Gulf Conflict*, Chapter 19.

[84] Freedman and Karsh, *The Gulf Conflict*, Chapter 21.

[85] Elaine Sciolino, "After the War: For US and Iran, a Chance for Ties," *New York Times*, March 12, 1991.

[86] By late January 1991 Iraqi internal documents indicated that desertions from the army were becoming a serious issue and were damaging unit morale. In early February Iraqi military reports showed a growing breakdown of discipline in units, with officers selling food and fuel rations and orders to execute deserters: Ibrahim Al-Marashi, "The Nineteenth Province: The Invasion of Kuwait and the 1991 Gulf War from the Iraqi Perspective," MA thesis, Oxford University, July 2004, pp. 295–304.

captured the small Saudi town of Khafji, about twelve miles from the Kuwait border. Saudi and Qatari forces counterattacked on January 31 and retook the town after two days of fighting. While the capture of the Saudi town was a brief propaganda victory for Saddam Hussein, the inability of the Iraqi army to follow up on its victory or reinforce the contingent there was an indication that it would be no match for coalition forces.[87]

As the air campaign continued, there were growing worries internationally about the extent of civilian casualties in Iraq. On February 13 American bombers destroyed a bunker in a Baghdad residential neighborhood. More than 300 Iraqis, many of them women and children, were killed. The Iraqi government highlighted the incident in its propaganda, and there were protests in a number of Arab countries. While the number of civilians killed in the air war was surprisingly small, given the duration and ferocity of the campaign, the daily televised pictures of damage to civilian targets in Iraq were having a mounting political effect in many parts of the world.[88]

At about the same time, the Soviet Union initiated a new diplomatic effort to end the hostilities, before coalition forces launched their ground attack. Gorbachev's special envoy Yevgeny Primakov met with Saddam in Baghdad on February 12. On February 15 the Iraqi Revolutionary Command Council issued a statement saying that Iraq was prepared to discuss compliance with UN Security Council resolutions on Kuwait, but presented a number of unacceptable conditions, including Israeli withdrawal from the occupied territories. Still, it was the first time that Iraq had given any public indication of a willingness to withdraw from Kuwait. Tariq Aziz arrived in Moscow on February 17 to continue the discussions. Aziz took a Soviet proposal back to Iraq, amid contradictory signals of Saddam's intentions. Aziz returned to Moscow on February 21 with an Iraqi response that accepted the principle of withdrawal but added a number of points to the Soviet proposal. Gorbachev telephoned Bush on February 22 in hopes of getting American approval to continue the negotiations on this basis.[89]

---

[87] Freedman and Karsh, *The Gulf Conflict*, pp. 364–66.

[88] Iraqi government figures put the number of civilians killed in the war at 2,278 and wounded at 5,965: Freedman and Karsh, *The Gulf Conflict*, pp. 324–29. Human Rights Watch estimated between 2,500 and 3,000 civilian Iraqi casualties during the air war. This does not include Iraqis who died subsequent to the war, in the uprisings against the regime and as a result of diseases exacerbated by the destruction of the Iraqi water and power infrastructure during the war: Human Rights Watch, "Needless Deaths in the Gulf War," 1991, www.hrw.org/reports/1991/gulfwar.

[89] Freedman and Karsh, *The Gulf Conflict*, Chapter 27.

The Bush administration was losing control of the diplomatic process. While the Soviet proposal might have gotten an interested hearing in Washington earlier in the crisis, by now the administration and many of its coalition allies were looking to deal Saddam a devastating defeat.[90] The talk of a diplomatic settlement threatened to save the bulk of Saddam's military on the eve of its destruction. President Bush responded to the Iraqi announcement of February 15 by calling it a "cruel hoax" and called on the Iraqi military and people to "take matters into their own hands" and force Saddam from power. This was the first time that the president had explicitly called for the overthrow of the Iraqi leader.[91] His reaction to Gorbachev's diplomatic initiative was to announce publicly on February 22 (before he had spoken to Gorbachev on the telephone) that Iraq had twenty-four hours to begin an unconditional withdrawal from Kuwait. Gorbachev was unable to assure Bush that Saddam Hussein had actually accepted the Soviet withdrawal proposal, having only Tariq Aziz's assurance that Saddam would agree, and the Iraqis had just that day begun to torch Kuwait's oil fields. With Kuwait ablaze and Gorbachev unable to assure that he had Saddam's agreement, it was not hard for Bush to reject the last-minute Soviet diplomatic gambit.[92]

The ground war began on February 24, with coalition forces smashing the dispirited Iraqi resistance and pushing into Kuwait and southern Iraq. On February 25 Baghdad Radio announced that Iraq had ordered its army to withdraw from Kuwait. By February 27 coalition forces were inside Kuwait City. Amid televised scenes of coalition air forces attacking Iraqi troops on the road out of Kuwait, President Bush ordered a halt to the offensive, to take effect at midnight, Washington time, in the morning of February 28. The ground war ended 100 hours after it began. It subsequently became clear that the magnitude of the coalition victory was not as overwhelming as it appeared at the time. General Norman Schwarzkopf, the American commander, told the press that coalition forces trapped two Republican Guard divisions with 700 tanks. "The

---

[90] President Bush reports that, when he heard the news report that Iraq had announced that it would comply with the withdrawal resolution, "instead of feeling exhilarated, my heart sank" (Bush and Scowcroft, *A World Transformed*, p. 471).

[91] This quote became a sore point for President Bush after the war, when the United States did not support the uprisings against Saddam. The call for the Iraqis to "take matters into their own hands" was, according to President Bush and NSA Scowcroft, an "ad lib" that was not part of the president's prepared remarks: Bush and Scowcroft, *A World Transformed*, pp. 471–72. The "cruel hoax" quote came in a separate statement by the president later in the day. "War in the Gulf: Excerpts from 2 Statements by Bush on Iraq's Proposal for Ending Conflict," *New York Times*, February 16, 1991.

[92] On the content of the telephone call, see Baker, *The Politics of Diplomacy*, pp. 405–06; Bush and Scowcroft, *A World Transformed*, pp. 475–77.

gate is closed," he said; "there's no way out." In fact, those Guard divisions did have an escape route across the Euphrates River. They slipped out of coalition control and helped put down the uprisings against Saddam's rule that erupted after the defeat. Still, the ground offensive had been an enormous success. Kuwait had been liberated with minimal coalition casualties. Total coalition battle deaths for the entire Iraqi operation, from the beginning of the air war, were only 240 (776 wounded). With by far the largest contingent in the coalition, US forces took the majority of those casualties, with 148 dead (458 wounded).[93] It is impossible to estimate with any degree of accuracy Iraqi military casualties, or to separate war deaths from those that occurred during the uprising after the war. One reputable source, admitting that its estimate was based on circumstantial evidence, estimates total Iraqi battle deaths during the entire war at 35,000.[94]

The Iraqi *intifada* and the aftermath of the Gulf War

Immediately upon the defeat of the Iraqi army, large sections of the north and south of Iraq rose up against Saddam Hussein's government. Baghdad lost control of much of the country as the Ba'th regime teetered on the brink of collapse. However, Saddam and his regime were able to restore their control over most of the country in a few bloody weeks of fighting, while the United States stood aside. For the rest of the decade, Iraq suffered under the most onerous regime of international economic sanctions in the modern era, but Saddam was able to cling to power. Meanwhile, the United States converted its victory in the Gulf War into a series of military bases in the Arabian Peninsula monarchies. There were important changes in Iran's regional role during the 1990s and interesting fluctuations in the world oil market that in turn affected relations among the Gulf states. However, the rest of the 1990s were characterized by stability much more than change in the international politics of the Persian Gulf.

The Iraqi intifada *and the American reaction*

Iraqi soldiers retreating from Kuwait began the revolt against Saddam Hussein's regime, which (like the Palestinian revolt against Israeli occupation) came to be called the *intifada* (from an Arabic word meaning a shaking

---

[93] Freedman and Karsh, *The Gulf Conflict*, pp. 403–06, 409.
[94] Freedman and Karsh, *The Gulf Conflict*, p. 408.

off or shaking out). Some sources report that the first manifestation of the revolt was in Zubayr, a small town just north of the Kuwait–Iraq border.[95] Others say that the revolt began in Basra, the major city in southern Iraq.[96] Sources agree that the uprising started on February 28, the day the Bush administration declared the cease-fire, and that the spark was Iraqi soldiers firing at and defacing the ubiquitous portraits and statues of Saddam. The revolt spread throughout the south of Iraq in a matter of days, with the major cities falling out of government hands within a week. In the Kurdish north, the revolt began a few days later. By March 20 every major city in the Kurdish region and the contested city of Kirkuk were lost to government control, though the mostly Arab city of Mosul, the largest city in the north, did not fall. While Basra was one of the earliest, if not the earliest, site of rebellion, government forces never completely lost control of it.

The revolt in the south was an unplanned and uncoordinated event. There were no indigenous opposition parties on the ground able to establish a leadership role; Saddam's regime had extirpated them. The Iranian-backed Supreme Council of the Islamic Revolution in Iraq quickly sent its forces and sympathizers across the border into Basra and other Iraqi cities, bearing portraits of Ayatollah Khomeini and the SCIRI leader, Ayatollah Muhammad Baqir al-Hakim. Iranian forces remained on their side of the border.[97] Without coordinated leadership, the southern revolt devolved into anarchy, as local crowds took revenge upon agents of the Ba'thist regime and looted government buildings. In Najaf, Ayatollah Abu al-Qasim al-Khoei, the leading Shi'i religious figure in Iraq, issued a *fatwa* (religious ruling) on March 8 calling for an end to looting and violence. Three days later he appointed a committee to assume governance of the city.[98] Al-Khoei had been the most apolitical of clerics, a necessity in Saddam's Iraq, but also apparently out of conviction. He was opposed to Khomeini's theory of *velayet al-faqih*, that the clerics should also be political rulers. Given the complete breakdown of authority, however, he felt compelled to intervene. Other cities in the south lacked even this rudimentary level of leadership.[99]

---

[95] Faleh Abd al-Jabbar, "Why the Uprisings Failed," *Middle East Report*, No. 176, May/June 1992, pp. 8–9; Andrew Cockburn and Patrick Cockburn, *Out of the Ashes: The Resurrection of Saddam Hussein* (New York: Harper Collins, 1999), p. 15.

[96] Kanan Makiya, *Cruelty and Silence: War, Tyranny, Uprising and the Arab World* (New York: W. W. Norton, 1993), p. 59.

[97] Abd al-Jabbar, "Why the Uprisings Failed," p. 10; Cockburn and Cockburn, *Out of the Ashes*, p. 21; Makiya, *Cruelty and Silence*, pp. 93–95.

[98] Makiya, *Cruelty and Silence*, pp. 63–76. Cockburn and Cockburn, *Out of the Ashes*, say "In Najaf and elsewhere, euphoria at the overthrow of the regime was followed by anarchy" (p. 20).

[99] "In the south ... [c]haos ruled the land" (Makiya, *Cruelty and Silence*, pp. 89–90).

The revolt in the Kurdish areas was somewhat more organized by the two major Iraqi Kurdish parties, the Kurdish Democratic Party (KDP) led by Masoud Barazani and the Patriotic Union of Kurdistan (PUK) led by Jalal Talabani. As the Gulf War was being waged, these two leaders were planning for the fall of the regime. They had contacted elements of the pro-government Kurdish militia, known colloquially as the *jahsh* (donkeys in Kurdish), to suborn them to their side. They also had coordinated with the SCIRI leadership in Iran on plans for post-war Iraq.[100] On March 5 the *jahsh* in a small Kurdish town revolted against the police and Ba'th Party officials. The rebellion spread, culminating in the capture of Kirkuk on March 20. Many of the *jahsh* and regular Iraqi army units in the area either came over to the rebels or peacefully dissolved.[101] While the KDP and the PUK were able to provide some amount of order in the liberated areas, there were still considerable amounts of violence against officials and symbols of the old regime.[102]

Saddam's regime quickly reorganized to put down the rebellions. The focus at the outset was on restoring control over the south, by any means necessary. By March 9 Republican Guard units, including those that General Schwarzkopf had claimed were trapped by coalition forces, were beginning the counterattack on Karbala, the Shi'i holy city where the third Shi'i imam, Hussein, is buried. Saddam sent instructions to Ba'th Party officials around the country to act on the basis of "kill or be killed."[103] The tanks that entered Najaf to retake the city had the words "no Shi'a after today" painted on them.[104] Government forces used missiles, artillery, helicopters, tanks and chemical weapons against rebel-held cities and were indiscriminant in their use of violence. In both Karbala and Najaf considerable damage was done to Shi'i shrines.[105] Ayatollah al-Khoei was captured by the government forces and transported to Baghdad, where he was forced to appear on television next to Saddam Hussein on March 20, condemning the rebellions and expressing support for the

---

[100] Cockburn and Cockburn, *Out of the Ashes*, pp. 18–19; Makiya, *Cruelty and Silence*, pp. 81–83.

[101] Abd al-Jabbar, "Why the Uprisings Failed," pp. 11–12.

[102] "Rebels and their sympathizers in both the north and south of Iraq openly took credit for executing personnel of the security forces and intelligence agencies during the uprisings. While many were killed in the heat of battle, hundreds, perhaps thousands, were executed while in custody or after summary trials": Human Rights Watch, "Endless Torment: The 1991 Uprising in Iraq and Its Aftermath," June 1992, Chapter 2, www.hrw.org/reports/1992/Iraq926.htm.

[103] Party instructions quoted in *al-Hayat*, October 2, 1991, pp. 1, 4.

[104] Makiya, *Cruelty and Silence*, p. 96.

[105] Human Rights Watch, "Endless Torment," Chapter 3. On the use of chemical weapons in the south of the country, see the Duelfer Report, p. 25.

government.[106] By the end of March, the south of the country was back under government control.

The Iraqi government's efforts to retake the north began shortly after the tide had turned in the south. Just one day after Kirkuk had fallen to the Kurdish rebels (March 20), Iraqi army tanks and helicopters bombarded the city. On March 27 government forces reentered Kirkuk and by March 28 had the city under control. The government then ordered the remaining Kurdish population of Kirkuk to leave the city.[107] The recapture of Kirkuk was followed by the fall of other Kurdish towns. The well-founded fear of violent reprisals, combined with the brutal history of the Anfal campaign of the late 1980s, terrified the Iraqi Kurdish population. As the rebellion collapsed, nearly 2 million Kurds took refuge across the borders in Turkey (approximately 450,000) and Iran (approximately 1.4 million).[108] It is impossible to say with any certainty how many people died across Iraq in the *intifada*. Figures range between 25,000 and 100,000, but none of the estimates can be verified.[109]

There are numerous reasons why the Iraqi *intifada* failed to dislodge Saddam Hussein from power. The spontaneous southern rebellion lacked any kind of organizing structure. The Kurdish rebellion overextended itself, taking over cities such as Kirkuk and Irbil that are in the plains and thus more easily recaptured by Iraqi forces. The center of the country remained in government hands, with few instances of revolt, allowing the regime to send its forces south, then north, to put down the rebellion. The role taken by Iranian-supported SCIRI in the south allowed the regime to paint the rebellion in the south as both sectarian and foreign-inspired. The loss of Kirkuk, with its oil resources, must also have concentrated the minds of the regime elite to rally around Saddam.[110] But the single most important reason for the failure of the Iraqi *intifada* was the decision of the United States, which occupied considerable parts of southern Iraq as the rebellion was occurring, not to support it.

To some extent, the United States was unprepared to deal with the swift end of the conflict and the cascading events in Iraq that followed.[111] The

---

[106] *New York Times*, March 25, 1991, p. 8; Makiya, *Cruelty and Silence*, p. 96. Makiya reports the television appearance as March 21.

[107] Human Rights Watch, "Endless Torment," Chapter 4.

[108] Human Rights Watch, "Endless Torment," Chapter 1.

[109] Human Rights Watch, "Endless Torment," note 74.

[110] Abd al-Jabbar provides an excellent analysis of the internal causes of the failure of the intifada in "Why The Uprisings Failed." See also Phebe Marr, *The Modern History of Iraq*, 2nd edn. (Boulder, CO: Westview Press, 2004) pp. 241–53.

[111] "The end of effective Iraqi resistance came with a rapidity which surprised us all, and we were perhaps psychologically unprepared for the sudden transition from fighting to peacemaking": Bush and Scowcroft, *A World Transformed*, p. 488.

lack of planning was so complete that General Schwarzkopf was sent to the cease-fire negotiation on March 3 without orders from Washington about what to obtain from the Iraqis and without a political adviser.[112] Administration officials, after the fact, justified their inaction by arguing that the United Nations Security Council resolutions under which American forces were operating were limited to the liberation of Kuwait. This argument, while a useful public response to their critics, demonstrates a respect for the letter of UN resolutions that is not common in the history of American foreign policy. More to the point, there was a consensus within the American government that Saddam could not survive so devastating a defeat; that he would fall at the hands of the military or other members of the elite in a short time.[113] More direct American involvement was thus not necessary, they thought, to achieve the goal of ousting Saddam. There was also a clear desire by the US military to avoid involvement in civil conflict in Iraq. The military had won a relatively clean victory and had a clear exit strategy – liberate Kuwait, restore the Kuwaiti government and start going home.

However, the most important reason that Washington did not support the Iraqi *intifada* was fear that Iran would benefit from upheaval in Iraq, particularly upheaval among Iraqi Shi'a. Secretary of State Baker wrote in his memoirs: "Just as fears of Iranian expansionism helped shape US prewar policy toward Iraq, this same phobia was a significant factor in our post-war decision-making."[114] President Bush and National Security Adviser Brent Scowcroft were even more explicit about the geopolitical basis for backing away from the Iraqi revolts: "While we hoped that a popular revolt or a coup would topple Saddam, neither the United States nor the countries of the region wished to see the break-up of Iraq. We were concerned about the long-term balance of power at the head of the Gulf."[115]

In the light of the collapse of Iraq after the 2003 American invasion, the first Bush administration's decision to remain aloof from the internal Iraqi

---

[112] Christian Alfonsi, *Circle in the Sand: Why We Went Back to Iraq* (New York: Doubleday, 2006), Chapter 5, gives a general account of efforts to plan for the post-war situation; see pp. 187–88 on the lack of instructions to Schwarzkopf on the cease-fire negotiations.

[113] President Bush reports in his memoir: "Almost every leader in the coalition had told me that in defeat Saddam would not be able to keep his hold on power" (Bush and Scowcroft, *A World Transformed*, p. 472). That view was shared within the US intelligence community. Cockburn and Cockburn quote "a former very high-ranking CIA official" thus: "A collective mistake. Everybody believed that he was going to fall. Everybody was wrong" (*Out of the Ashes*, p. 37).

[114] Baker, *The Politics of Diplomacy*, pp. 437–38.

[115] Bush and Scowcroft, *A World Transformed*, p. 489. Alfonsi, *Circle in the Sand*, reports that Bush originally resisted Scowcroft's view that regime change should not be part of the American war termination goals (pp. 155–63).

conflict in 1991 has come to be seen by many in the United States as a wise bit of statesmanlike restraint. At the time and through the 1990s, however, it was severely criticized on both moral and strategic grounds. President Bush did himself no favors in answering his critics by insisting that, in fact, he did not call on Iraqis to overthrow Saddam. In their joint memoirs, Scowcroft wrote: "It is stretching the point to imagine that a routine speech in Washington would have gotten to the Iraqi malcontents and have been the motivation for the subsequent actions of the Shiites and Kurds."[116] The testimony of Iraqi rebels indicates that it was not a stretch at all. Sayyid Majid al-Khoei, son of Ayatollah al-Khoei, said, "The biggest reason for the *intifada* is that they [the rebels] thought the Americans would support them."[117]

The administration's focus on Iran also helps explain its seemingly contradictory actions on the Iraqi Kurdish issue. After staying out of the Iraqi rebellion, at least in part because they feared that it would lead to the break-up of Iraq, the administration then took steps which promoted the de facto independence of the Iraqi Kurdish area. For Washington, Kurdish autonomy was not seen as redounding to the immediate benefit of Iran, and thus it was acceptable. Hundreds of thousands of Iraqi Kurdish refugees were fleeing into Turkey, an ally in the North Atlantic Treaty Organization (NATO) which had been extremely cooperative throughout the crisis. (Many more fled to Iran, but that was not a serious problem for Washington.) Their plight was brought to the television screens of the world in real time, sullying the American victory. As early as April 8 the European Community called for the creation of a protected enclave in Iraq to which Iraqi Kurds could return.[118] American politicians and pundits, taken aback by the success with which Saddam Hussein had put down the revolts, also called for the administration to do something.[119] The Turkish leadership, fearing the domestic consequences among its own restive Kurdish minority, pushed Washington for a solution that would return the Iraqi Kurds. Moreover, Secretary of State Baker personally seems to have been greatly affected by his visit to a Kurdish refugee camp in Turkey immediately following the war.[120]

---

[116] Bush and Scowcroft, *A World Transformed*, p. 472.
[117] Cockburn and Cockburn, *Out of the Ashes*, pp. 22–23.
[118] Alan Riding, "Europeans Urging Enclave for Kurds in Northern Iraq," *New York Times*, April 9, 1991.
[119] The domestic political pressure the administration was feeling on this issue is captured in Alfonsi, *Circle in the Sand*, pp. 212–34.
[120] Baker, *The Politics of Diplomacy*, pp. 430–35. See also Alfonsi, *Circle in the Sand*, pp. 221–22.

But to protect the Kurdish refugees, Washington had to involve itself in domestic Iraqi politics in a way that it had avoided just a month before. President Bush ordered the American military to supply humanitarian aid to the Kurdish refugees. To safeguard American forces providing that aid, on April 5 Washington established a "no-fly" zone for Iraqi aircraft in the north of the country. On April 16, Bush agreed to send ground forces into northern Iraq to secure a protected area for the return of the refugees. American, British, French and other coalition forces moved into northern Iraq (at its peak the force numbered 23,000), and the air forces of the three major coalition partners patroled the no-fly zone.[121] The coalition forces in the north operated under the somewhat fuzzy UN legal cover of Security Council Resolution 688, adopted on April 5, which called on the Iraqi government to end its repression of its own people, specifically mentioning the Kurds, and to allow humanitarian relief agencies to operate in the country.[122] UN officials negotiated a memorandum of understanding on April 18 with the Iraqi government to allow the setting up of the enclaves. By June 1991 most of the Iraqi Kurdish refugees in Turkey and many in Iran had returned to Iraq, and coalition forces left the area, though coalition aircraft continued to patrol the no-fly zone.

Emboldened by this turn in their fortunes and protected by coalition air cover, the KDP and the PUK began to assert their control over Kurdish towns. In October 1991 the Iraqi government decided to withdraw its forces to a defensive line south of major Kurdish population centers. It conceded the cities of Irbil and Suleimaniya and large swaths of territory in the north and northeast of the country to the Kurds, but maintained control over Kirkuk. Baghdad also imposed an economic blockade on the Kurdish region. The KDP and the PUK consolidated their control over the area, holding legislative elections in April 1992 and forming a local Kurdish administration.[123] A falling out between them in 1994 led to a split in the administration, with the KDP controlling Irbil and the northern section of the Kurdish area while the PUK controlled Suleimaniya and the southern part of the area. Iraqi Kurdistan became, de facto, independent of Baghdad under the protection of the American air force and would remain that way through the 2003 Iraq War.

---

[121] Sarah Graham-Brown, *Sanctioning Saddam: The Politics of Intervention in Iraq* (London: I. B. Tauris, 1999), p. 29.

[122] Graham-Brown, *Sanctioning Saddam*, p. 106.

[123] David McDowall, *A Modern History of the Kurds* (London: I. B. Tauris, 2000), pp. 373–83; Marr, *The Modern History of Iraq*, pp. 253–59; Graham-Brown, *Sanctioning Saddam*, Chapter 1.

The sanctions regime and Iraqi–American confrontations
in the 1990s

On April 3 the UN Security Council adopted Resolution 687, setting out the terms under which the regime of Saddam Hussein would have to deal with the international community. The economic sanctions placed on Iraq in August 1990, including a ban on Iraqi oil sales, were maintained pending Iraqi acceptance of a number of conditions. The most important of those conditions was Iraq's giving up all chemical, biological and nuclear weapons capabilities and missiles with a range of more than 150 kilometers. UNSC 687 established UNSCOM (the UN Special Commission for the Disarmament of Iraq) to carry this out. (The International Atomic Energy Agency handled the nuclear file.) Other conditions included acceptance of a UN-drawn border between Iraq and Kuwait and an Iraqi obligation to pay compensation to individuals, entities and countries harmed by its occupation of Kuwait.[124] Iraq formally accepted UNSC 687, leading to the withdrawal of American forces from southern Iraq in April 1991.

The sanctions were the centerpiece of Iraq's dealings with the international community and the United States for the next decade. One can hardly imagine an issue characterized by more hypocrisy, skullduggery and unsolved puzzles. The biggest of those puzzles came to light only after the Iraq War of 2003. Shortly after sanctions were imposed, Saddam Hussein in effect ordered the dismantling of his chemical, biological and nuclear weapons programs. Yet he went to great lengths to hide this from UNSCOM for over a decade despite the fact that, if he had come clean, the sanctions very likely would have been lifted. This bizarre behavior will be discussed in the next chapter, which deals with the 2003 war. When UNSC 687 was adopted, the United States did not think that Saddam would be in power very long. The sanctions were part of the effort to weaken the regime and encourage a coup against it. As months turned into years and Saddam was still in power, the Bush administration and then the Clinton administration were forced into a transparent hypocrisy. Washington claimed that, if Saddam disarmed, sanctions would be lifted. But the United States held firmly to a policy of encouraging the overthrow of Saddam's regime from within, and sanctions were part of that policy. It became increasingly clear that, as long as Saddam remained in power, the United States would not approve the lifting of the sanctions. Since the United States has a veto on the Security Council, it could block any resolution to that effect. By the end of the 1990s, international support

---

[124] Text of the resolution can be found at www.fas.org/news/un/iraq/sres/sres0687.htm.

for the sanctions was fraying, in part because other international actors, particularly Russia and France, were interested in doing business with Saddam, though, in another hypocrisy, those governments framed their impatience to have the sanctions lifted in international legal and humanitarian terms.

The sanctions were a political football kicked around by governments, but they were also a brutal reality for the Iraqi people. Iraq's oil wealth had transformed the country in the 1970s into a relatively prosperous place with a large middle class. The Gulf War and the sanctions destroyed the Iraqi economy. While the Iraqi regime exaggerated the effects of the sanctions, particularly in areas such as infant mortality, to rally international pressure for their lifting, there is no doubt that the sanctions caused tens of thousands of preventable deaths in the country.[125] The Iraqi middle class was gutted, with the emigration of those with marketable skills or the right connections and the progressive impoverishment of those who remained. The human toll helped to mobilize public opposition to the sanctions, particularly in the Arab world but elsewhere as well.

The story of Iraq after the Gulf War is the story of the interplay between the sanctions issue and disarmament efforts. The United States confronted Saddam Hussein militarily on a number of occasions and made numerous efforts to encourage his overthrow. At the same time, Washington accepted a number of modifications to the sanctions regime in an effort to alleviate some of the suffering of the Iraqi people and to maintain international support for the isolation of Saddam. The twists and turns of the story occupied much of the international attention in the region during the 1990s. However, the political reality did not change: Saddam Hussein, though weakened, was still in power at the end of the Clinton administration.

As it became clear that Saddam Hussein would not quickly fall from power, the Bush administration sought ways to hasten that event. The Central Intelligence Agency (CIA) sought out elements of the Iraqi opposition, something the United States had not done in the lead-up to the war, cobbling them together in an umbrella organization called the Iraqi National Congress (INC). The INC was headed by an Iraqi exile named Ahmad Chalabi.[126] The organization proved ineffective in coordinating

---

[125] See the careful analysis by Amatzia Baram, "The Effect of Iraqi Sanctions: Statistical Pitfalls and Responsibility," *Middle East Journal*, Vol. 54, No. 2 (Spring 2000), pp. 194–223. Cockburn and Cockburn, *Out of the Ashes*, present a number of telling anecdotes about the sanctions' effects (Chapter 5).

[126] Cockburn and Cockburn, *Out of the Ashes*, Chapter 2.

the various Kurdish, Shi'i, ex-Ba'thist and independent Iraqi opposition groups. It did become the vehicle for Chalabi's ambitions, his platform for insinuating himself into American political deliberations in the lead-up to the Iraq War of 2003. Washington also maintained military pressure on Saddam. It established a southern no-fly zone in August 1992 on the model of the northern zone. American aircraft regularly struck Iraqi military installations in both the south and north of the country, to degrade anti-aircraft capabilities and punish Iraqi recalcitrance on a range of issues.

The new Clinton administration basically continued the previous administration's policies toward Iraq – maintaining sanctions and military pressure, supporting efforts to destabilize the regime from within but not committing the full weight of American power to these efforts. In June 1993 President Clinton ordered a missile attack on the headquarters of Iraq's intelligence service in Baghdad in retaliation for a purported plot by Baghdad to assassinate former president Bush on a visit to Kuwait. In October 1994 he ordered the deployment of nearly 30,000 American troops into Kuwait when Iraq moved troops toward the border.[127] The Clinton administration continued the covert efforts to overthrow Saddam from within, supporting at first Chalabi's INC and later funneling support to another exile group, the Iraqi National Accord, headed by ex-Ba'thist (and future Iraqi prime minister) Iyad Allawi. Both groups were penetrated by Iraqi intelligence, which foiled a number of coup plots.[128] In late August–early September 1996, taking advantage of conflict between the KDP and the PUK in Iraqi Kurdistan, Saddam's forces moved north (in cooperation with KDP forces) and routed the elements of the INC that were headquartered there. The Clinton administration responded on September 3–4 with another volley of cruise missiles aimed at Iraqi military and intelligence installations, a relatively weak response to Saddam's daring attack on the United States' Iraqi allies.[129] As the 1990s progressed, Saddam seemed more and more secure domestically, even as his people suffered under economic sanctions.

---

[127] Most analysts believed that Saddam's movement of troops toward the Kuwaiti border in 1994 was simply a feint. However, al-Bazzaz reports that Saddam was serious about launching a second attack: *Ramad al-hurub: asrar ma ba'd harb al-khalij* [The Ashes of Wars: Post-Gulf War Secrets] (Amman, Jordan: Dar al-Ahliya, 1995), pp. 273–81, quote from p. 281.

[128] Cockburn and Cockburn, *Out of the Ashes*, Chapters 7 and 9; Baram, *Building Toward Crisis*, pp. 55–58.

[129] Cockburn and Cockburn, *Out of the Ashes*, Chapter 10; Graham-Brown, *Sanctioning Saddam*, pp. 231–34.

While covert American efforts to overthrow Saddam continued in the shadows, the world followed the more public confrontations between Iraq and UNSCOM. Iraq followed a strange and erratic strategy with the weapons inspectors. At times Iraqi officials would appear the souls of cooperation, turning over documents and standing by as the UNSCOM teams inspected Iraqi sites. At other times the Iraqis would stonewall, blatantly lying to UNSCOM and physically preventing access to certain buildings and areas. Iraqi officials on numerous occasions claimed that WMD materials had been destroyed, claims that ultimately turned out to be true, but were unable to produce documentary evidence to that effect, raising the suspicions of UNSCOM, since UNSC 687 called for any disposal of WMD-related material to be conducted under UNSCOM auspices. There were well-publicized standoffs between UNSCOM personnel and Iraqi security forces in September 1991 and July 1992 and numerous other confrontations over the years. Meanwhile, Iraq was turning over what it claimed was a complete record of its WMD activities. But when Iraqi defectors were debriefed by UNSCOM, the weapons inspectors discovered that the Iraqi government was hiding evidence of more extensive WMD programs. These cat-and-mouse games continued throughout the 1990s.

The most spectacular of these episodes was the defection to Jordan in August 1995 of one of Saddam's closest aides, his cousin and son-in-law Hussein Kamil Hassan. Since the late 1980s Hussein Kamil had been minister of industry and military industrialization, overseeing Iraq's WMD programs. His defection led to revelations about Iraqi nuclear, chemical and biological programs before and during the Gulf War that went far beyond what UNSCOM had been able to find. The story had an operatic denouement. Unable to rally any support, either in the exiled opposition or within Iraq, Hussein Kamil found himself increasingly isolated and ignored in Amman. In what can only be considered an unbalanced mental state, he agreed in February 1996 to return to Iraq, ostensibly with a guarantee of safe passage from Saddam. He was killed almost immediately on arrival.[130]

The Clinton administration found itself increasingly pulled in two directions on Iraq. In the United States, Republicans took control of both the Senate and the House of Representatives in the 1994 elections. Many congressional Republicans (and a number of Democrats) pushed Clinton to take a harder line toward Saddam Hussein, as the latter began

[130] For the story of Hussein Kamil, see Cockburn and Cockburn, *Out of the Ashes*, Chapter 8; Dilip Hiro, *Neighbors, Not Friends: Iraq and Iran After the Gulf Wars* (London: Routledge, 2001), Chapter 3.

to maneuver from 1997 to expel the international weapons inspectors from Iraq. In October 1998 Congress adopted the Iraq Liberation Act, allocating nearly $100 million to support Iraqi opposition forces. The administration was clearly uncomfortable, not having much confidence in the ability of the Iraqi opposition to threaten Saddam's regime. However, not wanting to appear "soft" on Saddam, President Clinton signed the legislation.

While pressured to be tough on Iraq at home, the Clinton administration faced increasing international pressure to lift, or at least modify, the sanctions regime that was creating enormous suffering for Iraqis. To try to maintain international support for the sanctions, Washington agreed to a series of modifications aimed at lessening their effects on the Iraqi people. The first was UN Security Council Resolution 986, adopted in April 1995, which established the "oil for food" program. Under this program, Iraq would be able to sell oil up to a fixed dollar amount every six months. The proceeds from those sales would go to a UN account, which would be used to purchase food, medicine and other essential items for distribution to the Iraqi people. Distribution would be the responsibility of the Iraqi government, though under UN auspices and, at least theoretically, ultimate UN control. Saddam Hussein finally accepted "oil for food" in November 1996.

While the oil-for-food program represented an improvement in the situation of the Iraqi people, it hardly restored living standards to their pre-war level. Two United Nations administrators of the program, Denis Halliday and Hans von Sponeck, resigned their positions (Halliday in August 1998, von Sponeck in February 2000) in protest against its inadequacies and the human cost of the sanctions on Iraq.[131] In response to continuing anti-sanctions sentiment internationally, the United States in March 1998 supported an expansion of the amount of oil Iraq could sell under the oil-for-food program, thus increasing its revenue. Finally, in December 1999 the United States accepted, in UN Security Council Resolution 1284, the lifting of all limits on Iraqi oil sales under the program. These compromises failed to change the increasingly widespread international perception that the economic sanctions were simply unjustifiable.

While these compromises had the advantage of somewhat mitigating the severe human costs of the sanctions, they also lessened whatever pressure the sanctions were bringing to bear on Saddam Hussein, thus giving him more confidence to challenge the weapons inspections regime.

---

[131] For a thorough analysis of the economic sanctions regime on Iraq through 1998, see Graham-Brown, *Sanctioning Saddam*, Chapters 2, 7 and 8.

In October 1997 he ordered all American members of UNSCOM out of Iraq. Through 1997 and in early 1998 Iraq declared a number of locations "presidential sites" and prohibited UNSCOM investigations of them. While an agreement between Saddam and UN secretary-general Kofi Annan in February 1998 ostensibly solved the presidential sites issue, in August 1998 Iraq announced the end of cooperation with UNSCOM. Once again, in the fall of 1998, under the threat of American military action, Iraq allowed UNSCOM inspectors to return. However, in December 1998, after a report from UNSCOM chairman Richard Butler that Iraq was not cooperating with his commission's efforts, American and British forces conducted four days of air and missile strikes on Iraqi targets in Operation Desert Fox. This marked the end of UNSCOM's access to Iraq.[132]

It took an entire year of diplomacy for the Security Council to address the collapse of UNSCOM. In December 1999 the council adopted Resolution 1284. Russia and France were so unenthusiastic about it that they abstained in the vote. Along with lifting the limits on the amount of oil Iraq could sell under the oil-for-food program, UNSC 1284 established a successor organization to UNSCOM, the United Nations Monitoring and Verification Commission (UNMOVIC) and offered Iraq the prospect of a possible lifting of sanctions if it permitted the new organization to operate in the country.

Baghdad was not interested in testing those possibilities. It already had the weapons inspectors out. With oil prices rising in 1999 and 2000 and limits on Iraqi oil production lifted, there were no immediate economic incentives for Saddam Hussein to permit the return of weapons inspectors. In January 2001, the UN Iraq escrow account contained $12 billion, with $5 billion of that amount not committed to specific contracts.[133] With the momentum seemingly moving toward further international pressure on the United States to loosen the sanctions, Baghdad was content to ignore the opportunity that the new resolution presented. When Bill Clinton left office in January 2001, Saddam Hussein was still in power. The international regime put in place after the Gulf War had eroded substantially. There were no weapons inspectors in Iraq. While economic sanctions still weighed heavily on the Iraqi people, Saddam's regime had learned to live with them, chip away at them and use them to mobilize international opposition to US policy toward Iraq.

---

[132] For an account by UNSCOM's last director of these matters, see Richard Butler, *The Greatest Threat: Iraq, Weapons of Mass Destruction and the Growing Crisis of Global Security* (New York: Public Affairs, 2000).
[133] *Petroleum Intelligence Weekly*, January 1, 2001, pp. 1, 2.

The American strategic buildup, Iran and oil

The most important strategic change in the international politics of the Persian Gulf to come out of the Gulf War, after the destruction of Iraq's offensive military capability, was the development of a new infrastructure of American military power in the region. Two important changes solidified this direct American military presence, converting it from an occasional and temporary surge into a permanent presence. The first was in American policy itself. The Bush administration took on a long-term commitment to contain and pressure Iraq militarily. The Clinton administration added to the military mission with its "dual containment" policy. Not only would the United States take primary responsibility for containing Saddam's Iraq, but it would also seek to contain the influence of Iran in the region.[134] Dual containment required the stationing of American naval, air and ground forces in the region on a long-term basis.

The second change was in the politics of the Gulf monarchies. Before the Gulf War, those states had been reluctant to play host to American military forces. They were all closely tied to the United States but shied away from hosting American military bases. Saudi Arabia had shut down the American air base at Dhahran in the early 1960s, bowing to Arab nationalist pressure. Bahrain continued to provide a home port for the American naval force in the Gulf, but until the late 1980s that consisted of three or four small vessels. Oman in the early 1980s agreed to provide facilities for the American military, but found itself criticized within the GCC for doing so. The Gulf monarchs preferred to have American forces "over the horizon," close enough to come to their defense but far enough away to allow some political space between them and the United States.

The Gulf War eliminated this reluctance. Kuwait enthusiastically welcomed American forces into the country. Throughout the 1990s there were usually about 5,000 American troops in Kuwait at any given time, about two dozen attack aircraft and prepositioned heavy equipment, including over fifty tanks. A new, onshore headquarters for the American naval force in the Gulf was built in Bahrain. That force, upgraded to fleet status as the Fifth Fleet in 1995, averaged fifteen vessels, including an aircraft carrier, on station in the region during the 1990s. Qatar permitted the prepositioning of heavy equipment for a mechanized brigade, including over 100 tanks. A major American airbase was built outside Doha at al-Udaid. The United Arab Emirates allowed prepositioning of military equipment and American access to airbases and ports. The United States

---

[134] The policy was set out by National Security Adviser Anthony Lake in "Confronting Backlash States," *Foreign Affairs*, Vol. 73, No. 2 (March 1994), pp. 44–55.

had access to Omani airbases and ports from the early 1980s, and Oman also allowed the United States to preposition military equipment on its territory. Along with the forces onshore, the United States normally maintained about 10,000 military personnel aboard ships in the region.[135]

Saudi Arabia was the only Gulf monarchy not to sign a formal security agreement with the United States after the Gulf War – a testimony to how sensitive the issue of foreign forces in the country was to Saudi public opinion. The lack of a formal agreement, however, did not block greater Saudi–American military cooperation in the 1990s. A number of new arms agreements were signed immediately after the war. More significantly, Riyadh permitted the United States to use Saudi air bases to patrol the southern no-fly zone in Iraq. That mission, dubbed Operation Southern Watch, required a squadron of American fighter aircraft and between 5,000 and 6,000 air force personnel. Unlike the new American military presence in the smaller Gulf states, which met with little overt public opposition (and, in Kuwait, a fair amount of public support), the American military presence in Saudi Arabia was controversial. Usama bin Laden, about whom more will be said in Chapter 5, made the issue a centerpiece of his indictment of the Saudi regime. In November 1995 Islamist militants bombed a US training mission attached to the Saudi National Guard in Riyadh, killing five Americans and two Indians and wounding scores. Saudi authorities executed four men for that attack in May 1996. In public statements before their execution, they referred to bin Laden and other activists who shared his perspective, such as the Jordanian–Palestinian preacher Abu Muhammad al-Maqdasi, as their inspiration.[136] In June 1996 a truck bomb exploded in front of the Khobar Towers apartment complex where American personnel assigned to Operation Southern Watch in Saudi Arabia's Eastern Province were housed. Nineteen Americans were killed and over 400 Americans, Saudis and third-country nationals were wounded. After the explosion, Operation Southern Watch was transferred to Prince Sultan Airbase in the desert south of Riyadh, remote from population centers.

---

[135] On the American military presence in the smaller Gulf states, see Geoffrey Kemp and Robert E. Harkavy, *Strategic Geography and the Changing Middle East* (Washington, DC: Brookings Institution Press, 1997), Chapter 7; Anthony H. Cordesman, "Saudi Arabia, the US and the Structure of Gulf Alliances," Center for Strategic and International Studies, February 25, 1999, www.csis.org/media/csis/pubs/saudialliances.pdf; Rachel Bronson, "Beyond Containment in the Persian Gulf," *Orbis*, Vol. 45, No. 2 (Spring 2001), pp. 193–209; and the descriptions of the individual facilities used by Central Command provided by the GlobalSecurity.Org website, www.globalsecurity.org/military/facility/centcom.htm.

[136] Edward Cody, "Saudi Islamic Radicals Target US, Royal Family," *Washington Post*, August 15, 1996.

'The identity of the Khobar Towers bombers remains a matter of controversy. Some expatriate Sunni opponents of the regime made the claim that their local allies were responsible.[137] However, American and Saudi officials soon came to the conclusion that the perpetrators were Saudi Shi'a with Iranian support. The investigation led to serious tensions in Saudi–American relations. The Saudis were reluctant to give American investigators access to suspects and evidence for fear that Washington would implicate Riyadh in retaliatory strikes against Iran. Not until two years after the attack did Riyadh begin to cooperate in more than a very limited way with the American investigation. In September 1999 President Clinton sent a letter to Iranian president Muhammad Khatami requesting Iranian cooperation in locating suspects in the Khobar Towers bombing who were believed to be in Iran. Finally, in June 2001 an indictment was handed up by a federal grand jury accusing thirteen Saudis and one Lebanese, members of the Saudi Shi'i opposition group Saudi Hizballah, of involvement in the Khobar Towers attack. Attorney General John Ashcroft said that "elements of the Iranian government inspired, supported and supervised" the attack.[138] It was subsequently revealed that the United States retaliated against Iran covertly, revealing the identities of a number of Iranian intelligence operatives to other governments and thus ending their viability.[139]

The American military buildup in the Gulf was as much about countering Iran as it was about containing Saddam's Iraq. Iran certainly gained the most, relatively, among the regional powers from Saddam Hussein's defeat in the Gulf War. With Iraq greatly weakened, Iran emerged as the most powerful regional state. However, it was not in a mood to try to exploit that strategic change to its own benefit. The Islamic Republic played a cautious

---

[137] Youssef M. Ibrahim, "Native Saudi Rebels Linked to Bombing of US Base," *New York Times*, August 15, 1996. The most prominent source of this theory is Saad al-Faqih, the head of the Movement for Islamic Reform in Arabia, a Saudi veteran of the Afghanistan war against the Soviets and a Sunni opponent of the regime. The 9/11 Commission, while accepting that the principal elements behind the bombing were Iranian-supported Saudi Shi'a, reported that "there are also signs that al-Qaeda played some role, as yet unknown": *The 9/11 Commission Report* (New York: W. W. Norton, 2004), p. 60.

[138] Richard A. Clarke, *Against All Enemies: Inside America's War on Terror* (New York: Free Press, 2004), pp. 112–21; Daniel Benjamin and Steven Simon, *The Age of Sacred Terror* (New York: Random House, 2002), pp. 224–25, 300–02. All three served on Clinton's National Security Council and all put responsibility for the attack on Saudi Shi'i opponents of the regime with an Iran connection. For the Clinton letter of September 1999, see "US Message to Iran," *New York Times*, September 30, 1999. Attorney General Ashcroft's statement when the indictment was issued can be found at www.fas.org/irp/news/2001/06/khobar.html.

[139] On the anti-Iranian operation, codenamed Operation Sapphire, see Barbara Slavin, "US 'Outed' Iranian Spies in 1997," *USA Today*, March 30, 2004. Richard Clarke hinted that the United States undertook even more serious covert responses: *Against All Enemies*, pp. 120–21, 128–29.

role in regional politics in the 1990s. That caution was certainly induced, in part, by the American success in the Gulf War and the American military presence in the area. But it was also the product of internal dynamics. Iran was still recovering from the Iran–Iraq War and adjusting to the death of Ayatollah Khomeini in 1989. Its government during the 1990s pursued a path of more normal diplomatic relations with its monarchical neighbors, deemphasizing the imperative of spreading the revolution. It did not abandon the revolutionary mission completely, continuing to support the Supreme Council of the Islamic Revolution in Iraq, Hizballah in Lebanon and Hamas in the Palestinian territory. It continued to oppose any normalization of Israel's regional role. As the Khobar Towers incident demonstrates, elements in the Iranian power structure were willing to take risks and use violence to oppose American power in the Gulf. Moreover, the convoluted political situation in Iran, with multiple centers of power within the regime, meant that there was frequently more than one policy line being pursued by different actors in Tehran at the same time. Despite these issues, Iran's overall stance in the Gulf during the 1990s was much different than that of the 1980s: it was more a normal player in the power game than a revolutionary challenger to the status quo.

Iran's careful and studied neutrality in the Gulf War was the avenue to improved relations with the Gulf monarchies. Kuwait, which had been among the most pro-Iraqi of the Arab states during the Iran–Iraq War, now viewed Iran as an important counterbalance to Iraq. Saudi Arabia and Iran restored diplomatic relations, broken in 1987 over the riots at the pilgrimage to Mecca, in March 1991. There have been no major incidents involving Iranian pilgrims' behavior during the pilgrimage since the renewal of relations. There were episodic crises in Iran's relations with the Gulf monarchies, including an assertion of Iranian power on Abu Musa Island, also claimed by the UAE, in 1992 and Bahrain's contention in 1996 that Iran was supporting the uprising by Shi'i opposition forces. These incidents, and Khobar Towers, however, did not escalate into major confrontations. Relations between Iran and the Gulf states were placid compared to the 1980s.[140]

Iran's stance in the Gulf War also raised the prospect for a new turn in Iranian–American relations after more than a decade of post-revolutionary hostility. However, that opportunity was not grasped. Washington still saw Tehran as a regional rival. The Clinton administration codified that inclination formally in its "dual containment" policy. Anti-Iranian feeling remained strong in the US Congress. In December 1995 Congress

---

[140] Christin Marschall, *Iran's Persian Gulf Policy: From Khomeini to Khatami* (London: Routledge Curzon, 2003), pp. 100–42.

appropriated $18 million for covert actions against the Iranian regime. In 1996 President Clinton signed the Iran–Libya Sanctions Act (ILSA), a measure adopted overwhelmingly in Congress, which in effect cut off the possibility of American trade with and investment in Iran while attempting to put roadblocks in front of other countries' investments there. The ILSA came after President Clinton had blocked by executive order a deal by the Canadian subsidiary of the American oil company Conoco to invest in the development of an Iranian gas field.[141] Meanwhile, Iran pursued policies guaranteed to raise hackles in Washington. It vocally objected to the Arab–Israeli peace process and supported its Palestinian (Hamas) and Lebanese (Hizballah) opponents. Of course, Khobar Towers would not encourage an Iranian–American rapprochement.

The surprise victory of reformist candidate Muhammad Khatami in the Iranian presidential election of May 1997 led to hopes of a new era in regional politics. Khatami, though a cleric himself, ran as an alternative to the candidate supported by the ruling clerical establishment and won an overwhelming victory. On foreign policy, he spoke of dialogue, even with the United States, and emphasized the need for cooperation with Iran's Gulf neighbors. While his predecessor, Ali Akbar Hashemi Rafsanjani, had initiated the new policy of accommodation with the Gulf monarchies, the Khatami election was seen by the Gulf rulers as potentially a real break from Iran's revolutionary past, and thus an end to Iranian opposition to their own rule in their states. Saudi Arabia immediately moved to reciprocate Khatami's gestures. Crown Prince Abdallah, the de facto ruler of the country (King Fahd had been incapacitated by illness since 1995), attended the Islamic Conference Organization summit in Tehran in December 1997, the first time a Saudi ruler had been to Iran's capital since the revolution. He met with Khatami and Khamenei during the summit and later welcomed Rafsanjani, who remained an important player in Iranian politics, on a visit to Riyadh. The atmospherics between Tehran and Riyadh were quite good, as if Khobar Towers had never happened.[142]

Khatami's election ushered in the first real prospect of a breakthrough in Iranian–American relations since the revolution. He made a number of positive comments about the United States, referring at one point in public to "the great American people." In January 1998, he called for "a

---

[141] Gary Sick, "The United States in the Persian Gulf: From Twin Pillars to Dual Containment," in David Lesch (ed.), *The United States and the Middle East: A Historical and Political Reassessment*, 4th edn. (Boulder, CO: Westview Press, 2007), pp. 325–26; Hiro, *Neighbors, Not Friends*, pp. 218–20; Shaul Bakhash, "Iran Since the Gulf War," in Robert O. Freedman (ed.), *The Middle East and the Peace Process: The Impact of the Oslo Accords* (Gainesville: University Press of Florida, 1998), pp. 242–50.

[142] Marschall, *Iran's Persian Gulf Policy*, pp. 143–45; Hiro, *Neighbors, Not Friends*, pp. 229–31.

crack in this wall of distrust" between the two governments.[143] The Clinton administration definitely noticed. In June 1998 Secretary of State Madeleine Albright gave a speech on Iran which dropped the rhetoric of past statements and called for exploring "ways to build mutual confidence and avoid misunderstandings."[144] Washington also took some tangible steps to signal its willingness to improve relations. In May 1998 it waived the penalties it could have imposed on the French oil company Total under the Iran–Libya Sanctions Act for Total's investments in Iran. In March 2000 the United States lifted trade restrictions on the import of Iranian carpets, caviar, dried fruit and pistachios into the United States. In announcing these steps, Secretary Albright admitted that Washington had made a number of mistakes in its policy toward Iran in the past, including its support for the 1953 royal coup against Prime Minister Mossadegh and its support for Iraq in the Iran–Iraq War. While not an "apology," as some in Iran had demanded, Albright's speech was as close to one as any great power was going to issue.[145]

The possibility of a rapprochement in the late 1990s was, however, not realized. Serious issues between the two sides could not be resolved. Iran's opposition to the Arab–Israeli peace process continued while Washington put enormous emphasis on negotiating Arab–Israeli agreements in this period. The United States was becoming increasingly concerned about the Iranian nuclear program. Khobar Towers was still an open file.[146] Iran, asserting that regional security could come only from regional states, could not accept the American military presence in the area. Tehran also objected to the continued American economic sanctions on the country. On both sides domestic politics pulled the leaders away from pursuing better relations. Khatami's conservative opponents used his opening to the United States to rally their supporters against his reform agenda. As they progressively limited Khatami's powers domestically, they also constrained his freedom to maneuver in foreign policy. On the American side, Congress unanimously passed in 1999 the Iran Non-Proliferation Act, aiming to cut Iran off from suppliers for its nuclear industry, a signal that it was not as enthusiastic as the Clinton administration about pursuing an

---

[143] Hiro, *Neighbors, Not Friends*, p. 231.

[144] Sick, "The United States in the Persian Gulf," pp. 326–27. Albright herself reported in her memoirs: "From my earliest days as Secretary of State, President Clinton and I were intrigued by the possibility of better relations with Iran" (*Madam Secretary* [New York: Miramax Books, 2003], p. 319).

[145] The text of Albright's March 2000 speech can be found at www.aghayan.com/alb031700.htm.

[146] Albright highlights these issues as stumbling blocks in her memoirs: *Madam Secretary*, pp. 323–24.

opening with Tehran.[147] When President Clinton left office in January 2001, American–Iranian relations had taken a few steps forward, but not many. The opportunity presented by Khatami's election for the relationship to take a new direction was lost.

While the Khatami opening did not lead to a new American–Iranian relationship, it did improve Saudi–Iranian relations. The tangible issue which underlay that improvement was the mutual interest of Tehran and Riyadh in stabilizing the falling price of oil. The world oil market in the 1990s favored the buyers, not the sellers, in part because of decisions made by Saudi Arabia during and immediately after the Gulf War. The Iraqi invasion of Kuwait and the subsequent UN sanctions had the immediate effect of taking about 5 mbd of Iraqi and Kuwaiti oil off the world market.[148] The table was set for another world oil crisis. Saudi Arabia, with help from the UAE, prevented that third crisis from occurring. It increased its oil production by 3 mbd; the UAE increased its production by 400,000 bd. Together they replaced two-thirds of the production lost from the Iraqi invasion.[149] Oil prices spiked immediately in August and September 1990 toward $40 per barrel but, by the time Iraqi forces retreated from Kuwait in February 1991, prices had dropped to approximately what they had been just before the invasion, below $20 per barrel.[150]

The Saudis were certainly bowing to American and international pressures to avoid an economic crisis in taking these moves, but they also had selfish reasons for doing so. During the 1980s they had sacrificed their share of world production in a failed effort to prop up prices. As was discussed in the previous chapter, they abandoned that policy in 1985. However, they were not able to recover all of their lost production capacity, given market softness and OPEC quotas of the late 1980s. The Gulf War brought Saudi production back up to around the levels it had reached in the early 1980s. Riyadh was not about to give up its share of the market, even as Kuwaiti production returned to its pre-war level. Between

---

[147] On the domestic impediments to improved relations on both sides, see Hiro, *Neighbors, Not Friends*, pp. 256–64, 275–79.

[148] Iraq was producing 3.5 mbd in July 1990; Kuwait was producing 1.9 mbd. Once sanctions hit, their total combined production was about 500,000 bd: US Department of Energy, Energy Information Administration, *Monthly Energy Review*, March 2004, Table 11.1a.

[149] Saudi Arabia was producing 5.4 mbd in July 1990. By December 1990 it was producing 8.4 mbd. The UAE went from a little less than 2.1 mbd to a little less than 2.5 mbd in the same period: US Department of Energy, Energy Information Administration, *Monthly Energy Review*, March 2004, Table 11.1a.

[150] Robert Looney, "Oil Prices and the Iraq War: Market Interpretations of Military Developments," *Strategic Insights*, April 1, 2003, www.ccc.nps.navy.mil/rsepResources/si/apr03/middleEast.asp.

the end of the Gulf War and 1998 oil prices remained relatively low and relatively stable, fluctuating between $15 and $20 per barrel.[151]

The Asian financial crisis, which began in the summer of 1997 and extended into 1998, cut world demand for oil. At the same time, Iraqi production was coming back onto the world market under the oil-for-food program. Moreover, OPEC completely misread the early signals of the Asian crisis. At the OPEC meeting in Jakarta in December 1997, the member states raised their quotas by a collective 2 mbd, just as the Asian crisis was biting into Asian oil demand. This combination of factors drove prices down considerably. In 1998 the Brent marker price averaged $12.72 per barrel, falling more than $6 per barrel from its 1997 average. In December 1998 prices fell below $10 per barrel.[152] All the oil producing states, including Saudi Arabia, were facing serious fiscal crises if prices stayed so low. As prices continued to fall through 1998, Riyadh reached out to Tehran. In March 1999 those negotiations led to a new agreement on deeper production cuts among OPEC and non-OPEC producers, taking 2 mbd off the world market. Iran was brought on board through a Saudi concession: letting Iran calculate its reduction from its "official" production level, which was higher than its actual production, thus sparing Iran the full brunt of the cutback.[153] These Saudi-led, Iranian-backed production cuts, combined with the earlier-than-expected recovery of the Asian economies and galloping American economic growth, pushed oil prices up in 1999 to an average of nearly $18 per barrel and $28.50 in 2000.[154] Riyadh and Tehran discovered that setting aside political differences to cooperate on oil issues could benefit both of them.

Conclusion

Quite a bit happened in the Persian Gulf between August 2, 1990, and September 11, 2001, but not that much changed. The biggest challenge to the regional status quo, Saddam's invasion of Kuwait, was turned back with surprisingly few major repercussions internationally. The regimes of

---

[151] British Petroleum, *Statistical Review of World Energy 2007*, Spot Crude Prices table, www. bp.com/sectiongenericarticle.do?categoryId=9017906&content Id=7033467.

[152] British Petroleum, *Statistical Review of World Energy 2007*, Spot Crude Prices table, www.bp.com/sectiongenericarticle.do?categoryId=9017906&contentId=7033467; US Department of Energy, Energy Information Administration, Petroleum Navigator, World Crude Oil Prices, http://tonto.eia.doe.gov/dnav/pet/pet_pri_wco_k_w.htm.

[153] F. Gregory Gause, III, "Saudi Arabia Over a Barrel," *Foreign Affairs*, Vol. 79, No. 3 (May/June 2000), pp. 89–90.

[154] British Petroleum, *Statistical Review of World Energy 2007*, Spot Crude Prices table, www. bp.com/sectiongenericarticle.do?categoryId=9017906&contentId=7033467.

all the regional states, including a weakened but resilient Saddam Hussein in Iraq, were still in power. Iraq could no longer vie for regional dominance, but the other regional contender, Iran, did not take advantage of Iraq's weakness to make its own play for regional hegemony. The United States was more entrenched militarily in the Gulf monarchies than it had been before the Gulf War, but its presence was intended to solidify the status quo, not challenge it. Clinton administration policy was about containment, not change. Washington did not like the governments in Baghdad and Tehran, but was not willing to do what was necessary to get rid of them. Iranian policy, first under Rafsanjani and then under Khatami, largely (though not completely) abandoned the goal of exporting the revolution in the Gulf, further consolidating the regional status quo. The world oil market avoided a third oil crisis during the Gulf War and was relatively placid, at least from the consumers' point of view, thereafter. Local producers were shaken by the price collapse of 1998, but they all weathered that difficult period, with Riyadh and Tehran finding common ground to meet that challenge. It was an eventful period, but not a revolutionary one.

Two developments during this period did set the stage for the tumultuous regional events that would follow the attacks by al-Qaeda upon the United States on September 11, 2001. The first was the consolidation of the system of American military bases in the region. Without the American military presence in the Gulf, it is possible (though we will never know) that Usama bin Laden would not have plotted attacks against the United States. Without those bases, and of this we can be more sure, the Iraq War of 2003 would not have been possible. What had been in the 1990s a military buildup to preserve the Gulf status quo became the instrument for a wildly ambitious effort to change it after 2001. The second development was the hollowing out of Iraqi society. The toll of international sanctions and of increasingly repressive and sectarian government domestically created the conditions for the brutalities Iraq would suffer after the fall of Saddam Hussein's regime. While the sufferings of the Iraqi people in the 1990s were "acceptable" to all the international players involved, including their own government, those sufferings debilitated and reduced a thriving middle class and encouraged ethnic, sectarian and tribal political identities to come more powerfully to the fore. The sanctions and Saddam's misgovernment in the 1990s set the stage for the Iraqi civil war that followed the American invasion. It is to these developments that we turn in the next chapter.

The 9/11 plot was hatched in Afghanistan and implemented in the United States, but both its origins and its repercussions were centered directly in the Persian Gulf. Usama bin Laden is a Saudi and his animus toward the United States originated largely, though not completely, in his opposition to American policy in the Gulf. Fifteen of the nineteen 9/11 hijackers were Saudis and two were from the UAE. Saudi Arabia was the source not only of the personnel who carried out the attacks, but also of much of the ideological fervor and many of the logistical networks that underlay the growth of the *salafi* jihadist movement in the 1980s and 1990s. The attacks led to the most serious crisis in the Saudi–American relationship since the 1973–74 oil embargo. The American invasion of Iraq also stemmed directly from the attacks. Absent the shock of 9/11, it would not have been possible for the Iraq war hawks in the Bush administration to carry the day, either within the administration, in Congress or in American public opinion. The Iraq War and the subsequent American occupation of Iraq dramatically changed the power realities of the Gulf. While Iraq remains profoundly unsettled, the outlines of a new regional power configuration were forming by the end of 2008. That new configuration, however, is hardly what the Bush administration imagined it might be in the heady days after the fall of Saddam's regime in 2003.

9/11 and the Persian Gulf

The irony of the 9/11 attacks is that they had their origins in the two great successes of contemporary Saudi–American cooperation: the jihad in Afghanistan against the Soviet Union in the 1980s and the Gulf War of 1990–91.

Afghanistan is a complicated and compelling story.[1] For the purposes of our narrative, I treat it only as it plays into the background to 9/11. The

---

[1] On the internal dynamics of Afghanistan and the international factors that led to the collapse of its government, the rise of the Communist regime and the development of the Islamist opposition, see Barnett R. Rubin, *The Fragmentation of Afghanistan* (New

Soviet Union sent forces into Afghanistan in December 1979, at the request of the communist government it had helped install in Kabul. The Afghan jihad against the Soviet occupiers was quickly taken up as a cause by both the United States and Saudi Arabia. Support for the Afghani resistance helped the Saudis counter the challenge of the Iranian revolutionary regime. For some time Riyadh had a monopoly on "Islam" in regional politics. Its rivals, most notably Arab leftists like Nasser and the Ba'th, were secular nationalists. Ayatollah Khomeini challenged the Saudi claim to speak for Islam at the international level, questioning the legitimacy of the Saudi monarchical regime and its international alliance with the United States. The Afghan jihad gave Riyadh a perfect opportunity to demonstrate to the Muslim world that it, not the Iranian revolutionaries, could deliver support when a Muslim country was under attack. The fact that Afghanistan is a largely Sunni country gave the Saudis a natural advantage over Shi'i Iran in developing local allies. Support for the jihad also served a domestic purpose for the Saudi rulers, still shaken by the 1979 takeover of the Grand Mosque in Mecca by Juhayman al-'Utaybi and his followers. What could be a clearer signal of the leadership's devotion to Islam than its support for a righteous jihad?

The Saudis therefore jumped at the chance to cooperate with the United States and Pakistan in supporting the Afghan jihad. Saudi society was mobilized, from the top down and the bottom up, to support the Afghan jihad with money and volunteers.[2] It was in this atmosphere that Usama bin Laden became involved in the issue. He was a religiously devout young man and interested in politics. As one of the numerous sons of Muhammad bin Laden, founder of what is now the largest construction company in the Middle East, he had an entrée into the top levels of Saudi society. The Afghan jihad fired his imagination. Bin Laden recruited Saudi volunteers and raised money for the cause. In 1984, during a trip to Pakistan, bin Laden made his first foray into Afghanistan. After that, he and Abdallah Azzam, a charismatic Palestinian who had worked at King Abd al-Aziz University in Jidda and moved to Pakistan to support the jihad in 1981, set up the "Services Bureau" in Peshawar, Pakistan, the base for most of the Afghan resistance groups. The Bureau, financed by bin Laden, coordinated the activities of Arab volunteers in the jihad. In 1986 bin Laden brought his wives and children to live in Peshawar and

Haven: Yale University Press, 1995). On American and Saudi involvement in Afghanistan during the 1980s and 1990s and on Usama bin Laden's rise in the Afghan context, see Steve Coll, *Ghost Wars* (New York: Penguin Books, 2004).
[2] Coll, *Ghost Wars*, pp. 79–84.

set up the first camp in Afghanistan exclusively dedicated to training Arab volunteers.[3]

The last Soviet troops left Afghanistan in February 1989. But for bin Laden (and many others), the jihad was not over. Thousands of young Arabs came to take part in its later stages, even after the Soviet withdrawal. Bin Laden sought to take advantage of this surge of recruits by founding a new organization, called al-Qaeda ("the base" in Arabic), that would train and employ the best of those recruits for future missions. What those missions would be was a matter of intense, even violent, debate as the jihad against the Soviets wound down. Bin Laden became increasingly close to the Egyptian contingent among the Arab volunteers, led by Ayman al-Zawahiri. Al-Zawahiri, the founder of the Islamic Jihad movement in Egypt, argued that the jihad should now be focused against what he considered to be apostate regimes in the Arab world. However, in the immediate aftermath of the Soviet withdrawal the Arab fighters participated in the continued fighting against the communist government in Kabul (which fell in April 1992) and in the internecine fighting among the various Afghan resistance groups.[4]

Bin Laden, meanwhile, had returned to Saudi Arabia in the fall of 1989 a hero. His efforts in Afghanistan had the blessing of the Saudi leadership, and he consulted regularly with Saudi intelligence officials throughout the 1980s.[5] However, his Afghan experience had changed him in three ways that would increasingly trouble the Saudi rulers. First, Afghanistan changed him ideologically. He went there a pious Muslim, committed to the puritanical social mores of Saudi Wahhabism, but with no clear political platform. He left with the beginnings of an ideology that would come to be called *salafi* jihadism or, more simply, bin Ladenism. It was a mix of the social elements of Wahhabism and the political activism of the more extreme elements of the Egyptian Muslim Brotherhood. Bin Laden had begun to see many of the ruling regimes in the Muslim world as illegitimate and deserving of overthrow. Immediately upon returning home, he began to organize an effort to overthrow the communist government of South Yemen (People's Democratic Republic of Yemen),

---

[3] These details on bin Laden's early career are taken from Lawrence Wright, *The Looming Tower: Al-Qaeda and the Road to 9/11* (New York: Alfred A. Knopf, 2006), Chapters 4–6; and from Peter L. Bergen, *Holy War Inc.: Inside the Secret World of Osama bin Laden* (New York: Free Press, 2001), Chapter 2.

[4] Wright, *The Looming Tower*, Chapter 6; Coll, *Ghost Wars*, Chapters 9–10; Rubin, *The Fragmentation of Afghanistan*, Chapter 12.

[5] Coll, *Ghost Wars*, pp. 87–88, 153. Ahmad Badeeb, a high-ranking official in Saudi Arabia's General Intelligence Department (the Saudi equivalent of the CIA), said of his relationship with bin Laden during the Afghan jihad: "I loved Osama and considered him a good citizen of Saudi Arabia" (p. 87). See also Wright, *The Looming Tower*, p. 154.

recruiting and funding volunteers to infiltrate the country and begin a guerrilla war. He continued those efforts after the unification of the two Yemeni states in May 1990 because the communists were included in the new governing coalition. The Saudi government quickly put an end to this venture, the first time bin Laden had been brought up short by a Saudi establishment that had, until then, celebrated him.[6]

The Afghan experience also broadened bin Laden's view of the crisis of the Muslim world. Peshawar, the headquarters of the Afghan resistance, became the equivalent of an international Islamic university of jihad. Volunteers came not only from the Arab world, but also from Pakistan, India, Chechnya, Central Asia, Southeast Asia – all over the Muslim world. Bin Laden learned that Muslims were being attacked not only in Afghanistan and Palestine, the favorite cause of most Arabs, but in Central Asia, Kashmir and the Philippines as well. Afghanistan taught him that the jihad was global, not local, and that Islam was under threat everywhere.

Second, during his time in Afghanistan bin Laden developed the organizational networks that would underpin al-Qaeda. It was there that he recruited the followers who would form the organization at its outset. The recruiting and fundraising networks he developed in the Afghan jihad came to support his subsequent activities. He got to know Afghan leaders who would provide him a base in the 1990s when he could no longer remain in the Arab world. Without the Afghan experience, he could not have built the al-Qaeda organization.

Third, and perhaps most importantly politically, the Afghan experience gave bin Laden an exalted view of what he and his movement could accomplish. In his mind and in the minds of his followers, they had not merely defeated a superpower. After the collapse of the Soviet Union in 1991 they could say that they had *destroyed* a superpower. Heavily out-manned and outgunned, but armed with faith in God, the *mujahidin* had performed a miracle. In that light, it is not so strange that bin Laden could think that he could take on the United States. The success of the Afghan jihad was an object lesson to many in the Arab world who had been disappointed by the political and military failures of other Arab ideologies. It was the most important recruiting tool bin Laden had.

These changes in bin Laden's ideology, organizational role and political ambitions were still inchoate on his return to Saudi Arabia. The Gulf War helped to crystallize them. Riyadh's decision to invite American and other foreign forces into the kingdom infuriated bin Laden. He proposed to

---

[6] Wright, *The Looming Tower*, pp. 153–54; Coll, *Ghost Wars*, pp. 221–22.

senior Saudi princes that he raise an army of *mujahidin* to expel Iraqi forces from Kuwait. He was received respectfully but the Saudi leaders were incredulous at his proposal. When one pointed out to him the size of the Iraqi army, he replied, "We pushed the Soviets out of Afghanistan." Bin Laden also confronted the Saudi clerics who issued a *fatwa* approving the regime's decision to invite the foreign forces, with as much effect as his offers to the princes.[7] The presence of American forces in Saudi Arabia turned him against his own regime and the United States.

In July 1994 bin Laden established an office in London, the Committee of Advice and Reform (ARC), to publicize his critique of the Saudi regime. In its founding declaration, the committee was highly critical of the regime, blaming it for the "scandalous decline" of the country and accusing it of "defaming the image of Islam and making war against those who call for Islam and work for it."[8] Over the course of the declarations that followed, bin Laden came closer and closer to declaring the Al Saud an apostate regime. He focused particularly on its treatment of religious scholars (the regime had arrested a number of the activist clergy in 1993 and 1994), its support for the communist secessionists in the Yemeni civil war of the summer of 1994 and its participation in the Arab–Israeli peace process. Finally, in a ten-page declaration (no. 17) dated August 3, 1995, he cut whatever thin thread kept him attached to the regime. He addressed King Fahd directly, accusing his regime of "departing ... from the requirements of 'no god but God' and its necessities which are the difference between unbelief and faith." His indictment made two general charges, that the king governed outside Islamic law and that his regime was in thrall to the infidels and hostile to the Muslims.[9]

Bin Laden could afford to take such a confrontational tone with the Al Saud, because he had left Saudi Arabia some years earlier. In either 1991 or early 1992 he returned to Pakistan and then settled in Sudan. It was from Sudan that he began his campaign against American influence in the Muslim world. Al-Qaeda operatives planted explosives near hotels in Yemen in December 1992 which were believed to house American troops

---

[7] Wright, *The Looming Tower*, pp. 154–58, quote on p. 158; Coll, *Ghost Wars*, pp. 222–23.

[8] I have a copy of the founding declaration of the ARC, along with a covering note signed by bin Laden announcing the establishment of its London office. I received it by fax in July 1994, probably because I was on the fax list of the Committee for the Defense of Legitimate Rights, an earlier Saudi opposition effort that had set up an office in London. For a careful assessment of the ARC, see Mamoun Fandy, *Saudi Arabia and the Politics of Dissent* (New York: Palgrave, 1999), Chapter 6.

[9] The quotes are from the copy of Declaration No. 17 in my possession. Wright contends that bin Laden tried to maintain a cordial relationship with Crown Prince Abdallah, sending him a letter in 1995 on the possibility of reconciliation: *The Looming Tower*, pp. 199, 201–10.

being deployed to Somalia. Bin Laden also claims to have sent al-Qaeda fighters into Somalia against American troops. He broadened his array of contacts with jihadist and extremist groups in Africa, the Middle East, Southeast Asia, Central Asia and Bosnia.[10] A number of Arab governments pressured the Saudis and the Sudanese to bring bin Laden to heel. King Fahd revoked his Saudi citizenship in March 1994 and ordered the bin Laden family to cut off his access to family funds.[11] As the pressure from Washington and Riyadh mounted, bin Laden's Sudanese hosts began to consider their guest more a liability than an asset. In May 1996 bin Laden departed Sudan and returned to Afghanistan.[12]

In September 1996 the Taliban consolidated their control of the country. They had no particular obligation to bin Laden, but they did have very close relations with Saudi Arabia. The Saudi government and the Pakistani intelligence service, the ISI (Inter-Services Intelligence), supported their formation and their efforts to impose order on the country. Saudi private donors helped to fund the schools in Pakistan from which the Taliban arose and recruited members. The Saudis saw in the Taliban not only a reliable partner, after being disappointed by their previous Afghan clients, but also an ideological ally that professed an austere brand of Sunni Islam very similar to Saudi Wahhabism. The Taliban asked Riyadh what they should do with bin Laden. The reply was that they should hold on to him and keep him quiet. In the meantime, bin Laden sought to ingratiate himself with his new hosts.[13]

Shortly after his arrival in Afghanistan, in August 1996, bin Laden issued his "Declaration of Jihad Against the Americans Occupying the Land of the Two Holy Mosques."[14] Since the jihad against the Soviet Union, many of the "Arab Afghan" veterans and those inspired by them had tried to replicate that success in Arab countries, seeking to replace what they saw as apostate regimes with "real" Islamic governments. They

---

[10] For a discussion of bin Laden's activities in Sudan, see Wright, *The Looming Tower*, pp. 174–75, 188–89; *The 9/11 Commission Report* (New York: W. W. Norton, 2004), pp. 57–60; and Daniel Benjamin and Steven Simon, *The Age of Sacred Terror* (New York: Random House, 2002), pp. 109–24.

[11] Wright, *The Looming Tower*, p. 195.

[12] Benjamin and Simon, *The Age of Sacred Terror*, pp. 131–33. The 9/11 Commission reports that Sudanese officials broached to the Saudi government the possibility of expelling bin Laden to Saudi Arabia, but only if the Saudis agreed to pardon him, which the Saudis refused: *The 9/11 Commission Report*, pp. 62–63, 110, note 6. Coll, *Ghost Wars*, says Sudanese sources report that the request for a pardon for bin Laden was not a condition for the turnover and that Saudi officials did not want bin Laden to return: pp. 324–25.

[13] Wright, *The Looming Tower*, pp. 226–29; Coll, *Ghost Wars*, pp. 294–97, 332.

[14] For an excerpt of the declaration in English, see Bruce Lawrence (ed.) and James Howarth (trans.), *Messages to the World: The Statements of Osama bin Laden* (London: Verso Press, 2005), pp. 23–30.

had no success in Algeria, Egypt, Saudi Arabia or anywhere else they mounted armed opposition to the state. Bin Laden himself had concentrated his energies mostly on altering the domestic politics of Saudi Arabia, with little to show for it. His 1996 declaration represented a strategic shift from giving priority to attacking local regimes to giving priority to attacking what he had come to see as their essential foreign ally, the United States.[15]

The declaration is notable for themes that characterized bin Laden's thought from that point. The first is the concentration on the United States and the "Judeo-Christian alliance" which he holds responsible for an international campaign against Islam. He mentions not only Iraq, Palestine and Lebanon, but also Tajikistan, Burma, Kashmir, India, the Philippines, Somalia, Chechnya and Bosnia as areas where Muslims suffer at the hands of the "blatant imperial arrogance of America." The second is his contention that "the greatest disaster to befall the Muslims since the death of the Prophet Muhammad" is the "occupation" of Saudi Arabia by American forces. The third is that the only solution to this problem of the entire Muslim world is to wage jihad against the United States, on the model of the victorious jihad against the Soviet Union in Afghanistan.[16]

In Afghanistan, bin Laden was able to recover his fortunes – reestablishing the fundraising networks he had developed during the Afghan jihad, setting up training camps and recruiting followers and, through shrewd use of the media, portraying himself as the center of a worldwide movement.[17] From a shaky beginning, he also developed a strong relationship with the Taliban leadership. In February 1998 he announced the formation of the "World Islamic Front for Jihad Against the Jews and the Crusaders." The Front brought together al-Qaeda with Ayman al-Zawahiri's Jihad Group from Egypt, another Egyptian jihadist group, a Pakistani group and a Bangladeshi group. Where the 1996 Declaration of Jihad was florid and verbose, the 1998 declaration of the World Islamic Front was terse and specific. Citing the American "occupation" of Saudi Arabia, American policy in Iraq and American support for Israel as evidence of "a clear declaration of war against God, His Messenger and the Muslims," the Front declared that "to kill the Americans and their allies – civilians and military – is an individual duty incumbent upon every

---

[15] For a discussion of the general turn from concentration on the "near enemy" to the "far enemy" in *salafi* jihadist circles, see Fawaz Gerges, *The Far Enemy: Why Jihad Went Global* (Cambridge: Cambridge University Press, 2005).

[16] Quotes from Lawrence and Howarth, *Messages to the World*, pp. 24–30.

[17] Wright, *The Looming Tower*, Chapters 15–16: Benjamin and Simon, *The Age of Sacred Terror*, pp. 144–45.

Muslim in all countries."[18] On August 7, 1998, al-Qaeda was able to achieve its first major attack against the United States with the bombings of the American embassies in Kenya and Tanzania. Those bombings killed 231 people, including 12 Americans, and wounded hundreds more.

Washington responded with cruise missile attacks on training camps in Afghanistan and on a factory in Sudan that reportedly belonged to bin Laden.[19] It also began to pressure the Taliban to deliver bin Laden for trial. Saudi Arabia had also concluded that bin Laden's presence in Afghanistan was more troublesome for them than they had anticipated. In June 1998, shortly before the embassy bombings, Prince Turki Al Faysal, the head of the kingdom's foreign intelligence agency, flew to Afghanistan to begin negotiations with the Taliban about handing over bin Laden. While the Taliban leader, Mullah Omar, was coy about his intentions, Prince Turki left under the impression that the Taliban were willing to do the deal. The Saudi relationship with the Taliban continued, including the supply of financial aid and equipment that allowed the Taliban to capture Mazar e-Sharif, the center of the Afghan Shi'i minority, in August 1998, amidst the slaughter of between 5,000 and 6,000 people. After the embassy bombings, Prince Turki returned to Afghanistan in September, accompanied by the head of Pakistan's ISI, to demand that Mullah Omar turn bin Laden over to Saudi Arabia. The Taliban leader refused. After that, Saudi Arabia withdrew its ambassador from Kabul, though American intelligence sources believed that wealthy Saudis continued to support bin Laden's jihad.[20]

Bin Laden was now ensconced in Afghanistan, protected by his growing relationship with the Taliban and benefiting from the global publicity that accompanied the embassy bombings. Planning for the 9/11 attacks began in early 1999.[21] Al-Qaeda operatives failed in a number of operations against American targets, but succeeded spectacularly in October 2000 in Yemen. On bin Laden's orders, an al-Qaeda team was able to severely damage the USS *Cole*, a guided missile destroyer at anchor in the harbor of Aden in Yemen. Seventeen American sailors died in the attack and thirty-nine were wounded.[22] The al-Qaeda offensive against the United States

---

[18] Quotes taken from Lawrence and Howarth, *Messages to the World*, pp. 58–62.

[19] The factory's connection to bin Laden has been questioned by a number of sources. See Bergen, *Holy War, Inc.*, pp. 123–26; and *The 9/11 Commission Report*, pp. 116–18. For a defense of the targeting of the factory, see Benjamin and Simon, *The Age of Sacred Terror*, Chapter 9.

[20] Coll, *Ghost Wars*, pp. 397–402, 414–15; Wright, *The Looming Tower*, pp. 266–68, 288–89.

[21] *The 9/11 Commission Report*, pp. 154–55.

[22] Wright, *The Looming Tower*, p. 331; *The 9/11 Commission Report*, pp. 190–93.

culminated with the attacks of September 11, 2001, on the World Trade Center in New York and the Pentagon in Washington.

9/11 and the Saudi–American relationship

The immediate ramifications of the 9/11 attacks for the international politics of the Persian Gulf were in the Saudi–American relationship. With the occasional exception (most notably the oil embargo of 1973–74), the relationship between Riyadh and Washington had been conducted far from the public eye, managed by elites on both sides who preferred it that way. After 9/11, Americans wanted to know how a country that had been so close to the United States, which American forces had gone to defend just a decade earlier, had produced both the mastermind of the attacks and most of the perpetrators. It is little wonder that, according to a poll taken in December 2001, only 24% of Americans viewed Saudi Arabia favorably and 58% unfavorably.[23]

Saudi reactions to 9/11 did little to reassure a shaken American public. The first response of officials in the Saudi government was to deny any Saudi responsibility for them, even to deny any Saudis were involved (noting that bin Laden, stripped of his citizenship, was no longer a Saudi).[24] The focus on Saudi Arabia in the American media led a number of Saudi officials, including Crown Prince Abdallah, to complain that the kingdom was being targeted in a "campaign" against it.[25] Americans felt aggrieved and looked to assign blame. The Saudis were the natural target. The Saudi leadership was in a defensive crouch, unwilling to admit to any, even unintentional and indirect, role in the sequence of events leading to 9/11, which infuriated Americans. What is remarkable, however, is how little the relationship has changed in the years since 2001. Elites on both sides worked to tone down the heated public rhetoric and maintain the relationship against its critics. The fact that the Saudi–American

---

[23] Those numbers basically reversed a pre-9/11 poll, taken in January 2001, in which 56% of those polled viewed Saudi Arabia favorably and 28% unfavorably (poll cited in Dr. James J. Zogby, "New Poll Shows Damage Done," December 24, 2001; accessed via "GulfWire" e-newsletter, www.arabialink.com).

[24] As late as December 2001, Saudi interior minister Prince Nayif ibn Abd al-Aziz Al Saud told an American reporter: "Until now, we have no evidence that assures us that they [Saudis on board the airplanes] are related to Sept. 11" (Douglas Jehl, "Saudi Minister Asserts That Bin Laden Is a 'Tool' of Al Qaeda, Not Its Mastermind," *New York Times*, December 10, 2001). It was not until February 2002 that Prince Nayif publicly admitted that Saudis were involved: "15 of 19 Suicide Hijackers were Saudi," *Associated Press*, February 6, 2002.

[25] For one example, see Karen DeYoung, "Saudis Seethe Over Media Reports on Anti-Terror Effort," *Washington Post*, November 6, 2001.

relationship was so little affected by an event as enormous as the 9/11 attacks is a testament to how central it is to the security strategies of each capital.

There is no denying that Saudi government policy did play a role in the events leading up to the attacks. During the Afghan jihad, it fostered an atmosphere in Saudi Arabia in which jihad was portrayed as a central, even *the* central, element of Islam. When the jihad in Afghanistan ended with the Soviet withdrawal, the Saudi government chose not to confront the ideological trend it had helped to create. It dealt sharply with *salafi* activists, such as bin Laden, who directly challenged the Al Saud's right to rule. It did not, however, do anything to rein in the jihadist ideas and networks created in the 1980s. It turned a blind eye to – and may even have been supportive of – efforts to redirect jihadist energies toward Bosnia, Chechnya, Kashmir and elsewhere. The top levels of the Saudi government ignored the global Islamic institutions they had created and fostered, allowing bin Laden sympathizers and other jihadists to gain control of parts of those institutions. Saudi decision-makers did little to monitor fundraising for Islamist causes.[26] They also ignored American intelligence community requests for greater information sharing on al-Qaeda.[27]

There is no evidence that anyone in the Saudi government supported bin Laden's attack on the United States or had any knowledge of it.[28] But it is equally clear that the Saudi political system permitted the fostering of resilient networks of support for Islamist extremism. The Bush administration might have concluded that it needed to pressure Riyadh for fundamental changes both at home and in the global Muslim institutions it supported – to treat the Saudis as a potential enemy rather than as a

---

[26] The 9/11 Commission, while exonerating the Saudi government of direct support for al-Qaeda, went on to say: "This conclusion does not exclude the likelihood that charities with significant Saudi government sponsorship diverted funds to al Qaeda" (*The 9/11 Commission Report*, p. 171). A task force of the Council on Foreign Relations concluded in October 2002 that "for years, individuals and charities based in Saudi Arabia have been the most important source of funds for Al-Qaeda. And for years, Saudi officials have turned a blind eye to this problem" (Council on Foreign Relations, *Terrorist Financing: Report of an Independent Task Force* [New York: Council on Foreign Relations Press, 2002], p. 15).

[27] "To our great frustration, the Saudis, who probably held more keys to unlocking the inner workings of al-Qa'ida than any other liaison service, were slow-rolling us on the feedback we kept requesting. Finally, at our request, Dick Cheney called the Saudi crown prince to break the logjam": George Tenet (with Bill Harlow), *At the Center of the Storm: My Years at the CIA* (New York: Harper Collins, 2007), p. 149. Tenet was referring to the pre-9/11 period.

[28] The 9/11 Commission reported: "we have found no evidence that the Saudi government as an institution or senior Saudi officials individually funded the organization [al-Qaeda]" (*The 9/11 Commission Report*, p. 171).

long-time ally. It did the opposite. In the face of both mass and elite opinion that was decidedly anti-Saudi, the administration worked to shield the bilateral relationship from political pressure and went out of its way to strengthen ties with Riyadh.

President Bush had some work to do on that score. His hands-off policy in the Arab–Israeli conflict had frustrated Riyadh. Israel's military move into the West Bank in the spring of 2001, and the lack of American response to that move, prompted Crown Prince Abdallah to write a strongly worded letter to Bush in August 2001. He said that differences between the two countries on the issue had grown so great that, "from now on, you have your interests and the kingdom has its interests, and you have your road and we have our road."[29] Saudi public opinion in the wake of 9/11 was strongly anti-American, as many Saudis saw the American war on terror as a war against Islam.[30] Reflecting the strained relations at both the public and governmental levels, the Saudi government very publicly denied American forces the right to use Saudi bases for the air campaign in Afghanistan (which began in October 2001), even while quietly allowing the United States to use the command-and-control center at Prince Sultan Airbase, south of Riyadh, to coordinate that campaign.

The repair job began with a Saudi–American summit in April 2002 at the president's home in Crawford, Texas. Crown Prince Abdallah, who in May 2001 had turned down an invitation to the White House, led the Saudi delegation, indicating that Riyadh was also anxious to avoid continued deterioration of the relationship. Just one month before, he had announced a Saudi initiative on the Arab–Israeli peace process, proposing that all Arab states recognize Israel if it withdrew from the occupied territories and a Palestinian state were established. While the proposal was a non-starter on the diplomatic front, it signaled that Riyadh wanted to improve its image in Washington. After the Crawford summit, more formalized channels of intelligence sharing between the two governments were established. The Saudis began to take steps Washington had urged regarding terrorist financing.[31] While Riyadh counseled the Bush administration not to go to war in Iraq, it quietly cooperated with Washington's war plan. It allowed American special forces to use Saudi bases near the

---

[29] Sulayman Nimr, "Qisat al-rasa'il al-mutabadil bayn al-amir abd allah wa bush" [The Story of the Letters Exchanged Between Amir Abdallah and Bush], *al-Hayat*, November 6, 2001, p. 7.

[30] Richard Burkholder, "The US and the West – Through Saudi Eyes," Gallup Tuesday Briefing, August 6, 2002, www.gallup.com/poll/tb/goverpubli/20020806.asp.

[31] Rachel Bronson, *Thicker Than Oil: America's Uneasy Partnership with Saudi Arabia* (New York: Oxford University Press, 2006), pp. 232–47; Tenet, *At the Center of the Storm*, pp. 247–50.

Iraq border (without announcing this publicly) and American planners once again to use the command-and-control center at Prince Sultan Airbase to manage the air campaign. Riyadh also permitted American warplanes unimpeded use of Saudi airspace.[32] A second summit between Bush and Abdallah, again at Crawford, in April 2005 cemented the recovery of the relationship, with both sides describing it as a great success.[33]

The relationship between the United States and Saudi Arabia was not completely unchanged by the events of 9/11 and the subsequent Iraq War. In April 2003 the United States announced that it was ending its military operations in Saudi Arabia and withdrawing nearly all of its forces from Prince Sultan Airbase.[34] An American air wing had operated out of Saudi Arabia, patrolling southern Iraq, since the end of the Gulf War. Its departure was a backhanded recognition that the American military presence in the kingdom had become a lightning rod of opposition, a core of bin Laden's critique of the regime. Saudi officials had mixed feelings about the departure, relieved that they could no longer be pilloried for the American presence but worried that the American departure might seem a sign of weakening of US support for the regime. They also noted that the regional American air command-and-control center moved to the new American base in Qatar, signaling that the smaller Gulf monarchies would play a larger role in American regional strategy.

For a brief time the United States also publicly pressured the Saudi regime on the issue of democratic reform. This rather mild pressure for democratic reform was unprecedented in the Saudi–American relationship.[35] It led to the very minor initiative of elections to Saudi municipal councils (only half the members elected; the other half appointed by the government) in 2005. The Saudis had their own worries about the United States and its policies in the region. American policy in Iraq had strengthened Iran's regional role and placed Iranian allies in control of Iraqi politics. Riyadh worried about Tehran's efforts to spread its influence throughout the Arab world and Washington's unwitting assistance to Iranian ambitions. Arab–Israeli issues, as usual, led to some tensions.

[32] Michael Dobbs, "Saudi Rulers Walk Political Tightrope; Support for US Played Down at Home," *Washington Post*, March 14, 2003, p. 23; Craig Smith, "Reluctant Saudi Arabia Prepares Its Quiet Role in the US-led War on Iraq," *New York Times*, March 20, 2003.
[33] Bronson, *Thicker Than Oil*, p. 244.
[34] Mohammed Alkhereiji, "US Troops to Leave," *Arab News*, April 30, 2003.
[35] Some accounts of the history of the relationship contend that the John F. Kennedy administration pushed the Saudis for domestic reform. A careful look at the documents by Robert Vitalis has debunked that widely held idea: *America's Kingdom: Mythmaking on the Saudi Oil Frontier* (Stanford: Stanford University Press, 2007), Chapter 8.

However, the ultimate proof that the bilateral relationship had returned to steady ground was the American proposal of 2007 to sell the Saudis (and the smaller Gulf monarchies) $20 billion in weapons. With Iran a threat and Iraq a mess, Saudi Arabia was still the most important American ally in the Persian Gulf. For the Saudis, facing a chaotic Iraq and a resurgent Iran, the American security guarantee was still seen as its ultimate insurance policy. When it comes to Saudi–American relations, the more things change, the more they stay the same.

The Iraq War

The full effect of the post-9/11 change in American foreign policy in the Gulf came to be focused not on Saudi Arabia, but on Iraq. Chapter 6 discusses in detail the Bush administration's decision-making process on the war. Here I provide a brief narrative of events from 9/11 to the American defeat of Saddam's regime, and then a somewhat fuller discussion of the American occupation of Iraq.

The immediate focus of the Bush administration after the 9/11 attacks was on Afghanistan, al-Qaeda's base, and the Taliban government, bin Laden's ally. On October 7, 2001, the United States began air strikes. American special forces cooperated with the Northern Alliance, the most powerful Afghan opposition group, to drive the Taliban out of the country's major cities. On November 12, Kabul fell to the Alliance. On December 6, the southern city of Kandahar, Taliban leader Mullah Omar's power base, was captured. Bin Laden, Mullah Omar and their followers retreated to the mountainous area of the Afghan–Pakistan border. On December 22 the new government of American ally Hamid Karzai assumed power in Kabul. It was a remarkably swift military success, in the country that had frustrated the Soviet Red Army for nearly a decade. The Bush administration entered 2002 supremely confident and disdainful of critics who questioned the wisdom of its military plans.

Even while the United States was fighting to topple the Taliban, Washington was beginning to focus on Iraq. Before the end of September 2001 President Bush ordered the Pentagon to begin planning for a potential war against Iraq.[36] The State of the Union address in January 2002 marked the beginning of the public campaign to muster support for an attack on Iraq. President Bush identified Iraq, along with Iran and North Korea, as an "axis of evil" which supported terrorism and was developing weapons of mass destruction, which they could pass on to

---

[36] Glenn Kessler, "US Decision on Iraq Has a Puzzling Past," *Washington Post*, January 12, 2003, p. 1. See also *The 9/11 Commission Report*, p. 335.

terrorists.[37] During the spring of 2002 there were numerous media reports that military plans against Iraq were progressing.

The administration took a short detour on the road to war beginning in the summer of 2002. Secretary of State Colin Powell convinced President Bush to seek a United Nations cover for any action against Saddam Hussein.[38] The president used his address to the General Assembly in September 2002 to challenge the world body to force Saddam Hussein to implement the disarmament resolutions dating back to the Gulf War, hinting broadly that, if it did not, he would do so on his own. But he also pledged that Washington would work through the UN Security Council to seek the necessary resolutions for new action against Saddam. Iraq just days later agreed to the return of UN weapons inspectors. Just days later, also, the White House released its National Security Strategy, laying out the rationale for preventive war against countries that the United States believed were developing weapons of mass destruction and had links to terrorist groups.[39] The race between war preparation and diplomacy was now on.

The president and other members of the administration gave a number of speeches in the fall of 2002 asserting a link between Saddam Hussein and al-Qaeda and charging Iraq with developing WMD, including nuclear weapons. Just weeks before the congressional elections, on October 20, 2002, both houses of Congress approved resolutions authorizing the use of force against Iraq by margins much wider than the congressional votes of 1991 approving the Gulf War. On November 8 the UN Security Council unanimously adopted Resolution 1441. The United States and Britain had wanted the resolution to authorize force against Iraq if it did not cooperate fully with the weapons inspectors, who returned to Iraq that month. France and other members of the council objected to "automaticity" regarding the use of force and held out for another Security Council review before force was authorized. The end result did include an explicit reference to further Security Council review, but also stated that, if Iraq did not cooperate fully with the inspectors, it would be in "material breach" (the code-word for use of force) of council

---

[37] The text of the speech can be found at http://archives.cnn.com/2002/ALLPOLITICS/01/29/bush.speech.txt/. "No presidential oratory had been more bellicose in the forty-one years since John F. Kennedy committed the United States to 'pay any price, bear any burden' at the height of the Cold War": Todd S. Purdum and the staff of the *New York Times*, *A Time of Our Choosing: America's War in Iraq* (New York: Henry Holt, 2003), p. 22.

[38] Purdum *et al.*, *A Time of Our Choosing*, pp. 40–45, subsequently confirmed by a number of other sources.

[39] The document can be found at www.globalsecurity.org/military/library/policy/national/nss-020920.htm.

resolutions.[40] Washington would assert that 1441 gave it the legal authority to attack Iraq, but this was a decidedly minority opinion at the UN.

As American war preparations continued, with troops being deployed to Kuwait by the end of 2002, diplomatic attention focused on the weapons inspectors. The new UN inspections organization, UNMOVIC (the United Nations Monitoring, Observation, Verification and Inspection Commission), was headed by Swedish diplomat Hans Blix. The Iraqi nuclear file was still in the hands of the International Atomic Energy Agency (IAEA), headed by Egyptian international civil servant Mohammed El Baradei. On December 7, 2002, the Iraqi government, as required by UNSC 1441, released 12,000 pages of documents that it claimed demonstrated that it had no weapons of mass destruction. Blix told the Security Council on December 19 that Baghdad had "missed an opportunity" to give a full accounting of its WMD programs and pointed to a number of "inaccuracies" in the Iraqi claims.[41] However, both Blix and El Baradei reported on a number of occasions in early 2003 that Iraq was cooperating with the inspectors. Blix was cautious in his overall assessments of Iraq's chemical and biological programs, pointing to progress but also finding that Iraq was not fully compliant with Security Council resolutions. El Baradei was more definitive in his judgment that Iraq was not reconstituting its nuclear program.[42]

While the initial Iraqi declaration, and the skepticism which greeted it, strengthened Washington's case for war, the subsequent reports by Blix and El Baradei gave support to the countries on the Security Council, led by France and Germany, that were hesitant to approve the use of force. In response, US secretary of state Colin Powell gave an extended presentation of American evidence of Iraq's continuing WMD programs and links to al-Qaeda to the Security Council on February 5, 2003. Both Blix and El Baradei called into question some of Powell's evidence in subsequent reports to the council. Powell's presentation strengthened domestic support for the administration's policy, but swayed none of the foreign governments represented on the council. It became increasingly clear that the Bush administration would not be able to get a council resolution explicitly authorizing the use of force against Iraq.

In the absence of UN authorization, the Bush administration emphasized that it had the support of a number of countries in its Iraq policy.

[40] The text of the resolution can be found at http://daccessdds.un.org/doc/UNDOC/GEN/N02/682/26/PDF/N0268226.pdf?OpenElement. See also Purdum *et al.*, *A Time of Our Choosing*, pp. 60–62.

[41] Purdum *et al.*, *A Time of Our Choosing*, p. 65.

[42] Purdum *et al.*, *A Time of Our Choosing*, pp. 63–69.

Britain was Washington's closest partner, with Prime Minister Tony Blair articulating the case against Iraq with his customary eloquence and 45,000 British forces ready to join the Americans in the invasion. Spanish prime minister José María Aznar and Italian prime minister Silvio Berlusconi were also strong public supporters of the war effort. Both sent small military contingents to support the occupation of Iraq, though their soldiers did not participate in the invasion. A number of other countries offered political support and token forces for the invasion (Poland, Australia and Denmark) or sent forces to Iraq subsequently to support the American occupation (most notably, South Korea, Ukraine and the Netherlands among thirty-five participating countries). However, unlike the Gulf War, there was nothing like an international consensus supporting the military campaign. Russia and China both were opposed. Major NATO allies France and Germany were in vocal opposition.

In the Middle East itself, support for the American war effort was muted, in contrast to the open support from many Arab states in the Gulf War. Kuwait was the only Arab country to participate publicly in the campaign, serving as the jumping-off point and rear echelon base of the invasion. Both Saudi Arabia and Jordan opened their territory to small contingents of American special forces, and Riyadh allowed the United States to use its sophisticated air command-and-control center at Prince Sultan Airbase to coordinate the air war. But neither of these countries publicized their limited military cooperation with Washington. American warships transited the Suez Canal, but no Egyptian troops participated in the campaign. The Mubarak government, which had organized Arab support for the United States in the Gulf War, signaled its opposition to the Iraq campaign. The smaller Gulf monarchies permitted American forces to use their facilities for logistical and staging purposes, though like the Saudis they kept this quiet. The recently elected Justice and Development Party (AKP) government in Turkey pledged to allow American forces to use Turkish territory to enter northern Iraq. AKP, the moderate successor to a series of banned Islamist parties, had won a stunning electoral victory in 2002. Given the party's Islamist roots, Prime Minister Recep Tayyib Erdogan was particularly keen to reaffirm his commitment to close Turkish–American relations. However, in an embarrassing political setback for Erdogan, the Turkish parliament voted down the motion to allow the American forces into the country.

With this limited "coalition of the willing," the United States went to war. On March 17, 2003, President Bush publicly announced that Saddam Hussein had forty-eight hours to leave Iraq or face war. On the evening of March 19 (March 20 in Iraq), the United States launched an air strike on a target where Saddam Hussein was thought to be, hoping to end the conflict with a quick decapitation stroke.[43] American and British units crossed the border from Kuwait into Iraq in force hours thereafter. On March 21 American aircraft and missiles began bombing Baghdad in a campaign of "shock and awe," aimed at breaking Saddam's regime's will to resist.

After initial advances by the American forces in the first days of the conflict, progress slowed in the last week of March. Iraqi units, some regular forces but others part of paramilitary groups of regime loyalists which conducted guerrilla operations, engaged the Americans in the southern cities of Najaf and Nasiriya and harassed the exposed American lines of communication. British forces, tasked with taking the southern port city of Basra, were also encountering resistance. Those setbacks were brief. Najaf, where American forces had encountered the stiffest resistance, fell to the invaders on April 1. By April 4 Baghdad International Airport was in American hands. On April 9 American forces secured Baghdad and, in a bit of political theater broadcast around the world, helped Iraqis pull down a large statue of Saddam Hussein in a downtown square. On April 10, Kurdish forces allied with the United States took control of Kirkuk, and the next day Kurdish and American forces captured Mosul. On April 13 American forces attacked Saddam's home town, Tikrit. The next day, with Iraq seemingly under the control of American and allied forces, the Pentagon announced the end of major offensive attacks. On May 1, 2003, in a display of hubris that he later admitted regretting, President Bush stood on the deck of an American aircraft carrier under a banner reading "Mission Accomplished" and declared the end of "major combat operations" in Iraq.

Saddam Hussein's decision-making in the lead-up to the war and in the war itself seems almost irrational. However, viewed through his own distorted lens of regime security concerns, it becomes more comprehensible. The authors of the US military study on Iraqi perceptions in the war, who had access to the transcripts of interrogations of regime figures seized by American forces and to captured Iraqi documents, state that, even as American and international forces were massing on his border in late 2002 and 2003, Saddam assumed that "the greatest danger the regime faced was an internal coup."[44]

The most important puzzle surrounding Saddam's decision-making concerns the seemingly irrational policy on weapons of mass destruction.

---

[43] Michael R. Gordon and Bernard E. Trainor, *Cobra II: The Inside Story of the Invasion and Occupation of Iraq* (New York: Pantheon, 2006), Chapter 9. This is the most comprehensive source on the military campaign in Iraq outside official unit and service histories. The short narrative of the fighting presented here is based on it.

[44] Kevin M. Woods *et al.*, *The Iraqi Perspectives Report* (Annapolis, MD: Naval Institute Press, 2006), p. xvii. The authors of this report did not have access to Saddam himself. He was captured after they had completed the interview phase of their work: p. 179.

It is clear that he made the decision during the early to mid-1990s to suspend his nuclear, chemical and biological weapons programs. He wanted to maintain the infrastructure for such programs, so he would have the option to renew them if circumstances changed, but the combination of international pressures and intrusive weapons inspections led Saddam to believe that he had to suspend the programs themselves.[45] However, Saddam wanted all sorts of parties to believe that he actually did have WMD. He and the people around him thought that chemical weapons and missiles were critical to their ability to emerge from the Iran–Iraq War still in power. They also saw fear of WMD as playing a deterrent role in 1991, making the Americans wary about continuing the fight up to Baghdad. The regime had used chemical weapons on domestic opponents, both in Iraqi Kurdistan at the end of the Iran–Iraq War and against Shi'i opponents during the *intifada* of March–April 1991.[46]

In the end, Saddam could not square the circle of being willing to forego WMD to escape sanctions but wanting other parties to believe that he had WMD to deter their hostile intentions against him. He tried to keep this ruse up far too long, apparently believing that the Americans must have known that he really did not have WMD.[47] It is important to note that as it became clear that the United States was intent on war, he effectively gave up on trying to have his WMD cake and eat it, too. He accepted the return of weapons inspectors to Iraq in November 2002. He ordered his military commanders and senior officials in December 2002 to "cooperate completely" with the inspectors.[48] With Washington intent upon war by then, it is hard to imagine that any degree of Iraqi cooperation with the weapons inspectors could have averted the conflict.

During the 1990s and up to the Iraq War of 2003, Saddam saw Iran as the greatest foreign threat to his regime.[49] He wanted the Iranians to

---

[45] "Comprehensive Report of the Special Advisor to the DCI on Iraq's WMD," September 30, 2004, www.cia.gov/library/reports/general-reports-1/iraq_wmd_2004/index.html (hereafter referenced as the Duelfer Report, after Charles Duelfer, the special adviser). See pp. 8–9 of the "Transmittal Message" section.

[46] "Former Iraqi officials concluded, time and time again, that the threat inherent in their WMD arsenal and weapons delivery systems helped preserve Saddam's regime": Duelfer Report, pp. 24, 29–33, quote on p. 33.

[47] "Senior aides told interrogators that Hussein was convinced the US intelligence agency [CIA] knew he had no illicit weapons. Hussein assumed that the CIA had penetrated his regime": Bob Drogin, "Through Hussein's Looking Glass," *Los Angeles Times*, October 12, 2004.

[48] Duelfer Report, pp. 62–63.

[49] This is the conclusion of both the Duelfer Report (p. 29) and Woods *et al.*, *Iraqi Perspectives Report* (p. 25). While both reports were based on largely the same set of evidence – interrogations of captured Iraqis – the fact that both groups came to the same conclusion independently strengthens the reliability of their judgment.

believe that he still had WMD, because he thought that WMD (and missiles) were central to keeping the Iranians at bay during the Iran–Iraq War. He saw Iran developing its own nuclear program. Saddam clearly feared another Iranian military attack on Iraq, but his focus on Iran was not limited to state-to-state military threats. A number of Iraqi officials told American interrogators that Iran's political and ideological threat, given the country's close ties to Iraqi Shi'a, was as important as its military threat.[50] Tariq Aziz told his captors that by 2002 the regime saw SCIRI and the Iraqi Shi'a in general as the greatest internal threat to the Ba'thist regime.[51]

The focus on domestic regime security continued even as it became increasingly clear that the United States was preparing to invade Iraq. The Iraqi military was configured to fight internal enemies and prevent military coups, not to counter an American invasion. The proliferation of special units and forces in the 1990s had divided military resources and made a coordinated defense plan almost impossible. However, these units were believed to increase regime security, since they reported directly to Saddam outside regular military channels.[52] Units tasked with the defense of Baghdad were not permitted to contact each other, for fear that their generals would plot a coup. Even the Republican Guard, believed by outsiders to be particularly committed to the regime, was not permitted to deploy in central Baghdad. Only the Special Republican Guard could enter the city as war loomed.[53] The authors of the US military's study of Iraqi perspectives concluded that "the overwhelming bulk of the evidence indicates that even with US tanks crossing the border, an internal revolt remained Saddam's biggest fear."[54]

The poor performance by the Iraqi military in 2003 was not only the result of fears of internal threats. Saddam Hussein also grossly misunderstood the nature of the American threat. It was not until December 2002 that he came to believe that the United States would strike him. Even then, he thought that the attack would be limited to the air, on the model of Operation Desert Fox in 1998, because of the American aversion to casualties.[55] Then, as it became clearer to him that a ground war was

---

[50] Woods *et al.*, *Iraqi Perspectives Report*, p. 25. "In fact, the link between the primary external threat (Iran) and the most significant internal one (Iraqi Shi'ites) was never far from the considerations of Saddam and his closest advisers."

[51] Woods *et al.*, *Iraqi Perspectives Report*, p. 26.

[52] Woods *et al.*, *Iraqi Perspectives Report*, pp. 48–56.

[53] Woods *et al.*, *Iraqi Perspectives Report*, pp. 27–28.

[54] Woods *et al.*, *Iraqi Perspectives Report*, p. 31.

[55] Duelfer Report, p. 32, interview with Saddam Hussein, and p. 67, interview with Tariq Aziz.

coming, he believed it would be limited to the south of Iraq, as was the case in 1991.[56] No one was willing to convey accurate information to him for fear of how he would react to bad news. He also intervened directly in military planning on a number of occasions, to the detriment of his defenses. As late as December 2002 he ordered a whole-scale revision of the longstanding military plans for defense of the country.[57] One can hardly imagine worse political leadership for a country facing a war.

The American war in Iraq was a success, if success is measured by overthrowing Saddam Hussein's regime. It was a swift and decisive victory. The campaign did not, however, secure the country as a whole. The security and administrative apparatus of the Iraqi state dissolved with the fall of the regime. Looting began in Baghdad almost immediately after American forces secured the city. Secretary of Defense Donald Rumsfeld famously responded to questions about the looting at an April 11, 2003, press conference by saying, "Stuff happens ... And it's untidy, and freedom's untidy, and free people are free to make mistakes and commit crimes and do bad things." However, on the ground American officers were feeling the erosion of control. "A finite supply of goodwill toward the Americans evaporated with the passing of each anarchic day," wrote an American Marine officer who served in Baghdad at the time.[58]

The American occupation of Iraq

The lack of American preparation for the post-war administration of Iraq was part and parcel of the rosy assumptions the Bush administration brought to the war itself. I discuss these assumptions in more detail in Chapter 6. It is sufficient here to note that the administration assumed that the post-war transition to a new Iraqi government would occur very quickly. The Iraqi regime would be removed, but the Iraqi state would continue to function. The Iraqi people, grateful to be liberated from a brutal dictatorship, would accept the new arrangement. Secretary of Defense Rumsfeld was insistent that the American forces would not commit to an extended stay in Iraq. After the fighting, General Tommy Franks (the commander of Central Command and the architect of the war plan) ordered his officers to prepare to withdraw their troops within sixty days. New units would arrive to stabilize the country, but they would not stay longer than 120 days. The deployment of the army's First Cavalry

---

[56] Duelfer Report, pp. 66–67; Woods *et al.*, *Iraqi Perspectives Report*, pp. 30–31.
[57] Woods *et al.*, *Iraqi Perspectives Report*, Chapter 4.
[58] Both this quote and the Rumsfeld quote can be found in Thomas E. Ricks, *Fiasco: The American Military Adventure in Iraq* (New York: Penguin, 2006), p. 136.

Division to Iraq, part of the original war plan, was canceled on April 21, 2003. The secretary of the army later said, "Our working budgetary assumption was that ninety days after completion of the operation, we would withdraw the first fifty thousand and then every thirty days we'd take out another fifty thousand until everybody was back."[59]

The transition to Iraqi rule envisaged by the Bush administration was to be implemented by a small team of American civilian administrators, called the Office of Reconstruction and Humanitarian Assistance (OHRA), headed by retired Army general Jay Garner. General Garner had commanded the post-Gulf War effort to protect the Kurdish areas of northern Iraq, but had no other experience in Iraq or the Arab world. Bureaucratic infighting set back efforts of the OHRA, established just a few months before the war, to prepare for its role.[60] Garner and the OHRA arrived in Baghdad on April 18, 2003. They were so unprepared that Garner did not even have a translator with him and had to dragoon a junior Foreign Service officer into the role.[61] Garner and his supervisors in the Pentagon foresaw a relatively short and easy transition. They thought that it would take about ninety days to reconstruct utilities, get ministries working again, appoint an interim government, get a constitution ratified and have elections.[62]

They were quite wrong. The collapse of authority in Iraq after the fall of the regime was complete (with the exception of the Kurdish areas, which had been autonomous from Baghdad since 1991). Looting was widespread. The Iraqi police melted away; looters helped themselves to what was left in the police stations. The United States was unable to repair the infrastructure of the country. Electricity was limited, water and sewer services were erratic. Civil servants stopped coming to work. On top of the chaos in Baghdad, in Sunni Arab areas of western Iraq an anti-American insurgency was beginning. On May 1, 2003, seven American soldiers in Fallujah were wounded in a grenade attack. The day before, American forces there had killed seventeen Iraqis and wounded more than sixty, firing into a demonstration against the American presence.[63] By July, General John Abizaid, General Franks' successor as head of Central Command, said his forces in Iraq were under attack from "a classic guerrilla-type campaign."[64]

---

[59] Gordon and Trainor, *Cobra II*, pp. 458–61, quote on p. 461.
[60] For a full and depressing discussion of the bureaucratic politics surrounding Washington's limited pre-war planning, see George Packer, *The Assassins' Gate: America in Iraq* (New York: Farrar, Straus and Giroux, 2005), Chapter 4; and Rajiv Chandrasekaran, *Imperial Life in the Emerald City: Inside Iraq's Green Zone* (New York: Alfred A. Knopf, 2007), Chapter 2. See also Ricks, *Fiasco*, pp. 102–04.
[61] This story was related to me by a member of General Garner's staff.
[62] Packer, *The Assassins' Gate*, pp. 132–34.   [63] Gordon and Trainor, *Cobra II*, p. 462.
[64] Gordon and Trainor, *Cobra II*, p. 489.

Like the war, the chaos in Baghdad was broadcast live into American living rooms. Moreover, as days turned into weeks after the fall of Saddam, it was becoming increasingly clear that the United States would not find the extensive caches of weapons of mass destruction that had been the most important public justification for the war. Saddam Hussein, who had escaped from Baghdad before the city fell to the Americans, was still at large. General Garner was ill equipped to deal with post-war Iraq and had nothing to do with the WMD fiasco, but he became the scapegoat for these early failures. He was unceremoniously removed from his post less than a month after his arrival in Baghdad. His replacement, Ambassador L. Paul Bremer, arrived in Baghdad on May 12, 2003, to head the Coalition Provisional Authority (CPA). His arrival signaled a shift in the Bush administration's approach to post-war administration. Gone were the ninety-day transition plans. Bremer came as a proconsul, to take control of Iraq, govern it directly and change its politics. He told the head of the UN office in Baghdad, "I am the government of Iraq now."[65] With the May 22 vote by the UN Security Council (Resolution 1483) recognizing the CPA as Iraq's interim authority, he had the international cover to do it.

The extent of the CPA's ambitions was evident from the beginning. On May 16, 2003, CPA Order No. 1 decreed that no member of the top four ranks of the Ba'th Party (which had already been dissolved by the American military authorities in April) could hold a government job, whether they had been implicated in violent or criminal activity or not. Bremer estimated that this involved 20,000 people; others thought it was closer to 40,000. Everyone agreed that it would strip the new Iraqi government of the experienced cadre of managers who had made the old one work. They just disagreed on whether that was a good thing or not. Bremer contends that CPA Order No. 1 was the single most popular decision among Iraqis that he made during his tenure. Many of his own staff, who had been working under Garner to restore the operations of Iraqi ministries, and Garner himself, who was still in Baghdad, vehemently objected to it.[66]

A second order, issued May 23, disbanded the Iraqi armed forces, special armed units of the old regime and the intelligence services. With the fall of the regime, the army fell apart, with whole units dissolving back

---

[65] L. Paul Bremer III, *My Year in Iraq* (New York: Simon & Schuster, 2006), p. 36.
[66] On the de-Ba'thification decision, see Bremer, *My Year in Iraq*, pp. 39–45; Chandrasekaran, *Imperial Life*, pp. 68–73; Packer, *The Assassins' Gate*, pp. 190–93; Ricks, *Fiasco*, pp. 158–61; Douglas J. Feith, *War and Decision: Inside the Pentagon at the Dawn of the War on Terrorism* (New York: Harper, 2008), pp. 428–31.

into society. During Garner's brief tenure in Baghdad, American officers had begun working with Iraqi officers to reconstitute at least part of the army. The CIA estimated that the majority of the army could have been recalled within a two-week period and put to useful work.[67] Both Bremer and the Pentagon civilians overseeing the occupation, however, thought that the melting away of the army gave them another opportunity for root-and-branch transformation of Iraqi society. Iraqi exile politicians and the Kurdish leadership, whose constituencies had been the victims of the armed forces during Saddam's regime, encouraged the United States in this direction. As was the case with the de-Ba'thification decree, many of the American military and civilians already working in Iraq were opposed to the measure and flabbergasted when it was announced. It turned over 300,000 soldiers into disgruntled, unemployed potential recruits for the developing insurgency. The reactions were immediate, with demonstrations by former soldiers in Baghdad, Mosul and elsewhere. Bremer decreed a few weeks later that the cashiered soldiers would be eligible for cash payments, but the damage had been done.[68]

Bremer took other steps to transform Iraq as well. In September 2003 the CPA issued sweeping economic regulations, opening up the Iraqi economy (except the oil sector) to foreign investment on the most liberal terms in the Arab world and restructuring the tax system to encourage private enterprise.[69] Given the declining security situation, nothing much came of this initiative, with few if any investors willing to risk their capital in the uncertainty of Iraq. Confusion within the CPA over how to deal with Iraq's state-controlled industrial sector helped to keep factories (many of which had been looted in the chaos of April 2003) shuttered for months, if not years.[70] Bremer also put a halt to a series of planned conferences of Iraqis, put together by Garner and Zalmay Khalilzad, the White House's special envoy to the pre-war Iraqi opposition, aimed at creating a transitional government.[71] Instead, Bremer appointed in July

---

[67] Tenet, *At the Center of the Storm*, p. 429.

[68] On the disbanding of the military, see Bremer, *My Year in Iraq*, pp. 53–60; Chandrasekaran, *Imperial Life*, pp. 73–77; Packer, *The Assassins' Gate*, pp. 193–96; Ricks, *Fiasco*, pp. 161–65; Gordon and Trainor, *Cobra II*, pp. 479–85; Feith, *War and Decision*, pp. 431–34.

[69] Rajiv Chandrasekaran, "Economic Overhaul for Iraq, Only Oil Excluded from Foreign Ownership," *Washington Post*, September 22, 2003.

[70] Chandrasekaran, *Imperial Life*, Chapter 6; Ali A. Allawi, *The Occupation of Iraq: Winning the War, Losing the Peace* (New Haven: Yale University Press, 2007), Chapter 6.

[71] Khalilzad contends that the failure to follow through with his plan was a lost opportunity to prevent the insurgency and to "put an Iraqi face" on the administration of the country: Roger Cohen, "The MacArthur Lunch," *New York Times*, August 27, 2007. On the evidence of the first two conferences, which were not attended by major figures in any

2003 a Governing Council to assist the CPA in administering the country; the Governing Council in turn appointed a cabinet to administer the Iraqi government in September 2003. It was never clear just what exactly the distribution of power and responsibility among the Governing Council, the cabinet and the CPA was to be, and the relationship was characterized by tension.[72]

In place of the Garner–Khalilzad series of meetings, Bremer proposed a constitutional convention, whose members would be selected by CPA-appointed regional and provincial councils. Once the constitution was written and approved, there would be elections to a parliament and a turnover of authority by the CPA to a new Iraqi government.[73] The members of the Governing Council thought they should be empowered immediately. Bremer, having appointed them, could handle them. What he could not handle, in the end, was the opposition of the most important Shi'i religious figure in the country, Ayatollah Ali al-Sistani. Al-Sistani was absolutely insistent that the Iraqi constitution could be written only by an elected assembly (as a majority of the Iraqi population, his co-religionists would control that process). In June 2003 al-Sistani issued a *fatwa* demanding an elected constitutional assembly. Al-Sistani's position made it impossible for Bremer to get the support of the Shi'i members of the Governing Council.[74]

As the political maneuvering within the Green Zone (the area of Baghdad housing the American occupation headquarters and important Iraqi government facilities, walled off from the rest of the city) continued in the summer and fall of 2003, a full-fledged insurgency was developing outside it. The violence at the outset came predominantly from Sunni Arab opponents of the new order, partisans of the ousted regime of Saddam Hussein in uneasy alliance with Sunni Arab Islamists. The insurgents brought the fight to Baghdad in August 2003, with deadly explosions at the Jordanian embassy (one of the United States' quiet Arab allies in the war) and at the UN office. In late August Ayatollah Muhammad Baqir al-Hakim, the leader of the Supreme Council of the Islamic Revolution in Iraq, was killed in a car bombing in Najaf that took the lives of 125 others as well. Al-Hakim's group, which had been created in Iran during the Iran–Iraq War, was the best organized Shi'i force in the country and was cooperating with the American occupation. Al-Hakim

---

of the political organizations taking hold in the country, Khalilzad might have been optimistic. See Chandrasekaran, *Imperial Life*, pp. 52–54, for a brief account of the Baghdad meeting. Feith shares Khalilzad's view: *War and Decision*, pp. 435–41.

[72] See, for one example, Bremer, *My Year in Iraq*, pp. 201–02.

[73] Bremer outlined his plan in an article in the *Washington Post*, "Iraq's Path to Sovereignty," September 8, 2003.

[74] Allawi, *The Occupation of Iraq*, pp. 210–11; Bremer, *My Year in Iraq*, Chapter 8.

himself had returned to Iraq from his two-decade exile in Iran only in May 2003. American combat deaths increased as summer turned into fall and the number of insurgent attacks grew.[75] Eighty-two American soldiers died in Iraq in November 2003, the highest monthly total to that time.[76]

The sense that things were getting worse, not better, in Iraq as the United States approached an election year in 2004 led to another change of direction in Washington. On November 15, 2003, Bremer and the Governing Council announced a new plan, which would turn sovereignty over to an Iraqi government by July 1, 2004. Acknowledging al-Sistani's power, it envisaged national elections before a permanent constitution was written. The United Nations, sidelined by the Bush administration in the early months of the occupation, was invited to play a central role in brokering the transition. After just a few weeks of General Garner and the ninety-day transition, and then a few months of Ambassador Bremer and the idea of American-directed, root-and-branch change in Iraqi society, the Bush administration switched course yet again.[77]

Into this political breach stepped the new UN envoy to Iraq, Algerian diplomat Lakhdar Ibrahimi. Ibrahimi convinced al-Sistani that elections could not be organized before the transfer of sovereignty. He brokered in June 2004 the appointment of a transitional Iraqi government, with a Shi'i ex-Ba'thist who had broken with Saddam in the 1980s, Iyad Allawi, as prime minister. The CPA and the Governing Council produced a Transitional Administrative Law (TAL) in March 2004 to serve as a bridge document until an Iraqi constitution was written.[78] On June 27, 2004, the CPA formally handed control of the country over to the new Iraqi government.

While political power was now formally in the hands of Iraqis, the American military was still fighting a growing insurgency. While Saddam himself was finally captured in December 2003, the overall security situation was deteriorating. April 2004 was a particularly difficult month. After the killing of four American security contractors and the defilement of their bodies (recorded by television cameras) in Fallujah, a town in the Sunni Arab area of western Iraq, American forces launched

---

[75] For an account of the beginning of the insurgency, see Ricks, *Fiasco*, Chapters 8–12; and Ahmed S. Hashim, *Insurgency and Counter-Insurgency in Iraq* (Ithaca: Cornell University Press, 2006), Chapters 1 and 2.

[76] Figures from the extremely useful compendium of data, updated monthly, maintained by Michael O'Hanlon of the Brookings Institution: "Iraq Index," www.brookings.edu/iraqindex, pp. 17–18, of the August 27, 2007 pdf.

[77] On the November 2003 course change, see Ricks, *Fiasco*, pp. 254–55; Chandrasekaran, *Imperial Life*, Chapter 10.

[78] The most complete account of the political machinations of this period is in Allawi, *The Occupation of Iraq*, Chapters 11, 12 and 16.

an offensive against the city that lasted for several weeks. Newly con-
stituted units of the fledgling Iraqi army, brought to the battle, refused to
fight. Fighting would continue there, on and off, for months, until
American forces launched another offensive in November 2004, which
took the city.[79]

At the same time, the CPA decided to confront the Shi'i leader
Muqtada al-Sadr. Al-Sadr was the son of a prominent Shi'i ayatollah,
Muhammad Sadiq al-Sadr, who had been killed by Saddam's regime in
1999. The younger al-Sadr, remarkably, was able to maintain his father's
networks in the ensuing years, while operating deeply underground in
Saddam's Iraq. He emerged during the American occupation as a major
figure in Shi'i politics, challenging both the established Shi'i leadership of
Ayatollah al-Sistani and SCIRI and the American authorities. He introduced himself to the American occupiers shortly after Saddam's fall when
his followers killed Ayatollah Abd al-Majid al-Khoei. Al-Khoei, from a
very prominent Shi'i religious family in Iraq (his father had been the
leading Shi'i cleric in Iraq until his death in 1992), had spent many
years in exile in London. With the support of the United States and
Britain, he had returned to try to assume a leadership role. On his first
visit to the Shi'i pilgrimage city of Najaf, al-Sadr's followers killed him.[80]
Al-Sadr built his following into a militia, called the Mahdi Army, which
asserted control over parts of the country, including a sprawling Shi'i
neighborhood in Baghdad that was originally called Saddam City,
renamed Sadr City after the war. He was a thorn in the side of both the
CPA and the Shi'i exile politicians who led SCIRI. In April 2004 the CPA
finally decided to move against him, closing his newspaper and arresting
one of his closest aides. In response, his followers took over a number of
cities in southern Iraq and battled coalition forces through June, with a
resurgence of fighting in August.[81]

As violence escalated, the political process continued. In January 2005
elections were held for the Constituent Assembly, which would write the
new Iraqi constitution. The electoral system was based upon proportional
representation, with voters choosing among party lists, and parliamentary
seats being allotted according to the overall percentage of the national vote
for each list. Sunni Arabs by and large boycotted the voting. Ayatollah

[79] On the Fallujah battles, see Ricks, *Fiasco*, pp. 330–46, 398–406; and Allawi, *The
Occupation of Iraq*, pp. 275–79.
[80] For an account of the murder of al-Khoei and the 2004 Sadrist uprising, see Packer, *The
Assassins' Gate*, pp. 312–27.
[81] Other accounts of the Sadrist uprising can be found in Ricks, *Fiasco*, pp. 337–38; Hashim,
Insurgency and Counter-Insurgency in Iraq, pp. 261–64; Allawi, *The Occupation of Iraq*,
pp. 266–75 and Chapter 18.

al-Sistani, his political prestige at its height, brokered an uneasy coalition of the major Shi'i groups – SCIRI, the Sadrists, the Da'wa Party (the oldest Shi'i opposition group in Iraq, which had borne the heaviest brunt of Saddam's oppression) and Shi'i independents. They ran as the United Iraqi Alliance (UIA). Masoud Barazani's KDP and Jalal Talabani's PUK put aside their history of rivalry and constructed a single Kurdish list, the Kurdish Alliance. Prime Minister Allawi put together his own cross-sectarian, cross-ethnic list, the Iraqi List. The Shi'i list won a smashing victory, taking 51% of the popular vote and 140 of the 275 seats in the Constituent Assembly. The Kurdish Alliance swept the Kurdish vote, with 27% of the popular vote and 75 seats. Allawi's Iraqi List, despite the advantages of incumbency, scored a disappointing 14.5% of the popular vote and 40 seats (See Table 3).[82]

The United Iraqi Alliance (UIA) and the Kurdistan Alliance quickly formed a governing coalition. However, it took more than two months of internal deliberations among the component factions of the UIA to form a government, and nearly a month more to obtain parliamentary approval. Finally, in late April 2005 Ibrahim al-Jaafari of the Da'wa Party formed Iraq's first elected government since the Hashemite monarchy. Earlier that month Talabani was elected president by the Constituent Assembly, the first Kurd to be head of state in modern Iraqi history. The assembly's main task was to write a permanent constitution. The resulting document reflected the Shi'i groups' fear of the kind of strong central authority that had oppressed them in the past and the Kurdish desire for maximum autonomy. Most Sunni Arab political leaders condemned the document, contending that its provisions for a federal system with strong provincial and regional governments would lead to Iraq's disintegration. They urged their supporters to go to the polls and vote "no" in the constitutional referendum of October 2005.[83]

The constitution was overwhelmingly approved, with nearly 79 percent of the vote. However, in two mostly Sunni Arab provinces, Anbar and Salahuddin, the constitution was rejected by overwhelming majorities. In the mixed province of Ninevah, including the city of Mosul, 55 percent voted "no."[84] With the new constitution approved, parliamentary elections were held in December 2005. Sunni Arab political groups

---

[82] For descriptions of the campaign, see Packer, *The Assassins' Gate*, Chapter 12, and Allawi, *The Occupation of Iraq*, Chapter 22. For the distribution of votes and seats, see *al-Hayat*, March 17, 2005, p. 5.

[83] For a good summary account of the politics behind the writing of the constitution, see Allawi, *The Occupation of Iraq*, Chapter 23.

[84] Referendum results from the Independent Electoral Commission of Iraq, Polling Results, Referendum Results, www.ieciraq.org/English/Frameset_english.htm.

Table 3 *Results of Iraqi elections of 2005*

List	Jan. 2005 popular vote	Jan. 2005 seats (of 275)	Dec. 2005 popular vote	Dec. 2005 seats (of 275)
United Iraqi Alliance	51%	140	41%	128
Kurdish Alliance	27%	75	22%	53
Accordance Front	boycott	boycott	15%	44
Iraqi List	14.5%	40	8%	25
National Dialogue Front	boycott	boycott	4%	11

participated this time. A coalition of Sunni Arab groups with shared Islamist political inclinations formed the Iraqi Accordance Front; a more secular but still exclusively Sunni list, the National Dialogue Front, tried to mobilize what was left of the old Ba'thist constituencies among Sunni Arabs. The UIA and the Kurdistan Alliance received the vast majority of the votes from Shi'i Arabs and Kurds. Once again, the only cross-sectarian, cross-ethnic list was Allawi's Iraqi List.[85]

As was the case after the January 2005 vote, the December 2005 vote was followed by an extensive period of horse-trading and deal-making before a new government was formed. In April 2006 Nuri al-Maliki, also of the Da'wa Party, replaced al-Jaafari as prime minister. While the core alliance between the UIA and the Kurdish Alliance provided the parliamentary backing for the new government, the government Maliki finally put together in May 2006 included ministers from all the major parties, including the Iraqi List and the Accordance Front, and from all the component parts of the UIA, including the Sadrists.[86] At least on the surface, it seemed that, after three relatively successful elections and the entrance of Sunni Arabs into the political process, Iraq was moving toward the rebuilding of political community.

Unfortunately, the progress at the institutional level was accompanied by a continuing deterioration of security on the ground and increased sectarian tensions between Arab Sunnis and Shi'a.[87] The

---

[85] For official results of the December 2005 parliamentary elections, see the Independent Electoral Commission of Iraq, Polling Results, December 15 Results, www.ieciraq.org/ English/Frameset_english.htm.

[86] Kathleen Ridolfo, "New Government Already Facing Doubters," Radio Free Europe/Radio Liberty, *Iraq Report*, Vol. 9, No. 21, May 26, 2006,www.rferl.org/reports/ iraq-report/2006/05/21-260506.asp.

[87] For a general discussion of trends in 2004 and 2005, see Allawi, *The Occupation of Iraq*, Chapter 21.

International Crisis Group, a respected international non-governmental organization (NGO) which has monitored Iraq closely since the 2003 war, said in a report issued in February 2006 that "2005 will be remembered as the year Iraq's latent sectarianism took wings, permeating the political discourse and precipitating incidents of appalling violence and sectarian 'cleansing.'"[88] That trend escalated in 2006. Weekly attacks as recorded by the American military command increased substantially from the beginning of 2005 through 2006 and into 2007.[89] Much of the violence in 2005 originated from Sunni Arab groups opposed to the United States' presence in the country. While the vast majority of the Sunni insurgents were Iraqis organized into indigenous Iraqi groups, al-Qaeda was able to recruit a small but extremely violent group of Iraqis and foreign fighters. Al-Qaeda in Iraq (AQI) was led by Abu Musab al-Zarqawi, the nom de guerre of Ahmad al-Khalayla, a Jordanian recruit to al-Qaeda who had fought in Afghanistan and traveled to Iraq shortly before the American invasion in March 2003. He not only encouraged attacks on the American forces, he also sought to enflame sectarian conflict by deliberately targeting Shi'i neighborhoods and holy places.[90]

The most spectacular of those attacks occurred in February 2006, when the Askariya Mosque in Samarra was bombed. The mosque contained the tombs of two of the twelve Shi'i imams and was a destination of Shi'i pilgrims. However, it was in a predominantly Sunni city and thus AQI members would have had easy access to it. The Askariya Mosque bombing snapped what had been the pattern of relatively restrained reaction by Shi'i militias. Now those militias, particularly Muqtada al-Sadr's Mahdi Army, struck back at Sunni Arab civilians with a vengeance. Formerly mixed sectarian neighborhoods and areas were subject to sectarian "cleansings," creating an internally displaced population of more than 2 million Iraqis to go along with the more than 2 million who had left the

---

[88] International Crisis Group, "The Next Iraqi War? Sectarianism and Civil Conflict," Middle East Report No. 52, February 27, 2006, www.crisisgroup.org/home/index.cfm?id=3980&l=1.

[89] See slide 3 in presentation by General David Petraeus to congressional committees in September 2007, http://graphics8.nytimes.com/packages/pdf/world/20070911_POLICY/Petraeus_Slides.pdf.

[90] The United States in February 2004 released a letter obtained in Iraq, purportedly from al-Zarqawi to Usama bin Laden, in which the former lays out his strategy for the conflict, which includes targeting Iraqi Shi'a: "targeting and hitting them [the Shi'a] in their religious, political and military depth will provoke them ... If we succeed in dragging them into the arena of sectarian war, it will become possible to awaken the inattentive Sunnis" (English translation at www.state.gov/p/nea/rls/31694.htm). While some have questioned the authenticity of the letter, it certainly conforms to the strategy pursued by AQI.

country and taken refuge abroad.[91] According to the NGO Iraq Body Count, which takes a conservative approach in documenting Iraqi civilian casualties, the period from March 2006 to March 2007 was the most violent twelve-month period for Iraqi civilians since the American invasion, with 26,540 confirmed civilian deaths, compared to 14,910 in the previous twelve-month period.[92]

The year 2006 ended with the execution by hanging of Saddam Hussein, who had been captured in December 2003 and sentenced to death by an Iraqi court in November 2006. His execution was presided over by partisans of Muqtada al-Sadr, who taunted the former dictator and chanted their leader's name as Saddam's body swung on the gallows.[93] The execution further alienated Iraqi and other Arab Sunnis from what appeared increasingly to be a sectarian Shi'i government in Baghdad. Al-Qaeda in Iraq appeared to be consolidating its control over a growing number of Sunni cities and towns, under the banner of their "Islamic State in Iraq."[94] While there were some successes for American forces during this period, most notably the killing of Abu Musab al-Zarqawi in June 2006, it seemed at the end of 2006 that things in Iraq, on both the security and the political planes, were spinning out of control.

There was a clear sense in Washington at this time that there had to be some change in Iraq policy. The Democratic Party, running on a platform of opposition to President Bush's Iraq policy, won control of both houses of Congress in November 2006. Later that same month, the bipartisan Iraq Study Group (ISG), headed by former secretary of state James Baker and former congressman Lee Hamilton, issued its long-awaited report. It called for a reduction in American forces in Iraq and a major diplomatic effort to engage Iraq's neighbors, including Iran and Syria, in a regional solution to the Iraq issue.[95] The Bush administration, however, took the

---

[91] The United Nations High Commissioner on Refugees reported in September 2007 that there were 2,256,000 internally displaced Iraqis and nearly as many who had taken refuge outside the country: UNHCR, "Statistics on Displaced Iraqis around the World," September 2007, www.unhcr.org/cgi-bin/texis/vtx/home/opendoc.pdf?tbl=SUBSITES&id=470387fc2.

[92] Iraq Body Count, "Year Four: Simply the Worst," March 18, 2007, www.iraqbodycount.org/analysis/numbers/year-four/.

[93] John Burns and Marc Santora, "US Questioned Iraq on the Rush to Hang Hussein," *New York Times*, January 1, 2007.

[94] Karen DeYoung, "Al Qaeda Allies Claim Bigger Base of Support in Iraq," *Washington Post*, December 23, 2006. For a short background account of the development of al-Qaeda in Iraq and the Islamic State of Iraq, see Joseph Felter and Brian Fishman, "Al-Qa'ida's Foreign Fighters in Iraq: A First Look at the Sinjar Records," Harmony Project, Combating Terrorism Center at West Point, United States Military Academy, December 2007, www.ctc.usma.edu/harmony/pdf/CTCForeignFighter.19.Dec07.pdf, pp. 3–6.

[95] The text of the ISG report can be found at www.usip.org/isg/iraq_study_group_report/report/1206/iraq_study_group_report.pdf.

opposite tack. On January 10, 2007, the president announced that he would increase the number of American forces in Iraq by 20,000 (the actual increase was closer to 30,000) to try to restore order first in Baghdad, then in other parts of the country. He appointed a new commander in Iraq, General David Petraeus, who had served with distinction earlier in the war and who had just rewritten the army's counter-insurgency manual. President Bush emphasized that the "surge" in American forces was aimed at reversing the trajectory of events in Iraq, in order to allow Iraq's politicians to work toward settlement of their outstanding issues.[96]

The "surge" strategy, combined with a new approach to counter-insurgency, succeeded in arresting the downward security spiral in Baghdad in the second half of 2007. The number of weekly attacks in Iraq as a whole peaked in June 2007, steadily decreasing to levels below those of before February 2006 (though not to zero) after that.[97] Anecdotal accounts of Baghdad's neighborhoods began to paint a picture of a slow return, if not to normalcy, at least to a state where the activities of everyday life were not life-threatening. Equally important to the improved security situation was the revolt among many Sunni Arabs against the excesses of al-Qaeda in Iraq and its Islamic State of Iraq. In the latter half of 2006, before the surge was announced, there were indications that many Sunnis were chafing under the Taliban-like social strictures which AQI was enforcing in areas under its control. By June 2007 American forces were actively cooperating with Sunni groups which had turned against AQI in Anbar province, supplying them with money, guns and logistical support.[98] The American command sought to replicate the success of the Anbar model in other Sunni-dominated and mixed provinces, including Sunni areas of Baghdad, recruiting forces of "concerned local citizens" from tribesmen and insurgents and paying them directly from American funds. By the end of 2007, there were between 65,000 and 80,000 men in these local forces, with plans to expand the number to 100,000.[99]

---

[96] For an account of how the Bush administration came to the "surge" strategy, see Bob Woodward, *The War Within: A Secret White House History, 2006–2008* (New York: Simon & Schuster, 2008).

[97] See slide 3 in presentation by General David Petraeus to congressional committees in September 2007, http://graphics8.nytimes.com/packages/pdf/world/20070911_POLICY/Petraeus_Slides.pdf.

[98] John F. Burns and Alissa J. Rubin, "US Arming Sunnis in Iraq to Battle Old Al Qaeda Allies," *New York Times*, June 11, 2007; Thomas E. Ricks, "Deals in Iraq Make Friends of Enemies," *Washington Post*, July 20, 2007.

[99] Alissa J. Rubin and Damien Cave, "In a Force for Iraqi Calm, Seeds of Conflict," *New York Times*, December 23, 2007.

The rise of what came to be called the Awakening movement among Sunnis and its campaign against AQI highlighted the increasing complexity of civil conflict in Iraq during 2006–07. Underneath the overlay of the strong Sunni–Shi'i sectarian conflict in Iraq were serious intra-sectarian conflicts. The rivalry between the two major Shi'i militias, the Mahdi Army of Muqtada al-Sadr and the Badr Brigade of the Supreme Council of the Islamic Revolution in Iraq, also grew more deadly. (SCIRI changed its name in May 2007 to the Islamic Supreme Council of Iraq, ISCI.) Two provincial governors in southern Iraqi provinces, both members of ISCI, were assassinated in August 2007.[100] Later that month Mahdi and Badr fighters squared off in the Shi'i holy city of Karbala during a Shi'i religious festival, leaving forty-nine people dead. The fighting led Sadr to announce a six-month halt to Mahdi Army operations to allow for reorganization, which was later extended through 2008.[101]

In 2008 Iraqi prime minister Maliki steadily increased his power, as the improved security situation allowed him to extend government control over more of Iraq. American–Iraqi military campaigns in Basra, Maysan province and Sadr City during the year targeted Mahdi Army elements, weakening Sadr's position and helping Maliki extend his power in these areas. Toward the end of 2008 Maliki sought out opportunities to confront his political allies, ISCI and the Kurdish parties, in an effort to consolidate his own power base.[102] The ultimate political direction of Iraq will be greatly affected by elections in 2009, at the provincial level and the national level. It remains to be seen whether those elections will allow Iraq to settle fundamental questions such as the relationship between regional and central governance, control over oil resources, the role of Islam in Iraqi politics and society, and sectarian tensions peacefully, or whether the improved security situation of 2008 was simply a pause in an Iraqi civil war.

The improved security situation in Iraq contributed to the surprising agreement in late 2008 on a timetable for American military withdrawal from Iraq. The Bush administration had rejected past calls for such a timetable. However, the legal authority under UN Security Council resolutions for the American presence in Iraq was set to expire at the end of 2008. Intense negotiations between the Maliki government and Washington yielded a Status of Forces Agreement (SOFA) in the fall of

---

[100] Megan Greenwall, "Governor Assassinated in Iraq's Oil-Rich South," *Washington Post*, August 21, 2007.
[101] Joshua Partlow, "Sadr Orders 'Freeze' on Militia's Actions," *Washington Post*, August 30, 2007.
[102] Alissa J. Rubin, "Iraq Unsettled by Political Power Plays," *New York Times*, December 26, 2008.

2008 which called for the withdrawal of American combat forces from major Iraqi cities by the end of June 2009 and the complete withdrawal of American combat forces from the country by the end of 2011.[103] The agreement was ratified by the Iraqi parliament in November 2008. It can be amended if both sides agree, but it lays out a timetable for American withdrawal not that different from the one proposed by presidential candidate Barack Obama, who took office as president of the United States in January 2009.

Regional political dynamics since the Iraq War: Iran, Saudi Arabia and the oil market

In a region whose history of great power interventions is replete with ironies, it should not be surprising that the state that benefited the most from the American wars in Afghanistan and Iraq was Iran. Both the Taliban and Saddam Hussein were serious opponents of the Islamic Republic. With their removal and the subsequent domestic turmoil in both countries, Tehran was able to extend its influence into Afghanistan and Iraq in ways unimaginable under the old regimes.[104] This shift in the regional power structure led to worries about Iranian power and intentions not only in Washington but also in Arab and European capitals. Those worries centered on the Iranian nuclear program and on Iran's cultivation of allies in the Arab world, and fueled a serious "cold war" between Tehran and Washington in the years after the Iraq War.

That cold war was not inevitable. We saw in the last chapter that, at the end of the Clinton administration, Iran chose not to respond to tentative feelers from Washington about a new relationship. In the wake of the 9/11 attacks and the Afghan and Iraq wars, it was the Iranian side that tentatively explored a new opening toward the United States. Iran cooperated with Washington's military campaign in Afghanistan. It encouraged its local Afghan allies to work with the United States. After the fall of the Taliban, Iranian representatives joined with those of the United States, the United Nations and other international actors in the negotiations in Bonn, Germany, which produced the new Afghan government under Hamid Karzai. Iranian leaders, including President Khatami, spoke publicly about the Afghan issue as the opportunity to open a new relationship

---

[103] Text of the agreement can be found at http://graphics8.nytimes.com/packages/pdf/world/20081119_SOFA_FINAL_AGREED_TEXT.pdf.

[104] "Not since the early nineteenth century had Iran's political reach been so extensive. They were seemingly on the cusp of empire, and even staunch [Iranian] nationalists found this tonic intoxicating": Ali M. Ansari, *Confronting Iran* (New York: Basic Books, 2007), p. 209.

Map 4 Iraq's provinces and major cities

with the Americans.[105] The United States used the cover of the Bonn negotiations to establish a direct bilateral channel to Iran, with diplomats from the two countries meeting regularly for some time thereafter.[106]

Flushed with its success in Afghanistan and confident that it could recreate the political realities of the Middle East, the Bush administration seemed to reject the Iranian initiative. In his January 2002 State of the

---

[105] Ray Takeyh, *Hidden Iran: Paradox and Power in the Islamic Republic* (New York: Times Books, 2006), pp. 119–24; Ansari, *Confronting Iran*, pp. 181–84.

[106] Flynt Leverett, *Dealing with Teheran: Assessing US Diplomatic Options toward Iran*, A Century Foundation Report, 2006, http://tcf.org/publications/internationalaffairs/leverett_diplomatic.pdf, p. 11. Leverett served on the National Security Council as senior director for Middle East affairs from March 2002 to March 2003, having previously held Middle East positions at the State Department and at the CIA. He subsequently became a vocal critic of Bush administration policy.

Union address, President Bush included Iran in the "axis of evil" with Iraq and North Korea. Iranian supreme leader Ayatollah Khamenei responded by referring to the "drunkard shouts of American officials."[107] The door appeared closed on this second initiative.

But appearances can be deceiving. Both Tehran and Washington, or, better put, some people in both governments, continued to explore the possibility of further cooperation. The channel established in Bonn did not end with the "axis of evil" speech.[108] The Bush administration used this channel in early 2003 to consult with Iran about the upcoming war with Iraq.[109] The debate over engaging the United States in Iran became so intense that in the summer of 2002 the head of the Tehran judiciary issued a directive outlawing "discussions about discussions with the United States," to no avail.[110] Shortly after the toppling of Saddam Hussein, the Iranian Foreign Ministry sent to Washington, through Swiss diplomatic channels, a proposal for direct and public talks aimed at a comprehensive settlement of outstanding issues between the two countries. The Iranian proposal offered to put on the table Iran's nuclear program and Iran's opposition to the Arab–Israeli peace process if the United States would put on the table its economic sanctions against Iran and its pressure for regime change. There were no commitments to policy changes in the document, but there were tantalizing hints of Iranian willingness to reconsider its positions on a number of issues.[111] It subsequently came to light that, at this same time, Iran offered to turn over to the United States high-value al-Qaeda targets detained in Iran, if the United States would exchange them for leaders of the Mujahidin e-Khalq in Iraq. The administration turned down the offer on the grounds that it would legitimize the Iranian regime.[112] In May 2003 Washington

---

[107] Takeyh, *Hidden Iran*, p. 129.   [108] Leverett, *Dealing with Teheran*, p. 12.
[109] Glenn Kessler and Walter Pincus, "One Step Forward, Direction Uncertain: US Notes Iran's Cooperation in Iraq War," *Washington Post*, April 18, 2003.
[110] Ansari, *Confronting Iran*, p. 190.
[111] This Iranian offer has been the subject of serious controversy in the United States. It was first mentioned by Leverett in his *Dealing with Teheran* (p. 12), which came out in the summer of 2006. See also Flynt Leverett and Hillary Mann, "What We Wanted to Tell You About Iran," *New York Times*, December 22, 2006. In February 2007 the *Washington Post* published a copy of the fax from the Swiss ambassador in Iran to the State Department that contained the Iranian proposal: Glenn Kessler, "2003 Memo Says Iranian Leaders Backed Talks," *Washington Post*, February 14, 2007. The memo was posted at www.washingtonpost.com/wp-srv/world/documents/us_iran_1roadmap. pdf. It was also posted by *New York Times* columnist Nicholas Kristof, along with more background information on contacts during 2002 between Iranian diplomats at the United Nations in New York and American officials: http://kristof.blogs.nytimes.com/2007/04/28/.
[112] Dafna Linzer, "Al-Qaeda Suspects Color White House Debate Over Iran," *Washington Post*, February 10, 2007.

terminated the low-profile, direct channel that had begun with the Bonn negotiations, contending that Iran was harboring al-Qaeda members who had fled from Afghanistan and who were involved in organizing attacks on housing complexes in Riyadh that month.[113]

If there was a post-9/11, post-Saddam Hussein possibility for a "grand bargain" between Iran and the United States, it ended in 2003. The Bush administration was in no mood to accommodate Iran. Iranian politics were also changing. The Khatami era was coming to an end. In 2004 Khatami's reformist coalition was dealt a serious defeat in parliamentary elections, with the clerical elite reasserting its control and new Islamist populist politicians taking control of parliament. In 2005 Mahmoud Ahmadinejad, a veteran of the Iran–Iraq War and mayor of Tehran, was elected president, soundly defeating former president Rafsanjani. Ahmadinejad, the first Iranian president to come from the foot soldiers of the revolution, hoped to revive the revolutionary spirit of Khomeini. He rejected the more moderate international course Khatami had followed, pledged his fealty to Khamenei and, unlike Rafsanjani, made it clear that he saw no need for any rapprochement with the United States. On the contrary, he pursued an aggressive rhetorical campaign against American influence in the region and made incendiary comments questioning the historical reality of the Holocaust and about the need for Israel to disappear from the regional map.[114]

Ahmadinejad's more aggressive rhetoric exacerbated the existing concerns in Washington about Iranian efforts to take advantage of the changed regional situation. The three major issues for the United States in facing the newly empowered Iran after 2003 were Iraq, Arab–Israeli issues and the Iranian nuclear program. As the security situation in Iraq deteriorated from 2003, American officials increasingly warned about Iranian influence in Iraq and blamed Iran for encouraging anti-American violence in the country.[115] Those allegations became a major theme of American statements on Iraq in 2006 and 2007. While there is no doubt that Iran plays an important role in Iraqi politics, the actual extent of Iranian influence in Iraq and Tehran's ultimate goals there remain matters of controversy. Two of the major Iraqi Shi'i political parties, SCIRI (later ISCI) and the Da'wa Party, were supported by Iran during the Saddam

---

[113] Leverett, *Dealing with Teheran*, p. 12. See also Douglas Jehl and Eric Schmitt, "US Suggests a Qaeda Cell in Iran Directed Saudi Bombings," *New York Times*, May 21, 2003.

[114] On Ahmadinejad's and the regime's stance toward Israel, see Takeyh, *Hidden Iran*, Chapter 8.

[115] John F. Burns and Robert F. Worth, "Iraqi Campaign Raises Question of Iran's Sway," *New York Times*, December 15, 2004.

Hussein years. SCIRI was created by the Iranian government as an Iraqi "government in exile" during the Iran–Iraq War and its militia, the Badr Brigade, was armed and trained by Iran. However, both parties have made efforts to assert their Iraqi roots since the fall of Saddam's regime.[116] ISCI even went so far, in 2007, as to acknowledge the leadership of Ayatollah al-Sistani in Najaf, whose opposition to the Iranian system of direct clerical rule is well known. However, at the same time, the organization did not abandon its position that its religious leader (*marja' al-taqlid* – source of emulation) was the Iranian leader, Ayatollah Khamenei.[117] Moreover, ISCI continued, through 2008, to advocate a regional government of the nine provinces in the center and south of Iraq with strong Shi'i majorities, on the model of the Kurdish Regional Government in the north of Iraq. Such a quasi-independent regional authority was seen by many (particularly Sunni Arab Iraqis and Sunni Arab leaders) as a step toward the partition of Iraq and the creation of a Shi'i satellite state, beholden to Iran.[118]

Iran has also developed close relations with other Iraqi players. Perhaps the most difficult and controversial of those players was Muqtada al-Sadr. Sadr challenged Iran's client, SCIRI/ISCI, within the Shi'i community. He mocked those who had spent the hellish years of Saddam's rule outside the country and portrayed himself as the real Iraqi and Arab nationalist leader of Iraq's Shi'a. The fact that his family and the al-Hakim family, the leaders of SCIRI/ISCI, have a long history as rivals within the clerical leadership of Iraq added personal spice to their political competition. While Sadr clearly was his own man, with his own political and militia network, by 2005 the Iranians had developed a relationship with him in which they supplied his militia and exercised some influence over him. He was certainly not as close to Iran as SCIRI/ISCI, but just as clearly, at the end of 2007, he was a client of Tehran, if an unpredictable and unwilling

---

[116] For a detailed discussion of the history of SCIRI/ISCI and its relations with Iran, see International Crisis Group, "Shiite Politics in Iraq: The Role of the Supreme Council," Middle East Report No. 70, November 15, 2007, www.crisisgroup.org/home/index. cfm?id=5158&l=1.

[117] The declaration of the ISCI conference of May 10–11, 2007, can be found at www. almejlis.org/news_article_11.html. The first point of the declaration was praise for al-Sistani. For an analysis of the declaration, see Reidar Visser, "SCIRI More Flexible on Federalism, But Fails to Resolve Khamenei Ambiguity," May 12, 2007, www.historiae. org/khamenei.asp.

[118] There is a debate over whether the Iranian government wants a unified Iraq or whether it would prefer to see the de facto partition of Iraq. For the first position, see Takeyh, *Hidden Iran*, pp. 180–87; for a more mixed reading of Iranian aims, see International Crisis Group, "Iran in Iraq: How Much Influence?", Middle East Report No. 38, March 21, 2005, www.crisisgroup.org/home/index.cfm?id=3328&l=1, pp. 10–12, 22–23.

one.[119] Iran also maintains ties to both major Kurdish parties, particularly the Patriotic Union of Kurdistan, which since the 1991 uprisings has controlled the area in Iraqi Kurdistan bordering Iran. That relationship is hardly one of patron and client. There remain serious tensions between the Iraqi Kurdish leaders and Tehran, which worries about the demonstration effect of Kurdish autonomy on their own Kurdish minority.[120]

While Washington certainly did not like the expanded Iranian role in Iraq, it found itself in the unusual position of sharing not only some interests with Iran in Iraq (putting down the Sunni insurgency, avoiding all-out civil war) but also some clients. If SCIRI/ISCI and the Da'wa Party were Iranian allies, they were also American allies, the leaders of the American-supported Baghdad government. The United States' Kurdish allies also had relations with Iran. American officials in Iraq knew that Iran could create much more disruption and difficulties for the United States in the country than it had. On occasion, American officials even publicly acknowledged the positive role of Iran on some Iraqi issues.[121] Increased Iranian influence elsewhere in the region was not as complex for the Bush administration: it was a bad thing that needed to be contained and reversed. Iran's ties to Hizballah in Lebanon, and to Palestinian groups that rejected peace with Israel, long predated Ahmadinejad's election. However, the Iranian president's inflammatory rhetoric toward Israel raised Tehran's profile in the Arab–Israeli arena. The conflict between Israel and Hizballah in the summer of 2006 refocused regional attentions on the Levant and on Iran's role there.

In July 2006 Hizballah forces staged a daring raid across the Lebanese–Israeli border, killing six Israeli soldiers and capturing two others. Israel retaliated with a sustained air campaign against Hizballah, concentrated in southern Lebanon but extending to Beirut and even locations north of the capital. The air offensive was followed by a limited ground offensive by Israeli forces into southern Lebanon. Hizballah answered with rocket attacks on northern Israel. The fighting ended mid-August 2006 with a UN-brokered cease-fire. The Israelis utterly failed to crush Hizballah, ending up strengthening Hizballah politically in Lebanon and making

---

[119] "Iran in Iraq: How Much Influence?", pp. 17–18; Takeyh, *Hidden Iran*, pp. 179–80. For American official accusations of Iranian support for Sadr, see, for example, Thom Shanker and Steven R. Weisman, "Iran Is Helping Insurgents in Iraq, US Officials Say," *New York Times*, September 20, 2004.

[120] "Iran in Iraq: How Much Influence?", pp. 19–21.

[121] David Satterfield, the State Department's coordinator on Iraq, said in December 2007 that at least part of the decline in violence in Iraq "has to be attributed to an Iranian policy decision … at the most senior levels" to rein in Shi'i militias: Karen DeYoung, "Iran Cited in Iraq's Decline in Violence," *Washington Post*, December 23, 2007.

the pro-American Lebanese government (which came to power in the parliamentary elections of 2005, after the withdrawal of Syrian troops from the country) look weak and ineffectual in the process. Hizballah, supported by Iran and Syria, proceeded to lead a sustained challenge to the government which ended only in a 2008 agreement giving the group an effective veto over Lebanese government decisions.

In terms of Gulf dynamics, Hizballah's "victory" in its confrontation with Israel redounded to the benefit of its Iranian patron. Washington and its Arab allies in Cairo, Amman and Riyadh saw the crisis as confirmation that Iranian power was on the rise. The next Arab–Israeli crisis–the Hamas–Fatah fighting in Gaza in June 2007, leading to direct Hamas control of the Gaza Strip–was also seen as an indirect Iranian victory. Hamas, while not as close to Iran as Hizballah, is supported by Iran and shares the Iranian rejection of a negotiated peace with Israel. The Israel attack on Gaza in December 2008–January 2009 has the prospect, like its attack on Lebanon in 2006, of further strengthening Hamas politically in Palestinian politics, though the ultimate result of this conflict remains unclear as of early 2009.

Increased Iranian influence in Iraq and the Levant troubled Washington and its Sunni Arab allies in Saudi Arabia, Egypt and Jordan. Iran's nuclear program was, if anything, even more disturbing. The Iranian nuclear issue took on increased international salience in August 2002, when the Iranian opposition group Mujahidin e-Khalq revealed that Tehran was secretly developing two parallel nuclear programs: a uranium enrichment program at its nuclear facility at Natanz and a plutonium program at its facility at Arak. In February 2003 President Khatami publicly acknowledged the accuracy of the charges. Iran defended the programs, stating (correctly) that it was allowed to develop its nuclear industry for civilian purposes under the nuclear Non-Proliferation Treaty (NPT). Its critics, including the International Atomic Energy Agency, responded that Iran was obligated to report these programs to the IAEA under the terms of the NPT. The secrecy of the programs raised questions about Iran's goals.[122]

The United States saw the nuclear program as confirmation of Iran's hostile intentions. It advocated international pressure on, and isolation of, the Iranian regime until it ended its efforts to enrich uranium, an essential step on the road to a nuclear weapon. The United States' European allies, also troubled by this information, sought to engage Iran diplomatically in an effort to achieve the same goal. France, Germany and Britain, repre-senting the European Union (EU), began negotiations with Iran on the

---

[122] Ansari, *Confronting Iran*, pp. 197–201.

issue. In October 2003, Iran agreed to suspend uranium enrichment and accede to the Additional Protocol of the NPT, which allowed the IAEA to conduct more intrusive inspections of Iranian facilities. In November 2004 the EU-3 (as the German-French-British contact group came to be known) and Iran reconfirmed their earlier deal, with Iran continuing its suspension on enrichment and the EU-3 promising no UN sanctions against Iran.[123]

In early 2005, the United States began to take a more supportive position toward the EU-3's engagement with Iran, though it would not join the negotiations itself. Washington even indicated that it would drop its objections to Iran's entry into the World Trade Organization if the nuclear issue could be settled. The American strategy was to give the Europeans a final chance at halting the Iranian enrichment program and then, if the EU-3 failed, to consolidate a strong international consensus against Iran. In March 2005, Tehran did make a new offer to the EU-3 for a comprehensive settlement of the nuclear issue, but continued to assert Iran's right to enrich uranium for peaceful purposes.[124] With the election of Ahmadinejad in June 2005 and his subsequent bellicose statements about Israel and the United States, fears of Iranian intentions in Washington and in Europe increased. In February 2006, Iran resumed uranium enrichment.[125] The United States then began the long diplomatic process of persuading the Europeans, Russia and China to sanction Iran through United Nations Security Council resolutions. In March 2006 the Security Council, in a unanimous statement (but not a resolution with binding consequences) called on Iran to suspend uranium enrichment. President Ahmadinejad responded in April 2006 by announcing that Iran had increased the number of centrifuges operating at Natanz, publicly celebrating the resumption of enrichment. At the end of July 2006 the Security Council adopted Resolution 1696, calling on Iran to suspend enrichment by the end of August or face the possibility of sanctions.[126] Iran refused. In December 2006 UN Security Council Resolution 1737 imposed sanctions on Iran, restricting trade in nuclear materials and freezing the assets of individuals and institutions involved in

---

[123] Ansari, *Confronting Iran*, pp. 202–06, 221–25.   [124] Ansari, *Confronting Iran*, p. 225.

[125] David Albright and Corey Hinderstein, "The Clock is Ticking, But How Fast?", Institute for Science and International Security Issue Brief, March 27, 2006, www.isis-online.org/publications/iran/clockticking.pdf, p. 2: "On February 11, Iran started to enrich uranium in a small number of centrifuges at Natanz, bringing to a halt Iran's suspension of uranium enrichment that had lasted since October 2003." Ansari, *Confronting Iran*, contends that the decision to renew enrichment was made before Ahmadinejad became president (p. 231).

[126] Warren Hoge, "UN Sets Deadline for Iran to End Uranium Work," *New York Times*, July 31, 2006.

the nuclear program.[127] In March 2007, the Security Council banned arms sales to Tehran and extended the asset freeze to other Iranian individuals and entities in Resolution 1747.[128]

The combination of the deterioration of the Iraq situation, the nuclear issue and Ahmadinejad's election focused the Bush administration's attentions on Iran in a more direct way at the beginning of 2006. In his January 2006 State of the Union address, President Bush described Iran as "a nation now held hostage by a small clerical elite that is isolating and repressing its people." He called for regime change, telling the citizens of Iran: "We respect your right to choose your own future and win your own freedom. And our nation hopes one day to be the closest of friends with a free and democratic Iran." The president also vowed "the nations of the world will not permit the Iranian regime to gain nuclear weapons."[129] The White House's National Security Strategy document, issued in March 2006, said that "we may face no greater challenge from a single country than from Iran."[130]

Shortly after the 2006 Hizballah–Israel conflict, the Bush administration decided on a more confrontational approach toward Tehran. The president authorized American forces to kill or capture Iranian operatives in Iraq and permitted a wider array of covert actions to curtail Iranian influence across the Middle East and in Afghanistan.[131] There was at least circumstantial evidence of American support in 2007 for Iranian groups, particularly ethnic minority groups, such as the Iranian Party for a Free Life in Kurdistan (PJAK), which were opposed to the Tehran government.[132] The US Treasury Department conducted a widely publicized campaign to discourage other governments and foreign corporations from investing in or doing business with Iran, with some success.[133]

[127] Colum Lynch, "Sanctions on Iran Approved by UN," *Washington Post*, December 24, 2006.

[128] Thom Shanker, "Security Council Votes to Tighten Iran Sanctions," *New York Times*, March 25, 2007.

[129] For the text of the address, see www.cnn.com/2006/POLITICS/01/31/sotu.transcript/.

[130] *The National Security Strategy of the United States*, March 2006, p. 20. A pdf of the document is available at www.comw.org/qdr/offdocs.html.

[131] Dafna Linzer, "Troops Authorized to Kill Iranian Operatives in Iraq," *Washington Post*, January 26, 2007.

[132] Richard A. Oppel, Jr., "In Northern Iraq, Conflict Simmers on Second Kurdish Front," *New York Times*, October 23, 2007; Selig Harrison, "The US Meddles Aggressively in Iran," *Le Monde Diplomatique* (English edition), October 2007, http://mondediplo.com/2007/10/02iran.

[133] Steven Mufson, "US Cautions Europeans to Avoid Oil, Gas Deals with Iran," *Washington Post*, February 1, 2007; Jad Moawad, "West Adds to Strains on Iran's Lifeline," *New York Times*, February 13, 2007; Robin Wright, "Iran Feels Pinch as Major Banks Curtail Business," *Washington Post*, March 26, 2007.

Washington strongly supported the Lebanese government in its continuing standoff with Hizballah during 2007–08. It reengaged in the Arab–Israeli peace process, holding a high-profile conference of all the parties to the conflict, including Syria, in Annapolis, Maryland, in November 2007. It sought to revive a regional alignment of "moderate" states to balance Iran, leaking word of new arms sales to Egypt, Israel and the Gulf Arab states in the summer of 2007 and conducting an active diplomatic campaign to firm up the anti-Iranian front, culminating in the January 2008 visit of President Bush to Israel, the West Bank, Kuwait, Bahrain, the UAE, Saudi Arabia and Egypt.[134]

The rhetoric matched the policy steps. On August 9, 2007, President Bush raised the issue of regime change again, telling a press conference that "my message to the Iranian people is, you can do better than this current government."[135] On October 17, 2007, the president said that, if Iran obtained nuclear weapons, it could lead to "World War III."[136] Various reports about American war planning against Iran leaked to the press.[137] Tough talk from Washington was matched by a confident and confrontational Iran during this period. After the summer 2006 Hizballah–Israel conflict, President Ahmadinejad met with UN secretary-general Kofi Annan in Tehran. He told Annan that Iran would become the dominant player in the Middle East and consign the great powers to secondary status.[138] In August 2007 Ahmadinejad asserted that American power in Iraq was collapsing and "very soon we will be witnessing a great power vacuum in the region. We, with the help of regional friends and the Iraqi nation, are ready to fill this void."[139]

The atmosphere of Iranian–American confrontation was unmistakable. This made the December 2007 release of a report from the American intelligence community asserting that Iran had suspended its nuclear weapons program all the more surprising. The National Intelligence Estimate concluded, with high confidence, that Iran had suspended

---

[134] On the arms sales, see Robin Wright, "US Plans New Arms Sales to Gulf Allies," *Washington Post*, July 28, 2007.

[135] Paul Richter, "Maliki May Need a Talk on Iran, Bush Says," *Los Angeles Times*, August 10, 2007.

[136] Sheryl Gay Stolberg, "Nuclear-Armed Iran Risks World War, Says Bush," *New York Times*, October 18, 2007.

[137] "What War With Iran Would Look Like (and How to Avoid It)," *Time*, September 25, 2006, cover story; Seymour Hersh, "The Redirection," *New Yorker*, March 5, 2007, especially p. 57.

[138] Warren Hoge, "Diatribes and Dialogue in Mideast for Annan," *New York Times*, September 11, 2006.

[139] Megan Greenwall, "Riots at Iraqi Religious Festival Leave 28 Dead," *Washington Post*, August 29, 2007.

work on developing nuclear weapons in 2003 for a number of years and, with moderate confidence, that the suspension had continued through mid-2007. This conclusion reversed earlier American intelligence findings that Iran was actively pursuing nuclear weapons. While the NIE said that Iran was "continuing to develop a range of technical capabilities that could be applied to producing nuclear weapons," most notably uranium enrichment, it held that Iran did not have a nuclear weapons capability at the end of 2007 and was unlikely to be able to acquire one before 2015. Moreover, the American intelligence community found that the 2003 suspension was the result of international pressures on the Iranian regime, indicating that Iran's decisions "are guided by a cost–benefit approach rather than a rush to a weapon irrespective of the political, economic and military costs."[140]

With accusations of Iranian nuclear ambitions so central to the American case that Iran was dangerous and needed to be contained, the release of the National Intelligence Estimate caused confusion among the United States' Arab allies and consternation in Israel, where the Iranian nuclear threat was seen as more imminent than in Washington. Even at the IAEA, considered by many to be more lenient on Iran than the Bush administration had been, there were doubts that Iran should be given such a sweeping finding of good behavior.[141] However, the NIE findings reduced the likelihood that Iranian–American tensions would escalate to a military confrontation in the last year of the Bush administration. Realizing the costs that the United States could pay in Iraq, Afghanistan and the Gulf, the administration in early 2008 rejected an Israeli proposal for cooperation in an Israeli strike on Iranian nuclear facilities, though it did step up covert efforts to sabotage the Iranian nuclear program.[142] Washington in 2008 emphasized that Iran remained a major threat and that it was intent upon containing Iranian regional influence, but without a direct military confrontation.

Saudi Arabia shared the American worry about growing Iranian power during these years. It is no coincidence that, as world attention

[140] Office of the Director of National Intelligence, National Intelligence Estimate, "Iran: Nuclear Intentions and Capabilities," November 2007, www.dni.gov/press_releases/20071203_release.pdf.

[141] The *New York Times* quoted "a senior official close to the agency" as saying: "To be frank, we are more skeptical. We don't buy the American analysis 100 percent. We are not that generous with Iran" (Elaine Sciolino, "Monitoring Agency Praises US Report, But Keeps Wary Eye on Iran," *New York Times*, December 5, 2007).

[142] David Sanger, "US Rejected Aid for Israeli Raid on Iranian Nuclear Site," *New York Times*, January 11, 2009.

focused on the Iranian nuclear program, the Saudis and other GCC states very publicly indicated that they might try to develop nuclear power infrastructures themselves.[143] However, Riyadh pursued a different set of tactics to deal with the challenge from across the Gulf. As the Bush administration advocated a very public isolation of Iran, the Saudis sought to avoid an open confrontation with Tehran. They remembered the last time there was a sustained period of Saudi–Iranian tensions, during the 1980s, and had no desire to repeat that experience. High-ranking Iranian officials, including President Ahmadinejad, visited the kingdom in 2006 and 2007. The two sides publicly averred that they were cooperating to try to prevent the Lebanese crisis from escalating, even while the Saudis strongly backed the Lebanese government of Prime Minister Fouad Siniora against Iran's ally, Hizballah.

Like the Bush administration, the Saudis also wanted to see progress on the Arab–Israeli front to reduce the opportunities for Iran to fish in those troubled waters. King Abdallah, who chaired the Arab summit meeting in Riyadh in March 2007, pushed his fellow Arab leaders to reconfirm their support for his earlier 2002 initiative offering Arab recognition to Israel if the Israelis withdrew to the pre-1967 War borders and a Palestinian state were created. Unlike the Bush administration, however, the Saudis did not isolate Hamas, Iran's Palestinian ally, after the party's victory in the 2006 Palestinian legislative elections. In early 2007 they brokered a deal between Hamas and Palestinian Authority president Mahmoud Abbas, head of Fatah, on a coalition government. Though the deal fell apart in the summer of 2007, as Hamas and Fatah fought for control of Gaza, Riyadh continued to see a Hamas–Fatah reconciliation as the best way to limit Iranian influence in the Palestinian territories.[144]

Saudi policy toward Iraq in the years immediately following Saddam Hussein's fall was characterized by passivity, even paralysis. The Saudis could not support the Iraqi governments that emerged from the elections of 2005, seeing the SCIRI and Da'wa leaders of those governments as tools of the Iranians. However, they also could not throw their political and financial weight behind the Iraqi insurgency. Supporting the insurgents would put them in a direct confrontation with the United States.

---

[143] Dalia Dassa Kaye and Frederic M. Wehrey, "A Nuclear Iran: The Reactions of Neighbors," *Survival*, Vol. 49, No. 2 (Summer 2007), pp. 111–28; Roula Khalaf, "UAE Set to Launch Nuclear Programme," *Financial Times*, January 21, 2008.

[144] For a discussion of Saudi regional policy during this period, see my article, "Saudi Arabia: Iraq, Iran, the Regional Power Balance and the Sectarian Question," *Strategic Insights*, Vol. 6, Issue 2 (March 2007), www.ccc.nps.navy.mil/si/2007/Mar/gauseMar07.asp.

Moreover, a small but important element of the Sunni insurgency was al-Qaeda in Iraq, and the Saudis were fighting al-Qaeda sympathizers at home. So from 2003 through the end of 2006, the Saudis basically relied upon the United States to prevent what was, for them, the worst outcome in Iraq – complete Iranian dominance of the country.

Toward the end of 2006, there were signs of a more independent Saudi strategy toward Iraq emerging. The spur to that new strategy seemed to be the Iraq Study Group report issued in November 2006, following closely upon the Democratic victory in the congressional elections. Both events led to speculation that US forces might be leaving Iraq sooner rather than later. While that withdrawal did not occur, these events did get the Saudis thinking about how they could preserve their interests in Iraq independent of Washington. King Abdallah signaled this new approach at the Arab summit meeting of March 2007, when in a public address to the assembled leaders he declared the "foreign occupation" of Iraq to be "illegal."[145] Such a statement was calculated to appeal to Iraqi Sunnis who, while beginning to cooperate with the United States, continued to see the American occupation as illegitimate. There were a number of signs, though no direct Saudi confirmation, that Riyadh was encouraging and helping to fund the rise of the Awakening movements among Iraqi Sunnis in 2007.[146] The Awakening groups fit the Saudi model for Iraqi clients perfectly: anti-al-Qaeda, anti-Iranian and willing to work with the United States. Saudi Arabia also quietly supported efforts by former prime minister Iyad Allawi to construct an alternative majority in the Iraqi parliament, even as the Bush administration was urging regional states to support the Maliki government.[147] As in the case of Iran and the Arab–Israeli peace process, the Saudis shared Washington's overall goals in Iraq but pursued a different tactical approach.

The Saudi–Iranian pas de deux in the wake of the Iraq War, part contest for regional influence and part strained diplomatic encounter, promises to be a central theme in the international politics of the Persian Gulf for years to come, at least as long as Iraq remains a playing field for outsiders as opposed to a player in the regional power game. There is a very strong tendency to read the relationship between Saudi Arabia and Iran, and

---

[145] Hassan Fattah, "US Iraq Role Is Called Illegal by Saudi King," *New York Times*, March 29, 2007. The phrase Abdallah used in Arabic could also be translated as illegitimate.

[146] Abd al-Aziz al-Hakim, the head of ISCI and no friend of the Saudis, told reporters on a visit to Washington in December 2007 that the Saudis had used their influence in Iraq to help bring about the Awakening movements: David Morgan, "Shi'ite Leader Sees an Iraq With No Foreign Troops," Reuters, December 4, 2007.

[147] David Ignatius, "Cheney and the Saudis," *Washington Post*, May 9, 2007.

their larger regional rivalry, in sectarian terms.[148] Saudi Arabia has for decades promoted its brand of Sunni Islam around the Muslim world. Since the revolution, Iran has done the same with its brand of revolutionary Shi'ism. Given the sectarian coloration of the internal disputes in Iraq and Lebanon, and the fact that the Saudis back Sunnis and the Iranians back Shi'a in both countries, it is natural to conclude that sectarianism is the driver in their regional rivalry. However, a stronger case can be made that balance of power concerns, not sectarianism, drive the regional contest for influence. The Iranians have Sunni allies as well, most notably Hamas in the Palestinian territories. The Saudis' objection to the Maliki government did not rest on the fact that Maliki is a Shi'i. They have promoted the fortunes of Allawi, who is also a Shi'i. Riyadh objected to Maliki because it saw him as an Iranian client. The Saudis have also demonstrated that they are more than willing to engage the Iranians (and Iranian clients like Hizballah) in a diplomatic process if it suits their interests. Finally, and most convincingly on the sectarian issue, the Saudis' treatment of their own Shi'i minority in recent years has not reflected a renewed fear of Shi'ism as a regional force. The Saudis were playing a sophisticated game of containing Iran without confronting it, for classic balance of power reasons. While sectarianism is ever present in regional politics, given the sectarian nature of the Iraqi and Lebanese conflicts and sectarian tensions in other regional countries (such as Bahrain and Pakistan), it did not seem to be the driver of regional international relations.[149] It is entirely possible, however, that either one or both of the sides in this rivalry will play the sectarian card more openly in the future.

The fact that both Iran and Saudi Arabia were flexing their diplomatic muscles after the Iraq War was not simply the result of the power vacuum created by the post-Saddam mess in Iraq. The dramatic increase in the price of oil from 2003 to the middle of 2008 gave both Tehran and Riyadh the resources and confidence to assert themselves in the region. After a downturn immediately after the September 11, 2001, attacks, oil prices charted a steadily upward path. Spot crude prices fell from an average of $28.50 per barrel in 2000 to $24.44 in 2001 and $25.02 in 2002, recovering their 2000 level in 2003, at $28.83. From there, prices skyrocketed.

---

[148] The most cogent argument that the overall impact of the Iraq War has been a rise in Shi'i assertiveness, and that this is something that should not trouble the United States, is made by Vali Nasr, *The Shia Revival: How Conflicts Within Islam Will Shape the Future* (New York: W. W. Norton, 2006).

[149] For a more developed version of this argument, see Gause, "Saudi Arabia"; and Maximilian Terhalle, "Are the Shia Rising?," *Middle East Policy*, Vol. 14, No. 2 (Summer 2007), pp. 69–83.

The 2004 average was $38.27 per barrel, in 2005 $54.52 and in 2006 $65.14.[150] Prices at the end of 2007 were about $90 per barrel, and during the summer of 2008 briefly went above $140.[151] It was the third oil boom, dwarfing the booms of the early 1970s and the early 1980s in terms of total dollars flowing into the oil-exporting states.

With rising prices, there was little if any acrimony among the Gulf state members of OPEC. Both Saudi Arabia and Iran were happy to ride the price escalator up. The Saudis, far from being price moderates during this period, used their influence to prop up prices when they looked as if they might fall. This was particularly true in the second half of 2006. Prices fell from over $75 per barrel in August of that year to just above $50 per barrel in January 2007.[152] The Saudis led OPEC in two agreements to cut production, one in October 2006 and the other in December 2006. From August 2006 to February 2007, the Saudis cut their oil production by 700,000 barrels per day, from 9.3 mbd to 8.6 mbd. During that same period, Iran cut less than 150,000 bd and Kuwait and the UAE made similar-sized cuts.[153] Riyadh absorbed a 7.5% production cut over that period, compared to 4% for Iran and the UAE and 5% for Kuwait. With the Saudis taking the lead in fulfilling their OPEC commitments, oil climbed back above $70 per barrel by June 2007 and continued its upward trajectory.

As the global financial crisis struck in the fall of 2008, however, prices crashed, by January 2009 reaching a low of about $32 per barrel. The Saudis brokered three OPEC production-cut agreements in September, October and December 2008, aiming to take a total of over 4 mbd off the market, in an effort to put a floor under the price fall. Where the market would go, in the face of the uncertainty gripping the global economy, was an open question. The year 2008 probably marked the end of the third oil boom, with potentially dramatic domestic consequences for all the oil producers. But from a Gulf security perspective, it is important to note that oil politics were an area of cooperation, not competition, between Saudi Arabia and Iran in the 2000s, at least at the declaratory level. They basically cooperated on oil issues in OPEC when prices were high and when prices were

[150] British Petroleum, *Statistical Review of World Energy 2007*, Spot Crude Prices table, www.bp.com/sectiongenericarticle.do?categoryId=9017906&contentId=7033467.
[151] US Department of Energy, Energy Information Administration, Petroleum Navigator, World Crude Oil Prices, http://tonto.eia.doe.gov/dnav/pet/pet_pri_wco_k_w.htm.
[152] US Department of Energy, Energy Information Administration, Petroleum Navigator, World Crude Oil Prices, http://tonto.eia.doe.gov/dnav/pet/pet_pri_wco_k_w.htm.
[153] US Department of Energy, Energy Information Administration, *Monthly Energy Review*, January 2009, Table 11.1a, www.eia.doe.gov/emeu/mer/pdf/pages/sec11_4.pdf.

low. It remains to be seen, given the enormous pressures of the price collapse of late 2008, whether they will live up to their commitments on production cuts in 2009.

Conclusion

It is not possible to wrap this period of dramatic change in the international politics of the Persian Gulf up in a neat summary. Too many issues remain unresolved. Most importantly, it is not clear what the future of Iraq will be. It is possible that there will be a gradual increase in the capacity of the Iraqi state to manage its own affairs and some political accommodation among the Iraqi parties. It is equally possible that the improved security situation at the end of 2008 will be temporary and that the various Iraqi parties will engage in an even more intense struggle for power in the near future. While the likelihood of a confrontation between Iran and the United States decreased in 2008, the trajectory of Iranian–American relations and of Iran's efforts to increase its regional influence remains to be seen. The direction of the world oil market as of the beginning of 2009 remains unclear. This is an unfinished chapter in the history of the international relations of the Persian Gulf.

What is clear is that the pattern of Gulf international politics in the period before 2001 is over. The relative stability of the Iran-Iraq-Saudi Arabia regional power distribution, which lasted through two brutal regional wars, with the United States standing just off to the side, ready to intervene to protect the status quo, ended with the Iraq War. Washington is a direct, day-to-day player in Gulf politics now. Iraq is no longer a player, but a playing field, and will be so for some time. Saudi Arabia and Iran look at each other warily, competing for influence in the Gulf and the broader Middle East but at the same time anxious to avoid a direct confrontation. Unlike the three-cornered structure of Gulf international relations, this new disposition does not appear to be at all stable. How it will develop and change is anyone's guess. The enormous influence of the Iraq War on the region, however, calls for a close study of why the United States chose to fight it. That is the business of the next chapter.

6   The Iraq War: American decision-making

The story of the American decision to go to war against Iraq in March 2003 is straightforward. The attacks on the United States of September 11, 2001, changed the strategic outlook of President George W. Bush. He accepted the calls from some in his administration, for which he had previously shown no particular enthusiasm, that a military campaign to unseat Iraqi president Saddam Hussein was a vital American security interest in the context of the new "war on terrorism." Once that decision was made, arguments were marshaled (with less than rigorous regard for their factual accuracy and unseemly willingness to disregard the complexity and ambiguity of the Iraqi reality) to mobilize international, domestic public and congressional opinion in support of the decision. The international element of that campaign largely failed, while the domestic element was very successful. With the strong support of Congress and substantial American public opinion support, but with little preparation for what would come after, President Bush took the country to war.[1]

So why rehearse the story in any more detail? Because there is a strong suspicion that September 11 was simply a pretext for the Bush administration to implement a preexisting war policy toward Iraq. This is certainly the import of accounts offered by former Treasury secretary Paul O'Neill, former counterterrorism director Richard Clarke, and retired general Wesley Clark.[2] The Iraq War has been depicted as part of a larger program of American imperial expansion, as a blatant grab for oil and corporate

---

[1] This is basically the story told in two of the first books to treat the issue: Todd S. Purdum and the staff of the *New York Times*, *A Time of Our Choosing: America's War in Iraq* (New York: Henry Holt, 2003), and Ivo H. Daalder and James M. Lindsay, *America Unbound: The Bush Revolution in Foreign Policy* (Washington DC: Brookings Institution Press, 2003).

[2] Wesley K. Clark, *Winning Modern Wars: Iraq, Terrorism and the American Empire* (New York: Public Affairs, 2003); Richard A. Clarke, *Against All Enemies: Inside America's War on Terror* (New York: Free Press, 2004); and Ron Suskind, *The Price of Loyalty: George W. Bush, the White House and the Education of Paul O'Neill* (New York: Simon & Schuster, 2004). Suskind concluded that the overthrow of Saddam Hussein was "already a central mission" of the Bush administration upon coming into office (p. 87). However, his accounts of NSC meetings, based upon O'Neill's notes and recollections, show

profits and as part of a plan to secure Israeli dominance of the Middle East.[3] All of these explanations share the analytical perspective that 9/11 was simply a pretext, not a cause, for the war. The post-war failure to discover any weapons of mass destruction in Iraq, the major public rationale for the war, undoubtedly contributes to the sense that it was really about something else.

This chapter examines the sequence of events leading to the Bush administration's war decisions, and finds strong support for the centrality of 9/11 as a turning point in President Bush's views toward Iraq. There is no indication in the public record of a war decision before 9/11, and substantial support for the proposition that the president was undecided on the Iraq issue then. There is compelling evidence that, shortly after 9/11, he decided on a course of war with Iraq. In a textbook example of the well-documented psychological process, once that decision was made, the administration searched for substantiation of its suspicions about Iraqi WMD and Iraqi ties to al-Qaeda to justify the decision, ignoring the weakness and ambiguity of much of the data it generated to support those suspicions. It bolstered its decision by accepting rosy scenarios about the ease with which a post-war Iraqi transition could be accomplished, despite numerous sources both inside and outside the government calling those assumptions into question.

The chapter goes on to assess the administration's case that spreading democracy in the Middle East was an important part of the rationale for the Iraq War, finding that there is considerable evidence to support this contention. The chapter then examines an important alternative hypothesis about the causes of the American war decision: that the real reason for the war was securing Iraqi oil resources. The strategic importance of

substantial differences of opinion among the principals. General Clark admitted, "I'm not sure I can prove this yet", when pushed on his contention that September 11 was a pretext to launch a preexisting plan to reshape the Middle East: Peter J. Boyer, "General Clark's Battles," *New Yorker*, November 17, 2003, pp. 72–74. Richard Clarke's contention was based largely on the fact that, before 9/11, "more and more the talk was of Iraq, of CENTCOM being asked to plan to invade" (p. 264). CENTCOM is the US Central Command, the military command for the Middle East. This is consistent with my assertion that high-level officials supported military action against Iraq before 9/11, but that they had not convinced President Bush.

[3] The most serious case for an oil-based imperial explanation for the war is made by Michael Klare, *Blood and Oil* (New York: Metropolitan Books, Henry Holt, 2004). See also Jay R. Mandle, "A War for Oil: Bush, the Saudis and Iraq," *Commonweal*, November 8, 2002; and Paul Roberts, *The End of Oil: On the Edge of a Perilous New World* (Boston: Houghton Mifflin, 2004). Maureen Dowd wrote that: "The imaginary weapons and Osama link were just a marketing tool and shiny distraction, something to keep the public from crying while they went to war for reasons unrelated to any nuclear threat. The 9/11 attacks gave the neocons an opening for their dreams of remaking the Middle East, and they drove the Third Infantry Division through it" ("I Spy a Screw-Up," *New York Times*, March 31, 2005).

Persian Gulf oil has always been a factor in American policy in the region. However, the oil argument is absent from the available accounts of Bush administration deliberations, and American policy in Iraq since the war has not borne out the "centrality of oil" argument.

The war decision

There is no evidence that the Bush administration had decided on war against Iraq before 9/11. A number of high-ranking officials in the administration had publicly supported, before they entered office, a more confrontational American policy to topple Saddam Hussein's regime. Secretary of Defense Rumsfeld, his two top deputies at the Pentagon in the first Bush term (Deputy Secretary Paul Wolfowitz and Undersecretary for Policy Douglas Feith), Deputy Secretary of State Richard Armitage and the national security coordinator for the transition team Zalmay Khalilzad all signed a public letter to President Clinton in February 1998 calling for a "comprehensive political and military strategy for bringing down Saddam and his regime."[4] Neoconservatives did not hide their preference for a muscular use of American power to bring down Saddam Hussein. They put it on the front page of the *Weekly Standard*.[5] Secretary of the Treasury O'Neill reports that Secretary Rumsfeld, as early as the National Security Council meeting of February 1, 2001, told his colleagues that "sanctions are fine, but what we really want to think about is going after Saddam."[6]

However, they were not the only players on the Bush administration's foreign policy team. Secretary of State Colin Powell was the informal author of what has come to be known as the Powell Doctrine, a very restrictive set of conditions for the use of American force abroad: that it be massive and aimed at gaining a clear military victory, that it have decisive public and congressional support, that there be a clear exit strategy. As the new administration came into office, it was hard to see how a new level of American military pressure on Iraq could fit into the Powell Doctrine. Even more salient, in terms of the new president's thinking on Iraq, were the views of Condoleezza Rice, who became Bush's national security adviser. She showed no signs of urgency concerning policy toward Iraq in her 2000 article in *Foreign Affairs* laying out her general foreign policy views. She compared the Iraqi regime to that of

---

[4] The letter can be accessed at the website of the Center for Security Policy, www. centerforsecuritypolicy.org/index.jsp?section=papers&code=98-D_33at.

[5] The December 1, 1997, cover of the *Weekly Standard* bore the headline "Saddam Must Go."

[6] Suskind, *The Price of Loyalty*, p. 85.

North Korea, and said: "These regimes are living on borrowed time, so there need be no sense of panic about them."[7]

The central player, President Bush, gave somewhat mixed signals about Iraq before coming to office, but hardly could be said to have focused much on the subject. He supported the 1998 Iraq Liberation Act and argued for vigorous containment, including "tougher" sanctions on Saddam's regime during the 2000 presidential campaign. Asked during a December 1999 debate what he would do if it were discovered that Saddam had weapons of mass destruction, he replied "take him out." However, he immediately, in the follow-up question, asserted that he meant that he would take the weapons out, not Saddam himself.[8] His vice presidential candidate, Dick Cheney, had been secretary of defense during the Gulf War of 1990–91. When asked later, in a 1996 documentary, about Saddam Hussein remaining in power after the war, Cheney said that "the idea of going into Baghdad for example or trying to topple the regime wasn't anything I was enthusiastic about. I felt there was a real danger here that you would get bogged down in a long drawn out conflict." When asked whether he found Saddam's continuation in power "personally frustrating," Cheney replied, "No, I don't … I think that if Saddam wasn't there that his successor probably wouldn't be notably friendlier to the United States than he is."[9] During the campaign Cheney told NBC's *Meet the Press* that "we want to maintain our current posture vis-à-vis Iraq."[10] There is no evidence that, once in office and before 9/11, Cheney pushed for a policy of military confrontation with Iraq.[11]

---

[7] Condoleezza Rice, "Promoting the National Interest," *Foreign Affairs*, Vol. 79, No. 1 (January/February 2000), p. 61.

[8] Quoted in Daalder and Lindsay, *America Unbound*, p. 40.

[9] "The Gulf War," PBS Frontline, www.pbs.org/wgbh/pages/frontline/gulf/oral/cheney/2. html.

[10] Glenn Kessler, "US Decision on Iraq Has a Puzzling Past," *Washington Post*, January 12, 2003.

[11] "It is important to note that at this early stage [before 9/11], the neocons did not have the enthusiastic backing of Vice President Cheney. Just because Cheney had spent a lot of time around the Get Saddam neocons does not mean that he had become one, says an administration aide. 'It's a mistake to add up two and two and get 18,' he says. Cheney's cautious side kept him from leaping into any potential Bay of Pigs covert actions": Mark Hosenball, Michael Isikoff and Evan Thomas, "Cheney's Long Path to War," *Newsweek*, November 17, 2003. Michael R. Gordon and Bernard E. Trainor argue that Bush and Cheney were more focused on Iraq as the administration came into office, thinking that a new approach was necessary, but not committed to a particular plan: *Cobra II: The Inside Story of the Invasion and Occupation of Iraq* (New York: Pantheon Books, 2006), pp. 13–14. Ron Suskind contends that Cheney believed that the first President Bush "missed history's call" by not destroying Saddam Hussein in 1991, but he offers no source for this assertion: *The One Percent Doctrine: Deep Inside America's Pursuit of Its Enemies Since 9/11* (New York: Simon & Schuster: 2006), p. 25.

The differences within the administration's foreign policy team on Iraq were clear from the outset. One perceptive reporter identified Iraq as "an especially interesting test case of the new Administration's foreign policy, for the differences of opinion represent well-established splits in the Republican foreign policy world."[12] The pre-9/11 evidence indicates that Secretary of State Powell, not the Pentagon civilians, had won the first round of the bureaucratic battle. Iraq was on the agenda of the National Security Council almost immediately, at a meeting on January 30, 2001. The discussion, based on the recollection of Treasury Secretary O'Neill, reflected a desire to increase pressure on Saddam Hussein. CIA director George Tenet presented photographic evidence of what might have been a chemical or biological weapons facility. O'Neill, in retrospect, believed a major shift in Iraq was underway. However, his own account of the meeting indicated that Secretary of State Powell and General Hugh Shelton, chairman of the Joint Chiefs of Staff, were hardly enthusiastic about military action in Iraq. In the end, the president ended the meeting with directions to Powell to draw up a proposal for a new sanctions regime and the Pentagon to "examine our military options," including how US forces could support Iraqi opposition groups inside the country.[13] General Tommy Franks, the commander of American forces in the Middle East (Central Command) told the 9/11 Commission that he "was pushing independently to do more robust planning for military responses in Iraq during the summer before 9/11 – a request President Bush denied, arguing that the time was not right."[14] It is clear that the new president wanted to take a fresh and "tougher" look at Iraq, as he (and Vice President Al Gore) had promised in the campaign. But in his directions to his cabinet officials, he seemed to want to expand his range of options on both the diplomatic and military sides.

The first initiative of the Bush administration on Iraq was not a military response, or even a high-profile increase in support for the Iraqi opposition, but a diplomatic campaign to modify the Iraqi sanctions regime – the "smart sanctions" proposal. The Pentagon civilians were not pleased.

[12] Nicholas Lemann, "The Iraq Factor," *New Yorker*, January 22, 2001.
[13] Suskind, *The Price of Loyalty*, pp. 72–76. Later in the book, O'Neill reflected on the pre-9/11 "battle" between Powell and the Rumsfeld bloc, indicating that there was hardly a set policy line for war against Iraq (pp. 96–97). It was in this context that O'Neill mentioned a Pentagon intelligence document he had seen that mapped Iraq's oil fields and listed companies that might be interested in developing them. This document is sometimes cited as proof that there was a pre-9/11 plan in the Bush administration for war on Iraq. However, the fact that O'Neill specifies that it came from the Defense Intelligence Agency, "Rumsfeld's intelligence arm," seems to indicate more that the secretary of defense was thinking about a war with Iraq.
[14] *The 9/11 Commission Report* (New York: W. W. Norton, 2003), p. 336.

Deputy Secretary of Defense Wolfowitz reportedly told European diplomats that the proposal was not the last word on the administration's Iraq policy.[15] Their displeasure indicates that the smart-sanctions proposal was not a stalking horse for a subsequent belligerent stance toward Saddam, but a loss in the bureaucratic wars for the hardline position. In short, at the outset of his administration, President Bush chose a diplomatic and multilateral rather than military and unilateral course on Iraq.

"Smart sanctions" was not a plan to lift sanctions, but rather to change them in an effort to win back international and regional support for the containment of Saddam. Powell's proposal would have opened up trade in civilian goods, but the UN would still control Iraq's finances, as oil payments would still be made into the UN escrow account. His proposal also called for international inspectors to be stationed in the countries bordering Iraq to enforce the prohibition on dual-use imports. The international response to Powell's proposal was not enthusiastic. France was lukewarm and Russia opposed.[16] Iraq's neighbors were also reluctant to host a new international inspections regime in their ports and airports. Neither Jordan nor Syria signed on, and Syria continued to import Iraqi oil, in violation of existing UN sanctions.[17] Turkey also expressed reservations. So the smart-sanctions proposal died in the summer of 2001.

Meanwhile, the Bush administration continued its internal debate on how to increase the military and political pressure on Saddam Hussein. Between the end of May and the end of July 2001, the deputies' committee of the National Security Council met four times to work on Iraq policy. On August 1, 2001, the group presented to the NSC an Iraq policy paper entitled "A Liberation Strategy." The rather grandiose title belied the cautious policy recommendations it contained: phased increases in economic and diplomatic pressure, carefully calibrated increases in existing military pressure (increased American air patrols over the northern and southern no-fly zones in Iraq) and covert efforts to weaken Saddam's regime and encourage the Iraqi opposition.[18] The NSC, still split among its principal members, did not immediately adopt the policy proposed by the deputies. There is no evidence that any policy decisions had been reached by September 11. Bob Woodward, who had access to all the principals and to notes of Bush administration deliberations, reports

---

[15] Jane Perlez, "Bush Team's Counsel Is Divided on Foreign Policy," *New York Times*, March 27, 2001.
[16] Steven Mufson and Alan Sipress, "Deal on Iraq Sanctions Eludes US," *Washington Post*, May 31, 2001; "Russia Blocks Smart Sanctions," *Middle East Economic Survey*, Vol. 44, No. 28 (July 9, 2001), p. C1.
[17] *Petroleum Intelligence Weekly*, May 21, 2001; *al-Hayat*, June 5, 2001, pp. 1, 6.
[18] Bob Woodward, *Plan of Attack* (New York: Simon & Schuster, 2004), p. 21.

that "most work on Iraq stopped for the rest of August" as President Bush went on vacation. "A policy recommendation on Iraq was never forwarded to the president."[19] One senior administration official told a reporter, shortly before the beginning of the war, "Before September 11, there wasn't a consensus Administration view about Iraq. This issue hadn't come to the fore, and you had Administration *views*."[20] Ivo H. Daalder and James M. Lindsay, after reviewing the long history of neoconservative support for an aggressive American military policy aimed at deposing Saddam, concluded that this policy line "gained little traction in the first months of Bush's tenure."[21] Armitage, the deputy secretary of state, subsequently said, "prior to 9/11 we [the State Department] certainly were prevailing" in the bureaucratic fight over Iraq policy.[22]

Then September 11 happened. It should not be surprising that such a cataclysmic event would alter a president's foreign policy perspective. There is every indication it did so for George W. Bush, with direct implications for Iraq policy. The president himself told Woodward that he was not particularly happy with Iraq policy before 9/11, but that "prior to September 11, however, a president could see a threat and contain it or deal with it in a variety of ways without fear of that threat materializing on our own soil." He went on to say that the attacks changed his attitude toward "Saddam Hussein's capacity to create harm ... all his terrible features became much more threatening. Keeping Saddam in a box looked less and less feasible to me."[23] The Pentagon civilians, with their coherent view of the causes of anti-American terror and their clear prescription of military action to change anti-American regimes, convinced the president. From that point, he joined the hardliners on Iraq. Richard Clarke, the senior counterterrorism official in the White House, reports that on the evening of September 12, 2001, President Bush took him aside and told him to "look into Iraq, Saddam," for links to the attacks.[24] Bush told the National Security Council meeting of September 17, 2001: "I believe Iraq was involved [in 9/11], but I'm not going to strike them now. I don't

---

[19] Woodward, *Plan of Attack*, p. 23. "When the Administration did focus on Iraq, its initial deliberations were inconclusive": Gordon and Trainor, *Cobra II*, p. 14. This conclusion is supported by Douglas Feith in his memoir *War and Decision: Inside the Pentagon at the Dawn of the War on Terrorism* (New York: Harper, 2008), Chapter 6.

[20] Nicholas Lemann, "How It Came To War," *New Yorker*, March 31, 2003.

[21] Daalder and Lindsay, *America Unbound*, p. 130.

[22] Thomas E. Ricks, *Fiasco: The American Military Adventure in Iraq* (New York: Penguin Press, 2006), p. 28.

[23] Woodward, *Plan of Attack*, pp. 12, 27.

[24] Clarke, *Against All Enemies*, p. 32. The president told the 9/11 commissioners that he wondered immediately after the attack whether Iraq had a hand in it: *The 9/11 Commission Report*, p. 334.

have evidence at this point."[25] On that same day, Bush signed a directive to the Pentagon outlining the plan to go to war against Afghanistan. The directive included an order to begin planning military options for an invasion of Iraq.[26] Woodward identifies November 21, 2001, when the president asked Secretary of Defense Rumsfeld to begin to prepare a war plan for Iraq, as the real beginning of the march to war.[27]

Ordering that options be prepared is not the same as ordering a war, but it is an indication of a marked change in the president's thinking, one that would lead relatively quickly to a war decision. That shift was reinforced by the growing concern among senior administration officials that the next terrorist attack could be with weapons of mass destruction. The anthrax scare, which occurred in September and October 2001, with envelopes laced with anthrax sent to news organizations and senatorial offices, brought this issue to the top of the public agenda.[28] Vice President Cheney, who had been tasked before 9/11 to coordinate plans for defense against WMD, reported to the president shortly after the attacks that the United States was essentially defenseless against a biological weapons assault.[29] In late October, CIA director Tenet briefed the president and his top aides on the possibility that al-Qaeda could get WMD, focusing in part on reports that four Pakistani nuclear scientists were cooperating with bin Laden's group. Tenet put Iraq at the top of the list of countries that *could* assist al–Qaeda in this matter, despite the paucity of solid intelligence on Iraq–al-Qaeda ties. According to the *New York Times*, the Tenet briefing "sent the president through the roof."[30] At the same time, the administration passed on to the District of Columbia police and congressional intelligence committees a warning, based upon intercepted conversations and other intelligence, that terrorists might be planning a "dirty

---

[25] Bob Woodward, *Bush at War* (New York: Simon & Schuster, 2002), p. 99. Woodward had access to the notes taken at the NSC meetings in the period after 9/11.

[26] Kessler, "US Decision on Iraq Has Puzzling Past"; Gordon and Trainor, *Cobra II*, p. 17. Feith reports that Rumsfeld asked the military to begin preparing options for an attack on Iraq on September 29: *War and Decision*, p. 218.

[27] Woodward, *Plan of Attack*, pp. 1–3, 30.

[28] "By all accounts, the administration was quick to suspect a possible link between Iraq and the anthrax attacks that had shaken the nation in the fall of 2001": Purdum *et al.*, *A Time of Our Choosing*, p. 30.

[29] Jacob Weisberg, *The Bush Tragedy* (New York: Random House, 2008), p. 190. Based on his interviews with people in the White House, Weisberg concluded that "[i]nside the administration, the October bioterror attacks had a greater impact that is generally appreciated – one in many ways greater than 9/11. Without the anthrax attacks, Bush probably would not have invaded Iraq" (p. 189).

[30] Quoted in Daalder and Lindsay, *America Unbound*, p. 119. See also Carla Anne Robbins and Jeanne Cummings, "How Bush Decided that Hussein Must Be Ousted From Atop Iraq," *Wall Street Journal*, June 14, 2002.

bomb" (a bomb that uses conventional explosives to spew radioactive material) attack in Washington. The *Wall Street Journal*, in a June 2002 story in which National Security Adviser Rice was interviewed, concluded that "the knowledge that al-Qaeda was aggressively searching for weapons of mass destruction – and wooing outside support – transformed the President's thinking about America's enemies."[31]

The terrorism–WMD nexus also brought those closest to the president, Vice President Cheney and National Security Adviser Rice, around to the pro-war position. According to the *Washington Post*, Cheney became "consumed with the possibility that Iraq or other countries could distribute biological or chemical weapons to terrorists."[32] Woodward reports that the attacks of 9/11 made Cheney a "powerful, steamrolling force" encouraging war on Iraq, with an "intense focus on the threats posed by Saddam."[33] Ron Suskind relates a conversation among Cheney, Rice and Tenet in late November 2001 in which the three discussed reports that Pakistani nuclear scientists had been in touch with bin Laden. Cheney said that, if there were "a one percent chance" that al-Qaeda could obtain a nuclear weapon, "we would have to treat it as a certainty in terms of our response." He went on to say, "It's not about our analysis, or finding a preponderance of evidence. It's about our response."[34] The same *Washington Post* article referenced above asserts that Rice, within days of 9/11, "privately began to counsel the President that he needed to go after all rogue nations harboring weapons of mass destruction."[35] Rice was quoted in the *Wall Street Journal* in June 2002 arguing that hard evidence of a link between Iraq and al-Qaeda was not necessary to justify targeting Saddam Hussein: "It's not because you have some chain of evidence saying Iraq may have given a weapon to al-Qaeda … But it is because Iraq is one of those places that is both hostile to us and, frankly, irresponsible and cruel enough to make this available."[36]

---

[31] Robbins and Cummings, "How Bush Decided."
[32] Kessler, "US Decision on Iraq Has Puzzling Past."
[33] Woodward, *Plan of Attack*, p. 4. See also pp. 29–30.
[34] Suskind, *The One Percent Doctrine*, p. 62. Tenet reports the quote in his own memoir, *At the Center of the Storm: My Years at the CIA* (New York: Harper Collins, 2007), p. 264.
[35] Kessler, "US Decision on Iraq Has Puzzling Past."
[36] Robbins and Cummings, "How Bush Decided." Lawrence Freedman concludes that Iraq emerged quickly on the administration's agenda after the 9/11 attacks because "worst-case analysis had suddenly gained a new credibility": "War in Iraq: Selling the Threat," *Survival*, Vol. 46, No. 2 (Summer 2004), p. 16. Feith argues that it was not the mistaken belief that Iraq had chemical and biological weapons that drove the war decision, but the correct (in his view) belief that Saddam could easily develop those weapons and pass them along to terrorists: *War and Decision*, pp. 227–28.

Those within the administration recognized the centrality of 9/11 to changing the course of Iraq policy. In background interviews in different media outlets, "senior administration officials" highlighted the point: "Without September 11, we never would have been able to put Iraq at the top of the agenda. It was only then that this president was willing to worry about the unthinkable – that the next attack could be with weapons of mass destruction supplied by Saddam Hussein."[37] "The most important thing is that the president's position changed after 9/11."[38] Tenet held the same view.[39] Jack Straw, the British foreign minister, came to the same conclusion in a memo to British prime minister Tony Blair on March 25, 2002: "If 11 September had not happened, it is doubtful that the US would now be considering military action against Iraq … Objectively, the threat from Iraq has not worsened as a result of 11 September. What has however changed is the tolerance of the international community (especially that of the US), the world having witnessed on September 11 just what determined evil people can these days perpetrate."[40]

Serious planning for war on Iraq began *before* the end of hostilities in Afghanistan, with Bush's request to Rumsfeld and Rumsfeld's subsequent order that the military begin to reexamine its war plan for Iraq. General Franks, in the midst of the Afghanistan war, was less than pleased with the news.[41] The quick collapse of the Taliban regime, by early December 2001, allowed the Bush administration to focus all its military energies on Iraq. On December 28 President Bush met with General Franks to discuss military options in Iraq.[42] On January 28, 2002, Bush highlighted the nexus between terrorist groups and states possessing weapons of mass destruction in his "axis of evil" State of the Union address, and vowed to take preventive action against what he called "a grave and growing danger" because "time is not on our side." Iraq received more attention in that speech than any other country besides Afghanistan, where the war had just ended. The president asserted that

---

[37] Steven R. Weisman, "Pre-emption: Idea with a Lineage Whose Time Has Come," *New York Times*, March 23, 2003.

[38] Kessler, "US Decision on Iraq Has Puzzling Past."

[39] "After 9/11, everything changed … Still, had 9/11 not happened, the argument to go to war in Iraq undoubtedly would have been much harder to make. Whether the case could have been made at all is uncertain. But 9/11 did happen, and the terrain shifted with it": Tenet, *At the Center of the Storm*, pp. 305–06.

[40] PM/02/019, "Crawford/Iraq," Jack Straw to Tony Blair, 25 March 2002. This is one of a series of documents leaked to a British reporter in 2005 about the lead-up to the war. It can be accessed at: www.downingstreetmemo.com/docs/straw.pdf.

[41] Woodward reports that he asked one of his subordinates, "what the f– are they talking about?": *Plan of Attack*, p. 8.

[42] Daalder and Lindsay, *America Unbound*, p. 131; Woodward, *Plan of Attack*, Chapter 5; Gordon and Trainor, *Cobra II*, pp. 30–32.

Iraq "has plotted to develop anthrax and nerve gas and nuclear weapons for over a decade."[43] In February 2002 he ordered the CIA to undertake a comprehensive, covert program to topple Saddam, including authority to use lethal force.[44]

During the spring of 2002, the indications that the White House had decided to target Iraq militarily grew. Intensive military planning began, with General Franks visiting the White House to brief the president every three or four weeks.[45] By March 2002 the administration began to shift specialized military and intelligence resources from Afghanistan to the Iraq theater.[46] Recognizing that regional and European support for such a war required at least the appearance of American movement on the Arab–Israeli issue, the administration reversed its year-long "hands-off" policy toward the peace process. It sponsored UN Security Council Resolution 1379, adopted in March 2002, calling for a two-state solution to the Israeli–Palestinian conflict. In response to Arab protests against Israeli military reoccupation of parts of the occupied Palestinian territories in late March and early April 2002, the administration began consultations that would lead, in the fall of 2002, to the formation of a "roadmap" toward that two-state solution by the "quartet" of the United States, Russia, the EU and the UN.

Sometime in March 2002 President Bush ducked his head into National Security Adviser Rice's office as she was briefing three senators on the Iraq issue. "F– Saddam. We're taking him out," the newsmagazine *Time* reported the president saying.[47] In April 2002 President Bush told a British television interviewer that "I made up my mind that Saddam needs to go ... The worst thing that could happen would be to allow a nation like Iraq, run by Saddam Hussein, to develop weapons of mass destruction, and then team up with terrorist organizations so they can blackmail

[43] The text of the speech can be found at http://archives.cnn.com/2002/ALLPOLITICS/01/29/bush.speech.txt/.

[44] Michael Isikoff and David Corn, *Hubris: The Inside Story of Spin, Scandal and the Selling of the Iraq War* (New York: Crown, 2006), p. 9; Woodward, *Plan of Attack*, p. 108. Kessler, "US Decision on Iraq Has Puzzling Past," has the decision in January 2002.

[45] Much of Woodward, *Plan of Attack*, revolves around the various war plans that General Franks brought to Secretary Rumsfeld and President Bush during 2002.

[46] Barton Gellman and Dafna Linzer, "Afghanistan, Iraq: Two Wars Collide," *Washington Post*, October 22, 2004.

[47] Quoted in Daalder and Lindsay, *American Unbound*, p. 132. For another example of President Bush's extremely colorful vocabulary regarding Saddam, see Isikoff and Corn, *Hubris*, p. 3. In the realm of scatology, President Bush had a serious rival in General Franks. Woodward reports that in the same month, at a meeting with his commanders at Central Command headquarters in Florida, Franks told them: "This is f–ing serious. You know, if you guys think this is not going to happen, you're wrong. You need to get off your a–": *Plan of Attack*, p. 115.

the world. I'm not going to let this happen." When pressed on how he would achieve his goal, Bush replied, "Wait and see."[48] A briefing paper for a July 2002 meeting among British prime minister Tony Blair and his foreign policy and security ministers, leaked to the London *Times* in 2005, stated that Britain agreed to a regime change strategy in Iraq that included the use of military force at the April 2002 Bush–Blair summit in Crawford, Texas, provided certain conditions were met: formation of a coalition that could shape public opinion, quiet on the Israeli–Palestinian front and the exhaustion of options to eliminate Iraqi WMD through the UN.[49]

As spring turned to summer in 2002, indications grew that the White House was preparing to go to war. President Bush in June 2002 gave the graduation speech at West Point, saying that deterrence and containment were no longer sufficient to protect American security against the new threats it faced. While not mentioning Iraq by name, this new strategy of preventive war was clearly designed with Iraq in mind.[50] The official White House statement on the new strategy, quickly dubbed the Bush Doctrine, was issued in September 2002. At the July 2002 meeting among senior British officials referenced above, the head of British foreign intelligence told his colleagues that in Washington "[m]ilitary action was now seen as inevitable," a judgment seconded by Foreign Secretary Straw.[51] Jordan's King Abdallah met with the president on August 1, 2002. The king asked Bush, "Can I change your mind?," about war against Iraq. Bush responded, "No."[52] Richard Haass, director of policy planning at the State Department, in early July 2002 met with NSA Rice. He asked whether the administration was "really sure that we wanted to put Iraq front and center at this point, given the war on terrorism and other issues. And she said, essentially, that the decision's been made, don't waste your breath."[53]

A comprehensive American air campaign to disrupt Iraq's military command-and-control system, termed Southern Focus, was launched in mid-2002. The strikes were justified publicly as a reaction to Iraqi violations of the no-fly zone in southern Iraq, but were intended to prepare

[48] Quoted in Woodward, *Plan of Attack*, pp. 119–20.
[49] "Cabinet Office Paper: Conditions for Military Action," *Times* (London), June 12, 2005.
[50] The speech can be found at www.globalsecurity.org/military/library/news/2002/06/mil-020601-usia01b.htm.
[51] "The Secret Downing Street Memo," *Times* (London), May 1, 2005; also available at www.downingstreetmemo.com/memos.html#otherdocs.
[52] John F. Burns, "Jordan's King, in Gamble, Lends Hand to the US," *New York Times*, March 9, 2003.
[53] Lemann, "How It Came to War."

the ground for a land assault.[54] On August 29, 2002, President Bush approved the "goals, objectives and strategy" of the military plan for the Iraq War. The document said that the United States would work with an international coalition if possible, but would act alone if necessary.[55]

It is interesting to note that, as the momentum on the war decision grew, there was not a culminating meeting of the National Security Council at which a final decision on war was made. Rather, a number of smaller decisions began to cascade, giving the war option a sense of inevitability. That trend was interrupted in early August 2002. Secretary of State Powell met privately with President Bush and NSA Rice on August 5 to urge that an international cover, through the UN, be sought for any move against Iraq. Powell's argument was echoed in the public debate at the same time by former Republican foreign policy officials Brent Scowcroft, James Baker and Henry Kissinger. National Security Council meetings on August 14 and August 16 then set the policy line: continued preparation for war, but accompanied by a diplomatic initiative at the United Nations to force a confrontation with Iraq on disarmament.[56] This hardly signaled unanimity within the administration. Some saw the UN approach as a possible alternative to war, others as a step (perhaps not even a necessary one) to secure international and domestic support for war. Just a few days later, Vice President Cheney called into question the effectiveness of weapons inspections in Iraq in a public speech, despite the fact that administration policy was now aimed at forcing the return of those inspectors to Iraq.[57]

In retrospect, it is clear that the move to the UN was not a shift in policy, but a tactical move aimed at shoring up public support for the Iraq campaign in the United States and among potential allies.[58] President Bush had made the decision to change the regime in Iraq sometime

---

[54] Michael Gordon, "US Air Raids in '02 Prepared for War in Iraq," *New York Times,* July 20, 2003. Gordon cites a briefing by Lieutenant General T. Michael Mosley, identified as "the chief allied war commander" for air operations, and interviewed Mosley for the article.

[55] Rowan Scarborough, "US Rushed Post-Saddam Planning," *Washington Times,* September 2, 2003. The article cites a report prepared for the Joint Chiefs of Staff entitled "Operation Iraqi Freedom: Strategic Lessons Learned," which contains a timeline of events from the September 11 attacks through the Iraq War. See also Gordon and Trainor, *Cobra II,* pp. 72–73, for the contents of the document.

[56] Woodward, *Bush at War,* pp. 331–36; Woodward, *Plan of Attack,* pp. 148–57, 161–62.

[57] Purdum *et al., A Time of Our Choosing,* pp. 42–45.

[58] President Bush subsequently told Bob Woodward that his decision to go to the UN for a new resolution was partially the result of pressures from his coalition partners in Britain, Australia and Spain: "Blair had a lot to do with it" (*Plan of Attack,* p. 183). "Going to the UN could help the administration to gain support for the war not just overseas but at home as well. At the time polls consistently showed that the American people would support a war with Iraq only if it had the support of the international community": James Mann, *Rise of the Vulcans: The History of Bush's War Cabinet* (New York: Viking, 2004), p. 343.

between September 12, 2001, and the summer of 2002. Had Saddam Hussein given convincing evidence that Iraq no longer possessed weapons of mass destruction, perhaps the Bush administration's march to war could have been diverted. Had the inspections regime somehow led to a coup against the regime, perhaps Washington would have seen war as unnecessary.[59] However, the Iraqi weapons declaration of December 7, 2002, characterized by UNMOVIC head Hans Blix as "an opportunity missed," simply confirmed for the administration its belief that Saddam Hussein would not disarm. Despite numerous statements from Blix before the war that Iraq was mostly cooperating and his plea for more time to complete the inspections, the administration was convinced that Saddam would not disarm without war.[60] Woodward points to late December 2002 as the point when President Bush decided that war would be necessary to accomplish his aims, and he transmitted this decision to the major cabinet officers in early January 2003.[61] But the record indicates that he was set on war much earlier than that. Bush's contention that Iraq continued to maintain a substantial WMD capacity was the centerpiece of the administration's argument for war. The mounting evidence after the war that Iraq did not have such a capacity called into question both American intelligence capabilities and the Bush administration's credibility.

The war decision and assumptions about Iraqi WMD, terrorist ties and post-war Iraq

The Bush administration rested its public case for war against Iraq on two putative threats – Iraq's possession of weapons of mass destruction and its ties to al-Qaeda – which have subsequently been shown to be baseless.[62] Opponents of the war have taken this as proof that President Bush and

---

[59] Bush told Woodward that his goal with the return of weapons inspectors to Iraq was "a very intrusive inspection regime which Blair and I both were hoping would cause there to be a crumbling within the regime" (*Plan of Attack*, pp. 227, 315–16).

[60] Some in the administration, suspicious of the UN to begin with, believed Blix "was a liar" when he spoke of Iraqi cooperation: Woodward, *Plan of Attack*, p. 240.

[61] Woodward, *Plan of Attack*, pp. 254, 261, 269–70.

[62] The definitive statement of the absence of WMD is the "Comprehensive Report of the Special Advisor to the DCI on Iraq's WMD," September 30, 2004, www.cia.gov/library/ reports/general-reports-1/iraq_wmd_2004/index.html (hereafter referenced as the Duelfer Report, after Charles Duelfer, the special adviser). See the "Key Findings" section. On the lack of a link between al-Qaeda and Saddam Hussein, according to al-Qaeda members in American custody, see James Risen, "Captives Deny Qaeda Worked in Baghdad," *New York Times*, June 9, 2003; and Dana Priest, "Al Qaeda–Iraq Link Recanted," *Washington Post*, August 2, 2004. President Bush himself admitted on September 17, 2003, that there was no link between Saddam Hussein and the September 11 attacks: Dana Milbank, "Bush

those around him lied to the American public and the world in order to mobilize support for their war plans.[63] Subsequent investigations by congressional committees, by a special commission appointed by President Bush and by the media paint a more complex picture. It is difficult to establish with certainty the difference between good-faith but incorrect estimates of disputable facts and uncertain outcomes, and willful misrepresentation and exaggeration of those facts and outcomes for political reasons. It is difficult to discern just what the policy-makers knew and how certain they were of what they knew. Such intimate knowledge would be necessary to answer the question: did the Bush administration lie about the threat that Iraq posed?

I cannot answer that question. The principals can struggle over this issue in their memoirs and in other forums. I want to try to answer a more analytical question: how did very smart people come to such wrongheaded conclusions on a series of factual and interpretative issues, when they had access to substantial contrary evidence, or at least substantial reason to doubt the evidence supporting the incorrect conclusions? Here the vast literature on the intersection of psychology and foreign policy decision-making can provide some guidance.[64] It teaches us that, because of both motivated and cognitive biases, people tend to misinterpret information in predictable ways. If they are convinced of a conclusion, they tend to emphasize information that supports that conclusion and discount information that calls that conclusion into question. Without more recent information, they tend to overrely on "lessons" of the past, reading into the present such "lessons" as fact, even when there is little empirical data to support those conclusions. Such biases affect the perfectly sincere and the liars equally. Readers can make their own moral judgment about the Bush administration. What I hope to demonstrate is that these established psychological tendencies can go a long way to explaining how the Bush

Disavows Hussein–Sept. 11 Link," *Washington Post*, September 18, 2003. The staff of the 9/11 Commission concluded, in a staff report presented to the commission on June 16, 2004, that "we have no credible evidence that Iraq and Al Qaeda cooperated on attacks against the United States": www.9-11commission.gov/staff_statements/staff_statement_15.pdf.

[63] This is the clear implication of the vigorous case made by Chaim Kaufman, "Threat Inflation and the Failure of the Marketplace of Ideas: The Selling of the Iraq War," *International Security*, Vol. 29, No. 1 (Summer 2004), pp. 5–48.

[64] That literature is too vast to review here, and this work is not meant to be a full theoretical test of competing hypotheses of decision-making regarding this case. I simply want to suggest that the insights of the literature on psychology and foreign policy can provide plausible answers to the question I pose. For guidance on these theoretical issues, see Robert Jervis, *American Foreign Policy in a New Era* (New York: Routledge, 2005), particularly Chapters 3–5. For his specific analysis of the US intelligence failures, see his article "Reports, Politics and Intelligence Failures: The Case of Iraq," *Journal of Strategic Studies*, Vol. 29, No. 1 (February 2006), pp. 3–52.

administration deluded so much of the public, and most probably itself, about key issues regarding Iraq.

This chapter has already established the context in which Iraq was viewed by the Bush administration after 9/11. A number of important figures in the administration were already looking for an opportunity to remove Saddam Hussein from power. Even those who were not – President Bush, Vice President Cheney, National Security Adviser Rice – were disposed after 9/11 to see Iraq in a much more sinister light, given the generally held belief that Saddam Hussein still had some elements of his WMD program, the fact that he had in the past supported groups that the United States regarded as terrorists and the certainty that he harbored ill will toward the United States. We know that Bush and Cheney very quickly focused on Iraq in the post-9/11 period. We also know that the American intelligence community, called upon to produce new analyses of the potential Iraqi threat, was hamstrung by a lack of reliable information from sources within Iraq itself. The community was also haunted by past failures on Iraq, both before and after the Gulf War, when it underestimated the extent of Iraq's WMD programs.[65] As the Silberman–Robb Commission reported:

Lacking reliable data about Iraq's progress, analysts' starting point was Iraq's history – its past use of chemical weapons, its successful concealment of WMD programs both before and after the Gulf War, and its failure to account for previously declared stockpiles … In essence, analysts shifted the burden of proof, requiring evidence that Iraq did *not* have WMD. More troubling, some analysts started to disregard evidence that did not support their premise. Chastened by the effectiveness of Iraq's deceptions before the Gulf War, they viewed contradictory information not as evidence that their premise was mistaken, but as evidence that Iraq was continuing to conceal its weapons program.[66]

---

[65] Richard Kerr, who headed a team of retired CIA officials that reviewed pre-war intelligence about Iraq, said that intelligence analysts drew heavily "on a base of hard evidence growing out of the lead-up to the first war, the war itself and then the inspections process … We had a rich base of information and [after the inspectors left Iraq in 1998] we drew on that earlier base": James Risen, David E. Sanger and Thom Shanker, "In Sketchy Data, White House Sought Clues to Gauge Threat," *New York Times*, July 20, 2003. George Tenet confirms that the misjudgments of the late 1980s and early 1990s influenced intelligence judgments about Iraqi WMD: *At the Center of the Storm*, pp. 316, 330.

[66] The Commission on the Intelligence Capabilities of the United States regarding Weapons of Mass Destruction, "Report to the President of the United States," March 31, 2005, Chapter 1, p. 49, www.wmd.gov/report (hereafter referred to as the Silberman–Robb Commission Report). This was the special commission appointed by President Bush to investigate the intelligence failure on the WMD issue. The Senate Select Committee on Intelligence report shared this general conclusion: United States Senate, Select Committee on Intelligence, "Report on the US Intelligence Community's Prewar Intelligence Assessments on Iraq," 108th Congress, July 7, 2004 (hereafter referenced as Senate Intelligence Committee Report), pp. 18–20.

As will be demonstrated below, the Bush administration exaggerated the intelligence about the extent of the threat posed by Iraq, more in some areas (nuclear weapons, al-Qaeda link) than in others (chemical and biological weapons). Members of the administration also accepted exceedingly optimistic projections about the difficulties and costs of stabilizing post-Saddam Iraq, despite very credible reports from both inside and outside the government calling those projections into question. This section will examine these four issues – biological and chemical weapons, nuclear weapons, the al-Qaeda link and post-war Iraq – to see how the administration came to its mistaken judgments. I conclude the section with an assessment of the "politicization" of the intelligence on Iraq and my judgment about these issues generally.

Iraq's biological and chemical weapons

The baseline finding of the American intelligence community on the question of Iraqi biological weapons, before the 9/11 attacks, was that Saddam Hussein retained both stockpiles that were, or could easily be, weaponized and the ability to produce more such weapons. Certainly the decision-makers in the Clinton administration thought that Iraq had at least a biological weapons program, if not a weaponized biological capability itself. It emphasized that fact during Operation Desert Fox in December 1998. Though they did not have specific evidence, the community judged in an August 1999 National Intelligence Estimate that the biological weapons program was "being revitalized" in the absence of UN inspectors. In December 2000, an Intelligence Community Assessment reported, based upon a single source, that Iraq had constructed seven mobile biological weapons plants and was generally increasing its focus on biological weapons production. The December 2000 Assessment was a significant upgrading of the picture of Iraq's biological weapons capabilities, though it also contained caveats about the uncertainties surrounding the issue.[67]

It was subsequently revealed that the single source responsible for the upgrading of the warning on the Iraqi biological weapons program, particularly on the mobile plants, was an Iraqi defector code-named Curveball. He had defected in Germany, and his information was provided to the American intelligence community by its German counterpart. There were numerous questions raised about his credibility within the intelligence community. However, his information began to be used again in finished intelligence by July 2002, including in the October 2002

---

[67] Senate Intelligence Committee Report, pp. 143–45.

NIE that helped to make the case for war and in Secretary of State Powell's presentation to the United Nations Security Council in February 2003.[68]

When the 9/11 attacks occurred, therefore, the intelligence community judgment was that Saddam Hussein probably had biological weapons and the capacity to produce more of them. The "probably" part of the assessment disappeared from community reports as policy-makers began to focus more intently upon Iraq in the post-9/11 period. The October 2002 NIE stated with "high confidence" that Iraq possessed biological weapons.[69]

Despite the obvious failure of the intelligence community to adequately vet Iraqi defector sources such as Curveball, and its willingness to jettison the earlier cautions it had included in its assessment of the biological weapons threat posed by Iraq, the post-9/11 community judgment on this issue is not that different from its pre-9/11 judgment. It is simply stated much more definitively. The Senate Intelligence Committee Report, which was the most scathing assessment of the intelligence community's work on biological weapons, took the community to task more for not highlighting the uncertainties about its conclusions – for overstatement and lack of recognition of possible alternative explanations – than for absolutely misreading the biological weapons issue. The report found that the community's conclusions about Iraq's ability "to produce and weaponize biological agents are, for the most part, supported by the intelligence provided to the Committee."[70] While the community's judgments about Iraqi biological weapons were incorrect, they were not unreasonable given the baseline knowledge provided by the final report of the United Nations Special Commission on Iraqi Disarmament (UNSCOM), Iraq's past behavior and the widely held assumptions about Saddam Hussein's ambitions.

The story of the intelligence community's assessment of Iraq's chemical weapons program is similar. Pre-9/11 reporting emphasized that Iraq had the material and the capability to produce chemical weapons, particularly after the end of the UNSCOM inspections in December 1998. The Clinton administration had emphasized the continuing threat of Iraq's

---

[68] Senate Intelligence Committee Report, pp. 152–60; Silberman–Robb Commission Report, pp. 81–85.

[69] Jim Dwyer, "Defectors' Reports on Iraq Arms Were Embellished, Exile Asserts," *New York Times*, July 9, 2004. The Senate Intelligence Committee subsequently concluded that "the Iraqi National Congress (INC) attempted to influence United States policy on Iraq by providing false information through defectors directed at convincing the United States that Iraq possessed weapons of mass destruction and had links to terrorists": US Senate, Select Committee on Intelligence, "The Use by the Intelligence Community of Information Provided by the Iraqi National Congress," 109th Congress, 2nd Session, September 8, 2006, p. 113, http://intelligence.senate.gov/phaseiiiinc.pdf

[70] Senate Intelligence Committee Report, Conclusion 54 (p. 192).

chemical weapons capabilities during the December 1998 Desert Fox operation. The reliance of the community on the reporting of UNSCOM is highlighted by a September 1998 finding regarding Iraqi chemical weapons in a report prepared by the National Intelligence Council: "Gaps and inconsistencies in Iraqi declarations to UNSCOM strongly suggest that Iraq retains stockpiles of chemical munitions and agents."[71] In February 1999 a report produced by the CIA, the Defense Intelligence Agency (DIA) and Central Command concluded that "we believe that Iraq possesses chemical agent stockpiles that can be, or already are, weaponized and ready for use." While the report also found that Iraq retained the infrastructure to produce chemical weapons, it judged that Iraq had not resumed such production.[72]

As was the case with biological weapons, the post-9/11 intelligence judgments regarding chemical weapons dropped many of the qualifiers and stated their findings more definitively. The October 2002 National Intelligence Estimate stated that Iraq had chemical weapons and also asserted that Iraq had resumed production of a number of chemical weapons agents. Part of this new certainty stemmed from new imagery intelligence that showed trucks moving to and from suspected chemical weapons sites in Iraq, leading analysts to judge that activity around the sites had increased.[73]

There was a substantial, pre-9/11 basis within the intelligence community for policy-makers to believe that Iraq possessed biological and chemical weapons. That belief was shared by other governments and outside observers. In a paper prepared in March 2002, the Overseas and Defense Secretariat of the British Cabinet Office reported that "Iraq continues with its BW [biological weapons] and CW [chemical weapons] programmes, and, if it has not done so already, could produce significant quantities of BW agents within days and CW agents within weeks of a decision to do so."[74] UNMOVIC head Blix said that up to a month before the war, he still thought that the Iraqis were concealing banned weapons.[75] The *New York Times*, which opposed the Iraq War, editorialized in September 2003: "Like President Bush, we believed that Saddam

[71] Senate Intelligence Committee Report, p. 195.
[72] Senate Intelligence Committee Report, pp. 195–96. See also Silberman–Robb Report, p. 115.
[73] Silberman–Robb Commission Report, pp. 116, 123–26. See also Senate Intelligence Committee Report, pp. 200–01.
[74] "Iraq: Options Paper," Overseas and Defense Secretariat, Cabinet Office, 8 March [2002], www.downingstreetmemo.com/docs/iraqoptions.pdf.
[75] Warren Hoge, "Blix Says White House Had 'Set Mind' on Iraqi Weapons," *New York Times*, March 15, 2004.

Hussein was hiding potentially large quantities of chemical and biological weapons."[76] Even high-ranking Iraqis, members of the Revolutionary Command Council, were surprised when Saddam told them in late 2002 that Iraq had no weapons of mass destruction.[77] These assessments confirm the reasonableness of the American intelligence community's judgment that Iraq possessed biological and chemical weapons. Other observers, not wedded to either the political ends of the Bush administration or the analytical frameworks of the American intelligence community, reached roughly the same conclusion on the question.

For those policy-makers who had targeted Iraq before the 9/11 attacks, the intelligence on biological and chemical weapons simply confirmed their view that Iraq was a threat to the United States. For policy-makers such as President Bush, Vice President Cheney and NSA Rice, who did not exhibit strong inclinations on Iraq before 9/11, the intelligence on Iraq was seen through the new prism of their fears about terrorist attacks on the American homeland with WMD.[78] Having quickly come to the conclusion that the post-9/11 threat from Iraq was much more serious than they had previously thought, they were disposed to look to the intelligence community for stronger confirmation of that conclusion and to discount uncertainties and caveats about Iraq's chemical and biological capacity. The consequences of underestimation were too great, in the wake of 9/11. The fact that it was sincerely believed within the administration, and was not simply a pretext to gain public support, is demonstrated by the extensive preparations made by American forces to confront chemical and biological weapons on the battlefield.[79]

In response to these new concerns from the top level of the administration, the intelligence community stated its judgments about Iraqi chemical and biological weapons much more definitively after 9/11. The more definitive intelligence findings after 9/11 stemmed in part from new information, from human sources and technical sources, which proved to be inaccurate. They stemmed in part from preexisting beliefs about Saddam Hussein's intentions and capabilities, and an unwillingness to challenge those beliefs as the political process moved toward war with Iraq. The more definitive tone of the findings also came from the intense

---

[76] "The Failure to Find Iraqi Weapons," *New York Times*, September 26, 2003.
[77] Duelfer Report, "Regime Strategic Intent" section, p. 16.
[78] In July 2003 Secretary of Defense Rumsfeld told the Senate Armed Services Committee: "The coalition did not act in Iraq because we had discovered dramatic new evidence of Iraq's pursuit [of WMD]. We acted because we saw the evidence in a dramatic new light – through the prism of our experience on 9/11" – (Dana Milbank and Mike Allen, "Bush and Rumsfeld Defend Use of Prewar Intelligence on Iraq," *Washington Post*, July 10, 2003).
[79] Gordon and Trainor, *Cobra II*, p. 80.

interest top policy-makers showed in getting just such definitive findings, an issue to which I will return below in the section on politicization of intelligence. However, in the case of chemical and biological weapons, the Bush Administration did not have to push the intelligence community very far. Its pre-9/11 consensus already leaned very strongly to the conclusion that Iraq possessed these weapons. That consensus was wrong, but it was not unreasonable.[80]

Iraq's nuclear program

The nuclear issue was considerably different than the biological and chemical weapons issue, in that the intelligence consensus before 9/11 was that Iraq did not pose a serious nuclear threat. The intelligence community, in a number of reports prepared in the late 1990s, concluded that Iraq had not reconstituted its nuclear program. Saddam Hussein had the ultimate desire to rebuild his nuclear capabilities, the reports asserted, and Iraq retained the human and technological capital to operate a nuclear weapons program, but there were no indications that it was pursuing that path at that time. Moreover, UNSCOM and the IAEA had successfully destroyed or neutralized substantial portions of Iraq's nuclear infrastructure during the early and mid-1990s, making it very difficult for Iraq to stage a "nuclear breakout" over a short period of time.[81] As late as December 2000, a community assessment noted that Iraq "still does not appear to have taken major steps towards reconstitution" of its nuclear program.[82]

The only indication, before 9/11, of a change in the intelligence community's assessment of Iraq's nuclear capabilities came in a spring 2001 report that Iraq was seeking high-strength aluminum alloy tubes, judged by some analysts to be consistent with requirements for building centrifuges, the key part of the uranium enrichment process aimed at producing fissile material. That report also noted other indications of Iraqi procurement that were consistent with reconstituting the nuclear program.[83] The aluminum alloy tubes quickly became the center of a major analytical conflict within the intelligence community, to be discussed below. However, this report was the beginning of some rethinking within the community

[80] Robert Jervis comes to much the same conclusion, not just on biological and chemical weapons but also on the intelligence community's assessment of the Iraqi nuclear program: "Reports, Politics and Intelligence Failures: The Case of Iraq."
[81] Senate Intelligence Committee Report, pp. 84–85; Silberman–Robb Commission Report, pp. 53–55.
[82] Silberman–Robb Commission Report, p. 55.
[83] The Silberman–Robb Commission Report dates that report to March 2001 (pp. 55–56); the Senate Intelligence Committee Report gives a date of April 2001 (p. 88).

of the Iraqi nuclear program. The Silberman–Robb Commission reported that analysts began to worry that "they may again be facing a surprise similar to the one in 1991," when the American intelligence community had underestimated the progress Iraq had made toward acquiring a nuclear capability.[84]

In the wake of 9/11, the intelligence community reached very different judgments about Iraq's nuclear program. The October 2002 NIE stated: "Most agencies assess that Baghdad started reconstituting its nuclear program about the time that UNSCOM inspectors departed – December 1998."[85] This marked a significant upgrading of the Iraqi nuclear threat. The key indicator of reconstitution highlighted by the NIE was Iraq's interest in procuring the high-strength aluminum alloy tubes.

Far from being united in its assessment of the aluminum tubes, however, the intelligence community was divided on whether they were suited to centrifuge design, and thus an indicator of nuclear intent, or whether they were more likely intended for conventional, short-range rockets. One congressional investigator characterized the disputes within the community on the aluminum tubes as a "holy war."[86] The theory that the tubes were an indication of nuclear intent was championed by analysts at the CIA. Their counterparts at the State Department's Bureau of Intelligence and Research (INR) and at the Department of Energy (DOE) vigorously objected to the CIA conclusion.[87] In the NIE itself, INR officially dissented from the finding that Iraq was seeking to reconstitute its nuclear program. The DOE agreed that the country was attempting to restart the program, but not based upon the evidence of the tubes.[88] The DOE based its case largely upon intelligence reports, subsequently discredited, that Iraq was seeking to obtain yellowcake uranium from Niger. Ironically, the CIA had by the fall of 2002 begun to question the validity of the Niger information. So the majority opinion of the intelligence community on the reconstitution of Iraq's nuclear program was a bureaucratic compromise,

---

[84] Silberman–Robb Commission Report, p. 56. Tenet reports that the intelligence underestimation of the Iraqi nuclear program at the time of the Gulf War "had a profound impact on my views and those of many of our analysts … we were haunted by the possibility that there was more going on than we could detect": *At the Center of the Storm*, p. 316; see also p. 330.

[85] "Iraq's Continuing Programs for Weapons of Mass Destruction," National Intelligence Estimate, October 2002, declassified July 18, 2003, www.fas.org/irp/cia/product/iraq-wmd.htm.

[86] David Barstow *et al.*, "Skewed Intelligence on Iraq Colored the March to War," *New York Times*, October 3, 2004.

[87] The Senate Intelligence Committee Report has the most extensive and detailed account of the conflict within the community over the aluminum tubes, and a damning criticism of the CIA assessment that they were intended for centrifuge construction (pp. 87–119).

[88] "Iraq's Continuing Programs for Weapons of Mass Destruction," NIE, October 2002.

with the CIA basing its findings on evidence discredited by the DOE and the DOE basing its findings on evidence discredited by the CIA.[89]

The story of the Niger connection, the other major piece of evidence that Iraq was reconstituting its nuclear program, has had a much fuller public airing than the aluminum tubes issue. It became a *cause célèbre* after the Iraq War, when former US ambassador Joseph Wilson publicly criticized the Bush administration for citing Iraqi efforts to obtain yellow-cake uranium from Africa as proof of Iraq's nuclear intentions.[90] Wilson's public attack on the Bush administration was followed by a news report that identified Wilson's wife, Valerie Plame, as the CIA official who proposed that Wilson make the fact-finding trip to Niger. Although not in the field, Plame was at that time still an undercover employee of the CIA, and releasing her name to the press was a violation of federal law. A special prosecutor appointed to investigate the case subsequently obtained an indictment of Vice President Cheney's chief of staff, I. Lewis (Scooter) Libby, on charges of making false statements to a grand jury related to the case. Libby was tried and convicted.

The "Plame-gate" scandal had little to do with the development of the nuclear case against Iraq in the lead-up to the war, as Wilson's trip to Niger had little effect on the developing analysis. More central to the analysis was the publication of a British government White Paper on September 24, 2002, which stated "there is intelligence that Iraq has sought the supply of significant quantities of uranium from Africa." There was sufficient doubt in the US intelligence community about the source of the report that the National Intelligence Estimate prepared in October 2002 downplayed the Niger connection in its discussion of the Iraqi nuclear program. There was no mention of the African yellowcake connection in the NIE's "Key Judgments" section. In a section on "Uranium Acquisition" found on page 25, deep into the document, the NIE states that a "foreign government service" reported on the Niger–Iraq yellowcake deal. It went on to say "we do not know the status of this arrangement." It then referenced other reports of Iraqi efforts to obtain uranium ore from Somalia and "possibly" the Democratic Republic of the Congo. It concluded: "We cannot confirm whether Iraq succeeded in acquiring uranium ore and/or yellowcake from these sources."[91]

Almost immediately after the publication of the October 2002 NIE, an Italian journalist provided the American embassy in Rome with

[89] Barstow *et al.*, "Skewed Intelligence on Iraq Colored the March to War."

[90] For a detailed account of this issue, see Isikoff and Corn, *Hubris*, Chapters 5, 13–15, 17–19.

[91] "Iraq's Continuing Programs for Weapons of Mass Destruction," NIE, October 2002.

documents related to the alleged Niger–Iraq agreement. State Department analysts quickly judged the documents to be forgeries and conveyed that finding to the entire intelligence community. The IAEA, given copies of the documents by the United States, also concluded some months later, in early 2003, that they were forgeries.[92] Secretary of State Powell found the information to be sufficiently questionable that he left it out of his presentation about Iraq's WMD programs to the UN Security Council on February 5, 2003.[93] The CIA, however, did not independently analyze the documents. It continued to report in the months leading up to the war that Iraq was probably seeking to acquire uranium from African countries. The CIA director cleared President Bush's January 2003 State of the Union address, in which he asserted that "the British government has learned that Saddam Hussein recently sought significant quantities of uranium from Africa."[94] Both the White House and the CIA subsequently acknowledged that this assertion was based on false information, but that was after the Iraq War.

The intelligence community's findings on Iraq's nuclear program in the months leading up to the Iraq War were not nearly as certain or unanimous as its findings on chemical and biological weapons. While the issues of both the aluminum alloy tubes and the Niger yellowcake connection were accepted by some parts of the community as evidence of Iraqi efforts to reconstitute the nuclear program, they were vigorously challenged by other parts. Nowhere in the National Intelligence Estimate of October 2002 did the community say that Iraq had a nuclear weapon in the way it stated "with high confidence" that Iraq had chemical and biological weapons. Its "high confidence" finding was that Iraq "could make a nuclear weapon in months to a year once it acquires sufficient weapons-grade fissile material." However, it did not conclude that Iraq had acquired such material and was cautious in its assessment of the Niger and other African connections. It concluded with "moderate confidence" that Iraq "does not yet have a nuclear weapon or sufficient material to make one, but is likely to have a weapon by 2007 to 2009," while acknowledging that the State Department's Bureau of Intelligence and Research believed that Iraq was much further away from acquiring a nuclear weapon. It stressed the attempts to acquire aluminum alloy tubes as evidence of reconstitution, but acknowledged that the Department of Energy did not agree that they were compelling evidence.[95] On the whole, while incorrect about the extent

---

[92] Silberman–Robb Commission Report, pp. 77–78.
[93] Senate Intelligence Committee Report, p. 68.
[94] Senate Intelligence Committee Report, p. 66.
[95] "Iraq's Continuing Programs for Weapons of Mass Destruction," NIE, October 2002.

of Iraqi nuclear reconstitution, the intelligence community was much more cautious and much more clearly divided on the nuclear question in the lead-up to the Iraq War than it was on biological and chemical weapons.

Moreover, top officials in the Bush administration knew of these disputes and uncertainties. A senior administration official said that NSA Rice "was aware of differences of opinion" in the community on Iraq's nuclear program, specifically on the issue of the aluminum alloy tubes. CIA and administration officials told the *New York Times* that "dissenting views were repeatedly discussed in meetings and telephone calls" and presented to senior officials. CIA director Tenet told the newspaper that he had "made it clear" to the White House "that the case for a possible nuclear program in Iraq was weaker than that for chemical and biological weapons." In closed hearings in September 2002, members of Congress heard testimony on the debate over the aluminum tubes.[96] The administration had access to the testimony of Saddam's son-in-law, Hussein Kamel, who defected from Iraq in 1995 after being in charge of Iraq's WMD programs. Kamel told UN weapons inspectors that Iraq had had an active nuclear program before the Gulf War of 1990–91, but that it had not resumed nuclear efforts after that war.[97]

Yet, in their public statements, the top officials of the administration emphasized their certainty that Iraq was actively pursuing nuclear weapons. Vice President Cheney told the Veterans of Foreign Wars convention in late August 2002 that "many of us are convinced that Saddam Hussein will acquire nuclear weapons fairly soon."[98] A few weeks later, in a speech to Wyoming Republicans, he said that the United States had "irrefutable evidence" in the aluminum alloy tubes that Iraq was working on nuclear weapons. NSA Rice told CNN on September 8, 2002 that the tubes were "only really suited for nuclear weapons programs," adding that "we don't want the smoking gun [definitive proof of Iraq's WMD capability] to be a mushroom cloud." The IAEA inspectors, who had returned to Iraq in November 2002, found by January 2003 that the tubes were being used by the Iraqis for rocket construction. UNMOVIC reported to the UN Security Council on January 27, 2003, that it had found no evidence of a revived nuclear weapons program in Iraq. Despite these public findings, President Bush in his January 28, 2003, State of the Union address cited the tubes, which he said were "suitable for nuclear weapons production,"

[96] Barstow *et al.*, "Skewed Intelligence on Iraq Colored the March to War."

[97] Barton Gellman and Walter Pincus, "Depiction of Threat Outgrew Supporting Evidence," *Washington Post*, August 10, 2003.

[98] The text of the speech is available at www.newamericancentury.org/iraq-082602.htm. Tenet says that the speech, which was not cleared by CIA, "went well beyond what our analysis could support": *At the Center of the Storm*, p. 315.

as evidence, along with the African uranium connection, of Iraq's nuclear ambitions.[99]

The administration's willingness to accept the contested intelligence judgment that Iraq was reconstituting its nuclear weapons program is probably attributable to two factors. The first is the motivated psychological bias of accepting information that accords with your preconceptions and that supports conclusions you have already reached.[100] Saddam's Iraq had come close to developing nuclear weapons in the 1980s, and the intelligence community had misjudged how close Iraq was to nuclear capability then. Moreover, Iraqi defectors involved in the program had already gone public with accounts of Saddam's effort to reconstitute.[101] Why believe the hedged judgments of analysts who had been wrong in the past when officials inside the program had already come clean about it? The second factor is more instrumental. In mobilizing public support for war, the nuclear issue was galvanizing. The imagery NSA Rice evoked when she warned that the "smoking gun" proving Saddam's possession of WMD could be a "mushroom cloud" was powerful. For officials who strongly believed that Saddam Hussein possessed biological and chemical weapons, based upon seemingly airtight intelligence, the step to believing that he also was seeking nuclear weapons, despite the more divided intelligence assessments, was short. If the WMD threat was real, and the way to mobilize public opinion to deal with that threat was to emphasize an element of that threat where the evidence was not as strong, perhaps exaggeration could be justified as being in the best interest of the country.[102]

Iraq's ties to al-Qaeda

Perhaps the most politically effective argument made by the administration in its case for war with Iraq was the alleged connection between Saddam

---

[99] Barstow *et al.*, "Skewed Intelligence on Iraq Colored the March to War."

[100] Paul Pillar, the national intelligence officer for the Middle East at the National Intelligence Council at the time, has written: "The administration used intelligence not to inform decision-making, but to justify a decision already made" ("Intelligence, Policy and the War in Iraq," *Foreign Affairs*, Vol. 85, No. 2 [March/April 2006], pp. 17–18).

[101] The most notable was the account by an Iraqi scientist involved with the program: Khidhir Hamza and Jeff Stein, *Saddam's Bombmaker: The Terrifying Story of the Iraqi Nuclear and Biological Weapons Agenda* (New York: Simon & Schuster, 2000).

[102] One senior policy-maker with directly relevant responsibilities told the *Washington Post* after the war: "I never cared about the 'imminent [nuclear] threat' ... The threat was there in [Saddam's] presence in office. To me, just knowing what it takes to have a nuclear weapons program, he needed a lot of equipment. You can stare at the yellowcake all you want. You need to convert it to gas and enrich it. That does not constitute an imminent threat, and the people who are saying that, I think, did not fully appreciate the difficulties and effort involved in producing nuclear material and the physics package" (Gellman and Pincus, "Depiction of Threat Outgrew Supporting Evidence").

Hussein's regime and al-Qaeda. In the aftermath of 9/11, any link between the two, particularly any Iraq–al-Qaeda link that related to the 9/11 attacks, would be a clinching argument for American public opinion to support a war against Iraq. Administration officials repeatedly emphasized what Secretary of State Powell called, in his February 2003 presentation to the UN Security Council, the "sinister nexus" between Iraq and al-Qaeda.[103]

The intelligence community was extremely cautious in its analysis of the Iraq–al-Qaeda link in its pre-war analysis, despite the fact that the Counterterrorism Center of CIA was "purposefully aggressive in seeking to draw connections" between the two in the wake of the 9/11 attacks.[104] The culminating pre-war report of the intelligence community on Iraq–al-Qaeda links was prepared in January 2003 under the title "Iraqi Support for Terrorism." On the al-Qaeda link, it cited a number of reports about contacts and relations between the two, but also emphasized that many of these reports came from foreign governments or Iraqi opposition groups whose reliability was questionable.[105] The report's overall conclusion: "In contrast to the patron–client pattern between Iraq and its Palestinian surrogates, the relationship between Iraq and al-Qaeda appears to more closely resemble that of two independent actors trying to exploit each other." It further concluded that there was no evidence of Iraqi involvement in or foreknowledge of the 9/11 attacks.[106]

The CIA's analysis of the Iraq–al-Qaeda link was, however, not the only account of that relationship circulating in policy circles in the lead-up to the Iraq War. Shortly after the 9/11 attacks, Undersecretary of Defense for Policy Feith established a Policy Counter Terrorism Evaluation Group (PCTEG) in his office. Feith was a public proponent of ousting Saddam Hussein from power before taking up his position in the Bush administration. This small office (it consisted of two consultants, replaced in a few months by two naval intelligence officers, later joined by an analyst on loan from the DIA) was tasked with reevaluating information from the intelligence community regarding terrorist groups, state sponsors and the links among them. By November 2001 the PCTEG was briefing Pentagon officials on the link between Iraq and al-Qaeda, painting a much different and more alarming picture of the relationship than the intelligence community did. In early 2002 it produced an extensive presentation on the issue

---

[103] The text can be found at www.cnn.com/2003/US/02/05/sprj.irq.powell.transcript/.

[104] The quote is from the Counterterrorism Center's analytical paper "Iraq and al-Qaida: Interpreting a Murky Relationship," distributed in June 2002; cited in Senate Intelligence Committee Report, p. 305.

[105] Senate Intelligence Committee Report, pp. 304–49; the reliability of link reports is discussed on p. 326.

[106] Senate Intelligence Committee Report, p. 322.

in which it explicitly criticized the intelligence community's approach to the issue. That briefing was presented to Lewis Libby, Vice President Cheney's chief of staff, and Stephen Hadley, the deputy national security adviser, in September 2002.[107] While the office was established to review existing intelligence, it subsequently established its own channels of intelligence collection as well. Richard Perle, an advocate of the overthrow of Saddam Hussein and chairman of the Defense Policy Board, a Pentagon advisory group, brokered a connection between the PCTEG and the Iraqi National Congress, the exile Iraqi opposition group headed by Ahmad Chalabi.[108]

The crux of the PCTEG account of the Iraq–al-Qaeda link was a list of fifty purported instances of contact between representatives of the two sides, which amounted, in the words of the group's briefing slides, to a "mature, symbiotic relationship" between them.[109] Many of those contacts were reported by the intelligence community, but with warnings about the community's doubts about the reliability of the sources of the information.[110] The most notorious of these contacts was the purported meeting, reported by Czech counterintelligence, between 9/11 hijacker Muhammad Atta and the head of the Iraqi Intelligence Service office in Prague in April 2001. The PCTEG briefing included the assertion, based upon this meeting, that there were "some indications of possible Iraqi coordination with al-Qaida specifically related to 9/11."[111] That meeting became the centerpiece of the administration's public case implicating Iraq in the 9/11 attacks, despite the fact that "the CIA judged that other evidence indicated that these meetings likely never occurred."[112] Secretary of State

---

[107] Senate Intelligence Committee Report, pp. 307–12; Isikoff and Corn, *Hubris*, Chapter 6; James Risen, "How Pair's Finding on Terror Led to Clash on Shaping Intelligence," *New York Times*, April 28, 2004; Douglas Jehl, "CIA Chief Says He's Corrected Cheney Privately," *New York Times*, March 10, 2004.

[108] Risen, "How Pair's Finding on Terror Led to Clash on Shaping Intelligence."

[109] The content of the briefing was conveyed by Undersecretary Feith to the Senate Intelligence Committee in October 2003. It was subsequently leaked, its contents appearing in summary form in Stephen Hayes, "Case Closed: The US Government's Secret Memo Detailing Cooperation Between Saddam Hussein and Osama bin Laden," *Weekly Standard*, November 24, 2003, www.weeklystandard.com/Content/Public/ Articles/000/000/003/378fmxyz.asp. A declassified copy of the briefing slides used by the PCTEG to brief administration officials can be found at www.fas.org/irp/news/2007/ 04/feithslides.pdf. See slide 7 for the quote.

[110] Senate Intelligence Committee Report, pp. 321–33; Senator Carl Levin, "Report of an Inquiry into the Alternative Analysis of the Issue of an Iraq–al Qaeda Relationship," October 21, 2004, p. 16, www.levin.senate.gov/newsroom/supporting/2004/102104 inquiryreport.pdf.

[111] Slide 19, www.fas.org/irp/news/2007/04/feithslides.pdf.

[112] Senate Intelligence Committee Report, p. 340. As early as September 21, 2001, CIA director Tenet told President Bush that the intelligence community was "skeptical" about the reported meeting between Atta and an Iraqi intelligence official in Prague: Suskind, *The One Percent Doctrine*, p. 23.

Powell chose not to mention the purported Prague meeting in his February 2003 presentation to the UN Security Council. The 9/11 Commission subsequently reported that "the available evidence does not support the original Czech report" of a meeting between the two.[113]

The other major connection the administration pointed to in its case for an Iraq–al-Qaeda link was the presence of al-Qaeda affiliate Abu Musab al-Zarqawi in Iraq before the war. Secretary Powell, in his presentation to the UN Security Council, charged that Iraq "harbor[ed]" al-Zarqawi, implying a cooperative relationship. The PCTEG case included the assertion that Iraq provided safe haven to al-Zarqawi and that Saddam's regime had a "close relationship" with Ansar al-Islam, the Iraqi Kurdish Islamist group with which al-Zarqawi took refuge in the pre-war period.[114] The intelligence community emphasized in its reporting that al-Zarqawi and his group had relocated, after the fall of the Taliban in Afghanistan, to an area in northeastern Iraq controlled by Ansar al-Islam. It concluded that Saddam Hussein's regime undoubtedly had knowledge of the presence of al-Zarqawi's group in Iraq and that Saddam probably acquiesced to that presence, though he did not have control of the territory in which al-Zarqawi was operating. It also reported that al-Zarqawi probably spent some time in Baghdad in the period before the Iraq War, establishing a network of sympathizers. Despite the fact that a foreign intelligence service had informed Saddam's government of al-Zarqawi's presence in Baghdad, Iraqi intelligence contended to that service that it could not locate al-Zarqawi. While acknowledging the dangers of Iraqi–al-Qaeda cooperation presented by the al-Zarqawi information, the CIA did not conclude from this that there was any such cooperation on terrorist operations. CIA director Tenet told the Senate Intelligence Committee (on the relationship more generally, not specifically on the al-Zarqawi link): "These sources do not describe Iraqi complicity in, control over or authorization of specific terrorist attacks carried out by al-Qaida."[115]

While the PCTEG and the intelligence community were producing these different assessments of the Iraq–al-Qaeda link in the lead-up to the Iraq War, a new intelligence source on the issue emerged: captured al-Qaeda commanders. Unfortunately for intelligence analysts, these

---

[113] *The 9/11 Commission Report*, pp. 228–29.

[114] See slide 16 on the link between al-Zarqawi and the Iraqi regime and slide 17 for the links between Ansar al-Islam and the regime. The briefing also asserted that al-Qaeda elements had received training at Iraqi facilities and that there were indications of Iraq–al-Qaeda cooperation on biological and chemical weapons development: www.fas.org/irp/news/2007/04/feithslides.pdf.

[115] Senate Intelligence Committee Report, pp. 334–38, quote on p. 338.

debriefings provided "contradictory" evidence.[116] Ibn al-Shaykh al-Libi, an al-Qaeda commander captured in Pakistan in November 2001, said that Iraq had provided chemical and biological weapons training to members of the organization. He later recanted that assertion, though it cannot be established whether that recantation occurred before or after the Iraq War. However, there was evidence before the war that al-Libi was telling different stories to different people about Iraq–al-Qaeda links.[117] At least one report before the Iraq War from the intelligence community questioned al-Libi's credibility in making this claim.[118] On the other hand, Abu Zubaydah, an al-Qaeda commander captured in April 2002 in Pakistan, told his captors that he was not aware of a relationship between Iraq and his organization, though he admitted that any such relationship would have been highly compartmentalized, and he might not know about it. Khalid Shaykh Muhammad, the mastermind of the 9/11 attacks, was captured in Pakistan in March 2003, on the eve of the Iraq War. Information gleaned from him would not have been part of the intelligence analysis of Iraq–al-Qaeda links in the pre-war period. Like Abu Zubaydah, he contended that he was unaware of any link between bin Laden's group and the Iraqi regime.[119]

The conflicting accounts between the PCTEG and the intelligence community regarding Iraq–al-Qaeda links were never reconciled in the months leading up to the Iraq War. In August 2002 Undersecretary Feith and the group presented their findings, minus a briefing slide on the purported Atta meeting in Prague and a slide explicitly criticizing the intelligence community's work on the issue, to CIA director Tenet and a number of CIA officials and analysts.[120] The CIA analysts agreed to include some of the PCTEG's reports about purported contacts between Iraq and al-Qaeda, but did not change their analytical conclusion about the lack of a substantive relationship between the two sides.[121] Despite the differences between the two accounts, and unbeknownst to Tenet, the

---

[116] Senate Intelligence Committee Report, p. 323.

[117] Dana Priest, "Al Qaeda–Iraq Link Recanted," *Washington Post*, August 2, 2004. Isikoff and Corn report that al-Libi originally told his FBI interrogators that al-Qaeda had no links to Saddam, but that after the CIA had transferred al-Libi to Egyptian authorities he told his Egyptian captors that there was an al-Qaeda–Iraq link. When he was returned to FBI custody, he recanted the story he told the Egyptians. When asked why he had told the Egyptians there was a link, he said, "They were killing me. I had to tell them something": Isikoff and Corn, *Hubris*, pp. 119–24.

[118] Walter Pincus, "Newly Released Data Undercut Prewar Claims," *Washington Post*, November 6, 2005.

[119] Senate Intelligence Committee Report, p. 325.

[120] Senate Intelligence Committee Report, p. 310.

[121] Levin, "Report of an Inquiry into the Alternative Analysis of the Issue of an Iraq–al Qaeda Relationship," pp. 15–16.

PCTEG a few weeks later presented its findings to Libby and Hadley at the White House, including their conclusion that the Prague meeting did occur and including their direct criticism of the intelligence community's work on the Iraq–al-Qaeda relationship.[122] The Defense Department's inspector general subsequently found that the activities of Undersecretary Feith's group, while not illegal or unauthorized, were "inappropriate, given that the intelligence assessments were intelligence products and did not clearly show the variance with the consensus of the Intelligence Community ... As a result, OUSD(P) [Office of the Undersecretary of Defense for Policy] did not provide 'the most accurate analysis of intelligence' to senior Defense decision makers."[123]

Despite the clear differences between the conclusions of the intelligence community and the PCTEG, administration officials used the latter's analysis in making their public case that the Iraq–al-Qaeda tie justified war.[124] Administration officials regularly asserted in the period between 9/11 and the Iraq War that there was a long history of contacts between Iraq and al-Qaeda, without including the cautions of the community about the reliability of some of the reports and the overall conclusion that there was no operational relationship between the two sides. President Bush referred to Saddam as an "ally" of al-Qaeda in his May 2003 speech announcing the end of major combat operations in Iraq. Vice President Cheney in particular referred to the Prague meetings repeatedly in public, both before and after the war, despite the intelligence community's judgment that the information was not reliable.[125]

As in the case of nuclear weapons, two reasons explain the administration's acceptance of the more extreme findings of the PCTEG regarding Iraq–al-Qaeda links and its rejection of the more nuanced and less alarmist analysis by the intelligence community. The first is the motivated psychological bias of accepting information that accords with your

---

[122] Jehl, "CIA Chief Says He's Corrected Cheney Privately."

[123] United States Department of Defense, Office of the Inspector General, Deputy Inspector General for Intelligence, "Review of the Pre-Iraqi War Activities of the Office of the Undersecretary of Defense for Policy," Report No. 07-INTEL-04, February 9, 2007, www.fas.org/irp/agency/dod/ig020907-decl.pdf; quotes from pp. 15–16.

[124] The Senate Intelligence Committee subsequently concluded that the intelligence community's assessment of the lack of linkage between Saddam and al-Qaeda was accurate. "Postwar findings indicate that Saddam Hussein was distrustful of al-Qa'ida and viewed Islamic extremists as a threat to his regime, refusing all requests from al-Qa'ida to provide material or operational support": US Senate, Select Committee on Intelligence, "Postwar Findings about Iraq's WMD Programs and Links to Terrorism and How They Compare with Prewar Assessments," 109th Congress, 2nd Session, September 8, 2006, quote from p. 105; http://intelligence.senate.gov/phaseiiaccuracy.pdf.

[125] See the series of quotations collected in Levin, "Report of an Inquiry into the Alternative Analysis of the Issue of an Iraq–al Qaeda Relationship," pp. 30–41.

preconceptions and your goals with little critical review, while subjecting information that goes against your preconceptions and conflicts with your goals to much more stringent standards of acceptance. After 9/11, Bush administration policy-makers were clearly focused on Iraq and disposed to accept the worst interpretation of any information relating Saddam Hussein to al-Qaeda. They even created a special intelligence unit, the PCTEG, to develop information about the Saddam–al-Qaeda relationship when the intelligence community (unlike the case with WMD) did not produce analysis that confirmed their preconceptions. After the failure of the intelligence community to "connect the dots" regarding the 9/11 plot, policy-makers were clearly open to the PCTEG's much more aggressive effort to arrange fragmented and questionable information into a coherent picture of long-term contacts between Iraq and al-Qaeda. They chose to ignore the community's warnings about the reliability of the information on which the PCTEG's case was based.

The second reason is more political than psychological. Mobilizing American public opinion for war against Iraq would clearly be easier if the public believed that Iraq was linked to al-Qaeda. This was a winning political argument, and the administration was making it to a public that was disposed to believe it. A September 13, 2001, poll conducted for CNN and Time Magazine found that 78 percent of those polled suspected that Saddam Hussein was involved in the 9/11 attacks.[126] The administration sold the Iraq–al-Qaeda link hard, beyond what a responsible reading of the evidence would merit. But it was selling to an audience willing to believe. The exact balance between a cynical desire to manipulate the public and a sincere, though biased and incorrect, belief in an Iraq–al-Qaeda link undoubtedly varies among the senior policy-makers of the Bush administration. What is clear is that even the most committed believers in the relationship had to reject considerable contradictory evidence from the intelligence community to continue to hold on to their belief.

Assumptions about post-war Iraq

The most damaging assumptions the Bush administration brought to the Iraq War were not about Iraq's weapons or its ties to al-Qaeda, but about what Iraq would look like after the fall of Saddam Hussein and what the American role in post-Saddam Iraq would be. The incorrect assumptions about weapons and terrorist ties helped to get the United States into a war

---

[126] Poll result cited in Dana Milbank and Claudia Deane, "Hussein Link to 9/11 Lingers in Many Minds," *Washington Post*, September 6, 2003.

that turned out to be relatively easy to win. The assumptions about the post-war situation led to mistakes and miscalculations that ensnared the United States in a long, expensive and debilitating occupation. As was the case with Iraq's nuclear capability and its ties to al-Qaeda, there was considerable debate within the US government before the war about what post-war stabilization would require. There was also a vigorous public discussion about post-war plans that emphasized the costs and difficulties of stabilizing Iraq after the fall of Saddam. Top policy-makers cannot plead ignorance about the potential problems they faced in Iraq.[127] Yet they uniformly accepted the most optimistic assumptions about post-Saddam Iraq.[128] Accepting those assumptions left the United States woefully unprepared for what it found in Iraq after the victory over Saddam Hussein. But the acceptance of those assumptions is an important part of the story of how the United States decided to go to war in Iraq in March 2003.

The top policy-makers in the Bush administration thought that the post-Saddam political transition in Iraq would be relatively short and relatively easy. Retired general Jay Garner, the head of the ORHA, when asked shortly before the war in March 2003 about the overall duration of the American presence in Iraq, responded, "I'll probably come back to hate this answer, but I'm talking months."[129] The administration planned to fight a different war than the one fought by the United States in Iraq in 1991. Rather than aiming to destroy the Iraqi infrastructure, they would focus their military might against the regime and its security forces, leaving Iraqi society largely intact. They would be fighting a war of liberation on behalf of the Iraqi people, who would for the most part welcome their intervention. Once Saddam's regime was gone, Iraqi society would quickly recover, a political process would begin, and the United States would be able to leave. NSA Rice told the *New York Times* in 2004 that "[t]he concept was that we would defeat the army, but the institutions

---

[127] Yet some of them do. Tenet says, "What never happened, as far as I can tell, was a serious consideration of the implications of a US invasion … In looking back, there seemed to be a lack of curiosity in asking these kinds of questions, and the lack of a disciplined process to get the answers before committing the country to war": *At the Center of the Storm*, p. 308.

[128] Lawrence Freedman cogently notes: "Yet while worst-case analysis was rampant on the subject of Iraq, WMD and terrorism, best-case analysis was equally dominant as to what would follow Saddam": "War in Iraq: Selling the Threat," p. 34. This sentiment is echoed by Thomas Ricks: "It [the war] was made possible only through the intellectual acrobatics of simultaneously 'worst-casing' the threat presented by Iraq while 'best-casing' the subsequent cost and difficulty of occupying the country" (*Fiasco*, p. 4). Douglas Feith presents a number of memos that he wrote in the lead-up to the war in which he mentions potential post-war problems. He blames others for not heeding his warnings: *War and Decision*, pp. 363–66.

[129] Ricks, *Fiasco*, p. 104.

would hold, everything from ministries to police forces. You need to be able to bring new leadership but we were going to keep the body in place."[130]

The belief that the Iraqi state, and particularly parts of the Iraqi security forces, would essentially remain intact through the post-Saddam transition was a key assumption in the Bush administration.[131] Barham Salih, an official in Jalal Talabani's Patriotic Union of Kurdistan who went on to high office in post-Saddam Iraqi governments, said "[t]hey were expecting the police to work after liberation ... I said, this is not the NYPD. It's the Iraqi police. The minute the first cruise missile arrives in Baghdad, the police force degenerates and everybody goes home."[132] That belief underlay the administration's plans to draw down American forces in Iraq rapidly after the fall of Saddam's regime. As early as April 19, 2003, shortly after the fall of Baghdad, General Franks told his field commanders that it was time to make plans to leave. Thomas White, then the secretary of the army, later said: "Our working budgetary assumption was that ninety days after completion of the operation, we would withdraw the first fifty thousand and then every thirty days we'd take out another fifty thousand until everybody was back."[133]

The assumption that there would be little need to maintain a large American military force in Iraq after the war was not simply the result of excessive optimism. It also accorded directly with Secretary of Defense Rumsfeld's notions of how the American military should be reconfigured for the twenty-first century.[134] Rumsfeld wanted the military to become faster and leaner, able to fight on short notice with smaller forces all over the globe. He was particularly opposed to American military forces taking on long-term commitments to provide political stability and facilitate

---

[130] Michael Gordon, "The Strategy to Secure Iraq Did Not Foresee a 2nd War," *New York Times*, October 19, 2004.

[131] Peter Slevin and Dana Priest, "Wolfowitz Concedes Iraq Errors," *Washington Post*, July 24, 2003: "In addition to believing that Iraqi soldiers and police officers would help secure the country, they [Bush administration] thought that Iraqis would embrace the American invaders and a future marked by representative government, civil liberties and a free market economy, and that Iraqi bureaucrats, minus a top layer of Baath Party officials who would quit or be fired, would stay on the job. Within weeks, if all went well, Iraqis begin taking control of their own affairs and the exit of US troops would be well under way."

[132] George Packer, "Letter from Baghdad: War After the War," *New Yorker*, November 24, 2003, p. 62.

[133] Gordon and Trainor, *Cobra II*, p. 461.

[134] Packer writes: "The number of American soldiers in Iraq, which hovered around 135,000, sometimes spiking or dropping by ten or twenty thousand in response to events, reflected nothing other than Rumsfeld's fixed idea of military transformation": *The Assassins' Gate: America in Iraq* (New York: Farrar, Straus and Giroux, 2005), p. 245.

"nation-building," as they had in the Balkans during the Clinton administration. He repeatedly pressed the military, in the lead-up to the Iraq War, to reduce the number of troops in the battle plan.[135] In February 2003, on the eve of the war, Rumsfeld gave a public speech titled "Beyond Nation Building," in which he contrasted the large foreign peacekeeping presence in Kosovo, which he said had created a "culture of dependence," with the Afghanistan model, where the United States relied largely on the new Afghan army and troops from other countries to help keep the peace.[136] Undersecretary of Defense Feith confirmed that the decision to limit the number of American troops in the Iraq War "was strategic and goes far beyond Iraq. This is part of his [Rumsfeld's] thinking about defense transformation."[137]

Rumsfeld's strategic vision corresponded well with those in the Bush administration who believed that the Iraq War would leave behind a relatively unscathed Iraqi state and a largely cooperative Iraqi population, ready to take on the responsibilities of government. They combined to produce a plan for a war that would require comparatively few American military forces and little American money. Deputy Secretary of Defense Wolfowitz, the intellectual leader of the war hawks, famously summarized those assumptions before congressional committees. On February 27, 2003, he told the House Budget Committee that "it is hard to conceive that it would take more forces to provide stability in a post-Saddam Iraq that it would take to conduct the war itself and secure the surrender of Saddam's security forces and his army – hard to imagine."[138] On March 27, 2003, he told the Defense Subcommittee of the House Appropriations Committee that "the oil revenues of that country could bring between $50 and $100 billion over the course of the next two or three years ... We're dealing with a country that can really finance its own reconstruction, and relatively soon."[139] The administration's view on its role in post-war Iraq was neatly summed up by a senior US Agency for International Development officer on March 13, 2003. Wendy Chamberlain told representatives of NGOs: "It's going to be very quick. We're going to meet their

---

[135] Woodward, *Plan of Attack*, pp. 36–37, 40–41, 54–58, 75–76. See also Gordon and Trainor, *Cobra II*, pp. 4–5, 28–30, 36–37.
[136] Gordon and Trainor, *Cobra II*, pp. 151–52.
[137] Barbara Slavin and Dave Moniz, "How Peace in Iraq Became So Elusive," *USA Today*, July 22, 2003.
[138] US Congress, House of Representatives, Committee on the Budget, "Department of Defense Budget Priorities for Fiscal Year 2004," 108th Congress, 1st Session, February 27, 2003, p. 8.
[139] Dana Milbank and Robin Wright, "Off the Mark on Cost of War, Reception by Iraqis," *Washington Post*, March 19, 2004.

immediate needs. We're going to turn it over to the Iraqis. And we're going to be out within the year."[140]

These assumptions proved to be devastatingly wrong. They were also not in accord with many of the estimates within the US government about what post-war Iraq would look like and what the United States would be called upon to do there to establish a stable post-Saddam government. On security issues, many government agencies warned before the war that it was likely that public order in Iraq would collapse with the fall of the regime. The National Intelligence Council prepared two reports in January 2003 that highlighted the possibility that the war could produce a deeply divided Iraqi society prone to violent internal conflict and that an armed insurgency could arise against American forces and a new Iraqi government.[141] The CIA ran a series of war-game exercises beginning in May 2002 on Iraq, in which "one recurring theme ... was the risk of civil disorder after the fall of Baghdad."[142] A CIA spokesman said shortly after the war that the intelligence community warned "early and often" of the challenges the United States would face in the post-war environment.[143] The Future of Iraq Project, a State Department effort to bring together Iraqi exiles and technical experts to plan for post-war Iraq, also emphasized the challenges to maintaining security in the country after the fall of the Ba'thist regime.[144]

The warnings within the government about the likely collapse of public order in the wake of a successful war against Saddam Hussein were echoed in public debate during the pre-war period. Rend Rahim Francke, an Iraqi exile who later became post-Saddam Iraq's first ambassador to

---

[140] James Fallows, "Blind Into Baghdad," *Atlantic Monthly*, January/February 2004, pp. 52–74. See also Packer, *The Assassins' Gate*, pp. 132–33.

[141] Douglas Jehl and David E. Sanger, "Prewar Assessment on Iraq Saw Chance of Strong Divisions," *New York Times*, September 28, 2004. See also Slevin and Priest, "Wolfowitz Concedes Iraqi Errors."

[142] Fallows, "Blind Into Baghdad." I participated in one of them. If the chaos of the simulation was any indication, the intelligence community should have been well prepared for the chaos of post-war Iraq.

[143] Mark Fineman, Robin Wright and Doyle McManus, "Preparing for War, Stumbling to Peace," *Los Angeles Times*, July 18, 2003. Paul Pillar, the national intelligence officer for the Middle East, subsequently wrote that the intelligence community in the lead-up to the war "presented a picture of a political culture that would not provide fertile ground for democracy and foretold a long, difficult and turbulent transition" including "a significant chance that the groups [in Iraq] would engage in violent conflict ... and it anticipated that a foreign occupying force would itself be the target of resentment and attacks": "Intelligence, Policy and the War in Iraq," p. 18.

[144] Eric Schmitt and Joel Brinkley, "State Department Study Foresaw Trouble Now Plaguing Iraq," *New York Times*, October 19, 2003; Fallows, "Blind Into Baghdad." Feith contends that the Defense Department cooperated with the Future of Iraq Project and argues that it did not produce operational plans for post-war Iraq: *War and Decision*, pp. 375–78.

Washington, told the Senate Foreign Relations Committee on August 1, 2002, that "the system of public security will break down, because there will be no functioning police force, no civil service, and no justice system."[145] Phebe Marr, a long-time observer of Iraq in both the academic and government worlds, told that hearing that "the removal of the current regime in Baghdad, under certain circumstances, could result in a 'breakdown' of the central government, and its inability to exercise control over the country."[146] The Council on Foreign Relations, in a study issued on January 1, 2003, warned that "without an initial and broad-based commitment to law and order, the logic of score-settling and revenge-taking will reduce Iraq to chaos."[147]

Concerns about post-war stability related directly to the issue of the size of the force the United States was planning to deploy in the Iraq War. A number of internal American government studies indicated that much larger force levels than were being planned would be necessary to secure post-war Iraq. A 1999 exercise conducted by Central Command concluded that the United States would need a force of 400,000 to invade and stabilize Iraq. A February 2003 memo generated in the National Security Council found that, if the international mission in Kosovo was used as a model, 500,000 troops would have to be deployed in Iraq to secure the country after the fall of Saddam's regime.[148] The chief of staff of the Army, General Eric Shinseki, in February 2003 told the Senate Armed Services Committee: "Something on the order of several hundred thousand are probably, you know, a figure that would be required."[149] Two days later, Deputy Secretary Wolfowitz told the House Budget Committee in a public hearing that such estimates were "wildly off the mark."[150] Secretary of Defense Rumsfeld echoed that sentiment on March 3, 2003, saying "the idea that it would take several hundred thousand US forces, I think, is far from the mark."[151]

[145] US Congress, Senate, Committee on Foreign Relations, "Hearings to Examine Threats, Responses and Regional Considerations Surrounding Iraq," 107th Congress, 2nd Session, July 31–August 1, 2002, p. 179.

[146] "Hearings to Examine Threats," p. 171.

[147] Council on Foreign Relations, "Guiding Principles for US Post-Conflict Policy in Iraq," January 1, 2003, www.cfr.org/content/publications/attachments/Post-War_Iraq.pdf.

[148] Slavin and Moniz, "How Peace in Iraq Became So Elusive." See also Fallows, "Blind into Baghdad," for reference to the Central Command exercise. Gordon and Trainor report that CENTCOM's 1998 plan for occupying Iraq in the wake of a collapse of Saddam's regime and central authority called for over 400,000 troops: *Cobra II*, p. 26.

[149] Eric Schmitt, "Army Chief Raises Estimate of GI's Needed in Postwar Iraq," *New York Times*, February 25, 2003.

[150] "Department of Defense Budget Priorities for Fiscal Year 2004," p. 8.

[151] "Administration Fends Off Demands for War Estimates," CNN.com, March 3, 2003, www.cnn.com/2003/ALLPOLITICS/02/27/sprj.irq.war.cost/.

Senior officials in the Bush administration also grossly underestimated the cost of the Iraq War, in spite of both internal government estimates and public debate on the issue. Before the war, the administration steadfastly refused to estimate in public what the range of costs of the war would be. In April 2003, the director of the Agency for International Development said that the US cost for rebuilding Iraq would be $1.7 billion, in essence in line with Wolfowitz's earlier estimate that the reconstruction of Iraq would be self-financing.[152] However, within the administration itself officials were making more realistic estimates. The Energy Infrastructure Planning Group established by Undersecretary Feith in September 2002 reported that Iraq's oil industry was not nearly as healthy as Saddam's government had claimed and estimated a range of oil revenues that could be generated post-war. Administration officials always cited the high end of the estimate.[153] Colonel Sam Gardiner prepared an elaborate study of the fragility of Iraq's electricity and water systems before the war, and told high-ranking administration officials that both systems would collapse in the post-war period even if they were not targeted during the war itself.[154] The director of the National Economic Council, Lawrence Lindsey, told the *Wall Street Journal* on September 15, 2002, that the "upper bound" of the costs would be between $100 billion and $200 billion.[155]

In the public debate, more realistic estimates of the cost of the war were also being made. Yale University economist William Nordhaus published a widely discussed article in December 2002 that estimated the costs of war at between $120 billion, under the most favorable circumstances, and $1.6 trillion, under the most unfavorable circumstances.[156] The Council on Foreign Relations study of post-war Iraq referenced above warned that, even if no oil facilities were damaged, Iraq's total annual oil revenues would likely average between $10 billion and $12 billion, certainly far less than would be needed to finance the country's reconstruction.[157]

With so much evidence available calling into question their assumptions about post-Saddam Iraq, why did the senior policy-makers of the Bush Administration not plan for a more difficult and extended post-war

[152] Milbank and Wright, "Off the Mark on Cost of War, Reception by Iraqis."
[153] Jeff Gerth, "Report Offered Bleak Outlook About Iraqi Oil," *New York Times*, October 5, 2003.
[154] Fineman, Wright and McManus, "Preparing for War, Stumbling to Peace."
[155] Quoted in William D. Nordhaus, "The Economic Consequences of a War with Iraq," October 29, 2002, www.econ.yale.edu/~nordhaus/iraq.pdf; published in *New York Review of Books*, December 5, 2002.
[156] Nordhaus, "The Economic Consequences of a War," p. 37.
[157] Council on Foreign Relations, "Guiding Principles for US Post-Conflict Policy in Iraq," p. 22.

occupation? As was the case with WMD and the al-Qaeda link, the most plausible explanation is a combination of cognitive bias and political expediency. With most of the administration set on war against Iraq shortly after 9/11, senior officials would be disposed psychologically to welcome scenarios that painted a picture of a relatively easy post-war transition. If deposing Saddam Hussein was essential in the new strategic context, any projection that emphasized the costs and difficulties of that policy would be discounted. Once a decision is made, decision-makers tend to look for information and analysis that will bolster their choice and to reject information and analysis that calls their decision into question. They can even accept as fact scenarios that are most unlikely. President Bush, in January 2003, when it was increasingly clear that the war would not have a United Nations imprimatur, reportedly told a group of Iraqi exiles that "a humanitarian army is going to follow our army into Iraq," looking to NSA Rice for confirmation of that fact, which she provided.[158] Even during the war, in April 2003, the White House was still planning on significant numbers of foreign forces, including from the Arab world, taking part in post-war stabilization.[159] Assumptions of an easy post-war transition also fit very well into Secretary Rumsfeld's new vision for a US military that would not be bogged down with long-term tasks of nation-building. Rumsfeld and those who shared this vision would thus be particularly resistant to more pessimistic analysis of post-war Iraq. Moreover, they could point to the relatively successful, relatively easy and relatively cheap model of regime change (or so it appeared at the time) that they had just accomplished in Afghanistan, as Rumsfeld did in his February 2003 speech mentioned above.

Once the administration was set on war, it did not have much difficulty in finding supporting evidence and supportive analogies for its view about the ease with which the United States could transition to a stable post-Saddam Iraqi government. That supporting evidence bolstered it in its rejection of more pessimistic, and more accurate, projections of what post-war Iraq would require from the United States. I have no doubt that senior administration officials were sincere in their beliefs. It is inconceivable, given the political capital that they invested, that they would have deliberately chosen not to plan for contingencies that they believed likely. The administration did prepare for a number of ugly post-war eventualities: chemical and biological weapons attacks by Iraqi forces, oil field fires, massive refugee movements. Those preparations were costly and raised fears about the negative consequences that war might bring.

---

[158] Packer, *The Assassins' Gate*, p. 111.
[159] Gordon and Trainor, *Cobra II*, p. 457.

Those costs and fears did not deter the administration from preparing for them.

Undoubtedly it was politically convenient to sell the war to the American people as one that would be easy and cheap. That convenience undoubtedly bolstered the strength with which many of the administration's policy-makers held on to their rosy scenarios about post-war Iraq. But it is hard to escape the conclusion that they really believed that it would be easy, and that they believed this because they thought that deposing Saddam Hussein was absolutely necessary for American security. Those sincere beliefs led them to ignore the abundant warning signs, both in the government and in the public debate, that post-war Iraq would be much different than they thought. It was a tragic example of wishful thinking, and a textbook example of bad policy-making. That these misconceptions were held so sincerely by those making the decisions does not mitigate their responsibility for ignoring the contrary evidence and sending American forces into Iraq with no realistic plan for the post-war transition.

Politicization of Iraq intelligence

I have made the case that it was reasonable for the American intelligence community and American policy-makers to conclude that Iraq possessed chemical and biological weapons. I further argued that it was much less reasonable for them to conclude that Iraq was an imminent nuclear threat, that it had operational ties to al-Qaeda and that the post-war transition there would be short and easy. To what extent can these latter errors be attributed to the politicization of the intelligence process?

It is absolutely clear that Bush administration officials took an active role in pushing the intelligence community to find the kind of evidence and do the kind of analysis that the administration wanted to have. Analyses that called into question the administration's case for war were clearly not welcome. However, the extent to which this pressure from above affected the intelligence process is much less apparent. The community, despite political pressures, did not produce analysis that fit the administration's case on either the terrorism or the post-war Iraq issues. In these cases, the administration went outside the normal channels to establish its own intelligence and operational offices, in the Pentagon, to provide support for its arguments. On chemical and biological weapons, the community did not have to be pressed by its political masters. It had already come to the conclusion, before 9/11, that Iraq possessed these kinds of weapons. Had there been contrary views on chemical and biological weapons, they might have been squelched. However, there is no evidence that such contrary views existed. The one area where political pressure can be argued to have affected the intelligence process is on Iraqi nuclear capability, and even there it is not clear how much effect it had.

The real politicization of intelligence was in the way that the administration used intelligence product in making its case for war, and in the way it staffed those parts of the government dealing with Iraq. The exaggerations in the public statements on both the nuclear issue and the al-Qaeda link by administration officials were clearly efforts to mobilize public opinion in favor of war. The establishment of special bureaus in the office of the undersecretary of defense for policy to find an Iraq–al-Qaeda link and to plan for post-war Iraq was clearly an effort by neo-conservative ideologues to undercut established bureaucratic channels and monopolize control over these issues. These steps had real and damaging consequences for the American administration of Iraq after the fall of Saddam, but it is hard to argue that they had much effect on the war decision itself. They were the result of the decision to target Iraq, not the cause.[160]

"The analysts who worked [on] Iraqi weapons issues universally agreed that in no instance did political pressure cause them to skew or alter any of their analytical judgments."[161] This conclusion, reached by the Silberman–Robb Commission, is the basis of Bush administration claims that it did not exert undue pressure on the intelligence community. It is supported by a more informal, internal CIA investigation of its performance on the Iraq WMD issue.[162] However, the Silberman–Robb Commission also found that the community was working "in an environment that did not encourage skepticism about the conventional wisdom" regarding Iraqi WMD.[163] That environment was created not only by the community's past mistakes on Iraq, in the sense that it did not want to underestimate Iraqi capabilities as it had both before and after the Gulf War, but also by the intense interest demonstrated by top administration officials in the answers it was generating. According to a member of his staff, Vice President Cheney paid "approximately 10" visits to the CIA during 2002 to speak directly with analysts working on Iraq issues. One agency analyst remarked, on the question of politicization, "they don't

---

[160] This conclusion is shared by Freedman, "War in Iraq: Selling the Threat," pp. 38–39.
[161] Silberman–Robb Commission Report, p. 11.
[162] "My confidential interviews with CIA officials at several levels of the hierarchy did not find anyone excusing his or her errors as resulting from political pressure" (Jervis, "Reports, Politics and Intelligence Failures: The Case of Iraq," p. 35).
[163] Silberman–Robb Commission Report, p. 11. James Risen disagrees, arguing that CIA analysts' doubts about the existence of Iraqi WMD programs "were stifled because of the enormous pressure that officials at the CIA and other agencies felt to support the administration": *State of War: The Secret History of the CIA and the Bush Administration* (New York: Free Press, 2006), p. 109.

have to tell us to do that – we know what they want."[164] A number of experienced intelligence analysts pointed to the practice of administration policy-makers persistently questioning intelligence reports that did not correspond with their beliefs about Iraq and requesting repeated reexaminations of questions whose original answers they did not like as constituting, in their totality, political pressure on the community.[165]

The pressure was real. But its effects seem to have been limited. Paul Pillar, the national intelligence officer on the Middle East, and Richard Kerr, the former CIA official who conducted an in-house investigation of the Iraq intelligence failures, while complaining of administration political pressure, both echoed the Silberman–Robb Commission finding that community analysts did not alter their substantive findings in the face of this pressure. Pillar has written that on WMD "there was indeed a broad consensus that such programs existed." He was particularly critical of administration pressure on the community to find a Saddam–al-Qaeda link, which it refused to do.[166] Kerr said that, despite the pressures from above, "analysts' judgments were consistent over a long period of time, and reasonable, he thought, given the limited information available."[167]

It was not so much what the intelligence community said that reflected politicization as what it did not say. The battle over Iraq's nuclear program within the community, detailed above, was settled by a bureaucratic compromise based on an inherent contradiction: the CIA accepted evidence rejected by the Department of Energy and the Department of Energy accepted evidence rejected by the CIA. Yet this illogical conclusion was allowed to stand. By the time the National Intelligence Estimate on Iraqi WMD was being prepared, in the fall of 2002, many in the community had concluded that war with Iraq was inevitable, and that attempting to

---

[164] Bryan Burroughs, Evgenia Peretz, David Rose and David Wise, "The Path to War," *Vanity Fair*, May 2004, p. 242.

[165] "But when policymakers repeatedly urge the intelligence community to turn over only certain rocks, the process becomes biased": Pillar, "Intelligence, Policy and the War in Iraq," p. 23. Analysts who presented views contrary to administration desires "were subjected to barrages of questions and requests for additional information. They were asked to justify their work sentence by sentence ... [A]t a certain point, curiosity and diligence become a form of pressure": Kenneth Pollack, "Spies, Lies and Weapons," *Atlantic Monthly*, January/February 2004, p. 88. Richard Kerr, a retired CIA agent brought back in to assess the intelligence failures leading up to the war, said: "There was a lot of pressure, no question ... Not that they [analysts] were being asked to change their judgments, but they were being asked again and again to restate their judgments, do another paper on this, repetitive pressures. Do it again" Burroughs *et al.*, "The Path to War," p. 244. See also Suskind, *The One Percent Doctrine*, pp. 189–91, for a telling anecdote.

[166] Pillar, "Intelligence, Policy and the War in Iraq," particularly pp. 20–21, 23–24.

[167] Burroughs *et al.*, "The Path to War," p. 244.

question the evidence for Iraqi WMD was futile. One Department of Energy analyst involved in composing the NIE told the Silbermann–Robb Commission: "DOE didn't want to come out before the war and say [Iraq] wasn't reconstituting."[168] There is no evidence that the community re-assessed its findings in light of UNMOVIC's failure to find evidence of ongoing Iraqi WMD programs after its inspectors went to Iraq in November 2002. Robert Jervis judges this a "significant failing" on the part of the community, and attributes it to the fact that "it was clear to the IC [intelligence community] that the US and the UK were committed to over-throwing Saddam and that any re-evaluations would be unacceptable."[169]

The political pressure from above undoubtedly, in Jervis' words, "created (and probably was designed to create) an atmosphere that was not conducive to critical analysis and that encouraged judgments of excessive certainty and eroded subtleties and nuances."[170] But there is no evidence that there were serious doubts present in the community on Iraqi possession of chemical and biological weapons. While there were differences of opinion about nuclear evidence and about how long it might take Iraq to develop a nuclear capability, all the major bureaucratic players, except the State Department, agreed that "Baghdad started reconstituting its nuclear program about the time that UNSCOM inspectors departed – December 1998."[171] On the al-Qaeda link, the community forthrightly opposed the administration's preferred conclusion, indicating that political pressure could be resisted by the intelligence agencies. In the end, the nuances of the analysis did not matter that much, as the political leaders had already decided that Saddam had to go.

The more serious effects of politicization of intelligence on Iraq were in the administration's use of that intelligence to justify the war and in its post-war planning. There is no doubt that the president and leading figures in the administration "cherry-picked" the intelligence in order to present the most lurid and frightening case about Iraqi capabilities and intentions, particularly on the nuclear and terrorist issues.[172] When Vice President Cheney told the Veterans of Foreign Wars in August 2002 that "many of us are convinced that Saddam will acquire nuclear weapons fairly soon,"[173] he did not talk about the differences of opinion within the

---

[168] Silberman–Robb Commission Report, p. 75; see also p. 190.
[169] Jervis, "Reports, Politics and Intelligence Failures: The Case of Iraq," p. 37.
[170] Jervis, "Reports, Politics and Intelligence Failures: The Case of Iraq," p. 36.
[171] Quote from the "Key Judgments" section of "Iraq's Continuing Programs for Weapons of Mass Destruction," www.fas.org/irp/cia/product/iraq-wmd.html.
[172] "The one action for which I cannot hold Administration officials blameless is their distortion of intelligence estimates when making the public case for going to war": Pollack, "Spies, Lies and Weapons," p. 90.
[173] See www.newamericancentury.org/iraq-082602.htm.

intelligence community about the quality of the evidence for that belief, nor did he mention the State Department's alternative view. When NSA Rice said on September 8, 2002, that "we do not want the smoking gun to be a mushroom cloud," she did not subsequently mention that the October 2002 NIE on Iraq's weapons of mass destruction stated "Baghdad for now appears to be drawing the line short of conducting terrorist attacks with conventional or WMD against the United States."[174] When President Bush used the same image in a speech in Cincinnati on October 7, 2002, he also neglected to mention the NIE's more nuanced judgments. When Secretary of State Powell spoke before the United Nations Security Council in February 2003 of the "sinister nexus" between Iraq and al-Qaeda, he did not reveal that his own intelligence agencies had not found any substantive and operational relationship between the two parties. When President Bush said in his January 2003 State of the Union address that Iraq "sought significant quantities of uranium from Africa," he did not acknowledge that his own secretary of state found the evidence for that assertion so weak that he left it out of his United Nations presentation just a few days later. The administration used bits and pieces of intelligence to build public support for a war that it had much earlier decided must be fought. In that sense, it "politicized" intelligence in the most egregious way.

The other extremely damaging consequence of the political uses of intelligence, and the political fights over the assumptions about post-war Iraq, was the monopolization of post-war planning (such as it was) by the civilians around Secretary of Defense Rumsfeld. On January 20, 2003, President Bush assigned responsibility for post-war Iraq to the Pentagon.[175] The responsible official was Undersecretary for Policy Feith, in whose office a recently formed Office of Special Plans had already been working on the issue, based upon the assumptions about post-war Iraq discussed above. Pentagon officials experienced in other post-conflict situations were excluded from the process. One Defense Department official told George Packer that "the senior leadership at the Pentagon was very worried about the realities of the postconflict phase being known, because if you are Feith or if you are Wolfowitz, your primary concern is to achieve the war."[176] Feith's office also made a point of discouraging participation by the Defense Department in planning exercises conducted elsewhere in the government.

---

[174] "Iraq's Continuing Programs for Weapons of Mass Destruction," www.fas.org/irp/cia/product/iraq-wmd.html.
[175] Packer, *The Assassins' Gate*, p. 120. See Chapter 4, "Special Plans," for an extended discussion of the problems in planning for post-war Iraq.
[176] Packer, *The Assassins' Gate*, p. 114.

Defense officials who participated in a May 2002 war-gaming exercise on Iraq sponsored by the CIA were reprimanded by their superiors and told not to participate in similar meetings.[177]

Feith's team was particularly concerned to block the efforts by those involved in the State Department's Future of Iraq Project from playing a role in post-war Iraq. The State Department projected that the reconstruction tasks would be much more complicated, time-consuming and expensive than the prevailing assumptions in Rumsfeld's office and the White House. Moreover, the Iraqi exiles involved in the State Department planning exercise were seen as rivals to Ahmad Chalabi and his Iraqi National Congress, which had the patronage of the Pentagon civilians.[178] The bureaucratic rivalry was so great that when retired general Jay Garner, the head of the ORHA, petitioned to have Tom Warrick, the State Department official who coordinated the Future of Iraq Project, included on his staff, he was refused. Secretary of Defense Rumsfeld told him to remove Warrick from his team, saying "I've gotten this from such a high level I can't turn it down." Garner enlisted Secretary of State Powell in an effort to get Warrick reinstated, but Powell was unable to do so.[179] When asked whether he or anyone else at the Pentagon had blocked Warrick's appointment, Feith replied, "I never met the guy. I wouldn't know him if he walked in the room."[180]

The fact that the Defense Department's senior official on post-war Iraq had never met the head of the State Department's planning effort on the same issue speaks volumes about the politicization of Iraq issues in the bureaucracy. Normal channels of interagency consultation and cooperation completely broke down in the lead-up to the war. The need to protect the assumptions held by senior Bush administration officials about the nature of the conflict and the character of post-Saddam Iraq from any challenge, either from within or from outside the government, led to a planning process that ignored expert advice and the evidence of the past, both the Iraqi past and recent post-conflict cases elsewhere. The costs of such politicized choices quickly became apparent after the fall of Saddam Hussein's regime, as Iraqi realities overwhelmed the American occupation authority.

A war for democracy?

As it became increasingly clear after the fall of Saddam Hussein's regime that Iraq was not the WMD threat that the Bush administration had

---

[177] Fallows, "Blind into Baghdad."
[178] Packer, *The Assassins' Gate*, p. 125.
[179] Packer, *The Assassins' Gate*, p. 124. See also Ricks, *Fiasco*, pp. 103–04.
[180] Fineman, Wright and McManus, "Preparing for War, Stumbling to Peace."

contended, officials put much more public emphasis on the importance of Iraq's democratic transformation as a major goal of the war. This transition was portrayed as the first step in the regionwide spread of democracy, and thus an essential part of the war on terrorism. A more democratic Middle East, the Bush administration argued, would allow opposition groups to play a constructive and public role, not suppress them and push them toward terrorism. A more democratic Middle East would also not have governments that sought to deflect their publics' anger toward the United States. A more democratic Middle East, in short, would not produce anti-American terrorism.[181] Some of its critics contend that the administration came to this emphasis on a democratic Middle East only after the war, to deflect attention from the intelligence failures on Iraqi WMD. It was a post hoc pretext for war, not a real administration goal.

The evidence points to a different conclusion. It is clear that the administration's post-9/11 focus on Iraq began with the nexus of WMD, anti-Americanism and support for terrorist groups which the Bush Doctrine declared intolerable. It was the WMD–terrorism connection that brought President Bush, Vice President Cheney and NSA Rice around to the position of those in the administration who had wanted to target Iraq for some time. However, as the build-up to war with Iraq progressed, the administration adopted a more expansive view of the benefits that would redound from Saddam's removal. Defeating Iraq would change not just the strategic picture of the Middle East, it would also change its political balance. Opponents of the United States would think more than once about challenging it, lest they face the same fate as Saddam. A democratic Iraq would be a force for change throughout the region, positive change for the United States.[182] President Bush emphasized this element of American war goals in a speech at the American Enterprise Institute on the eve of the war, on February 26, 2003: "The world has a clear interest in the spread of democratic values, because stable and free nations do not breed the

---

[181] Among the earliest post-war statements of this new American emphasis on spreading democracy in the Middle East are an article by NSA Rice, "Transforming the Middle East," *Washington Post*, August 7, 2003; and the November 6, 2003, speech by President Bush at the National Endowment for Democracy, www.ned.org/events/anniversary/20th.

[182] CIA director Tenet ultimately concluded that the transformation of the Middle East was a central, though not the only, motivation for the war: "The United States did not go to war in Iraq solely because of WMD. In my view, that was not even the principal cause. Yet it was the public face that was put on it. The leaders of a country decide to go to war because of core beliefs, larger geostrategic calculations, ideology and, in the case of Iraq, because of the administration's largely unarticulated view that the democratic transformation of the Middle East through regime change in Iraq would be worth the price" (*At the Center of the Storm*, p. 321).

ideologies of murder. They encourage the peaceful pursuit of a better life. And there are hopeful signs of a desire for freedom in the Middle East. A new regime in Iraq would serve as a dramatic and inspiring example of freedom for other nations in the region."[183]

This emphasis on democracy promotion in the Middle East was a new turn for President Bush and many others in his administration. However, one of the administration's main advocates for removing Saddam Hussein from power, Deputy Secretary of Defense Wolfowitz, had been a strong advocate of democracy promotion more generally for some time.[184] He had pushed for a democratic transition in Iraq throughout the Clinton years, championing Ahmad Chalabi and his Iraqi National Congress as the vehicles for such a transformation. Wolfowitz's vision of the strategic benefits of regime change in Iraq was not tied to the purported WMD threat posed by Saddam. Commenting on the administration's emphasis on WMD in its public case for war, he said: "For bureaucratic reasons we settled on one issue, weapons of mass destruction, because it was the one reason everyone could agree on."[185] A number of prominent neoconservatives outside the administration also strongly advocated the beneficial effects of a democratic regime change in Iraq for American interests in the region as a whole.[186]

The first sign that the Bush administration was reevaluating the role democracy promotion should play in its post-9/11 Middle East policy came in the Arab–Israeli arena. Reversing a longstanding American inclination to ignore the domestic arrangements of Arab states and groups as long as they were willing to negotiate with Israel, in June 2002 President Bush said that the United States would deal only with a new, democratic Palestinian leadership, not with Yasir Arafat. Once the Palestinians had moved toward democracy, Bush said, the United States would support the creation of a Palestinian state.[187] On August 29, 2002, President Bush signed a planning document outlining the broad goals of the war against Iraq, one of which was to aid the Iraqis in building "a society based on moderation, pluralism and democracy."[188] This democratic turn came to be reflected even in the public arguments for war of administration

---

[183] See www.globalpolicy.org/security/issues/iraq/attack/consequences/2003/0226bushspeech.
htms.
[184] Mann, *Rise of the Vulcans*, pp. 134–36, 351–52.
[185] Sam Tanenhaus, "Bush's Brain Trust," *Vanity Fair*, July 2003, p. 114.
[186] One cogent statement of the argument is Lawrence F. Kaplan and William Kristol, *The War Over Iraq: Saddam's Tyranny and America's Mission* (San Francisco: Encounter Books, 2003).
[187] Mann, *Rise of the Vulcans*, pp. 326–27.
[188] Gordon and Trainor, *Cobra II*, pp. 72–73.

officials not associated with the neoconservative view of the world. Vice President Cheney, in his August 26, 2002, address to the Veterans of Foreign Wars convention in Nashville, certainly emphasized the WMD threat from Iraq as the centerpiece of the American case for war. But he brought his remarks to a close by invoking not threats, but the promise of a new Middle East: "In the Middle East, where so many have known only poverty and oppression, terror and tyranny, we look to the day when people can live in freedom and dignity. And the young can grow up free of the conditions that breed despair, hatred and violence."[189] President Bush's February 2003 speech, as war was approaching, represented the culmination of this development inside the administration, staking American interests in the region as much on the spread of democracy as on the elimination of WMD and terrorist threats.

This new emphasis on democracy promotion was the outgrowth of the administration's struggle to come to grips with the causes of the 9/11 attacks and the appropriate American response. Those attacks were so calamitous for the United States that they must have deeply rooted causes, this line of thought held. Something so huge could not come from superficial political complaints about American policy in the region, nor simply from a stateless band of crossnational terrorists like al-Qaeda. Rather, it emerged from a civilizational crisis in the Muslim Middle East, and only policies that addressed the deep roots of that crisis could remove the terrorist threat to the United States.[190] The American quest for regional stability in past decades had simply allowed this crisis to fester. Dictatorship exacerbated this crisis; only democracy could help resolve it. Moreover, there was a firm belief in the administration (challenged by the intelligence community, as discussed above) that Iraq was a fertile ground for such a democratic transition.[191] Democracy promotion, at least in Iraq, it was assumed, would be relatively easy and trouble-free. If it would not be hard to establish an Iraqi democracy, if in fact the "default

---

[189] See www.newamericancentury.org/iraq-082602.htm.

[190] The intellectual ballast for this kind of analysis was supplied by the eminent Middle Eastern historian Bernard Lewis, who advised the administration in the post-9/11 period and was frequently quoted by administration officials. See his *What Went Wrong? Western Impact and Middle Eastern Response* (New York: Oxford University Press, 2002).

[191] In an interview with National Public Radio in February 2003, Deputy Secretary of Defense Wolfowitz responded to a question about the possibility that Iraqis would oppose an American military presence: "The Iraqis are among the most educated people in the Arab world. They are by and large quite secular ... We're seeing today how much the people of Poland and Central and Eastern Europe appreciate what the United States did to help liberate them from the tyranny of the Soviet Union. I think you're going to see even more of that sentiment in Iraq" (www.defenselink.mil/transcripts/2003/t02202003_t0219npr.html).

option" in a post-Saddam Iraq would be a democracy, then why should the United States not encourage that outcome?

That much of the democracy talk coming out of Washington in the lead-up to and immediately following the war concentrated (after Iraq) on Iran and Syria, the other major Middle Eastern states identified by neo-conservatives as anti-American, indicates that there were strategic as well as ideological rationales behind the democracy push. But the two impulses were complementary for the Bush Administration.[192] Policy-makers saw regional transformation as a necessity, as the regional status quo had produced 9/11.[193] As Thomas Ricks put it: "Stability wasn't their *goal*, it was their *target* ... They were determined to drain the swamp – that is, to alter the political climate in the region so that it would no longer be so hospitable to the terrorists inhabiting it."[194] But they were convinced that transformation in a democratic direction would serve American strategic interests, because they believed that democracies would be less anti-American and less likely to produce terrorists.[195] The democracy empha-sis was not simply a rhetorical cover for policy targeting the Iraqi, Iranian and Syrian leaderships. The administration pressured American allies Egypt and Saudi Arabia to open up their political systems in the wake of the war. The moves in both places were modest (in Egypt, direct elections for the presidency and somewhat freer parliamentary elections in 2005; in Saudi Arabia elections to municipal councils in 2005), but they would not have occurred without promptings from Washington. President Bush's rhetoric on democracy promotion in the Middle East continued to the end of 2008, even if the results of Arab democracy (Hamas' victory in the Palestinian elections of 2006; the Muslim Brotherhood's surprising gains in the Egyptian parliamentary elections of 2005) led the administration to deemphasize pressure for political reform on the United States' Arab allies after 2006.

This is not to argue that democracy promotion came to overshadow the WMD–terrorism nexus in the Bush administration's thinking about the Iraq War. Rather, it developed into a contributing argument. It reinforced

---

[192] For an similar argument about the centrality of ideas of transformation, democracy and American power in explaining the American war decision, see Andrew Flibbert, "The Road to Baghdad: Ideas and Intellectuals in Explanations of the Iraq War," *Security Studies*, Vol. 15, No. 2 (April–June 2006), pp. 310–52.

[193] After the war, one Cheney aide said: "The imminence of the threat from Iraq's WMD was never the real issue [for us]. WMD were on our minds, but they weren't the key thing. What was really driving us was our overall view of terrorism and the strategic conditions of the Middle East" (Burroughs *et al.*, "The Path to War," p. 283).

[194] Ricks, *Fiasco*, p. 48.

[195] For a critical assessment of the linkage, see my "Can Democracy Stop Terrorism?," *Foreign Affairs*, Vol. 84, No. 5 (September/October 2005), pp. 62–76.

the argument for war, and was completely consistent with the original rationale, in that a democratic Iraq would not be a WMD or terror threat to the United States. It was not emphasized in the administration's public arguments for war in the same way that the WMD–terrorism nexus was for two reasons. First, it did not poll that well with the American public. Public support for war to rid Iraq of WMD, strike at terrorists and remove Saddam Hussein from power was relatively strong. Public support for a war to spread democracy would not elicit the same levels of support. Second, putting democracy at the top of the war goals would complicate the difficulty the Bush administration was having getting cooperation from its non-democratic Arab allies, particularly Egypt and Saudi Arabia, both of which were opposed to the war.

The Bush administration's post-war public relations emphasis on democratic transformation of the region clearly was, in part, a response to the political problem caused by the absence of WMD in Iraq. But the commitment to democracy in Iraq, as a first step toward regional transformation, was not simply a post-war phenomenon. It had its roots in the administration's ongoing thinking about how the United States should respond to the challenge of al-Qaeda and anti-American terrorism emanating from the Middle East. Top administration officials, including the president, set out this rationale before the war not as its major justification but as an important ancillary one. It was not simply a post-war expedient to cover the absence of WMD in Iraq.

A war for oil?

The accusation that the "real" reason for the war against Iraq was securing the oil resources of that country cannot simply be waved away. Oil has been the core interest of the United States in its nearly sixty years of continuous engagement in the Persian Gulf region. The "war for oil" argument about the Iraq War takes two forms. The first is the crude assertion that the goal of the United States in fighting the war was to secure access to Iraqi oil resources for American oil companies. Saddam Hussein's regime had signed oil development deals with Russian and French companies during the 1990s, the implementation of which awaited the lifting of UN sanctions. It appeared that American companies would lose out on one of the biggest potential oil bonanzas of the twenty-first century. With the war and American occupation, the United States could insure that American companies developed Iraqi oil resources and, in the bargain, could break the power of OPEC in the oil markets by having a compliant Iraqi successor regime withdraw from the organization.

There is little available evidence about post-war oil planning in the deliberations within the administration in the pre-war period. In one of the few briefings given to President Bush on post-conflict issues, on February 24, 2003, a plan to establish a temporary oil authority with an Iraqi chief operating officer and an advisory board of Iraqi and international figures was proposed, with a shift to complete Iraqi control over the oil industry once a new Iraqi government was in power. The United States would not meddle with existing or future oil contracts or with Iraq's status in OPEC. The president agreed with the recommendation, indicating that he wanted Iraqis to have full control over the oil industry as soon as possible.[196]

Given the paucity of evidence of the administration's intentions on Iraqi oil going into the war, the best indicator we have is how oil issues were treated after the United States established control over Iraq. At the end of the Bush administration, the predictions generated by the hypothesis that the war was about American control of Iraqi oil have not been borne out. The essential first step for securing American commercial control of Iraqi oil resources would have been the privatization of the Iraqi oil industry. However, in the sweeping privatization regulations issued by the CPA in September 2003, the Iraqi National Oil Company (INOC) was pointedly exempted.[197] A State Department advisory panel had in February 2003 floated a recommendation that Iraqi oil be privatized, but added that such a move should wait until a sovereign Iraqi government was in place to take the decision.[198] Iraq under CPA control did not withdraw from OPEC. Iraqi officials in the newly reconstituted Oil Ministry indicated just the opposite, that they looked forward to resuming full OPEC membership once sovereignty was restored to an Iraqi government. With security problems persisting and the legal framework for foreign investment uncertain, American energy companies (and other companies) have not been rushing to make deals in Iraq. By the end of the Bush administration in January 2009, not a single American oil company had signed an oil development deal with the Iraqi government. If the "real" American motivation for this war were as depicted above, Washington was extremely negligent in allowing its period of direct control over Iraqi affairs to lapse without cementing American corporate control over Iraqi oil.

---

[196] Woodward, *Plan of Attack*, p. 323.
[197] Rajiv Chandrasekaran, "Economic Overhaul for Iraq, Only Oil Excluded from Foreign Ownership," *Washington Post*, September 22, 2003.
[198] Warren Vieth, "Privatization of Oil Suggested for Iraq," *Los Angeles Times*, February 21, 2003.

The second form of the "war for oil" argument is more subtle, based not on corporate interests but on more general strategic and economic considerations. Iraq is the largest undeveloped oil region in the Gulf, the result of quirks of the history of Iraq's relationship with British Petroleum and of twenty-five years of suspended oil plans under the Ba'th. So Iraq will have to be the source of a large part of the extra Gulf production the world will need to meet its petroleum needs. As long as Saddam Hussein was in power, not only could Iraq not play the role of reliable oil supplier in Washington's eyes, but it also was a threat to its southern neighbors, inhibiting oil investment in Kuwait and Saudi Arabia. After 9/11, the belief among many that Saudi Arabia was no longer a reliable oil ally for the United States added to the urgency of the need to find alternative sources of oil in the Gulf. For oil security and supply reasons, this argument concludes, Saddam had to go.

Michael Klare presents the most sophisticated version of this second form of the "war for oil" argument.[199] He begins his case with the National Energy Policy report prepared under the direction of Vice President Cheney at the outset of the administration, submitted to the president in May 2001. That report recognized that the Persian Gulf region would play a major role in meeting growing world demand for oil, and thus would remain a "primary focus" of American energy policy. However, Klare argues, the Persian Gulf in 2001 did not seem to be a secure source of increased oil production: Iraq and Iran were both hostile to the United States, and Saudi Arabia was weak and unstable. Therefore, Klare postulates, "in the months before and after 9/11, the Bush Administration fashioned a comprehensive strategy for American domination of the Persian Gulf." He termed this a strategy of "maximum extraction," and for it to succeed "Washington would have to ensure that these added supplies could be safely delivered to the United States and other major consumers – which means propping up imperiled allies in the Gulf and quashing any threats to American dominance in the region." Step one of such a strategy would have to be the removal of Saddam Hussein from power and his replacement with a stable pro-American government capable of substantially boosting Iraqi oil production.[200]

This sophisticated "war for oil" argument is consistent with the facts. The Persian Gulf is central to the world oil picture. American foreign policy has recognized that centrality for decades. It was unlikely, under United Nations sanctions and in a prolonged confrontation with the United States, that Saddam's Iraq could increase oil production.

---

[199] Klare, *Blood and Oil*, Chapter 4.
[200] Klare, *Blood and Oil*, pp. 78–84; quotes from pp. 82, 83–84.

However, there is no evidence from the public record that oil considerations played the kind of role Klare contends in the Bush administration's decision to go to war. Klare himself recognizes that his argument is not likely to be supported by administration documents or statements: "It is unlikely that this strategy was ever formalized in a single, all-encompassing White House document."[201] On numerous occasions he assumes that his analysis of the centrality of Persian Gulf oil and the concomitant need for American military action to secure it must have been shared by those in the White House, though he offers no direct evidence that administration officials shared his conclusions: "This circumstance no doubt weighed heavily on the deliberations of the NEPDG [National Energy Policy Development Group]"; "In the face of these problems and dangers, the Bush–Cheney team could draw only one conclusion."[202]

If the strategic necessity to get rid of Saddam based on the energy security rationale had been dominant, one would have expected to see some indication of administration moves in that direction before 9/11. Klare argues that the administration plan for Persian Gulf dominance was in train before then. At a minimum, efforts to prepare public opinion for a confrontation with Iraq should have been seen before the 9/11 turning point. An ideal vehicle for beginning that process would have been the National Energy Policy report with which Klare begins his analysis.[203] The media coverage of the report focused largely on its recommendation to open up areas in Alaska to oil exploration, questions about energy industry input into the report and the secrecy of the process of producing it. There is, however, a chapter on the international elements of American energy policy. Klare cites its conclusion that the Persian Gulf would remain a primary focus of American energy policy as a key finding underpinning what he sees as the new Bush strategy of Persian Gulf dominance. This chapter, presumably, would have been the place to make the argument for a new confrontational approach toward Iraq.

Iraq is not mentioned at all in the international chapter, nor in the summary of recommendations attached to the report. The bulk of the international recommendations revolve around efforts to encourage oil-producing countries in other areas of the world to open up their energy sectors to foreign investment. The report acknowledges the centrality of

---

[201] Klare, *Blood and Oil*, pp. 82–83.
[202] Klare, *Blood and Oil*, pp. 78, 82.
[203] Report of the National Energy Policy Development Group, May 2001. A full copy of the report is available at www.pppl.gov/common_pages/national_energy_policy.html.

the Gulf region to world oil supplies, but directs its focus toward developing alternative sources in other regions: "The Gulf will be a primary focus of US international energy policy, but our engagement will be global, spotlighting existing and emerging regions that will have a major impact on the global energy balance."[204] The section on the Gulf in the report is less than one page, shorter than the sections on North America, South America, Africa, the Caspian and Russia. The tenor of the international section of the report is on diversity of supply, rather than the risks present in the geopolitics of the Gulf.[205]

While results are not always the best indicator of intentions, it is useful to point out that, by the end of 2008, the war in Iraq had done nothing to increase Iraqi oil production. Iraqi production in September 2008 was 2.3 mbd; its 2002 average was just over 2 mbd.[206] Only one major contract for the development of a new Iraqi oil field had been signed as of the end of 2008, and that was with a Chinese company (though some new oil deals had been signed by the Kurdish Regional Government with energy firms from Turkey and Sweden).[207] It is possible that this is simply a matter of American incompetence. Certainly the post-war American occupation has been rife with examples of incompetence. Still, if increased Iraqi oil production had been the centerpiece of the war effort, it is surprising that so little progress would have been made on that front.

The strategic importance of Gulf oil for the United States has been a constant in American foreign policy since World War II. Undoubtedly that importance was part of the complex of reasons that the Bush administration decided to go to war in Iraq. Positive oil developments were expected from the war, just as strategic benefits and a new democratic impulse in the region were expected. It was a factor in the bureaucratic efforts to bring reluctant elements of the administration, the State Department and the uniformed military around to support for the policy.[208] It was the reason that the United States had a military infrastructure of bases in the Gulf to support the deployment, making the war logistically possible. Congress and the public had been conditioned to see

---

[204] Report of the National Energy Policy Development Group, Chapter 8, p. 5.

[205] Report of the National Energy Policy Development Group, Chapter 8, pp. 6–14.

[206] US Department of Energy, Energy Information Administration, *Monthly Energy Review*, December 2008, Table 11.1a, www.eia.doe.gov/emeu/mer/pdf/pages/sec11_4.pdf.

[207] Amit R. Paley, "Iraq and China Sign $3 Billion Oil Contract," *Washington Post*, August 29, 2008.

[208] After the war, Deputy Secretary of State Wolfowitz told a reporter that an "almost unnoticed but huge" benefit of the war was that it allowed the United States to remove its troops from Saudi Arabia, where their presence was a destabilizing element and a spur to al-Qaeda's hostility: Tanenhaus, "Bush's Brain Trust."

the region as centrally important to American economic and political interests for decades, particularly since the 1990–91 Gulf War.

The Iraq War fits in with the long-term logic of American policy in the Persian Gulf: the importance of oil, the need for the United States to be the dominant power there, the buildup of American capabilities in the area after 1979.[209] But the war itself was not the inevitable result of that logic. It was simply one of many possible results. A continuation of the pre-9/11 policy of military containment and economic sanctions aimed against Iraq and Iran, with a strong American military presence in the Gulf monarchies, was another possible result. There is an oil logic to the war. However, there is no evidence on the public record that energy security issues specifically drove the policy-making process in the lead-up to war. There is substantial evidence that the changed strategic perspective of the Bush administration after 9/11 did drive the war policy. The continuities of American policy in the Gulf set the table, but 9/11 turned on the stove. The counterfactual assertion suggested by both the crude and the sophisticated "war for oil" arguments, that the United States would have fought a war against Iraq for oil reasons had the 9/11 attacks not occurred, is not supported by the evidence.

Conclusion

The controversies surrounding the American war against Iraq in 2003 have spawned a vast literature, much more extensive than the sum total of the literature on the issues of Persian Gulf security for the three decades which preceded it. Analyzing the wealth of published information and opinion about the Iraq War is a task for a book in itself (many such works have been cited in the notes). This chapter has focused on the debate about the causes of the war. It has made the case that the primary cause for the Bush administration's decision to go to war against Iraq was the changed view of the potential threats emanating from the region after the attacks of 9/11. While one can question the wisdom of going to war against Iraq as part of the global war on terrorism, it is hard based on the evidence to question the sincerity with which President Bush, Vice President Cheney and those around them held their views. Their belief that Saddam Hussein's Iraq could potentially transfer weapons of mass destruction to terrorist groups intent upon striking the United States is open to criticism, but not to question. They believed it. Even if the probabilities of such a scenario were small, the consequences were so

[209] See the argument made by Sheila Carapico and Chris Toensing, "The Strategic Logic of the Iraq Blunder," *Middle East Report*, No. 239 (Summer 2006), pp. 6–11.

great – a WMD 9/11 – that preventive war was justified. They also believed that an American victory over Saddam Hussein would change the overall strategic picture in the Middle East in the United States' favor. At a minimum such a victory would warn other potential American foes of the consequences of their actions. More naively, they also believed that such a victory could lead to a democratic revolution in the Muslim Middle East that would greatly reduce the terrorist threat from the region.

The president and those around him came to these conclusions very quickly after the 9/11 attacks, with little regard for the specifics of the evidence regarding Iraqi WMD and Iraqi links to al-Qaeda. The decision came first; the analysis of evidence followed. Confirming evidence was emphasized; disconfirming evidence was rejected. Less plausible but more lurid threats were emphasized to the public, to rally support. Both cognitive biases and political expediency played a role in the way the policy-makers evaluated the evidence. The balance between these two forces – the psychological and the political – probably differed from person to person and issue to issue.

While the strategic importance of Persian Gulf oil plays a role in every American decision about the region, this was not a "war for oil" in any direct way. It is remarkable how little the oil factor appears in the accounts of Bush administration policy-making on the Iraq War. There is also no convincing evidence that the war was planned before the 9/11 attacks, with the administration simply looking for a pretext to rally public opinion for an attack on Iraq. Certainly some members of the administration favored a confrontational policy toward Saddam Hussein before 9/11. However, there is no evidence that they had won the day in the policy-making process before the attacks of that day. In a way that is strangely uncomfortable for many of the administration's opponents, the Iraq War was about what President Bush said it was about. Its wisdom is highly debatable; its origins are pretty straightforward.

The motivations for the American war on Iraq were much different than Saddam Hussein's war-time motivations, discussed in previous chapters. But the two sets of motivations do intersect at an interesting point: the centrality of domestic politics for explaining foreign policy decisions in and about the Middle East. Saddam Hussein was driven primarily by considerations of regime security in his war-making decisions. George W. Bush was driven to war against Iraq in large part because he believed that the character of domestic political regimes in the region was the key to understanding their foreign policies. Saddam Hussein was not deterrable, the way the Soviet Union had been on nuclear questions, because of the nature of his regime. Only regime change in Iraq would remove the potential for the WMD–terrorist nexus that underlay the Bush

Doctrine. Only a democratic wave in the Arab world could end the terrorist threat to the United States emanating from the region. Saddam believed that threats to his regime's security began at home, but were abetted by foreign actors who had to be attacked before they could work within his own society to undermine him. Bush also believed that the threats that mattered to him, the new threats to the American homeland, originated in the domestic politics of countries such as Iraq. To preserve his regime's security, Saddam thought he had to strike at the foreign sources of his domestic threats. To preserve his country's security, Bush thought he had to strike at the domestic sources of his foreign threat. The fact that both were probably mistaken in their judgments is irrelevant to the explanatory importance of those judgments in understanding the wars of the Persian Gulf.

7   Conclusions: war and alliance in the Persian Gulf

In this brief conclusion, I will highlight three important themes that emerge from the preceding chapters and then speculate on the future of the international relations of the Persian Gulf region based upon those themes.

War and alliance in the Gulf: transnational identities

One cannot understand the international politics of the Persian Gulf without appreciating the importance of transnational identities in the calculations of state leaders. The centrality of those identities – Arab, Kurdish, Muslim, Sunni, Shi'i, tribal – is a constant across the more than three and a half decades of events discussed in this book. Those identities are power resources in the hands of ambitious leaders. The Ba'thist regime in Iraq tried to use Arab nationalism to appeal to Arabs in Iran and the Gulf monarchies at various times in the 1970s and 1980s, and hoped that Arab nationalism would rally support for its invasion of Kuwait among Kuwaitis themselves and in the broader Arab world. The Islamic revolutionary government of Iran likewise used general appeals to Muslim identity and specific ties to Shi'i Muslims in Iraq, the Gulf monarchies and Lebanon to pressure other governments and expand Iranian influence. Iranian and Iraqi governments at various times have supported Kurdish groups on the other side of the border as leverage against the other's government. Even the United States has played at this game, if irregularly and idiosyncratically. American backing for Iraqi Kurdish groups, in league with the shah, was an element of Gulf international politics at the beginning of this narrative. The George W. Bush administration's efforts to pressure the Iranian regime, both through support for Iranian ethnic opposition groups (Kurds, Baluchis) and through its rhetorical support for democracy in Iran, are an element of Gulf international politics at the end of the narrative.

Saudi efforts to spread the *salafi*–Wahhabi interpretation of Islam are more important outside the Gulf than in it, though the growth of *salafi*

241

sentiment in Iraq and the smaller Gulf monarchies in the past two decades cannot be separated from the global Saudi proselytization effort. The Saudi venture into the global marketplace of ideas, however, demonstrates that such efforts are not cost-free. The religious/political movement nurtured by the Saudis came back to haunt them through the growth of al-Qaeda and the challenge it presents in Saudi Arabia itself. The United States suffered the same kind of blowback on September 11, 2001, as a political movement which got its start in the Afghan jihad of the 1980s, fighting the same fight as the American and Saudi governments, unleashed unprecedented violence on American soil. States have no monopoly on the use of transnational identities and ideologies as power resources.

The al-Qaeda example points out the important fact that transnational ideologies are not simply power resources in the hands of state and non-state actors. They are also threats to other state actors. These threats to the security of ruling regimes drove much of the international politics of the Persian Gulf in the period under study. Time and again, when faced with difficult choices in the security realm, states in the region (particularly the Arab states, which are subject to more serious transnational identity challenges than Iran) chose policies aimed at protecting regime security over other values. Ba'thist Iraq basically accepted Iranian terms in the 1975 Algiers Agreement in order to solidify the regime's control domestically. In both 1980 and 1990 regime security concerns played leading roles in Saddam Hussein's decisions to wage war. In their alliance decisions in the Gulf, Saudi Arabia, Jordan and Syria identified threats to regime security as being more salient than classic balance of power concerns such as military capabilities. The threats to regime security posed by transnational identities and ideologies drove many of the most important security outcomes in the region over the past decades.

A good case can be made that leaders have overestimated the seriousness of the threats posed by transnational identities. Saddam Hussein could not mobilize effective support from the Arab minority when he invaded Iran in 1980. Ayatollah Khomeini threatened leaders in Baghdad, Riyadh and elsewhere with the export of his Islamic revolution, but he could not replace them with sister Islamic republics. Neither Arab nationalist nor Islamist propaganda from Saddam in 1990–91 shook the regimes in Riyadh, Damascus and Cairo which stood against his annexation of Kuwait. The regional states themselves have their own resources – their oil money and the administrative and coercive apparatus which that oil money has allowed them to build – to blunt transnational appeals. It is a paradox: while transnational identities are strong, the states in the Persian Gulf have gained in strength (in terms of their control over their own societies) over the decades under study, with the obvious exception of Iraq. But leaders have erred on the side of caution, if not paranoia, in focusing on transnational threats to regime security. Understanding those perceptions, exaggerated though they may be, is a key to understanding the security dynamics of the Gulf.

The importance of cross-border political identities and ideas increases the likelihood of conflict and tensions in the Persian Gulf. Ambitious leaders think that they can use these identities against their neighbors to expand their power, to the extent even of finding support within neighboring populations for military adventures. Target governments worry not just about the military power of neighboring states, but also about the ability of neighboring leaders to interfere and intervene in their own domestic politics. The security dilemma, real enough already in an area where possession of territory can bring with it the riches of oil, is exacerbated by the political opportunities and threats presented by transnational political loyalties.

It is this intersection of idea and tangible interests that defines the security agenda in the Persian Gulf. In terms of international relations theory, classical Realist concerns about state power in an anarchic environment are hardly absent in the Gulf. States build large militaries and buy expensive weapons; they balance against threats through alliances with each other and with outside powers; war has been a frequent occurrence. But Realism cannot tell the whole story of the region's international politics. Ideas, just as much if not more than material factors, are power resources and threats to the Gulf's leaders. Constructivist approaches to international relations, which emphasize the independent causal power of ideas, capture some of this logic. However, the important transnational identities in the Gulf do not float freely. It is when they become tied to a powerful state that they become a power resource for some and a threat to others. It is in that nexus of ideas and state power that social constructions become weapons and threats, in that they can be used to increase one leader's ability to affect events beyond his borders or can be seen as threats to the domestic stability of regimes. Recognition of the importance of ideas does not negate Realist insights about anarchy, power and conflict in the Persian Gulf; it contextualizes those Realist insights by giving us a fuller understanding of how state leaders define their interests and understand the power resources at their disposal.

War and alliance in the Gulf: the American role

A second theme that knits together the narrative of international politics in the Persian Gulf is the American role in the region. During the period of this study, American involvement in the Gulf has increased steadily. The United States relied upon close regional allies, the shah's Iran and Saudi Arabia, to safeguard American interests after the British withdrawal of 1971. The Iranian Revolution marked the beginning of the upward trajectory of American direct involvement in the area, which was also spurred on by the Soviet invasion of Afghanistan. The military infrastructure that became Central Command was created in the early 1980s. A massive naval deployment occurred at the end of the Iran–Iraq War. The United States sent half a million soldiers and sailors to the area in 1990–91 to turn back Saddam Hussein's invasion of Kuwait. In the aftermath of that war, the Gulf monarchies welcomed full-scale American military facilities on their soil, a step many of them had been reluctant to take beforehand. This trend culminated in the Iraq War of 2003 and the American occupation of Iraq.

The story of escalating American military involvement in the Persian Gulf seems on the surface to be a straight line, with the Iraq adventure as the logical end point of a consistent upward pattern. That analysis, however, belies the profound change in the goals of American policy in the Gulf that the Iraq War represents. Up to 2001, American policy in the Gulf was oriented toward preservation of the regional status quo. The United States sought to limit the influence of the Soviet Union and its regional allies in order to maintain American dominance over the flow of oil. By the 1970s the American oil interest was less about commercial control than it had been in previous decades. Washington did not try to stop the nationalizations of American oil interests in the Gulf that followed the oil price revolution of the early 1970s. It did very little to try to reverse the price increases of that period. On the contrary, Washington accepted these enormous changes in the world oil industry, largely because the country's regional allies, Saudi Arabia and Iran, were the prime beneficiaries. A stronger, richer Iran and Saudi Arabia fit very nicely into the United States' Cold War strategy.

The Iranian Revolution changed the Gulf status quo enormously. Yet, Washington did little if anything to try to reverse the revolution. American policy adjusted to this profound reversal to its interests. Washington increased its direct military involvement, to be sure, but to safeguard its remaining regional allies, Saudi Arabia and the smaller Gulf monarchies. It played balance of power politics in the Iran–Iraq War, seeking to contain Iranian power while, on the side, trying to keep some avenue of communication open with Tehran, through the Iran–contra dealings. With the Iraqi invasion of Kuwait in 1990, the United States faced a challenge to the regional status quo that it could confront. It brought enormous military power to bear to restore Kuwaiti sovereignty, but sought no other changes from its victory. It even allowed Saddam Hussein's regime to remain in power, though much weakened and contained by international sanctions and by the increased American military presence in the region. The first Bush and Clinton administrations certainly hoped that Saddam would fall, but the removal of Saddam Hussein from power was not so important to Washington that it was willing to take many risks or pay much of a price to achieve it.

The Iraq War was a continuation of the use of American military means in the Persian Gulf, but it was fought for different goals. No longer was the overriding objective of American policy to protect a Gulf status quo. The Iraq War was about changing that status quo. For a number of reasons, not least of which was the Bush administration's flawed diagnosis of the causes of the 9/11 attacks, the United States decided that it could no longer tolerate Saddam Hussein's regime, after having tolerated it for more than two decades. Changing the domestic political regime of a Gulf state had not been at the top of the American agenda in the Gulf since the Mossadegh coup in Iran in 1953, and that was to restore friendly monarchical rule. The sustained American occupation of a Gulf country was unprecedented since World War II; the object of that occupation, to alter fundamentally the domestic politics of a Gulf country, was unique in the annals of American policy in the Gulf. The Iraq War was certainly a departure from previous patterns of American involvement in the Gulf. It remains to be seen whether it is an aberration or the beginning of a new pattern.

War and alliance in the Gulf: oil

One does not need to be a rocket scientist, or even a political scientist, to know that oil is why the outside world cares about the Persian Gulf. Even though I have argued that the United States did not launch the Iraq War of 2003 primarily to secure Iraq's oil resources, I fully concede that oil is a necessary (just not a sufficient) condition for that war to have occurred. Absent the strategic importance of the Gulf, a product of that oil, there would not have been an American invasion of Iraq in 2003 or an American military effort to turn back the Iraqi invasion of Kuwait in 1990–91. So oil undoubtedly increases the likelihood of regional conflict, because it attracts the attentions of the great powers.

But does oil affect the international relations among the Gulf states themselves? Oil increases the war-proneness of the region, and not only because outside powers are willing to fight over it. This is true for two reasons. First, control of territory is more valuable if there is oil underneath it. Thus, the potential benefits of war for the aggressor seem greater than they would be otherwise. While I argued that control of oil resources was not Saddam Hussein's primary objective in launching either the Iran–Iraq War or the Gulf War, I do not deny that the presence of oil across the border in both cases made the advantages of victorious war seem that much more substantial. Second, oil revenues provided all of the major regional states with the ability to build significant military forces and arm them with the most modern weapons. Having a big army increases the perception that war can be won, and thus increases the likelihood that ambitious rulers will see war as a rational choice. But oil is a constant. It cannot explain why specific wars happen at specific times. Other factors intervene to push leaders over the edge of the monumental decision to go to war. But the presence of oil in the Gulf has certainly made war there more likely than would have been the case otherwise.

Oil increases the likelihood of conflict, but it could also increase the likelihood of regional cooperation. All the major Gulf states are oil export-ers, as are most of the minor ones. While they might disagree about how high prices should go, they all have an interest in higher oil prices. That common interest is embodied in their common membership in OPEC. Four of the five founding members of OPEC are Gulf states (Iran, Iraq, Saudi Arabia and Kuwait); those four plus the UAE remain major actors in the organization. At times oil issues have brought them together. In the early 1970s Iran, Iraq and Saudi Arabia cooperated in oil negotiations with the major international oil companies. That cooperation helped smooth the geopolitical transition of 1971 represented by the withdrawal of British military protection from the smaller states and those states' independence. In the late 1990s the collapse of oil prices led to Saudi–Iranian cooperation, following nearly two decades of estrangement after the Iranian Revolution. With the price collapse of 2008, oil might be the only regional issue on which Riyadh and Tehran see eye to eye.

However, for the most part the incentives for cooperation present in oil issues have not been realized. Regional tensions over oil issues have been much more common than cooperation. That was obviously the case in 1990, when Iraq criticized Kuwait and the UAE for "overproduction" and used that as a justification to invade Kuwait. But those tensions were present even in situations that did not escalate to open conflict. While Saudi Arabia, Kuwait and the UAE were embargoing oil to the United States in 1973–74, Iraq and Iran were both selling as much as they could to whoever would buy. Iran, under both the shah and the Islamic Republic, has regularly criticized Saudi Arabia for producing more oil than it "should" and keeping prices down. The Saudis at various times used their surplus capacity to threaten other oil producers, including their Gulf neighbors, to hew to OPEC quotas. In 1986 Riyadh opened the spigots, driving prices down substantially, to punish the quota-cheaters in OPEC. This step had the added effect of weakening the Iranian economy in the midst of the Iran–Iraq War.

The possibilities of cooperation among Persian Gulf states on oil issues were only occasionally realized. Undoubtedly they would all have been richer and better off if they had cooperated consistently on oil production issues. However, more immediate concerns of short-term revenue maximization, security, competition and relative gain usually overcame the incentives for cooperation provided by oil.

The future of Persian Gulf security

There is no more important issue for the development of the security agenda of the Persian Gulf than what happens in Iraq. If the Iraqi state is able to reconstruct itself, resolving the political and physical battles over political power, extending its control over the country and finding a workable compromise on the constitutional questions about the relative power of the center and its regions, the entire region will be more stable. If the Iraqis fail to construct a viable state, then the country will remain a playing field for regional and international forces to extend their influence and fight their own proxy wars. There is a tension here between two important themes identified above: the salience of transnational identities and ideologies and the process of state-building. Stronger states are better able to vest the interests (and, eventually, the identities) of their citizens in the state and to fend off efforts by outsiders to exploit transnational ties and penetrate the polity. Weaker states not only are less able to do that, but the actors in weaker states – both the government and other political actors – have more incentive to invite foreigners into the country, to support them in their internal struggles for power.

In 2008, Iraq is a weak state. Foreigners, including Americans, Iranians, Turks, Saudis and al-Qaeda, have all played directly or indirectly in Iraqi politics, in collaboration with various Iraqi actors. If the Iraqi state remains weak domestically, the foreign interventions will continue. A perpetually weak and embattled Iraqi state increases the chances of Kurdish independence; it certainly solidifies Kurdish de facto autonomy. That means a high likelihood of further Turkish military incursions and political intervention in Iraqi Kurdistan in the future. Moreover, the longer that Iraq remains a playing field for others, the more likely it is that the interventions of these foreign players will develop into a proxy war among them. Iran and the United States are already playing out their own rivalries in Iraq, though on a complex Iraqi map that also sees them both supporting the Baghdad government. Saudi Arabia has been a late arriver to the Iraq political game. It has fewer allies in Iraq and fewer assets to deploy than either Iran or the United States. But to the extent that the United States begins to draw down its own presence in Iraq while the Iraqi state remains weak (if that happens), Saudi Arabia will become even more involved, to check what it sees as Iranian domination of the country. This will not be a military confrontation; it will be a confrontation between Iraqi proxies supported by their outside patrons.

Such a confrontation will undoubtedly take on a sectarian tone, as Sunni Arab Iraqis are the natural clients of the Saudis just as Shi'i Arab Iraqis are the natural clients of the Iranians, though both of these states are subtle enough to play the proxy game across sectarian and ethnic lines. Such sectarian tensions will spill over into other Gulf countries, raising the possibilities of domestic unrest in places such as Kuwait and Bahrain, as well as in Saudi Arabia and Iran themselves. It was in the context of Saudi–Iranian rivalry in the 1980s that the *salafi*–jihadist movement of which al-Qaeda is a part developed. A return to intense Saudi–Iranian ideological and political rivalry in the near future could help sustain the appeal of al-Qaeda and other extremist organizations, both Sunni and Shi'i, both in Iraq and throughout the region.

The prospect of Iran acquiring nuclear weapons is another important near-term regional security issue. I could simply scratch the surface of the debate on this issue in chapter 5 and do not intend to enter it in any detail here. Suffice it to say that the Iranian nuclear question will remain on the front burner of the Gulf security agenda for some time. I think that the effects of a nuclear Iran on the security dynamics of the Gulf can be exaggerated. But what I think about it is much less important than what people in Riyadh, Ankara, Jerusalem and Washington think about it. The two most likely, though by no means inevitable, reactions to an Iranian nuclear acquisition, or the imminent prospect of it, are an Israeli military strike and a Saudi decision to try to acquire their own nuclear arsenal. An Israeli strike would certainly be followed by Iranian retaliation against Israel. That retaliation could combine conventional military responses through Hizballah and other regional Iranian allies with asymmetric responses, through terrorist attacks and other indirect means. An Israeli attack would also help the Iranians in their current strategy of using their anti-Israeli position to rally support in Arab public opinion, thus putting pressure on Arab governments at peace with Israel. Iran would also see an American hand behind any Israeli strike and retaliate against American interests in Iraq, Afghanistan and the Gulf, again very possibly asymmetrically rather than through direct conventional military attack. An Israeli strike would greatly increase regional tensions and conflicts in the Persian Gulf and in the Arab–Israeli arena.

The Saudi reaction to an Iranian nuclear breakout would depend enormously on how Riyadh read American intentions and resolve. There would certainly be voices in the Saudi elite calling for the quick acquisition of an independent Saudi nuclear capability, most probably through purchase from Pakistan or some kind of Pakistani deployment in Saudi Arabia. If the United States extended a nuclear guarantee to Saudi Arabia, and made the continuation of a close security alliance with Riyadh contingent upon Saudi non-proliferation, that might dissuade the Saudis from trying to go nuclear themselves. Short of that, it is likely that Saudi Arabia would want to get its own nuclear weapons. If they do, there will certainly be tensions in the Saudi–Iranian relationship. However, as it is unlikely that Saudi Arabia and Iran would square off in a conventional military conflict, the likelihood of a real nuclear crisis between the two is low. The risks of nuclear accidents and other untoward consequences, however, are real and disturbing.

How would the United States react to an imminent Iranian nuclear breakout? That question leads to the third issue of importance for the future of Persian Gulf security – the role of the United States in the region. The Bush administration's turn away from the status quo policy of its predecessors was dealt a huge setback by the difficulties of the Iraq War. The likelihood that any American president in the near future will see the disruption of the Persian Gulf status quo, including domestic political change in its major states, as a key American interest is very slight. Even those in the United States who advocate a more confrontational stance toward Iran do not talk about using American ground forces to change the Iranian regime. It is unlikely that domestic political reform in Saudi Arabia, briefly on the agenda of the Bush administration after 2003, will have a prominent role in the Obama administration. The United States will have its hands full enough in the region without trying to midwife some kind of democratic transition in Riyadh.

On the other hand, there is no sentiment in the United States for a drastic change in the overall American commitment to the region. Whether oil prices are $140 per barrel or $40 per barrel, the strategic importance of the region is not questioned by American policy elites. Given the confrontational stance Iran has taken toward Israel, the American–Israeli relationship now requires a continuing US role in the Gulf as well. It is highly unlikely, even in the event of the withdrawal of all American forces from Iraq, that the United States will abandon its military and political role in the monarchical states. The system of bases constructed in the 1990s in the smaller monarchies was poured in concrete. A retreat from Iraq will be to Kuwait, Bahrain and Qatar, not to the United States. The Saudi–American relationship, having weathered the crisis of 9/11, does not seem likely to change substantially in the future.

All these factors seem to incline the United States back toward a status quo policy in the Persian Gulf – one aimed at minimizing the negative consequences of gradual withdrawal from Iraq and containing Iranian power. Yet the temptations of hegemony will still beckon, in a world where no peer competitor can challenge the use of American military force in the Gulf. The future of security in the Persian Gulf cannot be decided in Washington alone, but the decisions made in Washington about the Gulf will remain central for the foreseeable future.

Index